The Lost Peace

VIETNAMESE WOMAN
(Hoover Institution Archives)

The Lost Peace

America's Search for a
Negotiated Settlement of the Vietnam War

Allan E. Goodman

foreword by
William H. Sullivan
Ambassador

HOOVER INSTITUTION PRESS
Stanford University, Stanford, California

The Hoover Institution on War, Revolution and Peace, founded at
Stanford University in 1919 by the late President Herbert Hoover,
is an interdisciplinary research center for advanced study on
domestic and international affairs in the twentieth century. The views
expressed in its publications are entirely those of the authors
and do not necessarily reflect the views of the staff, officers,
or Board of Overseers of the Hoover Institution.

Hoover Institution Publication 173

For Danielle

Epigraph

I

When Hsüan-tsung became Emperor in 1425, the Chinese administration in southern Vietnam had been under siege for nine years. China's economic problems, the ineptness of her generals, the long sea and overland supply lines necessary for the war, coupled with Le Loi's (the Vietnamese emperor) guerrilla tactics and his ability to use the territory of what is today the country of Laos as a sanctuary, had combined to convince Hsüan-tsung that the war was unwinnable and that a negotiated settlement should be sought.

But Hsüan-tsung's ministers believed too much was at stake to compromise. One history of the period notes that the war so troubled the emperor that after a sleepless night he told his ministers of his desire to withdraw from the war and to grant autonomy to the Vietnamese. "He quoted the Ancestral Instructions' admonitions against offensive wars and said that the original intention [of his predecessors] was not to make Vietnam a Chinese province but to restore the legitimate . . . rulers." His ministers argued that to cease the struggle then, however, would "mean giving up twenty years of struggle and would also lessen China's prestige in the eyes of the world."

So the war continued.

By the winter of 1426, Le Loi alternated guerrilla attacks with conventional assaults on Chinese forts. The Chinese army suffered many defeats; in one battle alone, between 20,000 and 30,000 soldiers were lost. But it was Le Loi who proposed a truce: if the Chinese army withdrew, Le Loi would recognize as king a descendant of the dynasty the Chinese were seeking to restore to the throne. Hsüan-tsung's ministers branded Le Loi's proposal a ruse and argued that a reinforced army could yet win the war.

While the Chinese debated this, the Vietnamese defeated the reinforced army. When Hsüan-tsung's representatives finally reached Vietnam to negotiate, Le Loi refused.

The advocates of the war died in disgrace. But a hundred years later, Chinese historians said that Hsüan-tsung's wavering diplomacy had lost the war and had encouraged the barbarians to be contemptuous of Chinese power. "In war," Sun Tzu said, "let your great object be victory."

—*Based on an account compiled by Jung-pang Lo from the* Ming Hsüan-tsung Shih-lu *and the* Shu-yü Chou-tzu Lu

II

What will be the consequences if Viet-Nam and Cambodia do fall? It is a debate which has been going on for a long time. I believe, and the Administration believes, that if Viet-Nam falls as a result of an American decision to cut off its aid, that this will have, over a period of time, the most serious consequences for the conduct of our foreign policy. This will not be immediately apparent, but over a period of years it must raise the gravest doubts in the minds of many countries that have been associated with us, or of many countries to which the threat cannot be given a terminal date.

—Henry A. Kissinger, February 25, 1975

Contents

Illustrations

Foreword

The confrontation between the United States and the Lao Dong party in Indochina was incongruous in many ways. In the first place, there was the qualitative difference between the antagonists. The United States is the epitome of the Establishment among the nations of the world. It is also the world's oldest republic, its most stable nation, and its leading exponent of the need for international order and the rule of international law. The Lao Dong, on the other hand, is essentially a revolutionary movement—a political party with no fixed territorial base, a party dedicated to the violent overthrow of all existing order and all existing international law, on the grounds that they are falsely promised and prejudiciously applied.

In the quantitative sense, there were also enormous anomalies. The United States is the richest, most powerful nation in the world, and has the strongest military machine. The Lao Dong, by contrast, is able to call upon nothing more than some of the poorest, most undernourished and uneducated peasants in a poverty-stricken corner of the world. It commands no arsenals, has no industrial base, and cannot even feed the population under its control.

In moral terms, the United States bent over backward, in its application of military power in order to enforce the most scrupulous controls ever fashioned to the rules of warfare. Despite such occurrences as My Lai, no soldiers in the history of war have ever fought under such tight guidance (guidance designed to "civilize" the conduct of fighting men, especially with respect to the civilian population) as have the American forces in Vietnam. The Lao Dong, on the other hand, made the terrorization of civilians and the brutalization of military conduct a key element in its arsenal of belligerency.

Despite all these apparent disadvantages, the Lao Dong has been able to achieve most of its objectives in Indochina, and the United States has been forced to retreat, in a most humiliating fashion, from the goals and objectives that the American leaders publicly and piously set for themselves over nearly three turbulent decades of American political history.

Many military and political factors can be adduced to explain the outcome of the war in Indochina. Apologists and historians will be at work for many years examining circumstances that might have been. There were obviously better ways to have fought the war. In strictly military terms, it would have made more sense for the United States to have invaded North Vietnam and forced the Lao Dong to accept a more favorable outcome. In broader strategic terms, there arises the question whether there ever was any reason for the United States to have become engaged in a military confrontation in Indochina in the first place.

All of these issues lay in the background of the Indochina negotiations. They have been discussed in many of the volumes that have been written about Vietnam. It is timely, however, and valuable to have a book written about the negotiations as a separate and distinct phenomenon.

Dr. Goodman's record of the negotiations that took place sporadically from 1962 to 1973 describes the events of those years in objective detail. It makes clear that the United States had ambiguous objectives in Indochina and used ambiguous tactics to pursue them. We were interested in peace, justice, and the equilibrium of forces in Southeast Asia. On the other hand, we had doubts about the political, moral, and ethical qualities of our allies in the region. We respected some of the reasons that underlay the causes of our enemy's struggle in Indochina, even if we condemned the means they employed. We were, in short, ambiguous about our goals, our methods, and our allies in all contexts.

The Lao Dong, by contrast, never had a doubt. Its leaders and its members were convinced of their righteousness. They were also convinced that the correctness of their ends justified their means. How many times in the twelve years during which I negotiated with their representatives have I heard them use the adjective *correct* to justify their most outrageous and inhumane conduct! They had conviction; they had zeal; they had fortitude; and eventually they prevailed.

In examining the record of these negotiators and their result, we do not need to draw the conclusion that, just because the Lao Dong prevailed, or because it was constant, or zealous, it achieved justice. (Hitler's legions were also constant and zealous, and for a number of years they prevailed.) But, we do have to examine why, at least in the negotiating context, the Lao Dong was more successful than the United States.

Dr. Goodman's book offers a useful insight into this examination. It traces the many complex, sophisticated, and often obscure initiatives taken by the United States. It relates the many doubts, second thoughts, and nuances with which the United States was afflicted. It is a record of too much sophistication, too much solicitude, too much effort to outguess—and therefore to outnego-tiate—our opponents. It draws upon many sources that are more or less on the public record to document this perception of the American performance.

Goodman's sources of insight into the Lao Dong performance are understandably more limited and hence less detailed. But, even if they were better, the external evidence would seem to conclude that the Lao Dong, in contrast to the sophisticated, nuanced, "think-tank" effort that went into the American negotiating posture, had a primitive, simplistic system that was directed without diversion or equivocation toward the single goal of achieving political dominance in Indochina.

In retrospect, therefore, we can see that all the elaborate negotiating signals arranged by all the various men of good will who were called to Washington during this period were wasted on Hanoi. In most instances, it is probable that the signals were never even noticed, and many that were noticed were probably misinterpreted while those that were interpreted correctly were doubtless resented. They were resented because they were based on the presumption that the Lao Dong lacked conviction, or fortitude, or confidence in its goals. At the same time, because these signals were so ambiguous and reflected such ambiguous objectives, they could only generate contempt and the conclusion that they reflected an attitude of weakness.

By contrast, the Lao Dong objectives and its negotiating offers reflected simple, consistent, zealous dedication to a predetermined goal—the conquest of Indochina. While the Lao Dong may have dressed and redressed its proposals in ways that made them more attractive to the gullible, it never swerved from its ultimate goal and never fully receded from its "correct" objectives. Even when it was forced by the military measures in 1972 and by the strains of the Sino-Soviet confrontation to make tactical concessions in the final negotiations leading to the January 1973 agreement, the Lao Dong preserved a propaganda position that it subsequently used to renege on its agreements and brazenly condone its subsequent military assaults on South Vietnam and Laos.

It is not a rewarding experience for the professional negotiator to be engaged in an effort in which he is engulfed by ambiguities while his opponent is arrayed in constancy, conviction, and zeal. For the various relays of American negotiators who underwent this experience in various forms and in various forums for the decade of our agony in Vietnam, the frustrations were intense and the memories are searing. Dr. Goodman's book provides a narration of the events that encompassed that experience. It is a comprehensive, objective, and scholarly work that should become required reading for all students of this trying era in the history of the United States.

WILLIAM H. SULLIVAN
Ambassador to Laos, 1964–68
Deputy Assistant Secretary of State, 1969–73

Preface

It seems as inconceivable to me now as it did in 1965 that the United States would have become so deeply involved in the struggle in Vietnam—a country of so little strategic importance, and one with whose culture we were so thoroughly unfamiliar and about whose internal conflicts we understood so little. But in the early 1960s most Americans had a different view of our stake in internal conflicts beyond our borders. The widely held belief that every challenge to political order in changing societies was Communist-inspired and would, unless checked, advance Soviet and Chinese interests, thrust the struggle in Vietnam to center stage for nearly a decade.

In 1965, the security of the free world and the credibility of American power required our presence in Vietnam. By 1975, many thought these goals could best be served by liquidating our commitment to Vietnam altogether. The history of what the United States sought through fighting and negotiating in Vietnam is thus as profoundly affected by changes in the nature of support for foreign policy within the United States as by events on the battlefields of South Vietnam. In fact, to the statesmen quoted in this book the changes Vietnam wrought in American society were more shocking than the collapse of Saigon itself.

My sources—ranging from presidents to interpreters—included most of the Americans and non-Communist Vietnamese involved since 1962 in the search for a negotiated settlement in Vietnam. My discussions with them were not for attribution and were conducted off-the-record because many of these officials were still in office when I interviewed them.

I was unable to interview any officials of the DRV or PRG. While the State Department authorized travel to Hanoi, the North Vietnamese refused to issue me a visa. I then sought out several DRV officials posted abroad who were reported to be knowledgeable about the negotiations—one had read, I was told, Tad Szulc's account of the Kissinger-Tho talks that appeared in *Foreign Policy* magazine, and was prepared to comment on it to me. Our point of contact was to be the DRV Embassy in Vientiane, Laos. While I was given several appointments, they were always cancelled. So, what I have to say about Hanoi's diplomacy is based on what North Vietnamese leaders have written over the years for public consumption and on certain other material—clearly indicated in the text—that fell into the hands of U.S. and South Vietnamese forces on the battlefield. I also interviewed many who traveled widely to both North Vietnam and the PRG-controlled territory of South Vietnam in 1973 and 1974.

In any such account, of course, there are bound to be errors of omission. There is also a problem of perspective. By interviewing so many involved at different stages and staff levels in the negotiations, I may have compiled a picture that shows more detail than the one the principals actually had in mind when they were negotiating. That is why, whenever I could let a principal speak for himself, I chose to quote his remarks at length.

My most sincere thanks are due the officers and staff of the Hoover Institution for their generous support of my research and writing while a National Fellow in 1974–75. Dennis L. Bark and Alexander George, in particular, were constant sources of good advice and help. Several generous grants from the Francis A. Harrington Public Affairs Fund of the Department of Government and International Relations at Clark University where I served as chairman from 1971 to 1974 helped researchers to establish the collection of pertinent documents for this study, which are now available at the Hoover Institution archives.

Donald Brennan, Michael Cotter, and Samuel Harrington reviewed my early outlines and helped to improve them. Marsha Soloman served ably as my research assistant in 1974. Lynda Leiss and Ann Elliot cheerfully typed and retyped this manuscript, while W. Ann Garvey, a comparative literature major at Stanford University, edited my first draft. Sandy Sailer, my editor at Hoover Press, did a superb job in helping me prepare the manuscript for publication. I am also grateful to Jerry M. Silverman and Cung Thuc Tien, whose kind hospitality in Saigon during January 1975 greatly facilitated interviewing during a difficult and uncertain period. But without the insight and encouragement of my wife, Collette, who first gave me the idea, I would never have written *The Lost Peace*.

In every respect, this book is a product of my Vietnam studies, first at Harvard and then at Clark and Stanford universities. I wish to make it clear that only after completing *The Lost Peace* did I become associated with the Office of Political Research of the Central Intelligence Agency. Thus, this book is not the official view of the CIA or any other government agency.

Introduction

AMERICAN DIPLOMACY
AND VIETNAM

After more than a decade of struggle, those the United States supported in Indochina lost their attempted social revolution, their war, and their chance to bring peace to Vietnam. This book will show the peace the U.S. had sought for its South Vietnamese allies could not be prefabricated in Paris conference rooms. The peace that, as President Lyndon Johnson said on March 31, 1968, "will one day stop the bloodshed . . . [permit] all the Vietnamese people . . . to rebuild and develop their land . . . [and] permit us to turn more fully to our own tasks here at home" came only with the collapse of Saigon.

In *The Lost Peace* I have attempted to put together as much of the story as I could learn of the diplomacy behind the longest, most costly, least successful war in U.S. history. I have tried basically to reconstruct the most significant events and developments that affected Washington's search for a negotiated settlement and to explain how that search actually contributed to prolonging the war. My account is based almost entirely on interviews with decision-makers in Washington and Saigon; I wanted *Lost Peace* to tell the story of what happened and why, from their perspective.

The secret search for a negotiated settlement in Vietnam actually began with a meeting between U.S. and North Vietnamese representatives in 1962, reflecting President John F. Kennedy's belief that the international agreements that had just been reached concerning Laos would be meaningless without providing also for the neutralization of Vietnam. Neither President Kennedy nor his advisors believed Hanoi would oppose such negotiations. But Hanoi probably interpreted President Kennedy's initiatives as a sign that the United States was not prepared to fight another land war in Asia. And since the conflict in Vietnam was so wholly a struggle between two groups of Vietnamese, Hanoi's leaders probably reasoned that substantial U.S. involvement on behalf of the increasingly repressive and corrupt regime of Ngo

Dinh Diem was unlikely. What Hanoi did not anticipate was the degree to which the assassination of Diem in 1963—an event they thought would free the U.S. from any further need to be involved in Vietnam—made anything less than a substantial commitment of support to Diem's successors virtually unthinkable. Moreover, President Kennedy's assassination cut short the debate within the U.S. Government over whether the conflict in Vietnam was part of a worldwide Communist assault on democracy or a civil war. By the time President Johnson was prepared to make a decision on Vietnam, he believed that the political instability following the overthrow of Ngo Dinh Diem, coupled with the violations of the demilitarized zone by the North Vietnamese, left him little choice. The United States, President Johnson believed, had to stand firm on specific goals—namely, the cessation of Communist-sponsored violence in and the end of the North Vietnamese Army (NVA) infiltration into the south—that he realized were beyond the capabilities of Washington and Saigon to achieve on the battlefield. But President Johnson sought negotiations when they were least likely to occur; in 1964 and 1965, Hanoi still interpreted invitations to negotiate as a sign of U.S. weakness and still refused to take seriously U.S. threats that without a negotiated settlement the United States would be compelled to substantially increase its support to Saigon.

NVA attacks on U.S. forces in Vietnam during 1965, rather than promoting the realization in Washington that neither the United States nor the Government of Vietnam (GVN, the abbreviation commonly used to refer to the Saigon Government) could win a war, provoked an escalatory reaction aimed at protecting U.S. forces, discouraging Hanoi from continuing such attacks, and compelling Hanoi to negotiate. While the relationship between diplomacy and fighting during that year is too complex for facile summary here, President Johnson basically concluded that there was no practicable way to protect U.S. forces short of winning the war or withdrawing from it. A token U.S. military presence would not discourage Hanoi from continuing the war, and nothing could force Hanoi to negotiate (i.e., compromise) as long as it viewed negotiations as useful only after a position of strength on the battlefield and in the political arena of South Vietnam had been achieved. Eschewing the option of a unilateral U.S. troop withdrawal, the president sought to deprive Hanoi of the position of strength it sought by substantially increasing the size and mission of the American presence in Vietnam. In 1965, Mr. Johnson believed that time and force were on his side and that, rather than risk either destruction of the north or losing the war in the south, Hanoi would eventually negotiate.

As the war intensified in 1966 and 1967, however, the prospects for negotiations dimmed. Within the U.S. government, agreement could not be reached on an appropriate minimum position that would be acceptable to Hanoi. Hanoi remained adamant in refusing to enter talks as long as the bombing of North Vietnam continued. And the efforts of allies of both to arrange talks tended to convince each that the other was insincere about negotiations in the first place. During these years, the search for a basis for negotiation was also complicated by the fact that, to both Washington and Hanoi, the war appeared winnable—to Washington, largely because by 1967 the political and military situation in South Vietnam had dramatically improved over what it had been in 1964 and 1965; to Hanoi, because it was beginning to expand its political control to areas under the nominal authority of the GVN and it saw the U.S. presence (and thereby the U.S. impact on the long-term revolutionary struggle) as only temporary.

Unquestionably, it was the shock of the 1968 Tet offensive on the U.S. policy (and the reverberations of this shock on the principal advisors to President Johnson) that led to the change in the U.S. position on bombing. But as in Korea, the start of formal negotiations did not signal the beginning of the end of the war. The fact that negotiations were under way did not change the image each side had of the other's motives for negotiating.

The negotiations did coincide with the gradual withdrawal of U.S. forces and—with equally gradual changes in the U.S. negotiating position—these changes, coupled with the irreversible process of U.S. troop withdrawal, convinced Hanoi, that the longer it waited, the less likely it was that the United States and its ally would win the war, and the more concessions Henry Kissinger was likely to make in his secret talks with Le Duc Tho. When there was finally a breakthrough in the negotiations, misperception about how flexible each side could be (similar in nature to the misperception that had led to war in the first place) led to the breakdown of the negotiating process. Ultimately, the incompatabilities in the goals of both sides led to the breakdown of the 1973 Paris Agreement.

The Lost Peace tells the story of how the U.S. officials, who sincerely believed in the contribution negotiations could make to ending the war, tried to persuade Hanoi that negotiating could achieve more than fighting. *The Lost Peace* also attempts to explain why this approach failed.

The historical narratives that detail the secret search for a negotiated settlement outline the scope of each diplomatic initiative and its relationship to each side's war strategy and to the prevailing military situation. I pay particular attention to what Hanoi and Washington appeared to learn through diplomacy about each other's will to continue the war and strategy for fighting it. I stress this because I believe that the behind-the-scenes diplomacy, and later, the secret negotiations themselves, reinforced Washington's and Hanoi's images of each other's intransigence and of the correctness of their own basic strategy. In the end, Hanoi's strategy of negotiating in order to protract the fighting and Washington's counter-strategy of gradual escalation in order to raise the cost to Hanoi of fighting rather than negotiating contributed to both prolonging the war and vitiating efforts to end it with a negotiated settlement.

In particular, the U.S. strategy of escalation, more than Hanoi's strategy of protracted struggle, prolonged the war. Hanoi had little choice with respect to strategy. Its resources and political military capabilities in the south required a protracted war. Escalation (one of a number of ways the United States could have chosen to fight the war) provided Hanoi with a symbol (the bombing) with which to rally support for holding out. Escalation also gave Hanoi time to adjust to each new increment of force and—in terms of the public antipathy that each step up the escalation ladder generated in the United States from 1966 onward—a ready index of America's waning will to continue the war.

Consequently when an agreement was reached, Hanoi had not changed its view that it could still achieve its maximum goal: "liberation" of the south. As the provisions of the Paris Agreement broke down, as Hanoi expected they would, North Vietnamese forces consistently pushed for victory on the battlefield. It came, but at least a year sooner than Hanoi expected.

Many U.S. officials now firmly believe that, had the Nixon administration not been immobilized by Watergate and had Congress not voted to cut off funds for the air war in Indochina, the United States would have retained a credible capacity to discourage Hanoi from violating the Paris Agreement and pursuing a military victory. And, these officials believed, had Congress supported administration proposals for adequate assistance to Saigon, the Army of the Republic of Vietnam (ARVN)—and the GVN itself—would not have collapsed in the face of the threat of an NVA offensive. But there is nothing to suggest that, even with the requested level of the U.S. assistance in 1974 and 1975, the GVN would have undertaken the military, political, and economic reforms so necessary to arresting the internal decay of the Thieu government. Moreover, nothing in Hanoi's many pronouncements on the strategy it would pursue after the Paris Agreement was signed suggests that, without Watergate and with Nixon still in the White House, Hanoi would have behaved any differently than it did in 1975.

Because of the detailed nature of the substantive negotiations I describe, I urge the reader to keep in mind that no negotiation, regardless of how intense, secret, or technical its nature, is conducted in isolation. During the decade of the search for a negotiated settlement, U.S. relations with the Communist world changed, as did political forces within the Communist world itself. In addition, the shift from hostility to détente with the Soviet Union, the rapprochement with China, and the continued warfare in the Middle East— to mention only a few of the most critical developments constantly on policy-makers' minds—tended to heighten American desires to end the Vietnam war by negotiations, to demonstrate to allies and adversaries alike that conflicts could be resolved peacefully, and to reduce the drain on U.S. military and economic resources that the war entailed. Thus, while secret U.S. concessions to Hanoi often made no sense in terms of the battlefield situation (i.e., they conferred advantages on Hanoi that its military position did not actually warrant), these concessions were rationalized by referring to overall goals of U.S. foreign policy such as the need to eliminate "hotbeds of tension," to normalize relations with the Communist world, and to give the U.S. presence abroad its lowest profile since the end of World War II.

As the following pages will show, however, rather than serve as an alternative to warfare, the Vietnam negotiations were an extension of it. Each side delayed entering talks until it thought it had achieved a position of strength. When talks did begin, there was no negotiation: each side believed that the other would sign an agreement based on what had been achieved on the battlefield, not by bargaining over what it was legitimate to achieve in the political arena. Throughout the decade of Vietnam negotiations, moreover, both Washington and Hanoi believed in force, not diplomacy. When adversaries thus enter negotiations while still fighting, it is nearly always to reduce the costs of continuing the war, not to compromise on ways to end it.

For Communists, negotiating is a tactic of warfare. The American conception of negotiation is a process of bargaining and concession, and the outcome of negotiation is compromise, not victory. Americans expect to bargain, and we expect that a military stalemate will cause our adversaries to do the same.

Negotiating while fighting thus served Hanoi's purposes far better than it did Washington's. Hanoi used negotiation as a tactic of warfare, convinced that only a military victory, not concessions at a conference table, could end the war. But the United States lacked a strategy for winning the war or for depriving the North Vietnamese of the tactical advantages they sought in negotiations. Washington wanted the fruits of a military victory without actually having to win one. Washington sought the status quo ante: the end of Hanoi's military support to the Communist movement in South Vietnam. While Washington raised the cost to Hanoi of continuing to do this, U.S. spokesmen repeatedly assured Hanoi that the United States did not seek the destruction of North Vietnam. Escalation of aerial attacks against North Vietnam was viewed as the principal means of getting Hanoi to the conference table. But the more the United States bombed North Vietnam, the less there was to bomb, and the greater was Hanoi's will to resist. Consequently, Hanoi fought on, realizing that if Washington only wanted to restore the status quo in the south—a status quo that included the National Liberation Front as a political force—the North Vietnamese could not lose by continuing the war. Thus since Hanoi believed that a long war could not really hurt its interests but was precisely what Washington wanted to avoid, Washington was expected to make the concessions that would end it. And, indeed, nearly every time Washington made a negotiating offer to Hanoi, the U.S. terms softened. Every concession Washington offered Hanoi in private served as another wedge between Washington and Saigon. Every concession Hanoi hinted at in public, it rejected in private—and this widened the gap between the U.S. administration and the American public.

But, in retrospect, the real obstacle to a negotiated settlement was probably not Washington's diplomacy. As Hanoi maintained ever since its first direct conversation with Washington in 1962, the liberation of South Vietnam was an absolutely indispensable prerequisite for unification. North Vietnamese troops were not in the south for foreign adventurism or as a proxy for another Communist power. They were there to assure the outcome of a conflict fundamental to the success of the Vietnamese revolution. They would withdraw only when they had achieved victory. As a result, Hanoi repeatedly told Washington, there was basically nothing to negotiate about.

Beginnings, 1950–1966

THE BEGINNING
Part of the first shipment of U.S. military assistance to the French Union forces fighting the Viet Minh being transported through the streets of Hanoi in 1950. By 1954 the U.S. had provided some 500 aircraft, 440 naval vessels, and 360,000 small arms and machine guns. U.S. military aid to the French in Indochina totaled $2.6 billion by the time the Geneva Accords were signed. *(Courtesy of Jerry M. Silverman)*

A DECADE LATER
U.S. soldiers advising the army of South Vietnam. Shown during an inspection tour are (*right*) Army Chief of Staff General George N. Decker and (*center*) General Paul D. Harkins, head of the U.S. Military Assistance Command in Saigon. They are watching members of the Civil Defense Guard at fire practice. Official U.S. Army caption reads: "U.S. Army personnel are in Vietnam to advise and instruct in logistics, communications, and transportation. Personnel of the U.S. Army are not in combat status." *(U.S. Army photograph)*

PHASE OUT

Secretary of Defense Robert S. McNamara and General Lyman
Lemnitzer, chairman of the Joint Chiefs of Staff, during a 1962 inspection tour of Vietnam. McNamara was making plans to phase out all
U.S. advisers and to end U.S. logistical support to Saigon. When
McNamara asked how long it would take to eliminate the VC, he was
routinely told "one year." For planning purposes and thinking it best
to err on the side of caution, McNamara assumed that the defeat of
the VC could take as long as three years. *(U.S. Army photograph)*

THIS WAS THE ENEMY

Photograph of a Communist munitions "factory" captured by U.S.
forces during an operation. *(U.S. Army photograph)*

PLEIKU

A Johnson adviser recalled, LBJ believed that the Communist attack on this lonely outpost in the central highlands of Vietnam "was Hanoi's declaration of war against the United States." *(U.S. Army photograph)*

HAPPIER DAYS

June 1966, General Nguyen Van Thieu introduces his staff to General Fred C. Weyand, the commander of the U.S. Twenty-fifth Infantry Division in Vietnam. A decade later the two would meet, when the former's army was on the verge of collapse. A member of Weyand's party recalled of this last visit to Vietnam in early 1975: "After the first hour of our briefing, we knew that the situation was hopeless. We started doing what we could to make sure our Vietnamese friends would be evacuated." *(U.S. Army photograph)*

1962–1965: THE VIETNAM NEGOTIATIONS AND THE ROOTS OF THE WAR

The partition of Vietnam in 1954, despite the military defeat of the French in the battle for Dien Bien Phu, meant that the North Vietnamese achieved less at the conference table than they had won on the battlefield. They resolved to never let that happen again. By the early 1960s, the North Vietnamese had come to see negotiations only for their tactical value. Thus what Hanoi sought in direct talks with the United States was a way to improve its chances of winning a war, not a way of preventing or ending one.

FIGHTING AND NEGOTIATING: THE VIEW FROM HANOI

North Vietnam's strategy of fighting while negotiating reflects three principles they learned from experience.[1] The first principle General Vo Nguyen Giap called the "tradition of determination to fight and win," and it stemmed directly from the Dien Bien Phu experience. In the "pretalks" period this meant that Hanoi would not respond to U.S. offers made during bombing pauses; this was to avoid suggesting that bombing could affect North Vietnamese behavior. Once actually engaged in talks, Hanoi coordinated the military with the diplomatic struggle, so that negotiation became an extension of warfare. As Chief of Staff of the North Vietnamese Army, General Nguyen Van Vinh observed in a major speech in early 1966, "Fighting while negotiating is aimed at opening another front with a view to making the puppet army more disintegrated, stimulating and developing the enemy's internal contradictions, and thereby making him more isolated in order to deprive him of the propaganda weapons. . . ."[2]

Hanoi's second principle of fighting while negotiating was commitment to a protracted struggle. As one member of the Politburo observed:

> Time works for us. Time will be our best strategist. . . . To protract the war is the key to victory . . . if we prolong the war . . . our forces will grow stronger, the enemy forces will be weakened. . . . Those who want "lightening [*sic*] resistance war and rapid victory," who want to bring the whole of our forces to the battlefront to win a speedy victory and rapidly to decide the outcome of the war, do not profit from the invaluable experiences of history. . . . All they would achieve would be the premature sacrifice of the bulk of forces in a few adventurous battles; they would commit heroic but useless suicide.[3]

If negotiations were to be used as a tactic, then protracting them would be as essential as protracting the war itself. Protracted negotiations, Hanoi's leadership believed, would erode its adversary's will.

The third operational principle of Hanoi's fighting-while-negotiating strategy was that decisions about war and peace were to be insulated from the pressure of its allies.[4] Ever since the 1954 Geneva Conference, Hanoi had been fearful that Moscow and, to a lesser extent, Peking would promote negotiations that, given what could be achieved on the battlefield, were premature and that would be conducted according to an agenda not set by the Politburo in Hanoi. Consequently, the North Vietnamese were consistently unresponsive when Moscow acted as an intermediary or tried to promote negotiations. And, for its part, China did not try to act as a broker: Chinese leaders consistently told U.S. visitors to Peking that the question of whether or when to negotiate were issues on which Hanoi would accept no advice.

In 1960, Hanoi decided that, because of the growing strength of the Diem government and the political repression on which its authority rested, the south could be liberated only through a military struggle. This liberation struggle was to be fought by guerrillas in the jungle; the decline of governmental authority in the countryside would, Hanoi expected, precipitate Diem's collapse. The neutralist coalition of transition that then emerged would ask the United States to ends its military programs in South Vietnam. Thereafter, the National Liberation Front (NLF) would dominate the coalition and initiate the process of reunification.[5] The collapse of Diem and the departure of the Americans in its wake were thus "inevitable." From Hanoi's perspective, there would be no need to negotiate with the United States. At least this is what the leaders of North Vietnam probably thought when the United States first proposed negotiations to avoid war in Vietnam.

THE FIRST CONTACT

In July 1962, the overriding U.S. objective was to limit involvement in what President Kennedy and Secretary of Defense Robert McNamara believed was essentially a Vietnamese war. President Kennedy believed, moreover, that U.S. security interests were linked not to the fate of Indochina, but to developments in Europe and the Western Hemisphere. Thus, as the Geneva Accords on Laos were signed, President Kennedy asked the secretary of defense to initiate plans for a phased withdrawal of U.S. advisors from South Vietnam and a scaling down of the military assistance program. In part, the phased withdrawal program was rooted both in false optimism about the strength of the Diem government and the impact of the newly created strategic hamlet program, and in the belief that the NLF would continue to pose only a minor threat to the Government of Vietnam (GVN) in the countryside.[6] The president believed, however, that if any of these factors should change, the way to counter their effects was through diplomacy, not U.S. military intervention. Senator Mike Mansfield, who traveled to Southeast Asia in October 1962 at President Kennedy's request, agreed, suggesting that if the situation should change for the worse, "We may well discover that it is in our interests to do less rather than more than we are now doing. If that is the case, we will do well to concentrate on a vigorous diplomacy without bringing about sudden and catastrophic upheavals in Southeast Asia."[7]

Was an important opportunity to avoid war overlooked when Washington failed to follow up the Geneva Conference on Laos with one on Vietnam? The head of one Asian delegation to the conference later told me in an interview, "It was clear to us that the 1962 Laotian settlement would not work without some kind of agreement on Vietnam. All the diplomats at Geneva knew there would be a terrible war in South Vietnam unless Washington and Hanoi could reach a diplomatic accommodation. Washington was in a particularly anti-Communist mood, however; if communism wanted a fight in South Vietnam, the Americans boasted, it would be defeated in South Vietnam." But behind the scenes at Geneva the search for a diplomatic accommodation had already begun.

The president authorized W. Averell Harriman and his deputy William Sullivan (later a deputy assistant secretary of state deeply involved in the negotiations during the Johnson and Nixon administrations) to approach the North Vietnamese delegates at the Geneva Conference with an offer of secret talks. The president wanted Hanoi to know that Washington regarded the conflict in South Vietnam as an internal Vietnamese affair. Harriman and Sullivan were to suggest that the Laos Accords could serve as a model for an agreement guaranteeing Vietnam's neutrality.

This diplomatic overture to Hanoi had to be kept secret because, as one of Washington's emissaries put it, "To broadcast our meeting with North Vietnam would have alarmed the South Vietnamese who opposed such contacts. We knew if we were successful with Hanoi, we would have to bring Saigon around." The meeting and the site were arranged by the foreign minister of a neutral country attending the conference, and Harriman and

Sullivan took an elaborate detour through Geneva alleyways in order to avoid being seen by any of their South Vietnamese colleagues. They met with the foreign minister of North Vietnam and his military assistant, Colonel Ha Van Lau, who, like Sullivan, later participated in the secret Paris talks.

The ninety-minute session began with Harriman observing that he was the same age as Ho Chi Minh, and like Ho, shared the dream of enjoying old age with Vietnam at peace. A step in that direction could be taken that day, Harriman suggested. If agreement was possible on Laos, one should be no less possible on Vietnam.

The representatives from Hanoi responded that the Four-Point Manifesto of the NLF was the only basis for peace in Vietnam. This manifesto called, in part, for the immediate withdrawal of all "personnel of U.S. satellites and allies," and the establishment of a "national coalition government to guarantee peace, organize elections, promulgate democratic liberties, release political prisoners, and abolish all monopolies." If the United States wanted peace in the region, the North Vietnamese declared, all it had to do was withdraw its personnel from Vietnam and end its support to the Diem government. Because the United States was illegally supporting an illegitimate government, there was, from Hanoi's viewpoint, nothing to negotiate about. "I don't think they believed that we would stand firm or commit more troops than the 16,000 we already had in South Vietnam," one of the Americans at the meeting later told me in an interview. "They thought then that South Vietnam would be theirs in a matter of months or years and that, therefore, there was no need to enter negotiations to get what would certainly come through our default."

Further efforts to engage the North Vietnamese in talks were rebuffed for the next eighteen months as Hanoi, not without reason, expected the Saigon government to collapse. By the end of 1962, it was clear that the Diem government's tenuous hold on the countryside was slipping, the strategic hamlet program was failing, and Saigon's army was no match for the NLF's mobile guerrilla teams or for the small conventional units that could lure GVN troops into carefully planned ambushes.

By 1963, Hanoi saw political developments in Saigon as a prelude to a Communist-dominated South Vietnam. GVN repression had provoked a crisis between the Catholic elite and the urban Buddhists. Such repression alienated the Americans who, already upset with the inability of the Diem government to initiate long-promised administrative and political reforms, encouraged a coup against Diem. But once in power, the coup leaders could not agree on who should head the government or on how the army could be mobilized into an effective fighting force. The Communists expected the Americans to be further alienated by the squabbles between these South Vietnamese politicians and, consequently, to reduce support to Diem's successors. Loss of U.S. support would provoke yet another political crisis permitting the NLF to take the initiative in creating a Government of National Union, a coalition the Communists could dominate. The consolidation of Communist power in South Vietnam would be complete when the Catholics (their ranks thinned by assassination of anti-Communist leaders) adapted to life within a Communist state, and when the new Government of National Union in the south began talks with the DRV (Democratic Republic of Vietnam, i.e., North Vietnam) about unification.

Washington's secret diplomacy in 1962 and 1963 (as would be true a decade later) was not aimed at persuading Hanoi that its image of the future was incorrect; it was aimed at persuading Hanoi that the methods it had employed thus far—assassination, terrorism, use of the demilitarized zone for military purposes, and violation of the neutrality of Cambodia and Laos—constituted a threat to peace in Southeast Asia. The United States would respond, diplomats warned Hanoi, if peace continued to be threatened; aggression would be countered. Hanoi's diplomats did not, however respond to Washington's concern by suggesting that the conflict in Vietnam was strictly an internal affair. Their propaganda suggested, instead, that it was part of a worldwide struggle against imperialism. "At the time," one high White House official later recalled, "there was plenty of evidence to suggest that the domino theory was valid." Having thus inflated the significance of the conflict by the end of 1963, Hanoi's and Washington's diplomacy reinforced misperceptions that ultimately led to war.

PRESIDENT JOHNSON THOUGHT HE COULD GET NEGOTIATIONS ONLY THROUGH WAR

In 1966, I asked one of President Kennedy's most senior and trusted aides if there would have been a war in Vietnam if Kennedy had lived. He replied that he never stopped to think about that question. "The day after the assassination, I had to brief President Johnson about Vietnam. He realized that the administration had been deeply divided by the war and made it plain that encouraging the coup against Diem was a mistake, a product of these internal divisions. 'We can't get out of there while it's such a mess; at least Diem represented stability,' the president said. 'Now, I want no more backbiting and no more internal debate.' Johnson continued. 'I will set a policy soon and want it carried out firmly and with loyalty.'"

The assassination of President Kennedy deprived the country of a debate among policy-makers over the wisdom of becoming more deeply involved in the conflict in Vietnam. President Johnson did not encourage debate over the Vietnam involvement while Saigon bordered on the edge of anarchy—anarchy brought on, in Johnson's view, by the internal divisions within the U.S.

government that had led to U.S. support of a coup. Lacking any debate outside the White House and discouraging it within, President Johnson believed he had inherited a commitment, not the responsibility to decide if a commitment should be made.

The president thus believed his decision was whether Americans should fight a war for victory or whether they should fight for the very negotiations his predecessor had tried to start. If the United States sought military victory Americans themselves might have to fight a land war in Asia; if negotiations were sought, the United States had little guarantee in 1964 that Hanoi would be more willing to compromise in its struggle to liberate the south and unify Vietnam than it had been in 1962. Indeed, to Hanoi, the "correlation of forces" (the North Vietnamese term for the success of their social, political, and military struggles) from 1962 to 1967 was probably viewed as unfavorable for negotiations. This did not mean that Hanoi was stalemated militarily or that the government in Saigon had developed the administrative or military capability or the political support necessary to compete effectively with the NLF. Rather, Hanoi's refusal to negotiate reflected dissatisfaction with the success of its own military struggle and with the meager extent of the NLF's political control in the countryside.

To many of the president's advisors, Hanoi's intransigence was not entirely unwelcome. "That Saigon could have survived a negotiated settlement," one later told me in an interview, "seemed to us then inconceivable. We were in a terrible bind: if we started to negotiate, Saigon would refuse to stand and fight. Our first instinct was thus to build up their morale because we knew that weak states with neither the will nor the means to oppose communism in the first place would be swallowed up by communism after the negotiations were over."

Other officials thought that bolstering Saigon's morale by assisting them in fighting was a low-risk strategy that could actually improve the chances of a non-Communist government to survive a negotiated settlement. When London *Times* editor Henry Brandon asked Secretary of State Dean Rusk if the U.S. involvement in the war would escalate, Rusk replied simply: "Horse-shit."[8] What Dean Rusk and the rest of the U.S. government did not anticipate was the inability of Americans to have any impact on the GVN. As an unnamed analyst, who wrote the introduction to the section of the Pentagon Papers dealing with U.S.-GVN relations from 1964 to 1967, observed:

> In 1964 the U.S. tried to make the GVN strong, effective and stable, and it failed. When the U.S. offered more aid, GVN accepted it without improving. . . . When the U.S. offered a firmer commitment to encourage them, including possible later bombing of North Vietnam, the GVN tried to pressure

us to do it sooner. . . . When [U.S. Ambassador Maxwell] Taylor lectured them and threatened them, the ruling generals of GVN defied him.

. . . After several changes of government in Vietnam, the U.S. could set no higher goal than GVN stability. During the period, the USG [United States Government] was already starting to think about doing the job ourselves if our Vietnamese ally did not perform.[9]

By January 1964, President Johnson had ruled out further debate about the merits of underwriting the GVN when he decided that Vietnam would not prove amenable to the same kind of neutralization solution that President Kennedy had supported for Laos. Mr. Johnson's New Year's message to the junta then heading the GVN thus made clear that "the United States government shares the view of your government that 'neutralization' of South Vietnam is unacceptable. As long as the Communist regime in North Vietnam persists in its aggressive policy, neutralization of South Vietnam would only be another name for a Communist takeover."

What President Johnson did not say, but what a growing circle of officials knew to be the case, was that the neutralization solution—and nearly any other solution that could be envisioned—could not work because the GVN was already too weak (and getting weaker daily) to survive a negotiated settlement. The population under GVN control was indifferent and apathetic; army morale was low and the desertion rate high.

In March, the order implementing the phased withdrawal program of the Kennedy administration was rescinded. At that point, the urgency of the situation was such that an Inter-Agency Vietnam Committee was prepared to recommend to the president that "American personnel . . . be integrated into the Vietnamese chain of command, both military and civil. They should become direct operational components of the Vietnamese governmental structure."[10] Washington assumed that Hanoi would negotiate out of fear of both U.S. capabilities and the costs to the north of a prolonged war. But timing was the chief problem: the GVN had to be strong enough militarily to survive a cease-fire and organized enough politically to compete with the NLF. Either there had to be a favorable balance of forces when the negotiations began, or Washington would have to create one before they ended.

ENTER U.S. ALLIES

Hanoi believed that any negotiated settlement would fall considerably short of what could be achieved by frustrating the Americans militarily. Most officials in Washington did not believe U.S. military power could be so easily stalemated. As a result, in 1964 and 1965 Washington and Hanoi were telling each other they would fight to prove their point. At the same time, U.S. allies were telling Washington that a non-Communist South Vietnam might not be worth a war.

Undersecretary of State George Ball agreed with them, and he argued that our allies did not see Vietnam as a test case of U.S. counter-insurgency strategies or of the value of U.S. commitments abroad. In an October 1964 memorandum to Dean Rusk, Robert McNamara, and McGeorge Bundy, Ball pointed out:

> The assumption which has governed our planning with respect to South Viet-Nam has been that the United States must successfully stop the extension of Communist power into South Viet-Nam if its promises are to have credence. It is argued that failing such an effort our Allies around the world would be inclined to doubt our promises and to feel that they could no longer safely rely upon American power against Communist aggressive ambitions.
>
> We have by our own public statements contributed to such a reaction. (See, for example, Attorney General Kennedy's comment in Germany that if Americans did not stop Communism in South Viet-Nam, how could people believe that they would stop it in Berlin?)
>
> Against these concerns one must balance the view of many of our Allies that we are engaged in a fruitless struggle in South-Viet-Nam [sic]—a struggle we are bound to lose.
>
> They fear that as we become too deeply involved in a war on the land mass of Asia, we will tend to lose interest in their problems. They believe that we would be foolish to risk bogging ourselves down in the Indochina jungle. They fear a general loss of confidence in American judgment that could result if we pursued a course which many regard as neither prudent nor necessary.
>
> What we might gain by establishing the steadfastness of our commitments we could lose by an erosion of confidence in our judgment.[11]

Ball concluded, "We cannot assume that an escalation of the war in South Viet-Nam involving a more profound American engagement would be universally applauded by our friends and Allies or that it would necessarily operate to increase our prestige or the confidence placed in us."[12] He also did not think that escalating the war "would necessarily result in a more favorable political solution than a negotiation that was not preceded by such pressure."

What disturbed President Johnson most was that, while Ball might have been right, Hanoi's aggressive actions against South Vietnam gave the United States no choice but to increase military pressure in order to protect American lives while waiting for Hanoi to come to the conference table. Aides to the president later told me in interviews that Mr. Johnson realized that using force to compel the North Vietnamese to negotiate would only encourage them to continue fighting. But even if negotiations began, the president realized that Hanoi would use them only to win U.S. concessions, not to reach a compromise settlement. Consequently, the president said, he would only talk to the North Vietnamese when he was sure they had something to say.

Almost from the start the president discovered he could not follow his own instincts. U.S. allies believed it crucial that Washington and Hanoi talk out their differences. UN secretary-general U Thant, for example, thought that Hanoi and Washington equally misunderstood each other's resolve and that each perceived it was the action of the other that left it with no choice but to fight rather than negotiate. In October 1964, U Thant sought to arrange secret talks between the two governments. Hanoi "agreed" in November, but no response was received from Washington for over five months. When an answer was finally given, it was negative: UN ambassador Adlai Stevenson told U Thant that Washington had been assured that Hanoi was not interested in secret talks.

A year later, U Thant told President Johnson of his dismay that the initiative had not been followed. But the president had not even heard of Ho's offer or U Thant's efforts to arrange secret talks! The details of U Thant's efforts were released by Stevenson shortly before his death in an interview with CBS news commentator Eric Sevareid. Both Stevenson and Sevareid believed that the Johnson administration had let an opportunity for peace slip by.

Administration officials contend that the president was not informed of U Thant's initiative because it was not regarded as serious, because the other indications Washington had about Hanoi's intentions suggested no interest in negotiations, and because Mr. Johnson was suspicious of Mr. U Thant's efforts to arrange U.S.-North Vietnamese talks. Later, Hanoi denied that it had told U Thant it was willing to engage in secret talks. This was the first time Hanoi used the whipsaw technique of bargaining in which one North Vietnamese official would tell an intermediary something that another North Vietnamese official would contradict. While U Thant and others pressed the case for negotiations and assured U.S. officials that Hanoi was ready for talks, J. Blair Seaborn, head of the Canadian delegation to the International Control Commission (ICC), made five trips to Hanoi between June 1964 and June 1965 and reported just the reverse. The channel he established between President Johnson and DRV Premier Pham Van Dong remained open for nearly a year and directly contradicted what U Thant had told Stevenson in October.

Seaborn was to tell Pham Van Dong that the United States had limited objectives in Vietnam. The U.S. commitment was to the independence and territorial integrity of South Vietnam so that the people there could freely and

peacefully choose their form of government. U.S. military activities in
Vietnam were not aimed at North Vietnam, but rather at helping a duly
constituted government respond to a threat from forces of another government that was violating a demilitarized zone established by international
agreement. Seaborn was also instructed to say that Washington believed
Hanoi controlled the military operations of the NLF, as evidenced by the
nearly complete cease-fires that had occurred on Hanoi's orders at Tet (the
lunar new year holiday) in 1963 and 1964. Washington, consequently, wanted
Hanoi to cease and desist in its military support to the NLF. If Hanoi chose to
persist, Seaborn was instructed to say that President Johnson's patience was
wearing very thin and that he would stand up to aggression. "In the event of
escalation," Seaborn told Premier Pham Van Dong, "the greatest devastation
would . . . result from the DRVN [DRV] itself as a result of the air and
naval activities that would be taken against North Vietnam." These themes
were repeated during Seaborn's second visit to Hanoi in August 1964, when
he was instructed to warn Pham Van Dong that the Tonkin Gulf resolution
should serve as a warning that the United States could be provoked into war.

Seaborn was also to convey Washington's willingness to endorse a political
settlement if Hanoi ceased supporting the NLF's armed struggle. Washington's negotiating offer to Pham Van Dong included: (1) obtaining Saigon's
agreement to a resumption of north–south trade, (2) providing PL480 food
aid directly to the DRV, (3) lifting all foreign assets controls on the DRV
currency held in the United States, (4) reducing all trade restrictions to only
those in effect for the Soviet Union, (5) diplomatic recognition, (6) the
removal of all U.S. forces from South Vietnam except for the 350 advisors
permitted under the Geneva Agreement, and (7) a GVN announcement of
amnesty for all members of the NLF. Washington also offered Hanoi the
choice of announcing all of these U.S. concessions either at once or over a
three-month period.

Viewed against the background of South Vietnam's political instability and
the weakness of its army, U.S. government experts on Vietnam warned that, if
Hanoi accepted these concessions, communism would triumph in a matter of
months. As one put it, "The NLF would not have to fire a single shot. Saigon
politicians would do the job." But the president was convinced that if the
South Vietnamese were left alone and American economic aid continued, the
GVN would remain an independent and non-Communist government.

Pham Van Dong did not reject Washington's offer outright; he did so by
countering that the following was the only basis on which war could be
avoided: since the Geneva Accords had stipulated that Vietnam would be
free of all foreign military forces, the United States was an aggressor; the NLF
were engaged in a legitimate defense of the sovereignty and territorial
integrity of Vietnam; to avoid war, therefore, the U.S. must leave Vietnam

and end all support to the Saigon government.* There was, Pham told Seaborn, nothing to negotiate about.

AND THEN THERE WAS WAR

"After 125 Americans were wounded in the attack on Pleiku," one U.S. official recalled, "I knew we were into something big and something that would get much bigger. It was war." The February 1965 raid on the American advisors' barracks at Pleiku resulted in a decisive change in Washington's attitude toward the conflict. Until the attack, it had been possible for the president's advisors to press the case for not going to war over Vietnam. As one advisor later wrote (in the *Washington Post*) of McGeorge Bundy's fact-finding trip to Vietnam in February 1965:

> . . . after Bundy had been in Vietnam for several days, "getting out" still seemed possible. The chances were admittedly thin, but in the light of what Bundy had seen at first-hand, Johnson might just be convinced that America's interests would best be served by cutting loose as expeditiously and gracefully as possible—if the Communists laid low, at least as far as American personnel were concerned. Sunday, February 7 . . . promised to be a relaxed day. The Vietnamese New Year had not yet ended and it seemed peaceful enough for Bundy to pay a visit to the countryside. . . . We would leave the next morning for Anchorage where we would spend a day writing the final report. . . . [but] on that Sunday 10 years ago started the largest war in American history. Early that morning two hundred miles from Saigon in the town of Pleiku, a platoon of Viet Cong soldiers attacked an American airfield; eight American soldiers were killed, 125 wounded.[13]

The Pleiku incident meant that while diplomatic efforts continued, the United States no longer hesitated to use military force. U.S. dependents were evacuated from South Vietnam, and a series of reprisal air strikes were conducted over North Vietnam. It was at this point that plans were made also to land the first U.S. combat troops in Vietnam. Hanoi was not unprepared for U.S. aerial attacks on its homeland; it viewed them not as reprisals for actions taken against U.S. forces in South Vietnam, but as the beginning of a total war. As U.S. officials were to learn shortly:

> From the start of the U.S. air offensive . . . Hanoi . . . disbelieved protestations by the United States that the threat was a limited one in terms of targets and political objectives. Not only Hanoi's reporting and propaganda but also its actions indicated that it expected the United States to proceed to massive attacks on economic and population targets. Taken together, these actions

---

*The Geneva Accords and the Geneva Agreements refer to the same documents.—Author

added up to an urgent, comprehensive, and determined crash program to prepare the country for unrestricted air attack and possible ground invasion, and for a war of indefinite duration.[14]

Thus from the very start, the message Washington wanted Hanoi to get—that if it stopped its terrorist attacks on Americans (and later also ceased infiltration), the bombing would stop—was not getting through.

From the outset, intelligence experts did not anticipate that increased U.S. military pressure would either weaken Hanoi's will to fight or persuade the North Vietnamese to negotiate. For example, a month after the bombing of North Vietnam had begun, the director of Central Intelligence (DCI) noted that the bombing was not having an appreciable effect on North Vietnamese support to the NLF and that its continuation might encourage Moscow and Peking to increase military assistance to the DRV. Concerning the increased role of U.S. ground forces in the actual combat, the DCI warned: ". . . we will find ourselves mired down in combat in the jungle in a military effort we cannot win, and from which we will have extreme difficulty in extracting ourselves."[15] Civilian officials in the Defense Department agreed, as did air force generals faced with the job of waging the air war. As one put it in an interview, "Bombing doesn't work that way. You've got to hit the enemy hard the first time and carry through until there is a willingness to talk. If you turn the pressure on and off, the enemy can recover. He won't negotiate." The general was right.

1965–1967: THE SEARCH FOR NEGOTIATIONS PROTRACTS THE WAR

Once the United States was actually in the war, a negotiated settlement became less, not more, likely. U.S. officials believed that the war could be won and U.S. terms for a negotiated settlement stiffened. State Department and White House officials involved in the effort to start negotiations warned diplomats in touch with North Vietnamese that, if Hanoi continued to spurn all attempts to start talks, continued to reject all settlement offers, and continued to demand what amounted to U.S. capitulation, then the war might have to be fought until a weakened Communist movement no longer threatened Saigon's survival. At that time, these officials pointed out, Hanoi would be forced to settled on far less favorable terms than the ones currently being offered.

To Defense Department officials, in contrast, fighting the war for the GVN provided an interim solution to the thorny problem presented by the instability and ineffectiveness of Saigon. As Deputy Secretary of Defense John T. McNaughton put it, "Action against North Vietnam is to some extent a substitute for strengthening the government in South Vietnam. That is, a less active VC (on orders from DRV) can be handled by a less efficient GVN (which we expect to have)."[1]

Indeed, most U.S. officials I have interviewed recognized that, once in the war, Washington was there to stay until military developments persuaded Hanoi to cease and desist (the preferred goal) or at a minimum to enter talks with Washington about ceasing and desisting. As one official later told me, "The president and most of us quickly found that we had little trouble in finding reasons to keep the war going. We rapidly discovered that limited military pressure on Hanoi was not having any impact on their attitude toward negotiating. We could not cut our losses and get out because we had too much already sunk into the investment. If we called it quits, the American people would wonder about our wisdom, and our allies would begin to doubt the credibility of our commitments to them."

Once at war, Washington's strategy for terminating it depended on success on the battlefield. In President Johnson's mind, achieving a position of strength became an essential prerequisite for negotiations. The president quickly realized that such a position was not likely to be achieved rapidly merely by strengthening the GVN. It was essential at the same time to increase military pressure on North Vietnam and thus compel Hanoi to negotiate.

The North Vietnamese leadership, however, chose to refuse to negotiate because they were convinced the United States could not win the war as long as the NVA could choose the time and place of the major battles, that Saigon would not make the internal reforms necessary to compete politically with the NLF, and that U.S. and world public opinion would eventually force Washington to end the bombing of North Vietnam in return for the promise of negotiations. Consequently, when a basis for negotiation was proposed by the United States or suggested by an intermediary, Hanoi probably assessed the offer, not according to its fairness (i.e., how we wanted Hanoi to behave), but in terms of whether the immediate situation on the battlefield permitted the offer to be rejected.

The search for negotiations with Hanoi between 1965 and 1968 is one of the most fruitless chapters in U.S. diplomacy. White House sources estimate that as many as 2,000 individual efforts were made to initiate talks. On 432 of the 800-odd days of the air war against North Vietnam, U.S. planes were either restricted in their targets or completely prohibited from bombing in the hope of encouraging a favorable North Vietnamese response to a negotiating initiative. In his memoirs, Lyndon Johnson noted that there were some seventy-two negotiation initiatives he personally followed. He regarded those listed in table 2.1 as the most significant.

"As I look back," Mr. Johnson said of these efforts to start negotiations, "I think that we perhaps tried too hard to spell out our honest desire for peace. . . . These numerous appeals through so many channels may well have convinced the North Vietnamese that we wanted peace at any price."[2] Mr. Johnson was, in fact, pessimistic about a negotiated settlement from the start, believing that Hanoi would seek negotiations only to end the bombing and not the war. Mr. Johnson's characterizations of the search for negotiations are thus based on an increasingly embittering experience. As this account will show, Mr. Johnson had a fundamentally sound understanding of how Hanoi approached the war and negotiations. What Mr. Johnson failed to grasp was that U.S. goals—a successful outcome from a limited war and a political settlement—could be achieved neither by fighting nor by negotiating.

TABLE 2.1

PRESIDENT LYNDON JOHNSON'S ASSESSMENT OF THE MAJOR INITIATIVES IN THE SEARCH FOR NEGOTIATIONS WITH HANOI
1964–1968

Date	Initiative	Mr. Johnson's Assessment
June 1964–June 1965	Seaborn missions	Hanoi showed no interest in discussions.
May 1965	Five-day bombing pause (Project Mayflower)	Hanoi called the pause a trick. Just after the pause ended, North Vietnamese officials approached the French and discussed Hanoi's position on a peace settlement. French officials said this could "not be regarded as a valid offer of negotiations."
August–September 1965 November 1965 January 1966	An unofficial U.S. representative met with Mai Van Bo in Paris	Hanoi was unresponsive.
December 24, 1965– January 30, 1966	Thirty-seven-day bombing pause	Prime Minister Pham Van Dong in Hanoi called our peace effort a campaign of lies.
March and June 1966	Ronning missions	Hanoi authorities were totally negative with regard to any response on their part to a halt in the bombing. Hanoi repeated its insistence on its four points.
June–December 1966	The Government of Poland extends good offices to arrange direct talks (Project Marigold)	On December 13, the Poles informed the United States that Hanoi was not willing to have talks, and on December 15, the Poles terminated conversations on the possibility of direct talks, allegedly at Hanoi's insistence.
October 1966– February 1968	The government of Rumania extends good offices to report Hanoi's attitude toward talks	Hanoi's response was negative.
February 8–13, 1967	Wilson-Kosygin talks on extending the Tet bombing pause	Hanoi called the pause another trick.
July–October 1967	Four French friends of Henry Kissinger traveled to Hanoi to present what later became known as the San Antonio formula: The U.S. would stop bombing when this would promptly lead to productive negotiations	Hanoi gave final rejection in mid-October and increased offensive actions in Vietnam.

SOURCE: Adapted from "Major Peace Initiatives," in Lyndon B. Johnson, *The Vantage Point* (New York: Holt, Rinehart and Winston, 1971), pp. 579–89.

What follows is a year-by-year account of the most significant efforts between spring of 1965 and late fall of 1967 to start negotiations between Washington and Hanoi. The who, what, when, and how of each initiative is examined. I have also tried to explain the reasons for a particular initiative and the consequences of its collapse by drawing from interviews with those directly involved. My chief purpose has not been to provide a complete recounting of the diplomacy of the period, but to highlight what Washington and Hanoi learned about negotiating while fighting and why President Johnson ultimately came to believe that the search for negotiations prolonged the war.

1965: THE BOMBING FAILED EARLY

What the United States sought in Vietnam, President Johnson declared in an April 1965 landmark speech at Johns Hopkins University, was "an independent South Viet-Nam—securely guaranteed and able to shape its own relationships to all others—free from outside interference—tied to no alliance—a military base for no other country." Such a future for South Vietnam, the president said, could be achieved in many ways and the United States was ready for unconditional discussions with Hanoi to facilitate it.[3] But, from the start, administration officials did not know how negotiations could lead to the future the president had described. Hanoi offered Washington nonnegotiable demands, repeatedly telling Washington that the bombing has to stop before there could even be talks about talks. Washington insisted that the talks begin unconditionally, an indication of the president's unwillingness to stop the bombing, the bargaining chip he hoped to cash in for a political settlement.

Hanoi's basic position, the four points (see box, p. 27), was presented by Premier Pham Van Dong in a speech to the DRV National Assembly on April 8, 1965. The four points represented the minimum that had to be achieved in any negotiations with Washington. While Washington understood this in theory, it tended, in practice, to treat the four points as maximum demands, subject to modification through either tacit bargaining or formal negotiation.

Hanoi's four-point stand, however, linked ending the war to a political settlement of the struggle over power in South Vietnam. This represented something more than a shift of the conflict from the military into the political arena. Hanoi's insistence that the political and military issues could not be separated meant that, if negotiations were to end the war, Washington had to replace with a coalition the government in Saigon that it was trying to save from collapse. Hanoi maintained that U.S. intervention in 1964 and 1965 had dramatically affected the political situation in the south: the GVN had not been allowed to collapse as had been expected, and thereafter, the NLF had

NORTH VIETNAM'S FOUR POINTS
Presented by Premier Pham Van Dong
to the DRVN National Assembly
(April 8, 1965)

1. Recognition of the basic national rights of the Vietnamese people: peace, independence, sovereignty, unity, and territorial integrity. According to the Geneva Agreements, the U.S. Government must withdraw from South Viet Nam all U.S. troops, military personnel and weapons of all kinds, dismantle all U.S. military bases there, cancel its "military alliance" with Saigon. It must end its policy of intervention and aggression in South Viet Nam. According to the Geneva Agreements, the U.S. Government must end its war acts against the North and definitely end all encroachments on the territory and sovereignty of the Democratic Republic of Viet Nam.

2. Pending the peaceful reunification of Viet Nam, while Viet Nam is still temporarily divided into two zones, the military provisions of the 1954 Geneva Agreements on Viet Nam must be strictly respected: the two zones must refrain from joining any military alliance with foreign countries, and there must be no foreign military bases, troops, and military personnel in their respective territories.

3. The affairs of South Viet Nam are to be settled by the South Vietnamese people themselves, in accordance with the programme of the South Viet Nam National Front for Liberation, without any foreign interference.

4. The peaceful reunification of Viet Nam is to be settled by the Vietnamese people in both zones, without any foreign interference.

lost ground politically as well as militarily. By seeking both a political and a military settlement, Hanoi sought to restore to the Communist movement in the south the momentum that had been lost. This the United States was unprepared to permit.

Washington's diplomacy aimed at providing Hanoi (through pauses in the bombing of North Vietnam) chances to back down from the four-point stand and reformulate, either in public or in secret, its settlement proposals. The theory was that, once Hanoi had backed down enough to make it possible for the United States to enter talks, bargaining would ensue in substantive negotiations. But President Johnson never believed that those who advocated negotiations understood Hanoi or were realistic in their assessment of the chances that such unilateral initiative as stopping the bombing would actually lead to negotiations and a settlement. "If I were Ho Chi Minh," the president repeatedly told aides, "I would never negotiate."

Thus, while Mr. Johnson realized that negotiation was increasingly a domestic political necessity, he did not think it would lead to a settlement of the war. The president's skepticism had such an effect on the search for negotiations that, as one aide put it, "Every time we entered into a bombing halt, every time some third party reported to us that there might be a chance for talks with Hanoi, and every time Hanoi encouraged American citizens visiting North Vietnam to believe that it was willing to enter into productive talks, the president would just figure the odds. He never once saw a moment when, if he had been Ho Chi Minh, he would have responded positively to our effort to start negotiations. But we had to have some bombing pauses to show our critics at home and abroad that we were willing to take risks for peace and it was Hanoi, not us, that was putting up the obstacles."

The first bombing pause came in May 1965, some three months after regular air operations had begun over North Vietnam (see Appendix R), and lasted for only five days. In a telegram to Ambassador Maxwell Taylor in Saigon, the president summarized his purposes in the following terms:

> I have learned from Bob McNamara that nearly all ROLLING THUNDER [the code name for the air war against North Vietnam] operations for this week can be completed by Wednesday noon. . . . This fact, and the days of Buddha's birthday, seem to me to provide an excellent opportunity for a pause in air attacks which might go into next week and which I could use to good effect with world opinion. My plan is not to announce this brief pause but simply to call it privately to the attention of Moscow and Hanoi as soon as possible and tell them we shall be watching closely to see whether they respond in any way. My current plan is to report publicly after the pause ends on what we have done.[4]

Settlement terms—a set of propositions to which Hanoi could simply say yes—were not offered during pauses; instead, Washington offered Hanoi a chance to respond by modifying its four points or by deescalating the war. Average monthly indicators of the level of combat and of North Vietnamese military activity were established so that policy-makers could determine if Communist military activity did indeed taper off in response to U.S. initiatives. These statistics were seasonally adjusted to take into account the normal patterns of combat in the dry and rainy seasons.

The problem with this conceptualization of how Hanoi would respond to a U.S. initiative was that Hanoi's signaling interest in negotiations through restraining its military activities would be tantamount to signaling that the bombing could change DRV policy. Thus, Hanoi never appeared to be winding down the war. As one U.S. negotiator later observed:

> Every time Hanoi or one of its allies hinted that talks might be possible, we would look at the indicators. They always told us that Hanoi was far more interested in fighting than in talking. Those of us who favored negotiations could argue that infiltration had slowed; the military specialists would say that, while the rate of infiltration was lower than the previous month's, it was average for that particular month. Or we would say that the NVA appeared in the process of withdrawing some of its troops from the south and that this could be a sign of willingness to talk. But the military analysts would only see the NVA withdrawing to Laotian and Cambodian sanctuaries in order to regroup for the next attack.

Hanoi denounced the May 1965 bombing pause and all other bombing pauses, claiming that they were designed to rationalize the expansion of the war. Moscow generally refused to serve as an intermediary in the face of that reaction, and when Washington once sought to have a diplomatic note outlining the context of a bombing pause initiative delivered to Hanoi, a Soviet Foreign Ministry official tersely informed the U.S. ambassador in Moscow: "I am not a postman."

A few hours after the United States resumed the bombing of North Vietnam, however, Mai Van Bo, the highest ranking North Vietnamese diplomat accredited to a non-Communist government, asked the French Foreign Ministry to convey the following message to Washington: "Premier Pham Van Dong's Four Points of April 1965 should not be considered as prior conditions but rather as working principles for negotiations." What Bo had to say was significant, if ambiguous. Blair Seaborn had just returned from Hanoi convinced that the DRV was not interested in negotiations. Washington was slow to respond because, as one U.S. official involved in monitoring negotiation efforts put it, "We just couldn't believe that what Mai Van Bo was telling us was more authoritative than what the premier of North Vietnam, himself, had said to Seaborn." By midsummer, and after several conversations between Bo and the French, the State Department selected an unofficial representative to meet with Bo in Paris. His job was to convey Washington's desire to start talks, to avoid escalation, to see the war ended, and to add the view of a private citizen that, unless talks began soon, there would be a substantial domestic sentiment and support for widening the war.

At the first substantive meeting in the Paris apartment of Mai Van Bo, and after each side had communicated to the other the gravity with which the war was viewed in its respective capital, the U.S. representative proposed changes in the wording of the four points so that they could be used as the basis for negotiations. The first point of Hanoi's version provided for:

> Recognition of the basic national rights of the Vietnamese people: peace, independence, sovereignty, unity, and territorial integrity. According to the Geneva Agreements, the U.S. Government must withdraw from South Viet Nam all U.S. troops, military personnel and weapons of all kinds, dismantle all U.S. military bases there, cancel its "military alliance" with Saigon. It must end its policy of intervention and aggression in South Viet Nam. According to the Geneva Agreements, the U.S. Government must end its war acts against the North and definitely end encroachments on the territory and sovereignty of the Democratic Republic of Viet Nam.

The U.S. modification of this first point aimed at making the following issues subjects for "immediate, international discussions without conditions" (a reference to President Johnson's position in his April 1965 Johns Hopkins speech): (1) the withdrawal of all foreign military and quasi-military personnel from North and South Vietnam, (2) the dismantling of foreign military bases in North and South Vietnam, and (3) the military alliances in contravention of the Geneva Accords.

Hanoi's second point provided:

> Pending the peaceful reunification of Viet Nam, while Viet Nam is still temporarily divided into two zones, the military provisions of the 1954 Geneva Agreements on Viet Nam must be strictly respected: the two zones must refrain from joining any military alliance with foreign countries, and there must be no foreign military bases, troops, and military personnel in their respective territories.

Washington substantially agreed with this point, but argued that compliance with the military provisions of the Geneva Accords could now be achieved only with greatly improved inspection mechanisms.

Hanoi's third point concerned the political future of South Vietnam:

> The affairs of South Viet Nam are to be settled by the South Vietnamese people themselves, in accordance with the programme of the South Viet Nam National Front for Liberation, without any foreign interference.

Washington proposed substituting the phrase "in accordance with the programme of the South Vietnam National Front for Liberation" with only a general reference to "principles of self-determination." The program of the NLF called for, among other things, the overthrow of the government in Saigon, the imposition of a coalition, and the recognition of the NLF as the sole genuine representative of the South Vietnamese people. To thus recognize the NLF in advance of negotiations, U.S. officials argued, would concede something that Hanoi had been unable to achieve either on the battlefield or in the political arena.

Hanoi's fourth point provided:

> The peaceful reunification of Viet Nam is to be settled by the Vietnamese people in both zones, without any foreign interference.

Although Washington desired to change the wording of this point, there was no disagreement with it in principle.

Washington hoped its version of the four points could serve as a basis for unconditional discussions in a Geneva-Conference-type forum. By the end of his second meeting with the U.S. representative, Mai Van Bo agreed, in principle, with the idea of holding such a conference. Bo also suggested that the withdrawal of all forces from South Vietnam should be phased and balanced. But U.S. officials had difficulty in squaring Hanoi's private forthcomingness with what Ho Chi Minh had said in *Le Monde* on August 15, just as the second meeting with Bo began. In that interview, Ho declared: "The U.S. government must give tangible proofs that it accepts the four-point stand . . . it must immediately stop the air attacks against DRV territory, stop forthwith the aggressive war against the south of our country, and withdraw from there all U.S. troops and weapons." Given that definition of the significance of the four points—one clearly at variance with the flexibility Mai Van Bo suggested was possible—the U.S. representative wondered aloud if there was any point to further meetings. Bo answered that another meeting should indeed be held; he had not yet read the Ho interview in *Le Monde,* and he hinted that there might be some additional changes in Hanoi's position that would make negotiations possible.

The third meeting took place three days later. To Washington's very great surprise, Bo began by saying that his position, not the one outlined by Ho Chi Minh in the *Le Monde* interview, was the official DRV position. Bo did not insist that Hanoi's wording of the four points was the only form in which they could be expressed. However, Bo emphasized that Hanoi required tangible evidence (the end of the bombing of North Vietnam) that Washington accepted the four points in principle.

U.S. officials monitoring the talks in Paris realized the significance of how far Hanoi had come to meet some of Washington's basic objectives on mutual troop withdrawal and reunification. Nonetheless, there remained fundamental disagreements on the conditions under which the bombing of North Vietnam would cease and on whether the political future of South Vietnam could be decided by a process other than the one specifically called for in the NLF program. "These differences were not trivial," one U.S. official later told me in an interview, "but all of us thought that we at least had arrived at a point where negotiations were conceivable."

The closer Washington's and Hanoi's positions appeared in private, however, the further apart they appeared in public. At the end of August, while the secret talks in Paris were in recess, Pham Van Dong gave a particularly hard-line National Day address in which he reiterated Ho's views as they had been expressed in *Le Monde.* The premier called for Washington's acceptance of the DRV's four points before a settlement could be contemplated. He stressed that "no difficulty whatsoever could force our people to retreat, and no enemy whatsoever could intimidate us." He impugned the motives of President Johnson: "In a word, while President Johnson talks about peace the more he steps up the war." Then Pham Van Dong referred to an important lesson the DRV had learned in its efforts to reach a negotiated settlement with the French:

> Soon after the DRV's founding and even after the outbreak of the resistance war in South Vietnam, we entered into negotiations with the French colonialists on many occasions and concluded with them several agreements and a *modus vivendi* in an effort to preserve peace. But to the French colonialists the signing of agreements was only a move designed to gain time and to prepare military forces and make plans for further aggression. It was only when our victories had made it clear to them that they could never conquer Vietnam and subdue our people and that further military adventures would only result in still heavier defeats that peace could be restored on the basis of the recognition of our national rights. This is a clear lesson of history, and lesson on relations with the imperialists which our people will never forget.

When Mai Van Bo and the U.S. representative convened for a fourth meeting, Bo said Pham's speech was now the authoritative DRV position: Washington must accept Hanoi's version of the four points, U.S. troops must totally withdraw from South Vietnam, and the bombing of North Vietnam must stop. A fifth scheduled meeting was never held; the U.S. representative was informed that Bo was ill, and no substitute date for a meeting was suggested. Washington, however, kept this channel open for at least a year and replaced the original U.S. representative, who had to return to the United States, with a retired diplomat who had been persuaded to take up his pension in Paris. The new representative did meet once with Mai Van Bo and twice with his deputy, but Bo's demands did not change. Washington had had its first taste of Hanoi's leapfrogging between public and private positions.

President Johnson and his advisors believed that Hanoi used the secret talks to determine what the U.S. would concede to get negotiations started. Hanoi's objective, official Washington believed, was to get the bombing stopped in exchange for talks. Consequently, these officials recognized that there was an immediate need to make certain that the search for a basis for negotiation would neither restrict the American ability to fight the war nor restrict the bombing of North Vietnam when it was essential from a military viewpoint. Rightly or wrongly perceiving Hanoi's motives, the breakdown of the secret talks in Paris convinced most U.S. officials that the North Vietnamese were using negotiations as a ploy to get the bombing stopped. These officials thus argued that the bombing should continue until a negotiated agreement was substantially in sight.

From the May 1965 bombing pause, Hanoi learned how far the United States was prepared to go in private to reach a negotiated settlement—the U.S. version of the four points was far more conciliatory in substance and rhetoric than the Johnson administration's public position. But Hanoi misjudged this as a sign that there was considerable private flexibility to Washington's position. While Washington could be made to soften its terms in private, once those terms were spurned, the president realized that he had been "had." This not only discredited those who advocated negotiations in the future but also hardened U.S. terms again. In addition, Hanoi learned that the United States was committed to the survival of a non-Communist regime in South Vietnam and that nothing Hanoi was likely to offer Washington—for example, a decent interval before the NLF governed Saigon—would be acceptable as long as the United States thought the NVA could be contained and that the GVN could eventually neutralize the NLF. Hanoi probably concluded that the United States would have to be defeated militarily before it would be willing either to sign the kind of agreement Hanoi was prepared to offer or to withdraw its troops unilaterally. Indeed, from Hanoi's perspective, what had been learned in these particular contacts with Washington was that there might be no alternative to war—a view President Johnson had come to somewhat earlier.

Thus, efforts to start negotiations actually reinforced the view on both sides that the basic conflict would only be settled by fighting. Washington wanted Hanoi to cease firing before negotiations started. Hanoi wanted Washington to give up the only bargaining chip it had before negotiations began. Each interpreted the other's demands as an indication that negotiation was an extension of their war strategy, for each appeared to be seeking through negotiations the same goals they were seeking to achieve on the battlefield.

By the end of 1965, there were 185,000 U.S. soldiers in South Vietnam.

Their presence, along with 1,000 tons of bombs dropped on North Vietnam, was designed to bring an end to Hanoi's aggression—with or without negotiations. But President Johnson found that the bombing, had, as one of his aides later put it, "a short half-life. From the moment it started, there was pressure to have it stopped. Hanoi always reacted the same. The more we bombed, or the more we paused bombing, they would not negotiate. Thus, advocates inside the administration argued that the bombing should be stopped altogether because it was neither reducing Hanoi's capability to make war nor affecting Hanoi's will to fight."

Initially the bombing of North Vietnam was publicly justified as a measure to reduce Hanoi's capability to wage war in the south, not as a bargaining chip designed to affect Hanoi's willingness to seek a negotiated settlement. Nonetheless, it was instantly controversial for both military and diplomatic reasons. Civilian officials in the Office of the Secretary of Defense and in the Central Intelligence Agency argued that the bombing was not effective in reducing the flow of soldiers and supplies into South Vietnam or in persuading Hanoi to negotiate. World War II bomber pilots who had become generals by 1965 and 1966 argued that bombing could not reduce infiltration unless target restrictions were removed. Intelligence analysts estimated that more than three-quarters of the north's war-related industries and military supply systems had been insulated from air attack by such restrictions. State Department officials argued that removing target restrictions would bring China and possibly the Soviet Union into the war. Air force strategists insisted that the bombing would never persuade Hanoi to come to the negotiating table unless it were kept up around the clock until negotiations began. Allies in touch with Hanoi argued that only by stopping the bombing would Hanoi negotiate.

President Johnson had to find a balance between bombing for purposes of fighting the war and the potential impact of bombing on persuading the North Vietnamese to negotiate. Spared targets, coupled with an obviously restrained approach, were rationalized as reminders to Hanoi of what North Vietnam still had to lose. Pauses in the bombing were considered essential to give Hanoi time to calculate the costs of continuing to refuse to negotiate. Such pauses would last as long as Hanoi did not take advantage of a pause to pre-position supplies for a new wave of attacks. Finally, such pauses were intended to show both the North Vietnamese and the president's critics that the United States was genuinely committed to negotiating an end to the war and not to destroying North Vietnam.

The thirty-seven-day pause that began on December 24, 1965, followed the pattern that had been set in May. The pause was appended to a holiday. Every possible channel through which Hanoi could respond secretly was explored. High-level U.S. officials traversed the globe in a peace offensive, explaining U.S. aims to 115 governments and asking for help in bringing Hanoi to the negotiating table. Again, Washington did not offer Hanoi a new proposal for ending the war; it offered Hanoi a chance to indicate it was interested in doing so.

Telegrams from the secretary of state to all U.S. ambassadors able to approach a representative of Hanoi indicated that this Christmas pause could be extended if the North Vietnamese were willing to make "a serious contribution toward peace" and avoid any provocations (i.e., the resumption of fighting). The DRV ultimately accepted this message in the form of an *aide mémoire* through its representative in Burma who promised to transmit it to Hanoi for a formal reply. While the United States was waiting for some comment through this channel, Hanoi radio and other sources struck a public posture on the bombing pause that branded it a "deceptive peace campaign." "The facts have shown," a January 4, 1966, Hanoi radio broadcast pointed out, "that every time the U.S. authorities want to intensify their aggressive war they talk still more glibly about peace. The present U.S. peace efforts are also a mere attempt to appease public opinion at home and abroad." The radio broadcast once more stated that peace would come only when the United States accepted the four points and signaled their acceptance by stopping "unconditionally and for good" the bombing of North Vietnam.

Soviet officials, in informal discussions, confirmed what most U.S. officials expected — that there was almost no chance that Hanoi would even respond to the pause, let alone see it as an opportunity to enter into serious talks with Washington.

On February 1, 1966, some twelve hours after the bombing of North Vietnam had resumed, Hanoi's representative in Rangoon responded to the December *aide mémoire* by informing the United States that the position embodied in the radio broadcast quoted above was to be considered the DRV's official response. On that same day, Hanoi radio broadcast an extensive commentary on the bombing pause denouncing the U.S. search for negotiations as ingenuous as long as the bombing continued. The broadcast concluded by repeating the DRV's basic stand: "A political settle-ment . . . can be envisaged only when the U.S. government has accepted the four-point stand of the DRV . . . has proved this by actual deeds, and has stopped unconditionally and for good its air raids and all other acts of war against the DRV." Responding to the U.S. initiative after the bombing had resumed was consistent with Hanoi's policy of never negotiating while appearing to be on the defensive. By broadcasting the official DRV position, Hanoi also showed its disdain for the private channels in which both parties might be able to be more flexible.

"After this bombing pause collapsed," one of Mr. Johnson's advisors recalled in an interview, "the president said that as far as he was concerned the search for negotiations was pointless. 'We were fighting a war in Vietnam,' he would say, 'not trying to mediate a dispute.' " In his memoirs, Chester Cooper, another White House advisor, confirms the salience of this attitude: "The experience of January 1966 influenced the President's views on any further bombing cessations or other gestures toward Hanoi for the remainder of his tenure. He has been said to feel that he had been led down the garden path by doves among his advisors. His two close confidants and unofficial advisors, Abe Fortas and Clark Clifford, reportedly told him the January bombing pause was his 'worst mistake' in the Vietnam War."[5]

The futility of diplomacy in 1965 contrasted sharply with assessments of what might be achieved on the battlefield in South Vietnam. Walt Rostow had replaced McGeorge Bundy as the president's special assistant for national security affairs and he argued that other guerrilla wars had been "lost or won cleanly." Consequently, there was nothing inevitable about having to reach a negotiated settlement in Vietnam.

Rostow's basic hypothesis was that the guerrilla lost if he did not win;[6] Henry Kissinger would later argue the reverse. This fundamental difference in outlook explains, in part, why the Johnson administration took so long to make the concessions necessary to get North Vietnam to the conference table, and why the Nixon administration was at such pains not to let negotiations be strictly governed by what occurred on the battlefield. Johnson feared that negotiations would prolong the war, while Kissinger feared that the war—if it appeared to be winnable—would prolong negotiations.

1966: GOOD OFFICES BREED BAD FAITH

By 1966, Washington knew that Hanoi would not agree to accept any conditions for talks that required reciprocity. Through the DRV representative in Rangoon, Washington had been told authoritatively that Hanoi was not interested in negotiations at all. But to other intermediaries, Hanoi behaved differently. Between February and June, at least eleven heads of state or high foreign ministry officials, as well as UN secretary-general U Thant, were led to believe that Hanoi would enter talks with Washington without insisting on prior acceptance of the four points if the bombing were stopped. Western European diplomats in Washington urged the president to call Hanoi's bluff—end the bombing and await talks. But if this were done and Hanoi failed to respond (as was almost certain from the indications Washington had received from its secret contacts with Hanoi) the United States would be forced into a much more aggressive posture, and this President Johnson was trying to avoid.

In fact, when principal administration officials and advisors to the president were asked why they did not try to mobilize popular support for the war, nearly all said that they feared the consequences. As one put it in an interview, "We were trying to fight the war with an absolute minimum of force. We believed we could calibrate our use of force and find the precise mixture of men and bombs required to weaken Hanoi's will without destroying North Vietnam. To have whipped up public opinion—particularly as the numbers of American soldiers who were being killed increased—would have made it difficult to exercise any restraint at all. We did not, after all, want to defeat North Vietnam, only to discourage the Communist leadership there from continuing the war in South Vietnam."

Between January and June 1966, a debilitating political controversy in Saigon between the government of Nguyen Cao Ky and the Buddhist church made it difficult for U.S. officials to advocate political settlements; Saigon obviously lacked the cohesion essential for political competition with the NLF. In fact, Ky's government appeared likely either to lose control over the strategic northern five provinces of South Vietnam (where nearly all public officials had resigned to protest Ky's repression of the Buddhists) or to collapse in a wave of reaction from the right.

Queried about the significance, for American policy, of the political crisis in Saigon, 48 percent of those sampled in a May 21, 1966, Gallup poll thought that the South Vietnamese would not be able to establish a stable government, while another 54 percent thought that, if the warring South Vietnamese factions turned to arms and fought among themselves, Washington should withdraw all U.S. troops. And 72 percent thought that, if the GVN decided to stop fighting (that is, embrace the neutralism of those leading the protests against Ky), the United States should withdraw from the struggle.

Given both these attitudes on the part of the American public and the uncertainties inherent in the South Vietnamese crisis then brewing, Washington wanted to avoid contributing to further instability. Offering to negotiate with Hanoi was therefore to be avoided unless such negotiations would rapidly result in an agreement acceptable to Washington and Saigon. It should be remembered that Washington sought peace in Vietnam, but believed peace could only be achieved if there were a viable and thriving anti-Communist government in the south. The intense efforts of Washington's allies in 1966 and 1967 to start negotiations—negotiations U.S. officials regarded as premature—ultimately worked to Washington's disadvantage.

To America's allies, talking seemed preferable to fighting. In countless meetings with U.S. officials, foreign diplomats pointed out that, with such a preponderance of power on Washington's side, the risk would be low that Hanoi could take any appreciable advantage of an end to the bombing, which was, after all, only one aspect of the war. More importantly, they argued, if Washington refused to appear interested in negotiations and continued the bombing, world public opinion would portray the United States, not Hanoi, as the aggressor.

In 1966, there were two major efforts by third parties to use good offices to bring Washington and Hanoi to the conference table. The net effect of these efforts, however, was to deepen President Johnson's skepticism of Hanoi's intention to negotiate, to increase domestic and international pressure on the United States to stop the bombing, and to strengthen the president's belief that to stop the bombing or the war before a position of strength had been achieved would spell victory to Hanoi and reward its intransigence.

Chester Ronning traveled to Hanoi in March and June of 1966 as a special representative of the Canadian government, ostensibly for the purpose of getting new terms of reference for Canada's participation in the International Control Commission. With official Washington approval (though nearly everyone involved in staffing "the Ronning channel" was pessimistic), Ronning was, as he put it, in testimony during the Pentagon Papers trial, "an explorer to find out whether or not there was any possibility of bringing the two sides together for direct talks, but we had no function whatever in mediating or acting as an arbiter between the two sides."[7]

In Hanoi, Ronning met with Pham Van Dong, who told him: "We will come unconditionally to the peace table, unconditionally of [sic] the Four Points, two of which (we know) are absolutely impossible of acceptance by the U.S. We will come unconditionally to the conference table if the U.S. will stop, unconditionally stop, the bombing of North Vietnam."[8]

Ronning was so flabbergasted at what the North Vietnamese premier had said he asked that it be repeated. Ronning then repeated what he had heard to make certain he remembered the statement correctly. He was then told that the position expressed by Pham Van Dong was not new but was contained also in the statement issued by the North Vietnamese Foreign Ministry on January 4, 1966. But that January announcement did not say that at all. Thus, privately, Ronning downplayed the significance of Pham Van Dong's offer of unconditional talks, and after both of his missions remained pessimistic about the chances for a negotiated settlement within the year. Ronning knew that, in Washington's view, the North Vietnamese were not prepared to give enough to warrant a suspension of the bombing. They were only suggesting that in return for an end to the bombing they would agree to "talk". But, as they had made clear before, such talks would focus only on whether Washington would agree to the four points.

On June 29, 1966, a week after Ronning's second trip to Hanoi, U.S. bombers began attacking the POL (petroleum, oil, and lubricants) storage facilities at Hanoi and Haiphong. According to the Defense Intelligence Agency estimates, this bombing campaign had destroyed nearly two-thirds of North Vietnam's POL resources within a month. In the wake of this bombing, both Janusz Lewandowski (the chief of the Polish delegation to the ICC) and the Italian ambassador to Saigon approached Washington (appearing to U.S.

officials to be concerned about the widening of the war) with a reworded version of the U.S. position that, Lewandowski said, would be acceptable to Hanoi as a basis for secret talks in Warsaw. It now appears that Lewandowski's strategy was to establish a negotiating agenda incorporating those elements that would be acceptable to both sides in the long run, and then to rely on direct negotiations between them to resolve their differences over how an agreement would be implemented. Lewandowski made it clear that negotiations could not end the conflict; they could only shift it to the political arena.

In exchange for winding down the war, Lewandowski proposed that the NLF be assured a place in the politics and administration of South Vietnam. Lewandowski understood that Hanoi would not negotiate while the bombing continued and that Washington would not stop the bombing unless it could be assured that Hanoi was ready for substantive negotiations. If both could agree on the outcome of such negotiations in principle—and in advance—Lewandowski reasoned, then the bombing could be stopped. Once into the talks, a specific agreement could be reached. The first obstacle to such a scenario, Lewandowski recognized, was Washington: Would U.S. policymakers believe that Hanoi was ready to negotiate?

State Department and White House officials involved in secret efforts to arrange negotiations, as well as those in the Pentagon and in the intelligence services, agreed that it was highly unlikely that Hanoi was as inclined to negotiate as Lewandowski suggested. These officials pointed out that Hanoi's assessment of its position (as revealed in captured documents) characterized negotiations as premature. Beyond areas that had been loyal to the Communist movement for decades, the NLF had expanded its control in South Vietnam only with difficulty. Consequently, entering negotiations the outcome of which would be an agreement on the terms of a political struggle (that is, only a military and not a political cease-fire-in-place) would leave the NLF vulnerable in newly liberated areas to competition from pro-Saigon and other anti-Communist political forces.

The origin of Lewandowski's initiative lay in a conversation he claimed to have had with Ho Chi Minh in late June 1966. The details of the conversation were later leaked by Polish sources to the U.S. press, but they were never confirmed by the North Vietnamese. Ho, according to Lewandowski, indicated that the DRV would agree to talks if the United States suspended the bombing and agreed to have the NLF participate in the talks. This, Lewandowski recognized, was an offer Washington would be hard-pressed to refuse: Hanoi had previously insisted that the bombing stop and that Washington indicate its acceptance of the DRV's four-point stand. Ho now appeared to be saying that the bombing only had to be suspended and talks would begin. But this contradicted what Washington had learned from other contacts with Hanoi. To President Johnson, "The simple truth was that the North Vietnamese were not ready to talk with us."[9] This was later confirmed by Communist sources. A high-level Eastern European Communist who defected to the West indicated that Lewandowski was acting on his own, and Australian journalist Wilfred Burchett, who Washington knew had close ties with Hanoi, said in an interview that the Lewandowski initiative "had been concocted by 'well-meaning friends' of North Vietnam as an effort to draw up what might be acceptable to the United States and then sell it to Hanoi."[10]

Dean Rusk saw Lewandowski's proposals as leading not to an acceptable political settlement but to a Communist victory through diplomacy. Suspending the bombing would, according to Rusk, legitimize U.S. dissenters who would then push for its total cessation regardless of how forthcoming Hanoi actually was in negotiations, or whether talks were begun at all. In addition, to permit the NLF a role in negotiations would also legitimize those who Washington and Saigon were trying to convince the world were merely armed terrorists under the command of Hanoi. Moreover, if the negotiations produced an agreement, the NLF would have to be allocated a specific role in South Vietnamese politics. But Washington wanted the political evolution of Vietnam after a cease-fire to be left as ambiguous as possible, pending the strengthening of the GVN.

With these concerns in mind, Henry Cabot Lodge, the U.S. ambassador in Saigon, was instructed to pursue the Lewandowski-Ho contact (code-named Marigold) to establish both the extent to which Lewandowski was acting on Hanoi's specific instruction and what Hanoi would do to reciprocate for a suspension of the bombing of North Vietnam. Not once during the nearly seven months of Marigold was Washington to have answers to these basic questions.

Early in the contact, Lodge had also been instructed to inform Nguyen Cao Ky, then prime minister of South Vietnam, that Washington had received signals (Ky was told they were rumors) of Hanoi's interest in negotiations. Ky was told that, although these signals were under investigation, Washington did not think they were likely to prove significant. It was what Ky wanted to hear, for the GVN was not enthusiastic about a negotiated settlement. Saigon's basic objective was the status quo ante, and this it expected would come from military victory, not from negotiations. After Hanoi withdrew its troops, Ky argued, the NLF could participate in the political life of South Vietnam, provided it disbanded as a Communist political organization.

By the end of July 1966, officials in Washington believed that Marigold was moribund. Lewandowski, now acting on the instructions of his government, rather than allegedly acting on instructions of the North Vietnamese, informed Lodge that nothing of a substantive nature could be discussed until the bombing of North Vietnam was suspended. For the next two weeks, and through a series of parallel conversations between Lodge and the Italian ambassador in Saigon, and between the latter and Lewandowski, Washington learned that Hanoi was not interested in entering negotiations as an end to the war (it was not at all worried about the long-term outcome of the war); it was interested in entering negotiations as a way of altering the political situation in the south faster than it could alter it through warfare at that time. At a minimum, Hanoi was after a change in the personnel leading the GVN, if not in the character of the GVN itself. One acceptable consequence of this, according to Lewandowski, would be a coalition government as overwhelmingly neutralist as the one in Cambodia.

At the end of September, U.S. ambassador Arthur Goldberg indicated in a widely publicized speech to the UN General Assembly that the United States was "prepared to order a cessation of all bombing of North Vietnam—the moment we are assured, privately or otherwise, that this step will be answered promptly by a corresponding and appropriate de-escalation by the other side." On the issue of the role of the NLF during negotiations, Goldberg referred to President Johnson's dictum that, once de-escalation was apparent, the issue would not be an insurmountable problem. But if Lewandowski or Hanoi had hoped to discern through Marigold or through the Goldberg speech any substantial change in Washington's basic position, they were to be disappointed.

At the October conference attended by the United States, the GVN, and the countries contributing troops to the defense of the GVN, U.S. terms were once again made clear, and with them, the basic incompatibility between Washington's and Hanoi's demands became evident. The seven-nation Manila Declaration, issued on October 25, 1966, underscored the fundamental objective of the non-Communist participants in the conflict: "Our sole demand on the leaders of North Vietnam is that they abandon their aggression." This could be achieved, the declaration continued, "through discussion and negotiation or through reciprocal actions by both sides to reduce the violence." The essential elements of peace, the declaration concluded, were cessation of aggression, preservation of the territorial integrity of South Vietnam, freely chosen reunification, resolution of internal political problems once the war has stopped, removal of allied military forces ("as North Vietnam withdraws, infiltration ceases, and the level of violence thus subsides"), and effective international guarantees for "any negotiations leading to the end of hostilities."

Washington also proposed that there be two separate phases to mutual de-escalation; this later became known as the Phase A–Phase B formula. In Phase A, Washington would suspend the bombing. After a specific, mutually acceptable interval of time had passed, Washington and Hanoi would start to de-escalate the war in the south: U.S. and North Vietnamese forces would begin to withdraw, NLF attacks against populated centers would be curtailed, and U.S.-GVN military pressure against the NLF areas would lessen. But before any of these steps could be taken, Washington had to know concretely, if privately, of the precise steps Hanoi would take in response to a bombing suspension. This, Lewandowski stressed from the outset, was not a demand to which Hanoi would respond since it maintained that the bombing of North Vietnam was illegal in the first place and should be stopped as a matter of principle, not in return for concessions.

At the beginning of December, Lewandowski suggested a series of propositions designed to express the U.S. position in terms most likely to be acceptable to Hanoi. Lewandowski's formulation affirmed both Washington's interest in peacefully settling the conflict and its pledge not to establish a permanent military presence in Indochina; it also reaffirmed its support for a neutral South Vietnam, its willingness to abide by a peaceful reunification process, its support for an electoral process in South Vietnam that would permit all political forces to participate, and its unwillingness to indicate acceptance of Hanoi's four-point stand as then formulated. These propositions were acceptable to Washington.

But there were doubts over the Lewandowski propositions; they centered on the specifics of mutual de-escalation and political evolution in South Vietnam. The de-escalation process Lewandowski proposed to present to Hanoi as Washington's position (which, Lewandowski assured U.S. officials, was already acceptable to Hanoi for the purposes of initiating talks) involved not only ending the bombing but also dropping any insistence by Washington that there had been infiltration by the NVA into South Vietnam. Of equal concern to Washington was a statement that set the negotiation process in context. In order to assure Hanoi that a negotiated settlement would not be tantamount to negotiated surrender, Lewandowski proposed that Washington make clear it expected negotiations would require a change in the political situation then prevailing in South Vietnam—possibly through the creation of a coalition government. Lewandowski concluded his proposals to Washington by saying that, if these formulations were acceptable to the U.S. government, the United States could so indicate to the North Vietnamese ambassador in Warsaw.

Given Washington's publicly declared policy that Washington had to know precisely what Hanoi would do in response to the end of the bombing, it is not surprising that these privately made proposals were not fully acceptable. Washington was unable to discern either just what it was Hanoi was prepared to concede if talks occurred, or what Hanoi had done vis-à-vis its military activities in the south to warrant any U.S. flexibility in the first place. Moreover, Washington thought that several of Lewandowski's points could be subject to vastly different interpretations. Consequently, Washington asked Lewandowski to inform Hanoi that several of the points in the proposal—and especially those relating to de-escalation and the political evolution of South Vietnam—were bound to lead to different interpretations. These issues, Washington wanted Hanoi told, would obviously surface in the negotiations. Hanoi's position, as reported by Lewandowski, was that Washington should state its objections precisely and in advance of any talks. And there Marigold might have languished, had it not been for a resumption of bombing near Hanoi. Whether a pretext was needed or not, these bombings precipitated the termination of the brief and confusing inter-mediary role played by the government of Poland.

For two days in early December and for two days in mid-December, targets in an area ranging from five to sixteen nautical miles from the center of Hanoi were struck as part of the Rolling Thunder program. In the total picture of the air war, these raids on the POL storage and transport facilities near Hanoi were routine. But the attacks were symbolic in the secret search for negotiations, coming as they did, just before and after the United States announced its desire for negotiations. Reconstructing the event from inter-views with the principals, the bombing was neither inadvertent nor acciden-tal; it was the subject of a careful review of North Vietnamese targets by both the State and Defense departments—a review process conducted in an atmosphere filled with doubt about the veracity of the Marigold initiative. To policy-makers in Washington, the bombing was viewed as an inevitable outgrowth of a situation in which fighting was conducted simultaneously with efforts to start negotiations. That December, they pointed out later in interviews with me, attacks by both sides took place against Vietnamese cities.

U.S. diplomats were appalled at the bombing, despite the fact that Hanoi had never once responded to repeated queries about its willingness to negotiate. As one high-level State Department official observed, "LBJ seemed to harden every time he went to the ranch. There he thought a lot about the U.S. boys being lost and decided he just couldn't stand there and let them die while Hanoi tied his hands by not responding to get negotiations under way. So, the bombing was resumed."

When the Polish government informed Washington that there would be no direct talks and that the use of the good offices of Poland would be terminated in light of the previous day's attack on Hanoi, Washington replied that the bombing was inevitable as long as Hanoi kept up the fighting but that the United States was prepared to suspend all bombing for a circle with a radius of ten nautical miles from the center of Hanoi—an area of more than 314 square miles. However, Washington demanded that Hanoi respect a similar area surrounding Saigon and refrain from conducting rocket, mortar, and terrorist attacks against it. Setting such a condition for reciprocity brought the issue at the heart of Marigold full circle: Washington would not budge on the bombing without getting a de-escalatory action of equivalent value from Hanoi and this Hanoi was not prepared to do.

The president pessimistically surveyed the prospects for further diplomacy in the wake of the collapse of Marigold. He was convinced, he told aides then, that Ho Chi Minh was not interested in negotiating. He was wary of offers of help in arranging negotiations. He questioned the motives of some who sought to promote direct Washington-Hanoi talks (accused some of them of having Nobel Prize fever) and doubted the credibility of others. French help (the Quai d'Orsay had been involved in several of the secret channels of communication to Hanoi) was particularly vexing, since nearly every private indication Washington had received suggested that the kind of settlement France wanted to arrange in Vietnam reflected de Gaulle's desire to have Washington withdraw its troops under the least favorable circumstances. In Feburary 1967, de Gaulle had told Senator Robert Kennedy that U.S. troops should be withdrawn regardless of the consequences—even if it meant a Communist takeover in Saigon. In fact, discussion with French officials led Senator Kennedy to conclude that, at the top, the French government did not have the slightest interest in a negotiated settlement. In private, the senator was not even sanguine about the impact of an end to the bombing of North Vietnam. Bombing should be ended because it "did not accomplish any military purpose," the senator said, but it should be ended "in a way that . . . does not arouse false hope" about any unilateral initiative leading to negotiations.

For his part, President Johnson recognized a pattern to Hanoi's behavior vis-à-vis negotiations, and this pattern reinforced his cynicism. When secrecy was assured—i.e., in direct contacts—Hanoi was intransigent. But, in public and with third parties, North Vietnamese diplomats hinted that they would be flexible in negotiations if the United States stopped the bombing. Johnson called this Hanoi's whipsaw, and he believed that it was working. As the details of the Marigold initiative were leaked to the press, the effect was to shake the confidence of those who would continue to work to arrange talks between Washington and Hanoi. Whether Lewandowski was genuinely acting on Hanoi's instructions was less important to those working for negotiations than whether there was in Washington a core of advocates of a negotiated settlement with enough influence to prevail over those who argued that the war was winnable and should be won.

Marigold convinced many that the advocates of negotiations could not prevail. Could the bombing of North Vietnam be coordinated with diplomatic initiatives? Marigold convinced many that it could not. Would an exhaustive study of the initiative provide insight into what Washington could have done to maximize the chances for negotiations to begin?* "The State Department secretariat . . . plowed through the Marigold record . . . to determine what, if anything, had gone wrong," wrote two enterprising journalists who had set out to assess the reaction to Marigold. "The resulting post-mortem narrative account, some forty pages long, was xeroxed and distributed to officials for study. One official said: 'Those of us who saw the report agreed that the United States did everything that could have been done to keep Marigold alive, apart from cancelling the air strikes.' "[11] Other officials disagreed: "You will never get the inside story. . . . It makes our government look so bad."[12]

What had Hanoi learned from Marigold? It had learned the ease with which the slimmest straw in the wind concerning negotiations could lead to serious consideration in Washington; this suggested, that perhaps, the United States was war weary and anxious to end its involvement. Hanoi also learned that, as details of an unsuccessful effort at diplomacy were leaked to the press—the collapse of Marigold began to be reported only a month after the contact was terminated—it was Washington's intransigence over the bombing issue, not Hanoi's intransigence over reciprocity, that surfaced as the principal reason for the failure. Hanoi finally learned that, if there were to be negotiations at all, some degree of reciprocity would be necessary for a suspension of the bombing. In fact, the origins of the understanding reached in 1968, as a result of which the United States suspended all bombing of North Vietnam in return for a private pledge that Hanoi would cease its rocket and mortar attacks on Saigon, probably lie in the formula devised for implementing the ten-nautical-mile limit on bombing around Hanoi.

By year's end, the 148,000 sorties (a sortie is the attacking flight of a single aircraft) flown in the air (this was three times as many as in 1965) had dropped 128,000 tons of bombs (four times as many as in 1965) on all of the north's fixed targets. The estimated economic damage to North Vietnam increased threefold over that inflicted in 1965, while the cost of the United States doing this increased 50 percent over the 1965 level. Still Hanoi would not turn toward negotiations. The air war, as CIA analysts noted, was rapidly approaching a point of diminishing returns without producing the predicted effect. "The available evidence does not suggest," one intelligence assessment

---

*In the face of such contradictory assessments of how the U.S. government handled Marigold, I requested that, under the terms of the Freedom of Information Act, the report prepared in the State Department secretariat be reviewed for release. The State Department denied my initial request (and my appeal of that decision) on the grounds that the report was based on, and almost entirely comprised of, material given in confidence to the United States by other governments and this confidence had to be respected. While classification of a document for this reason is permitted under the terms of the Freedom of Information Act, by its decision the State Department continued to respect confidences that the other governments involved in Marigold had long ago leaked to the press.

concluded, "that Rolling Thunder to date has contributed materially to the achievement of the two primary objectives of air attack—reducing the flow of supplies to VC/NVA forces in the south or weakening the will of North Vietnam to continue the insurgency."[13]

1967: WITH VICTORY AT HAND

During 1967, the official Washington view about who was winning the war would change. Partly because many of the pessimists left office, partly because the American people could not conceive of half a million U.S. troops fighting a land war in Asia and not winning it, and partly because Saigon appeared to begin the processes of economic and political development essential to competing with the NLF, official Washington was becoming convinced that there was a light at the end of the tunnel. As a result, the search for negotiations with an intransigent adversary became less urgent in 1967.

Most visitors to Saigon during this period, including this writer, were initially struck with the sense of confidence exuded by the Americans and their Vietnamese counterparts. Those officials deeply involved in the secret efforts to get negotiations started felt, as one put it, "an air of confidence that victory and not a negotiated settlement was at hand." "The prospect of winning the war complicated the effort to end it by negotiations in 1967," another official told me. "It meant we had to prove to LBJ that what we could get at the conference table was better than what we could get on the battlefield."

By early February 1967, President Johnson was prepared to offer Hanoi not better terms but rather a range of ways in which to signal interest in negotiations. "There was no earthly reason why," one U.S. general told me later, "we should have made concessions. We were at last winning the war." However, as the details of the Marigold initiative began to leak out at Washington cocktail parties, the president did strike a more conciliatory tone in his press conferences, even though he felt he had been had by Lewandowski. Johnson declared willingness to go more than halfway to achieve a negotiated settlement; he wished the war were over. Hanoi, the president said, could take "just almost any step" toward reciprocating for a suspension of the bombing, and the negotiations that would ensue could take any of a variety of forms:

> We would be glad to see the unconditional discussions to which I referred in my statement of April 1965 at Johns Hopkins. We would participate in preliminary discussions which might open the way for formal negotiations. We are prepared today to talk about mutual steps of de-escalation. We would be prepared to talk about such subjects as the exchange of prisoners, the

demilitarization of the demilitarized zone, or any other aspect which might take even a small step in the direction of peace.

We should be prepared to discuss any points which the other side wishes to bring up along with points which we and our allies very much want to raise ourselves, or there could be preliminary discussions to see whether there could be an agreed set of points which could be the basis for negotiation.[14]

Harold Wilson took Lyndon Johnson at his word. British interest in promoting negotiations between Washington and Hanoi had long been evident, and in early February 1967, the Wilson government believed that the key might lie in joint action with the Soviet Union. On February 6, Soviet Premier Kosygin began a week-long visit to London, during which Vietnam was discussed extensively. Prime Minister Wilson would later say in the House of Commons that, during that week, "peace was in . . . grasp."

While Wilson and Kosygin were discussing Vietnam, a secret letter from President Johnson to Ho Chi Minh proposing negotiations was accepted for transmission to the North Vietnamese leader by Hanoi's embassy in Moscow. Both initiatives were made to reinforce what UN ambassador Arthur Goldberg had pledged in a New Year's Eve letter to UN secretary-general U Thant: "My Government is prepared to take the first step toward peace; specifically, we are ready to order a prior end to all bombing of North Vietnam the moment there is an assurance, private or otherwise, that there would be a reciprocal response toward peace in North Vietnam." Essentially, Washington was pushing its Phase A–Phase B proposal, which Hanoi had not yet specifically rejected and which the British supported.

But the conditions of the A-B proposal had changed since November 1966 when it first had been made known to the British. Then, the Phase A–Phase B formulation required that Washington receive an authoritative pledge from Hanoi that, in return for an end to the bombing, NVA infiltration would stop. In his letter to Ho, however, the president wrote that the bombing of North Vietnam would be ended "as soon as I am assured that infiltration into South Vietnam by land and by sea *has stopped* [my italics]." To the president, such a change seemed essential in light of the alarming buildup of North Vietnamese forces—two new NVA divisions had arrived just north of the DMZ in December, and a third division appeared ready to move south. NVA supply activities substantially increased during the Tet truce. These signs, while not necessarily indicative that an offensive was imminent, did alarm the president, who saw Hanoi in position to take advantage of the interval between Phase A and Phase B to attack the northern half of South Vietnam.

Since the bombing was clearly not hurting the North Vietnamese, U.S. officials feared that any interest in negotiations on Hanoi's part might be purely tactical. Indeed, in early 1966, North Vietnamese officials began to spell out the merits of entering a fighting-while-negotiating state in the war, and this line was disseminated to party and army cadres. The clearest publicly available statement of the tactical advantage to be gained from fighting while negotiating occurred in 1966 in a speech by the NVA's chief of staff, General Nguyen van Vinh: "Fighting while negotiating is aimed at opening another front with a view to making the puppet army more disintegrated, stimulating and developing the enemy's internal contradictions and thereby making him more isolated in order to deprive him of the propaganda weapons, isolate him further, and make a number of people who misunderstand the Americans clearly see their nature."[15]

Washington's suspicion that the British initiative would come to naught was also heightened by the fact that, previously, the Soviet Union had been entirely unwilling to play an intermediary role. Only four months before, Moscow had declined to convey to Hanoi precisely what Wilson was going to offer again: the Phase A–Phase B formula. In any case, mindful of the Korean experience in which more U.S. soldiers were killed in combat while cease-fire talks were going on than before they began, President Johnson was not inclined to cease the bombing without a concrete de-escalatory action by Hanoi.

To assure that he would not be discussing a subject without full knowledge of what had already transpired in the secret search for negotiations, Wilson asked President Johnson "to send a representative in whom he had confidence to put me fully in the picture before Mr. Kosygin arrived." The president sent Chester Cooper to brief the prime minister and, at the latter's request, to remain in London throughout the talks in order to facilitate communications with Washington. According to Wilson, Cooper described the U.S. position as follows:

> The American Government was hoping to pass proposals [the Phase A–Phase B formula] . . . to the DRV at a secret rendezvous, "under a palm tree," arranged for some eight or ten days hence, when the Tet truce became effective. But, and the President confirmed this to me direct, they wanted me to do all I could to get the Russians behind the proposals and, if the omens looked right, to get Mr. Kosygin himself to pass them on to the DRV administration. . . . Our hope was that Mr. Kosygin, with his special contacts with Hanoi, could impress on the North Vietnamese leaders the importance of giving the Americans a firm sign, during Tet, of a readiness to make a positive and visible response to a cessation of bombing.[16]

Chester Cooper's account, however, contradicts Wilson's with respect to President Johnson's enthusiasm for the initiative. In considering the following observations drawn from Mr. Cooper's book, the crucial element to remember is that LBJ's skepticism was not communicated to Wilson. Cooper writes:

Wilson's enthusiasm might have been somewhat dampened if he had known that President Johnson, Walt Rostow, and a few people in the State Department took a rather dim view of his eagerness to discuss Vietnam with Kosygin. There was a sense that the British Government was pushing hard, perhaps too hard, to undertake the role of mediator. To be sure, the British could claim both a right and responsibility to assume such a role; they and the Russians were co-chairmen of the 1954 Geneva Conference and of the 1961–1962 Laos Conference. But some of Wilson's American cousins felt his underlying motivation was to bolster his own and England's prestige. . . . There was another, less articulated but more deeply felt attitude about Wilson's imminent meeting that cooled Washington's interest and perhaps even contributed to the failure of the talks. After all the recent frustrations and disappointments of Warsaw and Moscow, the prospect that Wilson might be able to use American chips to pull off peace talks was hard for the President and some of his advisers to swallow. If the time was now ripe to get Hanoi to talk, Johnson, not Wilson, should get the credit.[17]

Johnson, in his own memoirs, makes clear that he "doubted . . . strongly" that London and Moscow could serve as mediators. "I believed," Mr. Johnson wrote, "that if the Soviets thought they had a peace formula Hanoi would accept, they would deal directly with us rather than through a fourth party." Strong doubts on Mr. Johnson's part rapidly turned to certainties as he received details of the Wilson-Kosygin talks and of Hanoi's continued military buildup in South Vietnam. "It became clear to me why the Soviets were willing to discuss Vietnam," Mr. Johnson wrote. "Kosygin was pressing Wilson hard to use his influence to persuade us to accept Hanoi's vague offer of possible talks in exchange for a bombing halt."[18]

Central to the misunderstanding that led to the collapse of his initiative was the fact that Wilson was not only unaware of the prevailing mood in the White House, but also did not know of the letter from President Johnson to Ho Chi Minh. Chester Cooper was in London to prevent just such an occurrence and, though aware that a letter might be sent to Ho, he ". . . left Washington . . . without knowing whether Johnson had approved [a version of the letter Cooper had seen] . . . or whether Johnson had decided to communicate directly and personally to Ho Chi Minh."[19] And when Cooper should have received instructions based on the Johnson-Ho letter—i.e., as he sought a routine confirmation of the A-B terms Wilson was preparing to offer Kosygin in writing—he did not. Washington-based officials, given the president's attitude toward the Wilson-Kosygin talks, did not expect them to develop into a contact with Hanoi and, hence, monitored their progress less carefully than they monitored the fate of the president's letter to Ho Chi Minh.

For the most part, the president's letter was written in a straightforward style and read well in Vietnamese. It began with a reference to a problem

Washington knew Hanoi shared: the number and conflicting purposes of intermediaries' motivations. Johnson observed:

> It may be that our thoughts and yours, our attitudes and yours, have been distorted or misinterpreted as they passed through these various channels. Certainly that is always a danger in indirect communication.
>
> There is one good way to overcome this problem and to move forward in the search for a peaceful settlement. That is for us to arrange for direct talks between trusted representatives in a secure setting and away from the glare of publicity. Such talks should not be used as a propaganda exercise but should be a serious effort to find a workable and mutually acceptable solution.
>
> In the past two weeks I have noted public statements by representatives of your government suggesting that you would be prepared to enter into direct bilateral talks with representatives of the U.S. Government, provided that we ceased "unconditionally" and permanently our bombing operations against your country and all military actions against it. In the last day, serious and responsible parties have assured us indirectly that this is in fact your proposal.

But in terms not likely to increase the chance that Hanoi would agree to talks, Mr. Johnson went on:

> Let me frankly state that I see two great difficulties with this proposal. In view of your public position, such action on our part would inevitably produce worldwide speculation that discussions were under way and would impair the privacy and secrecy of those discussions. Secondly, there would inevitably be grave concern on our part whether your Government would make use of such action by us to improve its military position.
>
> With these problems in mind, I am prepared to move even further towards an ending of hostilities than your Government has proposed in either public statements or through private diplomatic channels. I am prepared to order a cessation of bombing against your country and stopping of further augmentation of U.S. forces in South Vietnam as soon as I am assured that infiltration into South Vietnam by land and by sea *has stopped* [my italics].

The problem generated by this letter, once the British had been informed of it and had to pass its contents on to Kosygin, was that the U.S. position appeared to stiffen. Every public statement by U.S. officials placed the Phase A–B formula in the terms Wilson had originally passed on to Kosygin. According to Wilson's memoirs, these original terms were that "the U.S. were willing, over and beyond the two-phase formula previously discussed, to stop the build-up of their forces in the south if they were assured that the movement of North Vietnam forces from the north to the south *would stop* [my italics] at the same time. Essentially, therefore, the two stages [i.e., the unilateral halt in the U.S. bombing of North Vietnam and the steps described above] were kept apart. But, because the United States Government would know that the second stage would follow, they would therefore be able first to stop the bombing. . . ."[20]

Wilson believed what had happened "was, simply and tragically, a victory for the hawks," and he discounted the explanation that the change in wording was either a mistake or the result of bureaucratic confusion. "Such action," Wilson went on, "could only have the worst possible effect on the Russians. For the first time since the Vietnamese fighting had begun, they had shown willingness to use their good offices in Hanoi. . . ."[21] Now, Wilson said, Moscow might lose whatever influence it had had over Hanoi, and the actual evidence of a hardening of U.S. terms would weaken the position of those in Moscow and Hanoi who were arguing for a peaceful settlement of the conflict. Wilson cabled President Johnson directly: "You will realise what a hell of a situation I am in for my last day of talks with Kosygin. . . . I have to reestablish trust because not only will he have doubts about my credibility, but he will have lost credibility in Hanoi and possibly among his colleagues. . . ."[22]

Washington, by now less and less convinced that the Wilson-Kosygin talks or the direct letter to Ho Chi Minh would produce a forthcoming North Vietnamese response, wanted Wilson to understand that the change of tenses—from "would stop" to "has stopped"—was a conscious decision necessitated by the menacing military situation and the North Vietnamese Tet truce violations. The three NVA divisions poised above the demilitarized zone (DMZ) had to be prevented from taking advantage of the prospect of talks by infiltrating into South Vietnam without fear of bombing. Washington also considered that the proposal it had authorized Wilson to make—along with the change of tense—actually represented a step beyond the simple A-B formulation; namely, the United States was agreeing not only to end the bombing but also to end its augmentation of U.S. troops in South Vietnam. These two concessions required the assurance that NVA infiltration had stopped before the bombing would be halted. Presumably, Washington implied to Wilson, Hanoi could still have the offer that Washington was making in public—the bombing would stop in return for an assurance that infiltration would stop, with no cessation of the U.S. troop augmentation program. In fact, Washington's public and private proposals were not inconsistent, and the harder-line but more comprehensive proposal was made in private to facilitate Hanoi's acceptance. However, this permitted Hanoi subsequently to demand in public what the U.S. had already rejected in private; and by leapfrogging its public and private positions, Hanoi could call for an end to the bombing and all other acts of war, including augmentation of U.S. forces, in return only for talks. This practice made Washington appear the obstacle to talks; yet Hanoi actually was the one who opposed talks at this stage in the war.

Dealing with the immediate problem of the negotiations, Wilson informed President Johnson that "to meet his [Johnson's] expressed fear that, between the cessation of bombing and the stopping of infiltration, the DRV would rush three or four divisions through the DMZ, I proposed that the 'prior two-way assurance' [essential to implementing the A-B proposal] should contain a time-table, if possible underwritten by, or at any rate communicated through, the Russians, under which the DRV would agree in advance to stop the infiltration, say, six hours later, or an even shorter time-table if necessary."[23] This message was drafted and sent in the early hours of the morning of the twelfth of February; later that day, Wilson was to see Kosygin at a state dinner at which the communiqué on their visit was to be signed. It would be the last occasion on which they could act in concert as intermediaries. The details of that day are well known through both Mr. Wilson's memoirs and Mr. Cooper's book.

Wilson had pressed President Johnson to delay resumption of the bombing so that there could be one last effort to get a response from Hanoi to the new terms embodied in the Johnson-Ho letter and to the message Kosygin had sent to Hanoi. Washington's final position, cabled to Wilson, was that the bombing would not resume if before 10:00 A.M. London time (only nine hours after the cable had been received) Washington could have an assurance from North Vietnam that the infiltration of its troops and supplies had ceased. Wilson characterized it thus: "It was a formulation somewhere between the American Friday statement [demanding assurances that NVA infiltration had stopped] . . . and my own proposals [suggesting that the bombing stop in return for an assurance that NVA infiltration would stop within a specified few hours]. Given time, it might have been a basis for a move forward. But in my view, it was certain to founder on the utterly unrealistic time-table."[24] Kosygin shared Wilson's pessimism. The latter sought an extension from the president and received a grudging six hours, but it was to no avail. Hanoi failed to respond either to the offer stemming from the Wilson-Kosygin talks or to the one contained in the letter from Johnson to Ho Chi Minh.

Chester Cooper later learned some of the factors that contributed to the collapse of the Wilson-Kosygin initiative.

It was clear that Washington officials actually had little real interest in the London episode; they regarded it primarily as a sideshow to the main event they were trying to get under way in Moscow. My message [seeking what Cooper thought would be routine confirmation of the A-B formulation] had reached the State Department early Thursday evening; no one seemed to take it seriously enough to address himself to it, or even to flag it for priority attention. . . . When my message was finally brought to his attention, Johnson reportedly blew sky high. A group of advisors were quickly assembled. The meeting was held against a background of concern about the North Vietnamese troop movement. Indeed, Washington had been in a state of near panic during the previous several days. Perhaps this explains why the President's letter to Ho had been drafted in haste by Johnson and a few others at 2 o'clock in the morning.[25]

Bitterly, Cooper recalls, on the very day when the Phase A–B formulation was changed in private, UN ambassador Goldberg was making a speech emphasizing that U.S. policy was what Wilson had originally told Kosygin: "The United States remains prepared to take the first step and order the cessation of all bombing of North Vietnam the moment we are assured, privately or otherwise, that this step will be answered promptly by a tangible response toward peace from North Vietnam."

In his memoirs, President Johnson rationalized the failure of the Wilson-Kosygin initiative by downplaying the significance of any one effort by an intermediary to promote direct talks: "In many cases, they did not realize that the proposals they advocated so strongly had already been tried and had been rejected by Hanoi." The nub of the problem, Mr. Johnson explained, was that "most of those working so hard to find a peace formula carried no major day-to-day responsibilities in Vietnam or Southeast Asia. This lack enabled them to take a detached, above-the-battle stance." Positions would have been different during the Wilson-Kosygin talks, Mr. Johnson asserted, "if a brigade of Her Majesty's forces had been stationed just south of the demilitarized zone in Vietnam."[26]

Throughout this period, Hanoi's basic position remained unchanged from what its propaganda broadcasts had stressed during 1966. DRV foreign minister Nguyen Duy Trinh said in an interview with Wildred Burchett on January 28, 1967: "It is only after the unconditional cessation of U.S. bombing and all other acts of war against the DRV that there could be talks. . . ." This, President Johnson saw as but another indication of how steadfastly Hanoi was going to concentrate on the issue of ending the bombing. Trinh had only said talks *could* start if the bombing ended, not that they would start. This was a risk the president was not going to take.

To make negotiations as attractive to Hanoi as possible, given the fact that the president would not unconditionally end the bombing, Washington elaborated its maximum and minimum positions. By January 1967, the fourteen points first enunciated by the Department of State in January 1966 had come to read like a menu of ways the negotiations could proceed. They made clear that the 1954 and 1962 Geneva Agreements were "an adequate basis for peace in Southeast Asia," but this formulation did not rule out the possibility of ignoring them completely and forging a new type of agreement. There could be a conference "on Southeast Asia or any part thereof," thus assuring that the scope of the discussions could be chosen by Hanoi. Various types of negotiations would be acceptable—the negotiations without preconditions embodied in the nonaligned nations appeal of April 1, 1965, the unconditional discussions proposed by President Johnson on April 7, 1965, or "direct discussions or discussions through an intermediary." Should the discussions start unconditionally, then Washington would move quickly to de-escalate the conflict. Hanoi's four points would be on the agenda but could not serve as the agenda exclusively; preliminary discussions could be held to work out an agenda satisfactory to all. NLF participation in these discussions would pose no difficulty "if Hanoi . . . decides she wants to cease aggression."

The fourteenth point reflected the change of policy in the Johnson–Ho letter:

> We have said publicly and privately that we could stop the bombing of North Viet-Nam as a step toward peace although there has not been the slightest hint or suggestion from the other side as to what they would do if the bombing stopped;
>
> —We are prepared to order a cessation of all bombing of North Viet-Nam, the moment we are assured—privately or otherwise—that this step *will be answered promptly by a corresponding and appropriate de-escalation of the other side* [my italics]. . . .

Hanoi and its allies knew precisely what the last phrase meant: The bombing would stop when the infiltration stopped. Publicly, Washington would say that it was prepared to stop the bombing in accordance with the fourteenth point. Privately, it would now demand more than assurances. Publicly, Hanoi would say it would agree to talk only if the bombing were stopped. Privately, it refused to give the required assurances about infiltration by repeating its public position.

The elaborated fourteen-point statement was a strategy for beginning talks; insight into what Washington sought in a political settlement came a week later in a February 1967 speech by UN ambassador Arthur Goldberg at Howard University. Mr. Goldberg defined a political settlement as "a settlement whose terms will not sacrifice the vital interest of any party." Inherent in such a settlement was the need for compromise; this was, Mr. Goldberg asserted, what was lacking in the public and private communication Washington had with Hanoi. Operationally defined, in the period before talks began, compromise meant mutual de-escalation; thereafter, what was to be compromised was Hanoi's four-point stand. In his analysis of the four points, Mr. Goldberg suggested the broad outlines of those concessions Hanoi needed to make. The U.S. withdrawal called for in the first point would have to be matched by a similar step on the part of North Vietnam. The neutrality called for in the second point would have to apply to North Vietnam as well. The internal affairs of South Vietnam, the subject of the third point, should be determined, "through a process of mutual accommodation whereby nobody's vital interests are injured, which would be a political solution." No disagreement existed, Mr. Goldberg noted, with respect to the fourth point, which provided for the peaceful reunification of Vietnam.

Hanoi, however, saw a negotiation process involving three distinct phases, with entry into the second and third phases clearly dependent on the satisfactory outcome of the prior phase. Hanoi's insistence that there be talks to establish an agenda, negotiations to work out the modalities of an agreement, and a settlement in which those modalities were finalized and committed to paper struck Washington officials as needlessly cumbersome at best and at worst as evidence that Hanoi intended to use negotiations to stall while trying to improve its position on the battlefield.

On the same day that Ambassador Goldberg delivered his speech, Australian journalist Wilfred Burchett filed an AP report based on his conversations with North Vietnamese and NLF leaders. His report provided an unusually clear, frank, and authoritative account of how negotiations related to the future the Communists envisioned for Vietnam. Burchett asserted that the DRV would agree to talks in return for the end of the bombing of North Vietnam and that this was not contingent on prior acceptance of the four-point stand. He said, however, that the four points were the only basis on which the conflict could eventually be settled. DRV officials stressed to Burchett that Washington should see in the four points the following "important concessions": the "indefinite postponement of reunification" (implied in the fourth point), restrictions on the sovereignty of North Vietnam (implied in the second point, which required the north as well as the south to "refrain from joining any military alliance with foreign countries"), and because of the assurances given in private and public—in January, for example, Le Duan had advocated "Socialism for the North, Democracy in the South"—the DRV had in effect conceded that the spread of communism would be halted south of the seventeenth parallel. These appealing concessions were the essence of the four-point stand, one unnamed DRV official told Burchett, "to facilitate American disengagement."

Pending Washington's acceptance of the four points and the concessions they implied, a member of the NLF's Central Committee then told Burchett:

North and South Vietnam [would] remain autonomous in internal and foreign affairs. The north would remain Socialist and a member of the Socialist bloc. The south would be neutral, unallied to any blocs. Each would have its own foreign ministries and diplomatic representatives abroad. . . . For regulating north-south relations, there would be a type of general assembly, presumably nominated by the respective parliaments to handle questions important to both zones, such as trade, post and telegraph, interzonal travel, including sports and cultural exchanges. The question of negotiations between Hanoi and the Ky government in Saigon is seen as an impossibility. The latter is considered as representing no national interests or any section of the population and would die a natural death the moment serious negotiations started.

Washington interpreted the Communist position described by Burchett as a recipe not for the political settlement of the conflict but for a Communist victory.

Indeed, by the winter of 1967, visions of victory in the war overshadowed the secret search for negotiations. The consequence of this, coupled with the mutually reinforcing intransigence of Washington and Hanoi, was that their negotiating positions edged farther and farther apart, with each calling for what the other had over and over again refused to give. Five channels of communication existed with Hanoi during this time, each deadlocked over Washington's demand for reciprocity for a bombing halt and Hanoi's refusal to promise any. Four of these channels directly involved other governments—Rumania, Norway, Sweden, and Italy—and were viewed with skepticism by Washington. Each of the four had a definite interest in ending the war and each believed that the U.S. bombing of North Vietnam was the primary obstacle. One, the government of Rumania, thought that Hanoi was unlikely to honor any agreement in the long run and, therefore, Washington was trying to achieve the impossible. The Rumanians believed that the United States had too few strategic interests in Indochina to remain indefinitely as the guardian of South Vietnam. Eventually, they argued, the United States would have to leave the GVN to its fate. This would be easiest to do in 1967 or 1968 via a simple cease-fire agreement—one that provided, of course, for the return of U.S. prisoners and the withdrawal of U.S. troops.

But Washington did not want out; it wanted to win the war. Arriving in Vietnam to spend the summer of 1967 as a consultant to the State Department, I recall never once having thought about prospects for a negotiated settlement. "It appears unnecessary," I wrote in a kind of diary. "All the Americans and most of the Vietnamese I have talked to think they are winning the war. If they are, they argue, then there will be no need to negotiate. There have been so many efforts to get Hanoi into talks when the situation did not look quite so bad for them that now U.S. officials think that with the tide finally turning against the NLF, for Hanoi to enter talks would involve a serious loss of face." In Washington, however, pressure increased on the president to limit U.S. objectives in the war, restrict the bombing of North Vietnam, and begin the process of scaling down the American presence. Secretary of Defense McNamara in particular urged:

> The time has come for us to eliminate the ambiguities from our minimum objectives—our commitments—in Vietnam. Specifically, two principles must be articulated, and policies and actions brought in line with them: (1) Our commitment is only to see that the people of South Vietnam are permitted to determine their own future. (2) This commitment ceases if the country ceases to help itself.

> It follows that no matter how much we might *hope* for some things, our *commitment* is *not*:

>> to expel from South Vietnam regroupees [i.e., members of the NLF who went north in 1954 and later returned to "liberate" the South], who are South Vietnamese (though we do not like them);
>> to ensure that a particular person or group remains in power, nor that the power runs to every corner of the land (though we prefer certain types and we hope their writ will run throughout South Vietnam);
>> to guarantee that the self-chosen government is non-Communist (though we believe and strongly hope it will be); and
>> to insist that the independent South Vietnam remain separate from North Vietnam (though in the short-run, we would prefer it that way).

> (Nor do we have an obligation to pour in effort out of proportion to the effort contributed by the people of South Vietnam or in the face of coups, corruption, apathy or other indications of Saigon failure to cooperate effectively with us.)

> We *are* committed to stopping or off-setting the effect of North Vietnam's application of force in the South, which denies the people of the South the ability to determine their own future. Even here, however, the line is hard to draw. Propaganda and political advice by Hanoi (or by Washington) is presumably not barred; nor is economic aid or economic advisors. Less clear is the rule to apply to military advisors and war materiel supplied to the contesting factions.

> The importance of nailing down and understanding the implications of our limited objectives cannot be over-emphasized. It relates intimately to strategy against the North, to troop requirements and missions in the South, to handling of the Saigon government, to settlement terms, and to U.S. domestic and international opinion as to the justification and the success of our efforts on behalf of Vietnam.[27]

McNamara thus proposed that the president take the following steps in 1967 to transform the conflict into a political struggle with or without negotiations:

June: Concentrate the bombing of North Vietnam on physical interdiction of men and materiel. This would mean terminating, except where the interdiction objective clearly dictates otherwise, all bombing north of 20° and improving interdiction as much as possible in the infiltration "funnel" south of 20° by concentration of sorties and by an all-out effort to improve detection devices, denial weapons, and interdiction tactics.

July: Avoid the explosive Congressional debate and U.S. Reserve call-up implicit in the Westmoreland troop request. Decide that, unless the military situation worsens dramatically, U.S. deployments will be limited to . . . [484,000 U.S. troops in South Vietnam by June 1968 and no more than 508,000] (which, according to General Westmoreland, will not put us in danger of being defeated, but will mean slow progress in the South). Associated with this decision are decisions not to use large numbers of U.S. troops in the Delta and not to use large numbers of them in grass-roots pacification work.

September: Move the newly elected Saigon government well beyond its National Reconciliation program to seek a political settlement with the non-Communist members of the NLF—to explore a cease-fire and to reach an accommodation with the non-Communist South Vietnamese who are under the VC banner; to accept them as members of an opposition political party, and, if necessary, to accept their individual participation in the national government—in sum, a settlement to transform the members of the VC from military opponents to political opponents.

October: Explain the situation to the Canadians, Indians, British, UN and others, as well as nations now contributing forces, requesting them to contribute border forces to help make the inside-South Vietnam accommodation possible, and—consistent with our desire neither to occupy nor to have bases in Vietnam—offering to remove later an equivalent number of U.S. forces. (This initiative is worth taking despite its slim chance of success.)[28]

But Mr. McNamara's recommendations were not immediately endorsed by the president, and the events of the latter half of 1967 ultimately dictated another course of action. Johnson knew of the feud between the secretary of defense and the Joint Chiefs of Staff, and he believed McNamara's recommendations to be stimulated more by a desire to end U.S. participation in the war than by a cool assessment of whether the war would really wind down if the United States significantly reduced military pressure on Hanoi. The president, aides later told me, faced his most significant congressional criticism not from those who wanted to end U.S. involvement but from those who advocated a more aggressive policy. "To give in to McNamara now," one of the president's assistants put it, "was just politically too costly for the president."

The president concluded that the only way he could conceivably embrace what McNamara had recommended was if Hanoi had shown any intent to negotiate seriously. But by the summer of 1967, prospects for negotiations were bleak. Professor Henry Kissinger had told his Harvard classes the previous spring that as long as the United States had not succeeded in finding a strategy for winning the war, and as long as Hanoi continued to receive unlimited supplies from its Communist allies, there would be no negotiations. Nevertheless, at the June 1967 Pugwash meetings, Kissinger suggested that one of the participants with close personal contacts in North Vietnam ought to go to Hanoi to assess North Vietnamese receptivity to any of the formulas for negotiation that had been discussed at the conference. Kissinger's Pugwash colleague, biologist Herbert Marcovich, went, accompanied by a friend in whose house Ho Chi Minh had stayed at the end of the 1946 Fontainebleau Conference. In North Vietnam by July 1967, they had two substantive conversations with Pham Van Dong, as well as a visit with Ho.

Briefing Kissinger on their trip, both were convinced that Hanoi was ready to enter negotiations as soon as the United States stopped the bombing. President Johnson recalled: "They had the impression that the bombing halt need not be 'permanent,' or at least that the United States would not have to describe it as being permanent. A de facto stoppage would be sufficient, without public announcements."[29] Pham Van Dong had also told Marcovich that once the bombing stopped and negotiations began, Washington would find Hanoi forthcoming enough so that the bombing would never have to be resumed.

In mid-August, Kissinger was authorized to tell his contacts that the United States was willing "to stop all aerial and naval bombardment of North Vietnam when this will lead promptly to productive discussions. We, of course, assume that while discussions proceed, North Vietnam would not take advantage of the bombing cessation or limitation."[30] In essence, there should be no increase in the infiltration of men or supplies into South Vietnam. The word *productive* was used to emphasize the need for rapid agreement on settlement terms, for the United States sought to avoid the prolonged, fruitless negotiations that had deadlocked the Korean Armistice Conference.

While this proposal was being transmitted and considered by Hanoi, the air war continued unabated. There had been, unfortunately, raids that had damaged some of the water control systems in the north and three days of heavy bombing raids on Hanoi just before the U.S. proposal was passed to the DRV representative in Paris. Hanoi charged that these raids were evidence of Washington's bad faith and of an effort to use pressure tactics to force Hanoi into negotiations. Kissinger was instructed to explain that acts such as the bombing were both accidental and inevitable: Hanoi had insisted on secrecy about U.S.–North Vietnamese contacts and in Washington this required limiting knowledge of the secret initiative to as few people as possible; therefore, a certain lack of coordination was to be expected. Kissinger expressed his own personal dismay at Hanoi's attitude—after all, Hanoi was fighting the war without letup in the south.

Hanoi's rejection of the U.S. proposal came in mid-September. A month later, Hanoi moved to end the contact altogether. On October 17, Mai Van Bo transmitted a message arguing that, given the bombing and general escalation of the war, Washington's "words of peace are only trickery. At a time when the United States continues the escalation we can neither receive Mr. Kissinger nor comment on the American views transmitted through this channel." What happened next is described in President Johnson's memoirs:

> The North Vietnamese representative said that discussions could take place only when bombing of the North had ended "without condition." With this statement, I became convinced again that Hanoi had no interest in serious talk about peace except, as always, on its own stiff terms. But we wanted to leave no stone unturned. On October 18 I met in the Cabinet Room with Secretaries Rusk and McNamara, Walt Rostow, and Dr. Kissinger. We reviewed the entire record of the talks in Paris, and on the strong recommendation of my advisers, I agreed that Kissinger should return to France and make one more attempt to get into serious discussions. He flew to Paris and passed along to the French intermediaries our views and our sense of strong disappointment that nothing meaningful had happened. The Frenchmen immediately called Bo and asked to see him. They reported that the North Vietnamese representative's response was icy.

> "There is nothing new to say," he told them. "The situation is worsening. There is no reason to talk again." They pleaded with him. He repeated that "There is nothing new to say." Four times in all he said the same thing; Hanoi's answer was "no." The channel was dead. The door was closed and locked. On October 23, for the first time in two months, our planes hit a military target within ten miles of Hanoi.[31]

Kissinger came away from the experience convinced that the differences in the thought processes of the two adversaries were so fundamental that it had been impossible for either to imagine a negotiated—i.e., compromise—settlement. He believed that, as long as Washington and Hanoi were convinced that the war was winnable, moreover, the search for negotiations would be fruitless. The year 1968 thus marked the beginning of a new phase in the war, not a prelude to its end, and the Tet offensive was the first of a series of North Vietnamese assaults on the U.S. claim that it was winning the war.

1968: "WE WERE
DEFEATING OURSELVES"

The 1968 Tet offensive, Henry Kissinger observed,

brought to a head the compounded weaknesses—or, as the North Vietnamese say, the internal contradictions—of the American position. To be sure, from a strictly military point of view, Tet was an American victory. Viet Cong casualties were very high; in many provinces, the Viet Cong infrastructure of guerrillas and shadow administrators surfaced and could be severely mauled by American forces. But in a guerrilla war, purely military considerations are not decisive: psychological and political factors loom at least as large.

On that level the Tet offensive was a political defeat in the countryside for Saigon and the United States. Two claims had been pressed on the villages. The United States and Saigon had promised that they would be able to protect an ever larger number of villages. The Viet Cong had never made such a claim; they merely asserted that they were the real power and presence in the villages and they threatened retribution upon those who collaborated with Saigon or the United States.

As happened so often in the past, the Viet Cong made their claim stick. . . . the Tet offensive marked the watershed of the American effort. Henceforth, no matter how effective our actions, the prevalent strategy could no longer achieve its objectives within a period or with force levels politically acceptable to the American people. This realization caused Washington, for the first time, to put a ceiling on the number of troops for Viet Nam. Denied the very large additional forces requested, the military command in Viet Nam felt obliged to begin a gradual change from its peripheral strategy to one concentrating on the protection of the populated areas. This made inevitable an eventual commitment to a political solution and marked the beginning of the quest for a negotiated settlement.[1]

To President Johnson, Tet was less a defeat of U.S. strategy than a defeat of the nation's will. The president saw the roots of the psychological shock as stemming from the fact that the American people were ill prepared for the attacks he knew Hanoi had been planning. In his memoirs he wrote, "The blow to morale was more of our own doing than anything the enemy had accomplished with its army. We were defeating ourselves."[2] Tet became a symbol of how illusory the progress claimed in the war had been.

U.S. officials in Saigon, however, pointed out that Tet was a setback not a defeat, and that Tet indicated how severely hurt the NVA had been by allied combat operations and pacification in the summer and fall of 1967.[3] The NVA lost more than two-thirds of the troops it committed to the Tet attacks. Communist cadres were told that Tet was to be accompanied by a general uprising of political forces against the GVN. This, U.S. officials pointed out, did not occur. Instead, representatives of hitherto antigovernment organizations formed their own self-defense units and worked closely with GVN officials in reconstruction and recovery efforts. In essence, these officials pointed out, with U.S. support the GVN could recover and was already showing signs of doing so. But in the United States, there were already strong doubts about what the military claimed could be achieved. To many American officials, Tet offered vivid proof that the United States could not win the war and that a non-Communist government in South Vietnam would never be worth the price in American lives that the United States had already paid.

"What we wanted could neither be achieved through fighting nor negotiating," one of the president's senior advisors later observed in an interview. "If Tet convinced us that our force was not working against Hanoi, surely negotiations could not bring what force did not: the stability and permanency of General Thieu's government." Speaking for many within the administration, the president's speech writer Harry McPherson recalled that after Tet he "did not believe we could persuade or force North Vietnam to talk, or that we could win the war. I wanted to cut our losses, get the demonstrators off the streets, and reelect Lyndon Johnson."[4]

As the war thus entered the fighting-while-negotiating stage, the gap between the supporters of the war and its opponents within the U.S. government widened, as did the gap between Washington and Saigon. The turnaround in public and congressional support for the president and the war forced the United States to end the bombing of North Vietnam in return only for Hanoi's vague agreement to enter talks, not negotiations. From Hanoi's perspective, Tet confirmed the value of shifting to a fighting-while-negotiating strategy. Henceforth, attacks would be designed to have maximum impact on the war-weary American public and to capture territory that could later be given up as concessions should there actually be a need to reach formal agreement—that is, an agreement providing the United States a face-saving opportunity to withdraw from the war and abandon Saigon.

But Tet also compounded the tragedy of the conflict for the Vietnamese because it set in motion a recovery process that for the first time created vested interests in and support for an alternative to the NLF in South Vietnam. "It was a turning point all right," one embassy official told me in Saigon. "Tet turned us off the war and the GVN on to it."

THE POLITICS OF THE BOMBING HALT

Tet resolved a year-long debate within the administration that had led to the resignation of Robert McNamara. This debate had centered on the pros and cons of a unilateral end to the bombing of North Vietnam. Those in favor argued that a bombing halt would promote negotiations; those against, that it would prove too great a risk to take with the lives of U.S. soldiers. Before Tet, the hawks and the doves had been accommodated by varying the pace and intensity of the war. When there were prospects of secret contacts leading to negotiations, the president had curtailed the bombing of North Vietnam; when such initiatives had collapsed, the bombing was intensified. In early 1968, a systematic study on the "Political-Military Implications in Southeast Asia of the Cessation of Aerial Bombardment and the Initiation of Negotiations"[5] was undertaken within the Pentagon by the Joint Staff and the Office of International Security Affairs (which was both the center of dissent within the Pentagon on the bombing policy and the office most influential in shaping the Vietnam views of both Secretary McNamara and his successor, Clark Clifford).

The study's findings were significant in two respects. First, it suggested that, after two years of the air war, North Vietnam could, within two months, recover almost completely from the damage done to its strategic lines of communication (LOCs), and that, within half a year after the bombing ended, the DRV could gain the advantage in the military balance in the south. Second, the study was not sanguine about the prospects for productive negotiations, suggesting that—while negotiating—Hanoi could calibrate its fighting so that a level of violence would be kept up just below the threshold at which Washington might resume bombing. Hence, Hanoi could essentially continue those military actions that contributed most to the erosion of the ARVN and of American will. The study concluded that, from both a diplomatic and a military point of view, a bombing halt would be of doubtful value.

This finding was confirmed by the "A to Z" assessment of the U.S. role in the war that President Johnson had ordered the new secretary of defense, Clark Clifford, to undertake. The agencies responsible for drafting the report tended to agree that negotiations were likely to prove fruitless; that, because Hanoi was uninterested in negotiations, a bombing halt should not be expected to produce them; and that, in any case, the United States would not be entering talks from a position of strength. The document was, in essence, a compromise between the civilian and military tensions that the war had stirred up all along:

> . . . it was a compromise brought about by differences between the Assistant Secretary of Defense for International Security Affairs [ISA] and his staff, and the Chairman of the Joint Chiefs of Staff and his officers. Initially, ISA had prepared a draft Presidential memorandum which had indeed re-assessed U.S. strategy in VN, found it faulty, and recommended a new strategy of protecting the "demographic frontier" with basically the U.S. forces presently in-country. The Chairman of the Joint Chiefs of Staff found "fatal flaws" in this strategy, could not accept the implied criticism of past strategy in the ISA proposal, did not think that the Defense Department civilians should be involved in issuing specific guidance to the military field commander, and supported his field commander in his request for the forces required to allow him to "regain the initiative." The compromise reached, of course, was that a decision on new strategic guidance should be deferred pending a complete political/military reassessment of the U.S. strategy and objectives in Vietnam in the context of our worldwide commitments.[6]

Clifford was appalled at the outcome of what was supposed to be an agonizing reappraisal of Vietnam policy. He later recalled:

> When I reached the Pentagon and we were assigned the task of reexamining our entire posture, particularly in view of the fact that the Tet onslaught had occurred just shortly before I went into the Pentagon, and whereas we had felt that we were winning the war—and I remember so well in the late fall of '67 our two top men coming back from Vietnam, civilian and military, one of them saying there is light at the end of the tunnel and the other saying we can start to plan to bring our men back. And that coincided with what I had heard. With that very optimistic report, within two months or so after that the enemy, which was supposed to be in its last throes of desperation, staged the Tet offensive, which was a very, very serious defeat in the early stages for the United States and for the South Vietnamese. That shook me.

> So I had the opportunity then to discuss with the Joint Chiefs and with other top people in the Defense Department the request of the military to send another two hundred and six thousand troops. We already had five hundred and twenty-five thousand. So I had a number of questions, and we spent days at it. And that's all I did my first few days over there. I would ask the Joint Chiefs of Staff, "If we sent another two hundred and six thousand, is that enough?" They didn't know. "Well, if we send that, will that end the war?" "Well,

nobody knows." "Well, is it possible that you might need even more?" "That's possible." "Will bombing of the North bring them to their knees?" "No." "Is there any diminishing will on the part of the North to fight?" "Well, we're not conscious of it." Then, finally, "What is the plan for victory on the part of the United States in South Vietnam?" There wasn't any. I said, "There isn't any?" "No. The plan is that we will just maintain the pressure on the enemy and ultimately we believe that the enemy will capitulate." Well, that wasn't good enough for me after all the years we had been in there at enormous expense. I reached the conclusion that it was the kind of war that we were not ever going to win.[7]

And it was this conclusion, formed in the wake of the Tet offensive, rather than the conclusion embodied in the final report of the "A to Z" assessment that Clifford pressed home to the president.

TALKS ABOUT TALKS

On March 31, President Johnson announced that U.S. air attacks on military targets in North Vietnam would henceforth be confined to targets south of the twentieth parallel. "Even this very limited bombing of the north could come to an early end," the president declared, "if our restraint is matched by restraint in Hanoi."

On April 4, Hanoi denounced the partial bombing halt as "a perfidious trick . . . to appease public opinion," and responded: "It is clear that the U.S. government has not correctly and fully responded to the just demand of the DRV government, of U.S. progressive opinion, and of world opinion [to unconditionally cease all bombing]. However . . . the DRV . . . declares its readiness to send its representatives to make contact with U.S. representatives to decide with the U.S. side the unconditional cessation of bombing and all other war acts against the DRV so that talks could begin." Hanoi, in essence, was ready to talk about talks, not about the mutual de-escalation of the war.

Why Hanoi responded so quickly and to only a partial bombing halt remains a matter of speculation. As one U.S. official later observed, "Agreeing to talks cost the North Vietnamese four more years of war. While they achieved a bombing halt, the new administration would have done this anyway since public opinion was so opposed to continuing the air war. But the fact of negotiations and the gradual withdrawal of our forces made continuing the war at a lower level much more acceptable in the U.S. Hanoi soon not only had to fight us in South Vietnam, but in Cambodia and Laos as well." Most analysts of the then prevailing battlefield situation tended to agree that Hanoi's chief purpose in agreeing to talks was to end the bombing. This was necessary, these analysts point out, not because it had hurt Hanoi but because with the Tet offensive Hanoi had decided to fight a more conventional war. Fighting a conventional war with regular NVA soldiers in the south required long, secure supply lines and this meant that the bombing of North Vietnam had to be stopped. Thus, these analysts point out, in the wake of Tet, Hanoi itself had been ready to propose talks, and LBJ's speech only hastened this announcement.

There ensued a month of bickering over where the talks would be held—and when the Official Conversations, as they were called, between the United States and the DRV began in Paris, the atmosphere could not have been worse. The site for the talks themselves had been a compromise—and a poor one from the U.S. point of view. U.S. diplomats involved in the discussions over the conference site would have preferred another capital. "The reason was simple," one later told me. "When we were in Paris we were dependent on the French and the whole effort gave the appearance of one defeated colonial power arranging for a defeated imperialist power to extricate itself from Vietnam. Many of us believed, moreover, that de Gaulle wanted us out on worse terms than he had had to settle for."

The Official Conversations between North Vietnam and the United States that began on May 13 were sterile. "Our objective," said Averell Harriman, the head of the U.S. delegation, "can be stated succinctly and simply—to preserve the right of the South Vietnamese people to determine their own future without outside interference or coercion." In order for this to be achieved, Harriman suggested, the North Vietnamese should respect the demilitarized zone so that it could function as the Geneva Accords intended—that is, as a buffer zone between two hostile political forces rather than as a barrier separating two societies. There should be mutual troop withdrawals so that the level of violence could subside in the south and the bombing of the north could be halted completely. Finally, Harriman suggested that the neutrality of Laos and Cambodia would be respected as far as the United States was concerned.

What would Hanoi get in return for de-escalating the war? We reaffirmed "our offer [first made by President Johnson in his Johns Hopkins speech in 1965] to contribute to the cooperative development of the economic life of the peoples of Southeast Asia—an effort in which we hope North Vietnam would be willing to participate." Harriman proposed at the second meeting that both sides "look to the future and seek a basis for peace." There were, after all, important similarities in the positions articulated at the first meeting, and Harriman reviewed them:

First—we both speak of an independent, democratic, peaceful and prosperous South Vietnam. You also speak of a neutral South Vietnam. We have no problem with this if that is South Vietnam's wish.

Second—we both speak of peace on the basis of respect of the Geneva Accords of 1954—to which we add the 1962 Agreements on Laos.

Third—we both speak of letting the internal affairs of South Vietnam be settled by the South Vietnamese themselves—which we would clarify by adding, "without outside interference or coercion."

Fourth—we both speak of the reunification of Vietnam by peaceful means. In our view this must not only be peaceful but also through the free choice of the people of South Vietnam and of North Vietnam.

Fifth—we both speak of the need for strict respect of the military provisions of the 1954 Geneva Accords.

Hanoi's position, however, was that there could be no substantive talks until the bombing of North Vietnam and all other acts of war against its territory were stopped. What Xuan Thuy said in the first five minutes of his opening remarks at the May 13 meeting grated on the U.S. delegation and convinced many that the talks would come to naught. Xuan Thuy suggested that Hanoi viewed President Johnson's March speech in this context: "In view of the heavy defeats inflicted by the staunch fight for independence and freedom of the Vietnamese people in both zones, in view of strong protests from world opinion and progressive American opinion, President Johnson had to announce on March 31, 1968, the 'limited bombing' of North Vietnam." The bombing continued "over a region no less than 300 kilometers in length from the 17th to the 20th parallel with a population of 4,500,000 inhabitants." Reconnaissance aircraft constantly violated DRV air space— even though there had been a private understanding (later publicly denounced and disclaimed by Hanoi) that reconnaissance was not an act of war; U.S. ships violated DRV territorial waters; and the United States kept supporting the war-making capability of the GVN and continued to augment its illegal troop presence in South Vietnam.

At the second meeting, Xuan Thuy described how Hanoi visualized the phasing of the talks: U.S. aggression would end first; only afterward would the conference "turn to other questions affecting the two sides." Xuan Thuy then proposed that the following joint communiqué could be issued once the United States recognized that Hanoi was indeed only acting in self-defense: "The United States pledges definitely to cease bombing and all other acts of war against the entire territory of the Democratic Republic of Viet-Nam. The Democratic Republic of Viet-Nam pledges that it will in the future, as it has been [*sic*] in the past, abstain from bombing and all other acts of war against the territory of the United States."

From the start, the United States attempted to start secret talks. Harriman selected U.S. ambassador to Laos, William Sullivan, for this task. Sullivan, who had been hand-picked by Harriman to be the deputy head of the U.S. delegation to the Geneva Conference on Laos in 1962, flew to Paris and he and Harriman worked out a plan to get secret negotiations going. But in the midst of Sullivan's efforts, a student uprising swept through France's universities and immobilized Paris. Sullivan, ill from the pace of work in Laos, could not get his malady diagnosed and treated by French doctors because they had gone on strike in sympathy with the students. The French foreign office officials who had promised to assist in arranging the secret talks were suddenly engaged in negotiations with the local police to get their children released from prison. By early July, Sullivan had left Paris en route to a hospital in the United States.

As formal talks continued, the NVA launched an offensive that brought sharp warnings from U.S. spokesmen, a hardening of the president's position with regard to the risks involved in announcing a total bombing halt, and a deep suspicion of the negotiating-while-fighting process by the GVN. North Vietnamese statements stressed the familiar line that only their four-point stand was the correct basis on which the conflict could end. The U.S. stand, despite the dramatic turnaround of Clark Clifford, sounded remarkably like that of 1965 rather than 1968. Government spokesmen from Secretary of State Dean Rusk on down declared that Hanoi must cease and desist in its efforts to take over the south by force, respect the 1962 Accords on Laos by ceasing to use Laotian territory to infiltrate troops into South Vietnam, and allow its neighbors to live in peace.

By July, Harriman and Vance were convinced that the Official Conversations would never get down to matters of substance without a total end to the bombing of North Vietnam. In July, there was the usual lull on the battlefield—the Joint Chiefs argued that this was traditionally a time of regroupment for the NVA. Harriman and Vance wanted the president to declare that this was the restraint that Washington had been insisting upon for so long, and therefore the end to the bombing of North Vietnam was justified. "Harriman later explained that he was trying 'to pull a Tommy Thompson.' During the Cuban missile crisis, Thompson, the veteran Kremlinologist, had recommended to President Kennedy that he ignore the tough rhetoric in a Khrushchev message and respond only to the hopeful hints of a possible settlement; in other words, to take the optimistic track, assume the enemy wants peace, and help him achieve it."[8]

But there was to be no bombing halt that July. "Clifford, of course, backed Harriman and Vance, as did Vice-President Humphrey, who was about to be nominated for the Presidency and chafed more each day at the burden of defending the war. Katzenbach and William Bundy happened to be in Paris at the time. Moreover, the *New York Times* published an editorial on July 29 in which it advocated a similar tactic. The President, always quick to sniff a conspiracy, evidently persuaded himself that Harriman and Vance, in cahoots with Katzenbach and Bundy, were using the *Times* to put public pressure on him. He rejected the plan without further consideration."[9]

Harriman and Vance believed that the longer it took to reach an agreement, the more antipathy would build up and the more difficult it would be for Washington and Hanoi to agree. So they started regular secret meetings with the North Vietnamese. They proposed that in return for a total bombing halt (though not an end to aerial reconnaissance of North Vietnam) the DRV agree to stop violating the DMZ and to cease rocket and mortar attacks against South Vietnamese cities. An understanding to this effect was actually achieved by Cyrus Vance's reading from a talking paper that spelled out these terms, and then leaving the paper on the conference table for his North Vietnamese counterpart to pick up, signaling the tacit acceptance of terms.[10] As one of the participants in these talks recalled, "Hanoi impressed us as sincerely wanting to repair their war-damaged economy and to regain their independence from China and Russia, on whom they were dependent for aid." But, my source informed, "it turned out that our most difficult negotiations were with Washington and not Hanoi. The military would say that the bombing was essential to protect American lives; we would argue that a negotiated agreement would save lives. But we just couldn't convince the president that summer."

Advocates of a total bombing halt did prevail by fall, and President Johnson, against all of his instincts and convinced that Hanoi would not respond by reaching an agreement, consented to announce, on October 15, a total halt to the bombing of North Vietnam. But Mr. Johnson insisted that four-party talks be held within twenty-four hours of the end of the bombing of North Vietnam.

Saigon balked, however.[11] The GVN asked for more time in which to assess the military situation. Then Hanoi demanded that before talks could begin, the United States sign a secret "minute" stating that it had stopped the bombing unconditionally. Johnson refused. Hanoi had secretly agreed to cease its military use of the DMZ and its rocket attacks on Saigon and other cities in return for the end of the bombing, and the president simply refused to give Hanoi the chance to, as one aide put it, "re-write history." Two days later, Hanoi dropped its demand.

On the eve of the scheduled announcement of the bombing halt Saigon telegraphed the White House to say that it required additional time—three days—to organize a delegation and dispatch it to Paris. The president was furious at the prospect of further delays, but announced that expanded talks would now begin in Paris on November 6. The NLF delegation arrived early but no one from Saigon arrived; no one did until their mercurial vice-president, Nguyen Cao Ky, taking up a form of exile, arrived to head the

GVN delegation. Still talks did not begin. Ky refused to sit at a four-sided table because that would, he argued, imply that the NLF was separate from the DRV. The shape of the table was only agreed on four days before President Johnson was to cede the White House and the country to Richard Nixon.

As the "negotiations" dragged on, chances gradually diminished for an agreement to end the war along the lines of the one Harriman and Vance had proposed in the summer. Averell Harriman later told the Senate Foreign Relations Committee:

> If the talks had begun as scheduled in early November 1968, one of the first subjects of discussion, as Secretary Clifford stated, would have been the reduction in the level of combat and violence. We were encouraged to believe that progress in this direction could be made. In late October and early November, the North Vietnamese had taken ninety percent of their troops out of the northern two provinces of I Corps. Half of these troops had been withdrawn above the 20th parallel—some 200 miles to the north. Fighting almost stopped in this area which had previously been one of the most active. Because of this, General Abrams was able to move the 1st Air Cavalry Division from I Corps to III Corps to strengthen our position there.[12]

This action was taken, as Clark Clifford said on "Face the Nation" in mid-December 1968, as a signal that "Hanoi is ready to enter into certain military understandings with us that would result in the withdrawal of troops and a very substantial diminution in the level of the fighting."

U.S. officials in the field and military experts in Washington, however, saw the North Vietnamese troop withdrawals as a reaction to NVA losses after the May 1968 offensive. The division that was withdrawn, they argued, could no longer be supported and needed to be rested and refitted in North Vietnam. North Vietnamese officials compounded doubts about the troop withdrawals by characterizing them as a positive gesture long sought by the Johnson administration, one that should be reciprocated by a total bombing halt. "It was," one of the State Department's senior Vietnam experts told me, "a typical North Vietnam negotiating ploy. They give up something they really can't hold on to, label it a concession, and ask us to reciprocate by stopping the bombing."

Nonetheless, Clark Clifford envisioned a phased negotiating process in which Washington and Hanoi reached agreement about lowering the level of combat in South Vietnam while Saigon and Hanoi conducted more prolonged negotiations on a political settlement. "I am becoming inordinately impatient of the continued deaths of American boys in Vietnam," Clifford told his TV audience on "Face the Nation." "I would like to get going at the Paris Conference. I would like to get started on these plans to lower the level of combat. This isn't difficult to do. I would like to start getting our troops out of there. I would like to see a cease-fire. All of that can take place while . . . lengthy negotiations on a political settlement [are being held]."

But to Clifford, Harriman, and Vance, the GVN's continued objections to the negotiations gradually eroded the atmosphere of trust that had been established with Hanoi, and with it was eroded the chance they had so carefully nurtured to end the war. In congressional testimony, Harriman observed:

> Even after President Thieu some weeks later at last permitted his representatives to join the talks in Paris, the opening of negotiations was delayed further by Saigon's raising of fantastic procedural questions, such as the shape of the table. When these matters were finally settled before I left Paris in January 1968, we then expected serious negotiations to commence. My associate, Cyrus Vance, at considerable personal inconvenience, remained in Paris to assist in smoothing the way for Ambassador Lodge for one month. However, Thieu pulled the rug out from under the negotiations. He announced that his representatives would not take part in private meetings with the NLF, claiming that would give them undue prestige, although he knew full well that it was only in the private meetings that any progress could be made. Two months later he was finally persuaded to agree to participate, but at the same time he announced that he would not in any circumstances agree to a coalition government or permit the Communists to become a political party in South Vietnam. By then the NLF refused to sit down privately with his representatives and it has stubbornly maintained that position.[13]

Other U.S. negotiators suggest that the election of Richard Nixon also contributed to eroding the chance for a military settlement in the fall of 1968. As one put it in an interview: "President-elect Nixon made his own approach to Hanoi by sending his personal representative to the talks with the message that a negotiated agreement would have to be more than a simple armistice [this was a contrast to what Harriman and Vance were offering]. The whole tone of the talks with Hanoi changed thereafter. They realized that President Johnson wasn't going to make an agreement that he knew his successor did not favor. Our talks then went dead."

Perhaps the most significant lessons from Tet and the "negotiations" which ensued were drawn, not in Washington or Hanoi, but in Saigon. While in the United States, the bombing halt was viewed as a worthwhile risk for peace, high officials in the Saigon government told me it signaled the beginning of U.S. withdrawal in spirit, soon followed by withdrawal in body as well. President Johnson's actions foreshadowed the shape of an eventual agreement based on concessions by North Vietnam that were far short of those Saigon had sought. "At the highest level," one member of the South

Vietnamese cabinet told me later, "we began to suspect that Washington might not insist on the withdrawal of the NVA from South Vietnam. If domestic pressure had forced President Johnson to give away the bombing bargaining chip for nothing in order to get 'talks,' another president might be forced to accept less than we wanted in order to get an agreement." Another high level GVN official later explained how he thought events might unfold and why the GVN's attitude toward negotiation stiffened after Tet:

> We never had any illusions about how the Communists would use the negotiations. For them, it was a new way to fight the war, to weaken us, and they very carefully played it out according to the timing of your elections.
>
> By 1968, they wanted to get the bombing stopped, so they used the negotiations to do it. They needed an end to the bombing because they wanted to fight a conventional war, and this kind of war required long supply lines free from aerial attack and a secure rear base in the north where supplies could be marshalled. Before 1968 they followed the dictum of Mao Tse Tung: let the countryside encircle the cities. With Tet, they decided to attack the victim at its heart (the cities) rather than its arms and legs (the countryside). This was geared to their negotiating strategy. They would thereafter take areas they could not hold and give them back by withdrawing their troops when they wanted to create the impression of having made concessions to facilitate negotiations or improve the atmosphere in Paris. They "gave back" the cities in 1968 for an end of the bombing. They "gave back" Quang Tri in 1972 for a cease-fire-in-place.
>
> After March 1968, the U.S. never seemed to see that it was our side that was always being forced into making concessions.

What President Johnson had rejected in the summer of 1968, and what President-elect Nixon had rejected that fall was, in the minds of those closest to the negotiations, the only chance to end the war and shift the conflict from the military to the political arena that six years of secret efforts had produced. It should be stressed here that these officials were not sanguine about the future of Saigon. They did not favor a negotiated settlement (i.e., primarily a cease-fire between U.S. forces and the NVA and a POW exchange) because Saigon was ready for it, but because from the point of view of the American people U.S. withdrawal from the Vietnam war was long overdue.

By 1969, however, a new generation of U.S. embassy officers in Saigon believed that the GVN's police forces in the countryside and the joint U.S. and Vietnamese campaign against the Viet Cong infrastructure—the Phoenix Program—had done much to make winning the war possible again. "We are finally turning the corner," one high U.S. embassy official told me. "Tet made the Vietnamese anti-Communist." Indeed, instead of signaling the need for the kind of political accommodation with Hanoi that Harriman and Vance had envisioned, the 1968 Tet offensive stiffened Saigon's resistance to a negotiated settlement. And the Vietnamization program would encourage Saigon to seek a position of strength in the war to compensate for U.S. troop withdrawals. Thus, the war was far from over and a negotiated settlement far from being at hand as Richard Nixon entered the White House.

Fighting While Negotiating, 1968–1970

CAPTURE
An unknown Communist photographer recorded the capture of a U.S. infantryman. Hanoi believed U.S. POWs were a major lever in the negotiations, that is, Washington would eventually have to negotiate on Communist terms if it didn't want to appear to be abandoning the POWs. *(U.S. Army photograph)*

DEVASTATION
A main street in Hue, a result of the 1968 Tet offensive. *(Robert Turner Collection, Hoover Archives)*

THE OTHER SIDE OF VIETNAMIZATION
South Vietnamese air force cadets receive English language instruction
in Saigon prior to departure for pilot officer training in the U.S. In
April 1975, South Vietnam had the fourth largest air force in the
world. *(U.S. Army photograph)*

VIETNAMIZATION
The departure of the Third Marine Division in 1969. Members of the division
pause in memory of those who died. *(U.S. Army photograph)*

4

ENTER NIXON: "THE ONLY WAY TO END THE WAR BY NEGOTIATIONS IS TO PROVE SAIGON CAN WIN IT"

From the start Richard Nixon believed that the war had been fought incorrectly. In 1954, he advocated sending U.S. troops to replace those the French had lost. In 1955 he argued that Communist Chinese aggression in Vietnam and elsewhere should be halted with atomic weapons. By 1964, Mr. Nixon considered that too many compromises had already been made to the Communists in Indochina, and he urged retaliatory air strikes against Laos and North Vietnam. In 1965, he opposed the Johnson administration's efforts to start negotiations, fearing that Hanoi would interpret it as a sign of U.S. weakness. Negotiations should only take place, Mr. Nixon believed, after North Vietnamese withdrawal from South Vietnam—after the status quo ante had been achieved, and not before. In 1966 Mr. Nixon strongly disagreed with congressmen Gerald Ford and Melvin Laird when they said President Johnson made a serious mistake in committing the United States so deeply to the war in Vietnam. Constant calls for negotiations, Mr. Nixon said, would only encourage Hanoi to continue fighting, and he predicted that the war would go on at least through 1971.[1]

To Richard Nixon, the fate of a non-Communist Vietnam was important, and an American commitment to see the struggle through was essential to U.S. security. He wrote, for example, in a 1967 assessment of "Asia after Vietnam," that "without the American commitment in Viet Nam, Asia would be a far different place today. . . . Viet Nam has diverted Peking from other such potential targets as India, Thailand, and Malaysia. It has bought vitally needed time for governments that were weak or unstable or leaning toward Peking as a hedge against the future—time which has allowed them to attempt to cope with their own insurrections while pressing ahead with their political, economic and military development."[2] Because the United States had stood firm, he argued, Southeast Asia was now relatively immune to Chinese subversion, as the overthrow of Sukarno—and with it the Communist party in Indonesia—in 1965 had demonstrated. Now, Mr. Nixon declared, it was time to act decisively to end the Vietnam war.

He was deeply influenced by what he had learned in conversations with Asian leaders who wanted to see the war brought to a satisfactory conclusion. This did not mean, Nixon told aides, the decent interval sought by many Democrats, but a genuine peace in which a stable, economically viable South Vietnam could develop freely. Nixon had been deeply impressed by what he had seen of the anti-Communist spirit of the South Vietnamese and he resolved that they would not be forced to live under communism if he had a say in the way the United States ended its involvement in the war. In 1967, a group of northern Catholic Vietnamese refugees presented Nixon with a lacquer plaque commemorating his visit to Vietnam. Later it was to hang in the bedroom of the western White House as a constant reminder, the president would tell visitors, of the need to make sure that the people of Vietnam would not have to flee communism again.

As a presidential candidate, Nixon was particularly critical of the Johnson administration's gradualism in the use of force. He suggested that the thrust of U.S. diplomacy should be directed not at Hanoi but at Moscow, for he believed the Soviet Union had as much influence on the course of the war as what happened on the battlefields of South Vietnam. In the draft of a speech he intended to deliver in an evening radio address scheduled for March 31, 1968—and published later by a speech writer—Mr. Nixon observed:

> Today, the Soviet Union and the Communist states of Eastern Europe are providing fully 85 percent of the sophisticated weapons for North Viet Nam and 100 percent of the oil. It is Soviet SAMs and Soviet anti-aircraft guns that are shooting down American planes. It is Soviet artillery that is pounding the Marine fortress at Khe Sanh. Without Soviet military assistance, the North Vietnamese war machine would grind to a halt.

> The Johnson Administration has made a fundamental error in basing its policies toward the Soviet Union on the wishful assumption that the Soviets want an early end to the war in Viet Nam. Not the small, primitive state of North Viet Nam, but its great Soviet ally and protector inhibits the full exercise of America's military power. Not even the proximity of Red China's massive armies is as powerful a deterrent to U.S. actions as the presence of Soviet freighters in the port of Haiphong. North Viet Nam can hold out stubbornly for total victory because it believes it has total Soviet backing. Yet Washington's desire for a broad political accommodation with the Soviet Union—for détente—arouses a will to ignore or to minimize that backing.

Hanoi is not Moscow's puppet, but it must remain a respectful client in order to keep Soviet aid flowing and to balance the influence of nearby Peking. If the Soviets were disposed to see the war ended and a compromise settlement negotiated, they have the means to move Ho Chi Minh to the conference table.[3]

Later in the campaign, Mr. Nixon further amplified his intended approach by making clear that he would move aggressively on a variety of fronts to improve the chances of both meaningful negotiations and the survival of South Vietnam. In response to questions submitted by the editors of the *New Republic* in October 1968 Nixon declared: "What is needed now is not further military escalation, but rather a dramatic escalation of our efforts in the often-neglected nonmilitary aspects of the struggle—political, economic, psychological, and diplomatic."[4]

To candidate Nixon, the diplomatic challenge was to "awaken the Soviet Union to the perils of the course it has taken in Viet Nam. This should be done," Nixon continued, "not through belligerent threats, but through candid, tough-minded, face-to-face diplomacy." Nixon suggested that, when the U.S. strategy for a settlement in Vietnam was linked to other concerns that were of particular interest to the Soviet Union, Moscow would apply pressure on Hanoi. In his reply to the editors of the *New Republic* on the eve of the election, he clarified what he had in mind: "If the Soviet Union is in fact interested in such discussions and negotiations with us—on European security, on increased contacts, and on arms control measures—then, it would seem reasonable to assume that the Soviet Union would view with favor the 'liquidation' of this serious obstacle to peace. Thus, in the final analysis, the Soviet Union must recognize its own self-interest in ending the Vietnam war."[5]

Nixon entered the White House hopeful that diplomacy could end the war but resolved to use decisive political, economic, psychological, and even military action if diplomacy did not work. Nixon was not interested in finding either the easiest or the quickest solution to the conflict because he believed that the way the war was ended would determine whether another war would begin elsewhere. As he would have told the American public in his March 31, 1968, radio address:

The easiest way to end the war quickly would be for the United States to surrender on terms designed to conceal the fact. Senator Robert Kennedy probably could end the war quickly—but if his impassioned rhetoric is to be believed, he would do so in a way sure to lose the peace. The silence of defeat that would descend over the Viet Nam battlefield would soon be shattered by the roar of guns elsewhere. Not only the hard-liners in Peking, but also the hard-line doctrinaire faction in the Kremlin, which has recently recovered prestige and influence, would be greatly encouraged to support bolder and more dangerous adventures. Inevitably, the challenge to our power, interests and security would bring a clash, the possible consequences of which are too easily imagined.[6]

Writing in the summer of 1968, for an article to be published in the January 1969 issue of *Foreign Affairs,* Henry Kissinger agreed:

No war in a century has aroused the passions of the conflict in Viet Nam. By turning Viet Nam into a symbol of deeper resentments, many groups have defeated the objective they profess to seek. However we got into Viet Nam, whatever the judgment of our actions, ending the war honorably is essential for the peace of the world.[7]

But in his assessment of the Vietnam negotiations, Kissinger pointed to one of the "cardinal maxims of guerrilla war: the guerrilla wins if he does not lose. The conventional army loses if it does not win."[8] Unlike Nixon, Kissinger, as one of his aides later told me in an interview, was inclined to seek a negotiated agreement "that Hanoi would sign, that would get our POWs back, and that would end the U.S. involvement. He would not even entertain the notion that we could get better terms or that Saigon could ever win the war." In contrast, President Nixon believed, one of his aides told me, that "the only way to end the war by negotiations was to prove to Hanoi and to Saigon that Saigon could win it." While there was thus a fundamental difference between Nixon and Kissinger over what the long-term prospects were for a non-Communist government in South Vietnam, they nonetheless agreed on the necessity for forcefulness and decisiveness in the search for a negotiated agreement that would permit the United States to withdraw its troops.

BACKDROP FOR THE NIXON ADMINISTRATION'S VIETNAM POLICY: THE THOUGHTS OF DR. KISSINGER

Kissinger's 1967 "National Security Policy" seminar at Harvard was my introduction to the strategic issues involved in the Vietnam war. Kissinger told us he had been against the war from the start: "The U.S. had become deeply involved in Vietnam because of the American tendency to transform individual conflicts into crises with universal potential," Kissinger observed in class. Once in the war we Americanized it: "We forced the South Vietnamese to learn to fight the way we were trained; we trained them to depend not on their own resources but on a supply line extending thousands of miles across the Pacific; we encouraged them to report progress on maps that did not depict the real problem of who controlled the countryside at night; and we were demanding that civilians be given control over the government in Saigon at a time when only the military possessed the national organization required for a viable government." The consequence of this, Kissinger pointed out, was that the U.S. approach, "rather than countering a Communist war of national liberation had thus created two wars: one in which conventional American forces were pitted against, and nearly stymied by, conventional North Vietnamese forces, and one in which Saigon's forces were tied down and beginning to be chewed up by the Viet Cong guerrilla forces. Even a victory for the United States in the first war would not necessarily mean that our ally would win the second."

"North Vietnam will not negotiate," Kissinger said, "as long as it can endure punishment, and this depends on whether their Communist allies can maintain reasonably uninterrupted supply lines to the war in the south." Kissinger never put much faith in the U.S. capacity to hurt North Vietnam or to interdict seriously the flow of men and supplies into the south. Writing in *Foreign Affairs,* Kissinger noted that "by opting for military victory through attrition, the American strategy produced what came to be the characteristic feature of the Vietnamese war: military successes that could not be translated into permanent political advantage."[9] Kissinger was also not sanguine about the role the Soviet Union could play in pressuring Hanoi into negotiations. He wrote:

> For a long time, Moscow has seemed paralyzed by conflicting considerations and bureaucratic inertia. Events in Czechoslovakia have reduced Moscow's usefulness even further. We would compound the heavy costs of our pallid reaction to events in Czechoslovakia if our allies could blame it on a quid pro quo for Soviet assistance in extricating us from Southeast Asia. Washington therefore requires great delicacy in dealing with Moscow on the Viet Nam issue. It cannot be in the American interest to add fuel to the already widespread charge that the superpowers are sacrificing their allies to maintain spheres of influence.[10]

What lay ahead as a new administration entered the White House? Kissinger predicted "prolonged negotiations" progressing "through a series of apparent stalemates." From his involvement in secret contacts in 1967, Kissinger knew that

> North Viet Nam's diplomacy operates in cycles of reconnaissance and withdrawal to give an opportunity to assess the opponent's reaction. This is then followed by another diplomatic sortie to consolidate the achievements of the previous phase or to try another route. In this sense, many contacts with Hanoi which seemed "abortive" to us probably served (from Hanoi's point of view) the function of defining the terrain. The methods of Hanoi's diplomacy

are not very different from Viet Cong military strategy and sometimes appear just as impenetrable to us.[11]

From his involvement with the U.S. government, Kissinger also knew that

> where Hanoi makes a fetish of planning, Washington is allergic to it. We prefer to deal with cases as they arise "on their merits." Pronouncements that the United States is ready to negotiate do not guarantee that a negotiating position exists or that the U.S. government has articulated its objectives.
>
> Until a conference comes to be scheduled, two groups in the American bureaucracy usually combine to thwart the elaboration of a negotiating position: those who oppose negotiations and those who favor them. The opponents generally equate negotiations with surrender; if they agree to discuss settlement terms at all, it is to define the conditions of the enemy's capitulation. Aware of this tendency and of the reluctance of the top echelon to expend capital on settling disputes which involve no immediate practical consequences, the advocates of negotiations cooperate in avoiding the issue. Moreover, delay serves their own purposes in that it enables them to reserve freedom of action for the conference room.
>
> Pragmatism and bureaucracy thus combine to produce a diplomatic style marked by rigidity in advance of formal negotiations and excessive reliance on tactical considerations once negotiations start. In the preliminary phases, we generally lack a negotiating program; during the conference, bargaining considerations tend to shape internal discussions.[12]

The problems caused by the differences between the U.S. and Communist approaches to negotiations were compounded, Kissinger went on to say in *Foreign Affairs,* when Americans not only had to negotiate with an adversary, but with an ally as well.

> Clashes with our allies in which both sides claim to have been deceived occur so frequently as to suggest structural causes. . . . When an issue is fairly abstract—before there is a prospect for an agreement—our diplomats tend to present our view in a bland, relaxed fashion to the ally whose interests are involved but who is not present at the negotiations. The ally responds equally vaguely for three reasons: (a) he may be misled into believing that no decision is imminent and therefore sees no purpose in making an issue; (b) he is afraid that if he forces the issue the decision will go against him; (c) he hopes the problem will go away because agreement will prove impossible. When agreement seems imminent, American diplomats suddenly go into high gear to gain the acquiescence of the ally. He in turn feels tricked by the very intensity and suddenness of the pressure while we are outraged to learn of objections heretofore not made explicit. This almost guarantees that the ensuing controversy will take place under the most difficult conditions.[13]

Such conditions, in Kissinger's view, had already been created. The Paris talks began with a public rift between Washington and Saigon over the latter's reluctance to participate in negotiations in any forum where the Viet Cong were given equal status with the GVN. But more importantly, Kissinger also knew that the GVN's demands could not be achieved on the battlefield, let alone in negotiations with North Vietnam.

Kissinger concluded his assessment of the prospects for a negotiated settlement with concrete proposals that unwittingly widened the credibility gap between the United States and its South Vietnamese ally. Kissinger wrote: "If Hanoi proves intransigent and the war goes on, we should seek to achieve as many of our objectives as possible unilaterally. We should adopt a strategy which reduces casualties and concentrates on protecting the population. We should continue to strengthen the Vietnamese army to permit a gradual withdrawal of some American forces, and we should encourage Saigon to broaden its base so that it is stronger for the political contest with the communists which sooner or later it must undertake."[14]

When GVN officials read the article, their reaction was summarized by one cabinet minister who told me in 1970:

> We fear Mr. Kissinger does not understand the significance of the struggle to us. We do not want a less costly war; we want an end to the war and this will only come when Hanoi withdraws its forces and we are strong enough to keep them north of the DMZ. We do not want a political struggle with the Communists, we want the Communists to leave South Vietnam alone, and this will only happen when we have destroyed their infrastructure. Finally, we do not want to have to live on American aid forever, but our need for it will stop only when the Communists stop getting aid from their allies to continue to fight the war. We want peace, we want freedom from communism, and these two goals cannot come through negotiation. In negotiation you have to compromise and this we are unwilling to do.

It was a point Kissinger had yet to learn about Saigon and Washington, as well as about Hanoi.

But to Kissinger, the war had to be settled and U.S. involvement ended, despite what Saigon or Hanoi wanted. In sum, Kissinger's view of the Vietnam war was that it had thrown out of equilibrium the relationships between the major and hitherto hostile nuclear powers. It was a conflict, he pointed out, in which the United States had become involved for reasons that were no longer as compelling as the need to improve relations with the Soviet Union and China. U.S. initiative (for 500,000 U.S.—not Chinese or Russian—soldiers were in Vietnam) was required both in the direction of a détente and toward deflating the importance of the war so that Hanoi would agree to conditions that lowered the level of violence and permitted the

United States to withdraw its troops. Later, in fact, Kissinger would defend the Paris Agreement largely in terms of what it did to restore great-power equilibrium, not of what it achieved for the Vietnamese:

> Now, what this administration has attempted to do is not so much to play a complicated nineteenth-century game of balance of power, but to try to eliminate those hostilities that were vestiges of a particular perception at the end of the war and to deal with the root fact of the contemporary situation— that we and the Soviet Union, and we and the Chinese, are ideological adversaries, but we are bound together by one basic fact: that none of us can survive a nuclear war and therefore it is in our mutual interest to try to reduce those hostilities that are bureaucratic vestiges or that simply are not rooted in overwhelming national concerns.[15]

NIXON SETS THE GOAL: A NEGOTIATED SETTLEMENT

A precipitous withdrawal of U.S. forces from the war was an option Nixon and Kissinger ruled out before they entered the White House. In their view, such a withdrawal would demoralize the GVN, encourage Communist aggression elsewhere, and cause allies to question the credibility of U.S. commitments. Furthermore, the administration would be vulnerable to charges from its conservative supporters that it was not hardheaded enough in its dealings with Communists. And, unless the administration could appear tough, it would be practically impossible for Nixon to transform relations with Moscow and Peking from confrontation to cooperation and détente.

A military victory also was not an option, not because it was as inconceivable to Nixon as it was to Kissinger, but because both agreed that it would deepen and prolong domestic division in the United States. A negotiated agreement was, therefore, essential. As Kissinger later explained: "One reason why the president has been so concerned with ending the war by negotiation, and ending it in a manner that is consistent with our principles, is because of the hope that the act of making peace could restore the unity that had sometimes been lost at certain periods of the war, and so that the agreement could be an act of healing rather than a source of new division."[16]

In the search for that agreement, Nixon and Kissinger both believed that the only trump card the United States had left was its preponderant military power. "No matter how irrelevant some of our political conceptions or how insensitive our strategy, we are so powerful that Hanoi is simply unable to defeat us militarily. By its own efforts, Hanoi cannot force the withdrawal of American forces from South Viet Nam. Indeed, a substantial improvement in the American military position seems to have taken place. As a result, we have achieved our minimum objective: Hanoi is unable to gain a military victory. Since it cannot force our withdrawal, it must negotiate about it."[17]

To Kissinger, however, what would determine when an agreement could be signed was not when the GVN was militarily or politically capable of surviving it, but when Hanoi agreed to separate political from military issues. As one of Kissinger's aides told me in an interview:

> Henry was prepared to move as soon as Hanoi indicated any give, any change in its formulation of the issues such that the political problems could be negotiated separately from military problems. He wanted an agreement and he always believed one was around the corner, no more than six months away. Every time Hanoi agreed to meet with us secretly, Henry used to say, "This may be it." Every time, he was disappointed. Our biggest problem at first was to convince Henry that the North Vietnamese were not going to change what they had been insisting on for the better part of a decade simply because Henry was talking with them.

> Nixon, in contrast, sought something more and operated with a longer timetable in mind. He repeatedly told his aides and the American public that he wanted to achieve a peace, not an armistice—a peace that would last, a peace that would justify the sacrifices already made by the Americans who died in Vietnam. This required developing the capability within South Vietnam as American troops were withdrawn for the GVN's armed forces to handle what would be an obviously serious threat from the north for some time to come.

And this requisite, in turn, meant that Vietnamization should reduce U.S. casualties as quickly as possible (as was done by withdrawing the bulk of the forces engaged in actual combat within six months) and then taper off the withdrawals so that the GVN could adjust gradually. This was achieved by withdrawing 65,000 troops in 1969 but only 50,000 in all of 1970, and then pulling out 250,000 in 1971. As 1972 began, there were still 184,000 U.S. troops in South Vietnam.

Throughout this period both Nixon and Kissinger came to believe that the selective use of force was essential for compelling Hanoi to negotiate despite the U.S. troop withdrawals. Thus there was no disagreement between them on the necessity for the secret bombing of Cambodia in 1969, on the subsequent military operations in Cambodia and Laos in 1970, and on the 1972 mining of Haiphong Harbor and Christmas bombing in Hanoi.

But while Nixon saw these actions as improving Saigon's chances to survive, and therefore to actually achieve a negotiated settlement, Kissinger saw them only in relation to his secret negotiations with Le Duc Tho. The United States had to appear credible to the North Vietnamese by increasing the costs to Hanoi of prolonging the negotiations by refusing to separate the military and the political issues involved in the secret talks. Both Nixon and Kissinger, for example, thought that Vietnamization should proceed far more slowly than Secretary of Defense Melvin Laird advised. Again, Nixon saw Vietnamization as assuring that Saigon was given the maximum time possible to develop an effective self-defense capability.

As Hanoi proved intransigent and the talks dragged on without result, Nixon finally came to believe that Saigon stood a good chance of surviving the U.S. withdrawal. As one of the president's aides recalled in an interview, "We started out saying that Vietnamization was not a substitute but a spur to negotiations. When nothing happened in the talks, Vietnamization and not negotiation constituted our plan to end the war." This was necessary because, as the president explained, "The North Vietnamese view negotiations as an alternative route to victory, not a compromise with opponents. For them, negotiations are a continuation of the military struggle by other means, rather than an effort to bridge the gap between positions."[18] In contrast to Nixon, Kissinger saw Vietnamization as essential to assuring that when an agreement was at hand, Saigon would have little ground on which to argue that it was premature. But as the secret talks dragged on, he was concerned about the GVN's apparent success in the war. "The stronger Saigon appeared," one of Kissinger's aides told me later, "Henry believed the less likelihood there would be that Hanoi would sign an agreement."

By initially choosing Vietnamization (in order to reduce casualties) and negotiations (to mollify public opinion), the Nixon administration silenced the welter of conflicting intragovernmental advice unleashed by President Johnson's March 31 speech. Nearly all of the advocates of alternative policies in Vietnam—except for those who favored immediate withdrawal of all U.S. military forces and the end of U.S. assistance to the Saigon government— could see in the new administration's policy some element of their recommendations. The small army of consultants and political counselors, who had begun traveling to Vietnam in 1967 and who had discovered that local units of the NLF and government forces were making live-and-let-live deals, saw the possibility of such accommodations expanding to the national level as the fighting became an all-Vietnamese affair. Advocates of this course—their ranks included the high officials who favored the bombing halt in 1968 and most of the foreign policy experts of the Democratic and Republican parties—believed that the war would wind down as the process of accommodation proceeded; a cease-fire and a political solution would thus occur simultaneously.

Those who advocated keeping maximum military pressure on the North Vietnamese saw that Vietnamization was the only domestically acceptable way to do this. Their ranks included former secretary of state Dean Rusk; General Creighton Abrams (the new commander of U.S. forces in Vietnam); and U.S. ambassador to Saigon, Ellsworth Bunker. It was, they would argue, an appropriate American counter to the Communist tactic of fighting while negotiating. Other officials, who agreed with McGeorge Bundy that the United States should begin unilaterally withdrawing troops until no more than 100,000 remained in Vietnam, saw Vietnamization as leading to that goal as well. As one advocate of this position who was close to Kissinger told me, "At last we have separated the goal of reducing the American presence from factors we cannot ourselves control, namely, the level of combat in South Vietnam initiated by North Vietnam and Hanoi's intransigence in the Paris talks."

Nearly everyone giving the new administration advice in 1969 and 1970 saw Vietnamization as a feasible way to facilitate secret negotiations with Hanoi—negotiations aimed at mutual troop withdrawals (a tacit form of cease-fire) that would not involve loss of face for Hanoi and would ultimately pressure Saigon into reaching a political settlement with the Viet Cong. This was the course that Henry Kissinger favored in his *Foreign Affairs* article, and it was the way most people expected Kissinger to go about ending the war. In that essay, Kissinger pointed out:

> The limits of the American commitment can be expressed in two propositions: first, the United States cannot accept a military defeat, or a change in the political structure of South Viet Nam brought about by external military force; second, once North Vietnamese forces and pressures are removed, the United States has no obligation to maintain a government in Saigon by force.
>
> American objectives should therefore be (1) to bring about a staged withdrawal of external forces, North Vietnamese and American, (2) thereby to create a maximum incentive for the contending forces in South Viet Nam to work out a political agreement. The structure and content of such an agreement must be left to the South Vietnamese. It could take place formally on the national level. Or, it could occur locally on the provincial level where even now tacit accommodations are not unusual in many areas such as the Mekong Delta.[19]

What Kissinger and most other outsiders in 1968 did not realize was the difficulty the new administration would face in getting Hanoi to sign any agreement at all. While Vietnamization was responsive to domestic criticism of the costs of the war, it ultimately proved counterproductive to what Nixon sought from the negotiations. The more U.S. troops departed Vietnam without any progress in the negotiations, the less incentive Hanoi had to reach any agreement at all. Just as the United States had given up a bargaining chip by halting the bombing when it did, it was now doing this with the withdrawal of the troops. But the more U.S. troop presence diminished, the more intensely the president insisted that the war end through a negotiated settlement.

Instead, with Vietnamization, the war appeared to be ending with a momentum independent of the negotiations. By 1970–71, the level of combat declined, since the ARVN was far less aggressive than U.S. forces had been. South Vietnam appeared secure and at peace despite the lack of progress in the Paris talks. "It was dramatic. Suddenly we found that the Vietnamese were capable of defending themselves and stabilizing their government. They were more than adequately filling in the vacuum we feared the departure of so many American soldiers would create. For the first time in a decade, they were bringing peace to most of the countryside." These observations, made by a senior U.S. official in Saigon in 1970, summarize many observations that I heard during that period. Indeed, by the end of 1969 more than 90 percent of the South Vietnamese population found themselves living under relatively peaceful conditions. According to even the most conservative estimates, at least two-thirds of the population were living in relatively secure areas—areas in which government control was not challenged and in which there was little, if any, warfare. According to President Thieu, by 1970 South Vietnam was officially "crossing over into the postwar era."

By the end of 1971 there were many in Washington and Saigon who thought that the war would be ended without a negotiated settlement or with, at most, a secret agreement between Hanoi and Washington for the return of American prisoners of war. The return of POWs had surfaced as a political issue in 1969 with the mobilization of families of soldiers who were known to be POWs or who were believed to be missing in action in North Vietnam. But more than a few officials believed that so much progress had been achieved in strengthening the GVN and the Communist movement had been so badly set back that U.S. prisoners would never be returned because, as one put it, "Hanoi would have to talk under the most humiliating of circumstances, that is, on the verge of having been defeated in South Vietnam and by the South Vietnamese." It was essential, in Kissinger's view, therefore, to set up a means of communication with North Vietnam through which the United States could propose compromises without having them denounced by Saigon, Hanoi propagandists, or the hard-line factions in Washington, and through which threats could be made without Hanoi dismissing them as warmongering. The deadlocked talks in Paris, used as a propaganda platform by each side, were, thus, to be avoided in the search for a negotiated settlement.

THE PARIS TALKS: THEIR FAILURE WAS THE FAÇADE

North Vietnam came to the Paris talks with a fighting-while-negotiating strategy, not for ending the war but for winning it. It agreed to the talks believing it had achieved a position of strength; it was prepared to step up the fighting in the south as the surest route to a military victory. By 1967, North

Vietnamese cadres were instructed to think of negotiations as a tactic. A notebook captured by U.S. forces contains, for example, the following comments on a typical 1967 indoctrination program:

> Negotiations, if we are to have negotiations, will serve mainly to provide us the groundwork from which to launch our general offensive. Another reason is to expose the enemy's political attack upon us and to show that ours is the just cause and his the unjust. This means that the war will be settled only on the battlefield, not in the conference room. To have such negotiations, we must fight more fiercely. Only in such a situation can we authorize negotiations to take place. Thus, when hearing that negotiations are about to take place, we must attack the enemy more strongly all over the country.[20]

Hanoi's negotiating strategy was spelled out in subsequent internal party assessments of how fighting and negotiations were to be coordinated. The following extract from a document captured in March 1969 summarizes statements that can be found in hundreds of documents that were captured between 1967 and 1972:

> Now that the U.S. is compelled to halt the bombing of North Viet-Nam, we bring up another demand. "The U.S. must withdraw all their troops from South Viet-Nam." . . . And when the Americans are compelled to withdraw troops from South-Viet-Nam [sic] that means their aggressive will has been defeated.
>
> The following are the principal points that should be understood, while studying the substance of a decisive victory.
>
> —The U.S. will accept a withdrawal of all their troops only after they have been struck hard by us and when they realize that if they carry on the war, they will suffer heavier defeat.
> —Both our military and political forces must be stronger than the remaining puppet army and administration, and this is possible only by annihilating, disintegrating and disrupting a major part of their infrastructure organization through the use of all forms of violence available in the hands of the masses.
> —We must strengthen the mastership of the people, seize and restore power to the people through violence . . .
>
> We are attacking the enemy in the military, political and diplomatic fields. We must positively affirm that the strong position in which we attack the enemy militarily and politically, and our actual military and political forces *on the battlefield* [emphasis in original] will determine the attitude of the enemy at the conference table and the issue of the negotiations.
>
> We should not in any way disregard the effect of the diplomatic struggle, of the art of using stratagems in foreign relations, which did and will secure successes.

But we must not absolutely depend on and expect too much from the Paris
Conference, and nurse an illusion of peace.[21]

The new Paris meetings on Vietnam ended as they began: as a propaganda
platform and a façade for secret negotiations. There were 174 sessions
between January 25, 1969, and January 18, 1973, and not once is there a hint
in the record that either side thought their deliberations would actually
contribute to a settlement of the war. North Vietnam's participation at the
talks was consistent with its strategy of using the negotiations to increase the
reach of its propaganda, to discredit the Saigon government, and to accustom
world opinion to accepting the PRG as a legitimate governmental force in
South Vietnam. For Hanoi, a negotiated settlement was a contradiction in
terms. To them, negotiations should be undertaken only to facilitate military
victory; a settlement could be based only on what had been achieved on the
battlefield, not at the conference table.

This was clearly understood by official Washington. Indeed, no U.S. agency
that responded to the twenty-nine questions posed by Henry Kissinger in
National Security Study Memorandum No. 1 (NSSM-1)—the Nixon administration's first major Vietnam policy review—argued that Hanoi had come to
Paris out of weakness:

> All consider it unlikely that Hanoi came to Paris either to accept a face-saving
> formula for defeat or to give the U.S. a face-saving way to withdraw. There is
> agreement that Hanoi has been subject to heavy military pressure and that a
> desire to end the losses and costs of war was an element in Hanoi's
> decision. . . . The respondents agree that the DRV is in Paris to negotiate the
> withdrawal of U.S. forces, to undermine the GVN [Government of Vietnam]
> and USG [United States Government] relations and to provide a better chance
> for VC victory in the South. . . . Hanoi's ultimate goal of a unified Vietnam
> under its control has not changed.[22]

Deadlock at Paris was expected from the beginning. "The purpose of the
Paris Four-Party Conference," Hanoi's representative Xuan Thuy said in his
very first statement, "is to find a political solution to the Viet Nam problem on
the basis of respect for the Vietnamese people's fundamental rights, namely
independence, sovereignty, unity, and territorial integrity, recognized by the
1954 Geneva agreements on Viet Nam." Washington, of course, wanted to
separate the military from the political issues of conflict. The political solution
Hanoi proposed was its four-point stand of April 1965, the stand the United
States had repeatedly rejected. There were secret talks between the U.S.
delegation head, Henry Cabot Lodge, and Xuan Thuy before the Kissinger-
Tho channel was established in February 1970, but these talks closely

paralleled the semi-public ones. As Mr. Lodge observed in a statement on November 24, 1969,

> Mr. [Xuan] Thuy has been as intransigent in private meetings as he has been in public meetings. He has avoided engaging in any give and take. Instead, his position has been to insist on the U.S. withdrawing completely from South Viet-Nam without any indication of what the North Vietnamese would do. He has also demanded that the U.S. overthrow the present government in South Viet-Nam as we leave.
>
> For our part, we have made it clear that—far from rejecting—we are willing to discuss all questions relevant to peace. We have made every effort to have the parties concerned discuss all the issues. We have made our proposals and we have indicated that we are willing to discuss the proposals made by the other side. Contrary to the position of the other side, we do not make proposals on a take-it-or-leave-it basis.
>
> At one stage we set forth a list of all the subjects—military and political—that needed discussion if there was to be a peaceful settlement of the conflict. We also invited the other side to clarify their own proposals.
>
> We got nowhere because [Hanoi] either refused to consider our proposals—or demanded that we take unilateral actions without any parallel action by them. And they even declined to have any serious discussion in which the government of South Viet-Nam could participate.
>
> Mr. Thuy has tried to make it appear as if he has all along been ready to meet privately for serious discussion. The fact is that every private meeting which we have held has been at the request of the United States. If Mr. Thuy had any desire to meet, he managed to conceal that desire very well.

KISSINGER FORMULATES A NEGOTIATING STRATEGY

For Kissinger in 1969, the almost predictable sterility of the Paris talks was compounded by the difficulty of dealing with two adversaries for whom recognition of each other's existence would, in their view, be tantamount to acknowledging defeat. In addition, the deep divisions within the U.S. government over what could be achieved on the battlefield in South Vietnam made it nearly impossible to hope for agreement on what Washington's minimum position in the negotiations should be. Official Washington's recommendation to Kissinger, contained in NSSM-1, was that an agreement should be delayed as long as possible. A mid-January 1969 National Intelligence Estimate (reflecting the views of the Defense Intelligence Agency, the CIA, the State Department's Bureau of Intelligence and Research, and the National Security Agency) noted that "over the next several months, further progress in pacification will almost certainly not make the GVN much more able to cope with the VC. . . . A significant advance in this respect would probably require at least a year. And the terms of a settlement would undo virtually all that has been accomplished. . . ." Saigon's intransigence over dealing with the PRG, coupled with the reluctance of U.S. government agencies to see substantive negotiations occur before Washington and Saigon could regain the position of strength lost at Tet, convinced Kissinger that only through the process of completely secret face-to-face negotiations, first with Hanoi and then with Saigon, could an agreement be achieved.

To support these secret negotiations Kissinger needed to keep the Paris talks sterile and to develop an organizational system that fragmented the Washington bureaucracy so that the necessary staffing could be accomplished, drawing on expertise throughout the government while minimizing agency predispositions toward a particular settlement. This was achieved (see table 4.1) largely by the creation of interagency special groups that operated under Kissinger's control. "All arrows pointed to Kissinger," one participant recalled, "and this meant that he had created a minibureaucracy he could control and which would not sabotage the kind of agreement he was trying to reach. It was difficult enough coordinating what Hanoi was likely to agree to with what Saigon wanted so that the last thing Henry needed was to have to negotiate with our own government as well."

Indeed, in 1969, the gap between Washington's and Hanoi's known positions and between Washington's and Saigon's were equally wide, as tables 4.2 and 4.3 suggest. Having entered into talks with North Vietnam on the latter's maximum terms, Kissinger realized that there was little Hanoi would concede for the sake of moving from talks to negotiations. Having refused talks altogether at first, Saigon came to Paris reluctantly and with only its maximum demands to lay on the table. Thieu had instructed the delegation that there could be no thought of cease-fire-in-place and no political settlement until the NVA had withdrawn. When the delegation pointed out in a private message to Thieu that a cease-fire-in-place was the only way to end the war, Thieu recalled its head. "Thieu wanted the delegation in Paris," one of its members told me in an interview, "to follow orders, not to negotiate." And the longer the negotiations dragged on, Kissinger feared, the more intransigent Hanoi, Saigon, and Washington would become.

Kissinger believed, as one of his aides recalled in an interview:

> . . . that he really faced three obstacles in the negotiations: The first, of course, was Hanoi. The North Vietnamese had to have a reason to sign an agreement. This would come when they were stalemated on the battlefield. The second obstacle was Saigon. Thieu wanted not a negotiated settlement but

TABLE 4.1

NIXON AND THE NEGOTIATIONS: PRINCIPAL INPUTS TO HIS DECISIONS

The President decides:

"You listen to everybody's arguments, but then comes the moment of truth . . . I sit alone with my yellow pad and I write down on one side the reasons for doing it and on the other side the reasons for not doing it. I do this before every important decision." (Nixon to Henry Brandon, *The Retreat of American Power*)

Nixon-Kissinger conference:

"Kissinger himself told me that he would go over the options with the President once the NSC had produced its conclusions, and that the President on these occasions wanted to know all the consequences of each alternative." (Brandon, *Retreat*)

The Delegation to the Kissinger-Tho Talks

The National Security Council [NSC]	WSAG [Washington Special Action Group]	Vietnam Special Studies Group Before October 25, 1972	Vietnam Special Studies Group After October 25, 1972
"Its discussions put the issues in sharp focus and give me the counsel of my senior advisors as the final step in a process of comprehensive review before I make a decision." (Nixon, *U.S. Foreign Policy for the 1970s: The Emerging Structure of Peace*, February 9, 1972)	The principal drafting and coordinating group; it included Sullivan (State), Helms (CIA), Moorer (JCS), a USIA representative and another general. It met as often as twice a day and coordinated both the war and much of the diplomatic effort. Chaired by Henry Kissinger.	"Gathers and presents to the highest levels of the United States Government the fullest and most up-to-date information on trends and conditions in the countryside in Vietnam. This group is of key assistance in our major and sustained effort to understand the factors which will determine the course of Vietnamization." (Nixon, *U.S. Foreign Policy*) In 1970, the VNSG—"consisting of the Under-Secretary of State and the Deputy Secretary of Defense, high-ranking representatives of the CIA and the JCS, and other government experts—supervised a detailed examination . . . of three different kinds of cease-fire [in-place] in twenty of South Vietnam's forty-four provinces." (Kalb and Kalb, *Kissinger*, p. 173)	5 Working Groups—intelligence, military affairs, truce supervision, personnel, economic assistance—to assess the impact of the draft agreement and to determine what U.S. policy should be in the period after the cease-fire.

Hanoi's surrender. He wanted their troops to leave South Vietnam, he wanted the Viet Cong disbanded, and he didn't trust us to hold out for these basic demands. So our strategy was to give Thieu the maximum amount of time possible to get ready for an agreement and the maximum amount of support to defend himself. But, when we could get an agreement, we were going to be firm with Thieu. We also did not tell Thieu what progress we had made with Hanoi or the terms we were offering because we knew he would oppose them and then leak them to the press. This would imperil the process of negotiations with Hanoi that it had literally taken us years to establish. The third obstacle was in Washington. The military never would support a compromise. They always believed that with just a little more time and money they could find the right formula to win the war. And like Thieu, if they didn't approve of what we offered Hanoi, then they would have leaked it to the press.

Given these obstacles, Kissinger thought that the key to a negotiated agreement was for the United States to avoid seeking to win at the conference table what could perhaps have been won on the battlefield.

To the negotiators this meant, as one said in an interview, "convincing Saigon that by accepting an agreement it could lose nothing it already had and convincing Hanoi that unless it accepted an agreement it would have no chance of winning politically. Each had to believe that a negotiated agreement was an interim step toward victory." Implementing this strategy required both time to allow Thieu to get accustomed to fighting the war without U.S. forces, and continued warfare so that Hanoi could not be certain that simply by waiting out U.S. withdrawal the war would wind down, and with it, the need to negotiate anything at all.

What Kissinger most wanted to avoid in the negotiations with Hanoi was the mistake that had been made in Korea—the restriction of military action to defensive operations while armistice talks continued. "By stopping military operations," Kissinger observed in a book written shortly after the Korean war, "we removed the only . . . incentive for a settlement [that the enemy had]; we produced the frustation of two years of inconclusive negotiations. In short, our insistence on divorcing force from diplomacy caused our power to lack purpose and our negotiations to lack force."[23] Consequently, another Kissinger aide told me, "Henry believed that, unless the U.S. showed Hanoi it was willing to threaten the absolute destruction of North Vietnam, they would never negotiate. He would often say that North Vietnam could not be the only country in the world without a breaking point."

When Hanoi eventually said "uncle," those I interviewed expected events to develop this way: Le Duc Tho would introduce into the secret talks a revision of the North Vietnamese stand, hinting that an agreement could be reached on military problems, and drop his insistence on reaching a political settlement prior to the cease-fire. Then negotiations would begin. Legal

TABLE 4.2

HANOI *vs.* WASHINGTON: MINIMUM AND MAXIMUM POSITIONS ON KEY ISSUES IN THE NEGOTIATIONS

	For Talks/Negotiations	For Negotiated Agreement on:	
		Cease-fire	Political Settlement
Hanoi's maximum	For negotiations: Stop bombing permanently and unconditionally; accept four points	*Cease-fire not separable from political settlement* U.S. withdrawal; end to GVN aid; release of all prisoners—POWs and political; cease-fire thereafter	Replacement of Thieu with a coalition
Washington's maximum	Bombing will be stopped in return for an end of NVA infiltration and attacks against urban centers	Cease-fire, mutual troop withdrawal, and POW return	Status quo ante, pending plebiscite
Hanoi's minimum	For talks: Stop bombing permanently and unconditionally	U.S. withdrawal; cease-fire-in-place (revealed in October 1972)	Assurance that freedom of political organization and other democratic liberties would be respected by the GVN; National Council of Reconciliation and Concord (NCRC) to serve as coalition government of the transition
Washington's minimum	Bombing will be suspended if serious talks follow U.S. decision to suspend bombing, and if rocket attacks against Saigon cease	Cease-fire-in-place; prisoner exchange	Status quo ante pending NCRC formation

TABLE 4.3

WASHINGTON vs. SAIGON: MINIMUM AND MAXIMUM POSITIONS ON KEY ISSUES IN THE NEGOTIATIONS

| | For Talks/Negotiations | For Negotiated Agreement on: | |
		Cease-fire	Political Settlement
Saigon's maximum	For negotiations: Withdrawal of all NVA forces	Withdrawal of all NVA forces	Elections organized by a mixed electoral commission in which Viet Cong could participate if they renounced violence
Washington's maximum	Bombing will be stopped in return for end of NVA infiltration and attacks against urban centers	Cease-fire, mutual troop withdrawal, and POW return	Status quo ante, pending plebiscite
Saigon's minimum	For talks: Withdrawal of all NVA forces	Withdrawal of all NVA forces	National reconciliation for, and integration of, Viet Cong into political system once war ends and NVA withdraws
Washington's minimum	Bombing will be suspended if serious talks follow U.S. decision to suspend bombing, and if rocket attacks against Saigon cease	Cease-fire-in-place; POW exchange	Status quo ante, pending NCRC formation

experts would be called in to draft the articles and protocols on a crash basis, while Kissinger and Tho reached understandings about what each really thought the agreement meant. Until this stage was reached, Kissinger believed his primary job was to develop proposals for a long-term political solution so that, if Hanoi accepted one, the separation of the political from the military issues would have been essentially achieved. Kissinger also asked Soviet and Chinese intermediaries to assure Hanoi that the United States was not wedded to the Thieu government, and that as long as the war did not resume after the United States had withdrawn its troops, Washington would abide by whatever evolved in the political arena in South Vietnam.

5

1969–1972: THE SECRET SEARCH FOR A NEGOTIATED SETTLEMENT

"The peace negotiations . . . have been marked by the classic Vietnamese syndrome: optimism alternating with bewilderment; euphoria giving way to frustration." Henry Kissinger wrote, in January 1969, of the Johnson administration's efforts to negotiate with North Vietnam.[1] This was to be no less true for Kissinger's own secret search for a negotiated settlement with Hanoi. "There were waves of optimism," one participant at the secret talks later recalled, "but they would always peter out on the shoals of Hanoi's intransigence. Le Duc Tho would routinely begin a session by declaring that the subject on the agenda was not at issue because the U.S. position was generally acceptable to North Vietnam, but he would say that the real obstacle to an agreement was posed by another aspect of a settlement. We would then make a proposal we thought acceptable to them. They would then tell us what was wrong with our proposal from their point of view. We would then adjourn to study their remarks. We would make a counter-offer, and again they would tell us what was wrong with that. They never flatly rejected anything. Le Duc Tho would just say what we said was very interesting but we had to first stop all acts of war against the DRV and Thieu had to resign before the negotiations could go further."

It was Kissinger's belief that an agreement would only be possible if the negotiations were aimed not at changing Hanoi's behavior—behavior that was incompatible with a long-term peaceful settlement of the conflict—but at changing Saigon's. Kissinger saw the need to limit warfare and then to encourage Saigon to be more forthcoming in offering a political accommodation to the PRG. What Kissinger sought in his secret negotiations with Hanoi, then, was the beginning of a process of accommodation, not a clear-cut end to the conflict. "What had to be created," one of Kissinger's aides later told me, "was a way of talking to the North Vietnamese where we could try out various formulations for an agreement without them having to risk losing face in front of their people or their allies. Henry was profoundly disappointed when the North Vietnamese appeared to be using the secret talks for many of the same advantages they sought in the Paris talks: to probe to discover how far the Americans would go in making concessions to the North Vietnamese position." Despite continued North Vietnamese intransigence, Kissinger remained hopeful that "even in Vietnam there must be some realities that transcend the parochial concerns of the contestants and that a point must be reached where a balance is so clearly established that if we can make generous and farseeing proposals . . . a solution may be possible."[2] If such realities were to lead to an agreement, it would have to be negotiated in private.

HANOI LEARNS WASHINGTON WILL FIGHT WHILE NEGOTIATING

President-elect Nixon's contacts with the North Vietnamese in 1968 convinced him that the Vietnam war could not be ended quickly. Like Johnson, Nixon began by telling the North Vietnamese that their chances of victory would only lessen if they did not negotiate seriously. Operation Menu (the secret bombing of Cambodia that began in mid-March of 1969 and frequently accounted for more than half of all daily B-52 sorties) was meant, in part, to underscore this message. In eleven secret meetings in Paris, Ambassador Henry Cabot Lodge also tried to convey to his North Vietnamese counterpart the advantage of Hanoi's quickly accepting an agreement. In addition, conversations were held between Henry Kissinger and Soviet ambassador Dobrynin to emphasize the importance the United States attached to Soviet restraint in supplying Hanoi with the capacity to continue to expand the war. Kissinger told Dobrynin that, if Hanoi would only agree to negotiate the military and the political issues separately, the withdrawal of U.S. forces could be speeded up. But the Soviet response was not encouraging. True, the Soviet government was the major supplier of arms and assistance to the North Vietnamese, but this, Soviet representatives pointed out, did not confer leverage over the North Vietnamese Politburo, just as the same position had not always given the United States leverage over their client in Saigon.

In May, the president delivered a major speech on Vietnam in which he proposed a mutual withdrawal and cessation of hostilities and announced the departure of 25,000 U.S. troops. Kissinger showed Dobrynin an advance copy of the text, called the latter's attention to several key passages that concerned the consequences of delay, and then "translated these sentences into simple English. If the Russians 'didn't produce a settlement,' the United States would 'escalate the war.' "[3]

In July, Jean Sainteny, one of France's Indochina experts who personally knew Ho Chi Minh, transmitted a letter from Nixon to Ho urging Hanoi to reconsider negotiations. "You will find us forthcoming and open minded in a common effort to bring the blessings of peace to the brave people of Vietnam," the letter promised. Hanoi responded by agreeing to a secret meeting between Kissinger and Xuan Thuy to take place in Sainteny's Paris apartment on August 4. The exchange that took place was reminiscent of the one that had been held in Geneva some seven years before, when the secret search for negotiations began in 1962. "Hanoi was unyielding, clearly unready for serious negotiations," a participant later recalled. Three weeks later Ho Chi Minh's official reply to the Nixon letter reiterated what the U.S. negotiators had heard in secret: the U.S. troop withdrawal should be unconditional and a political solution should be negotiated solely on the basis of the proposals advanced by the Communist side.

Three days after Ho Chi Minh's letter was received in Washington, Ho himself was dead. With Ho's death came the hope that his successors would be inclined to negotiate. But at Ho's funeral 250,000 mourners took an oath to continue the struggle for liberation of the south and unification of Vietnam that Ho had begun, and the new leadership that ran North Vietnam appeared less, rather than more, inclined to negotiate with the United States.[4]

The American search for meaningful negotiations with Hanoi was thus stymied. The dominant view in Washington was that the United States had to get tough. In a key speech in November 1969, Nixon highlighted the efforts of his administration to arrange secret talks with Hanoi, castigated Communist intransigence, and concluded:

> The effect of all the public, private, and secret negotiations which have been undertaken since the bombing halt a year ago, and since this administration came into office on January 20, can be summed up in one sentence: No progress whatever has been made, except agreement on the shape of the bargaining table.

> Well, now, who's at fault? It's become clear that the obstacle in negotiating an end to the war is not the president of the United States. It is not the South Vietnamese government. The obstacle is the other side's absolute refusal to show the least willingness to join us in seeking a just peace.

> And it will not do so while it is convinced that all it has to do is to wait for our next concession, and our next concession after that one, until it gets everything it wants.

It was necessary, the president said, to develop an alternate means of ending the war, one that was not dependent on the good will of Hanoi, and this, he said, was the Vietnamization program. Vietnamization meant that the United States would withdraw its troops first from combat and ultimately from Vietnam, turning responsibility for the fighting and the war over to the

GVN in a way designed to be least discouraging to Saigon and other U.S. allies and least encouraging to Hanoi. Nixon asked for the support of "the great silent majority" of Americans for the search "for a just peace through a negotiated settlement, if possible, or through continued implementation of our plan for Vietnamization, if necessary. A plan in which we will withdraw all of our forces from Vietnam on a schedule in accordance with our program as the South Vietnamese become strong enough to defend their own freedom. . . . It is not the easy way. It is the right way. It is a plan which will end the war and serve the cause of peace, not just in Vietnam but in the Pacific and the world."

Nixon was unaware that the overwhelmingly favorable public response to his speech and to the policy direction implied in it was, in part, arranged by the Republican party. The president believed that now that U.S. casualties were being reduced, he had unlocked an untapped reservoir of support for himself and the war. As a result, the president rejected an effort by a group of former White House officials and liberal Republicans to design a peace package that called for both a Christmas cease-fire to be continued indefinitely and a substantial withdrawal of U.S. troops. Instead, by mid-December the president ordered a withdrawal of only another 50,000 U.S. troops—and this only after he had received word from Cyrus Eaton, who had just met with Soviet leaders and Le Duc Tho, that the death of Ho had indeed caused the Politburo to consider secret negotiations again.

Le Duc Tho was henceforth to become a figure whose importance in the negotiations equaled that of Kissinger and Nixon.[5] On the basis of his published statements, Tho was thought to favor reaching an agreement of the type that returned the NVA to a protracted-war footing, thus easing the drain of the conventional large-unit war on the DRV's economy. Tho was Kissinger's window on the North Vietnamese Politburo, and from their many private (save for an interpreter) and informal chats, Kissinger presumably assembled enough data to explain to Nixon why Hanoi could conceivably be interested in a negotiated settlement. It was on the assumption that at least some elements in Hanoi genuinely wanted to negotiate that Kissinger continued to devote his energies to the secret talks and conducted them in a spirit of cordiality and trust. "He did not think Le Duc Tho was setting him up," one of Kissinger's aides told me, "or that, if an agreement was achieved, Hanoi would grossly and blatantly violate it. The president, in contrast, took a much harder line toward Hanoi and the negotiations and believed that, if Hanoi would not negotiate seriously in private, the costs of their intransigence should be increased."

Nixon saw his November speech as a means of preventing Hanoi from hinting in public a willingness to reach an agreement it had ruled out in private, thereby creating the impression that the United States was the obstacle to negotiations. After he was convinced that secret initiatives produced no results, Nixon informed the American people of his efforts and provided an updated report of the progress of the Vietnamization program. Nixon did not want the public to forget that his administration was bringing U.S. soldiers home while it was striving for negotiations with Hanoi and strengthening the ability of the GVN to defend itself. In such speeches, a review of the administration's secret efforts for peace often was the peroration for an announcement either that the GVN had reached a milestone related to its own self-defense and, hence, more U.S. troops were being withdrawn, or that decisive military actions (e.g., the incursion into Cambodia, the extension of U.S. and South Vietnam military operations into Laos, the mining of Haiphong Harbor, the Christmas bombing of Hanoi) had to be taken in light of Hanoi's intransigence at the conference table.

Initially, Nixon's rhetoric did little to improve the atmosphere of the talks or to induce Hanoi to change its position. For example, in the second round of secret talks, which took place between late February and early April 1970, Henry Kissinger met with Le Duc Tho four times in Paris, and found that the North Vietnamese position had hardened. "Their belief in our sincerity was nil," one participant recalled, "and even the cordiality of the first meeting evaporated."

Why did Hanoi spurn an agreement in 1969 and 1970? Ever since the 1968 Tet offensive, the need to reestablish and consolidate the Communist infrastructure that had been destroyed at Tet had been central to Hanoi's approach to the war. Internal PRG planning papers and assessments later captured by U.S. and South Vietnamese forces in Cambodia and Laos indicate that from Hanoi's viewpoint far too little progress had been achieved in these tasks to create the position of strength essential for substantive discussions with Washington. A related problem was the limited extent of the PRG's population control in the south—even the most conservative U.S. estimates put the figure at less than 25 percent. These concerns by no means preoccupied the entire North Vietnamese Politburo, for some members presumably believed that Hanoi should never negotiate and, therefore, the question of achieving a position of strength for such a purpose was irrelevant. Members of the Politburo who subscribed to this view probably argued simply that what had not been won on the battlefield could not be won at the conference table. Other members of the Politburo presumably favored negotiations, but only insofar as a negotiated settlement provided the United States with no more than a face-saving way to withdraw its troops and to end its support to the Thieu government.

Throughout this period, the Nixon administration appeared locked into an ever-widening war, with each new development on the battlefield reinforcing Hanoi's basic mistrust of Washington, an atmosphere that later prejudiced the 1972 secret negotiations.

Of all the military campaigns of the war, the Cambodian incursion, lasting from April 20 to June 29, 1970, proved to be the most fruitless and the most embittering. Cambodia had long been a front in the Vietnam war because of both the strategic Ho Chi Minh trail complex and the sanctuary that North Vietnamese troops were permitted in the Cambodian provinces adjacent to South Vietnam. Operation Menu, the secret bombing of North Vietnamese supply centers in Cambodia, began in 1969 and South Vietnamese forces were known to conduct deep penetration raids routinely into Cambodia thereafter. It was difficult to justify the Cambodian incursion in strictly military terms. (Cambodian and U.S. officials used the term *incursion* in preference to *invasion* because U.S. troops were invited to conduct operations against NVA sanctuaries.) During the period of the incursion, the ARVN faced its greatest threat from North Vietnamese forces operating from a secure base in the northern part of South Vietnam that had been the home of one North Vietnamese division and the home of elements of several others for two decades. But the Cambodian incursion was meant to serve symbolic, not strategic, purposes. It was undertaken to reduce the significant military threat inside Cambodia to the new government there.

In an end-of-operation report, televised in July 1971, President Nixon recounted what had convinced him that military action in Cambodia was essential. "From a series of isolated enclaves, [North Vietnamese] bases were rapidly becoming a solid band of self-sustaining territory stretching from Laos to the sea from which any pretense of Cambodian sovereignty was rapidly being excluded." The completion of such a line of control would have had ominous consequences for the war in South Vietnam. One South Vietnamese official with whom I talked at the time summarized the concern of many: "We had always thought that all of Indochina would be won or lost by what happened in the struggle for South Vietnam. To suddenly find ourselves surrounded by three Communist states would mean that we had to defend not the few miles of demilitarized zone but more than a thousand." And General Creighton Abrams in his June 30, 1970, analysis of the Cambodian incursion suggested that the action was designed to maximize its impact on the struggles inside both Cambodia and South Vietnam. "One of the two American divisions standing guard against attacks from the enemy bases in Cambodia was going home soon under President Nixon's withdrawal program, shifting a major burden to Saigon's forces. With the rainy season approaching and the Lon Nol government unlikely to survive until fall, the time was right. An attack would help the South Vietnamese and assure further American withdrawals. With a third of the enemy forces moved west, the risks of American casualties were reduced."[6]

What impact did the Cambodian incursion have on the prospects for a negotiated settlement? From the Nixon administration's perspective, it bought time. U.S. officials in Saigon speculated that it set Communist plans

for launching a general offensive back at least a year (that is, to 1972). During
the period ahead, U.S. embassy officials believed that the South Vietnamese
army would increasingly be able to provide for the defense of the country
against the conventional offensive most officials believed would accompany
any attempt by the Communists to impose a military solution on the conflict.
Should that offensive fail, these officials also believed, there would then be a
turn toward serious negotiations. As this scenario unfolded, the president
became increasingly convinced that surgical uses of massive American force
could work to turn Hanoi away from the war and toward negotiations. As he
told a television audience in July 1970:

> Put yourself in the position of the enemy. Also, put yourself in the position of
> an historian—and all of you are historians [Nixon was speaking to three
> national network news correspondents]; you study these matters and you write
> about them, you think about them, and you commentate upon them. You will
> generally find that negotiations occur when one party or the other concludes
> that as a result of the shift in the military balance they no longer have an
> opportunity to accomplish their goal militarily and therefore, they had better
> negotiate.
>
> Now I think one of the positive benefits of the Cambodian operation is that it
> has changed the military balance. How much it has changed in the minds of the
> enemy remains to be seen.
>
> I do not say it will change it enough so that they will negotiate. I think it might
> help. Only time will tell. But . . . I am convinced that if we were to tell the
> enemy now . . . that by the end of this year all Americans will be gone [as
> provided in the then-pending McGovern-Hatfield Resolution], well, I can
> assure you that the enemy isn't going to negotiate in Paris at all. They are not
> going to talk. They are going to wait until we get out because they know that at
> the end of this year the South Vietnamese won't be ready to defend the country
> by themselves.
>
> But if, on the other hand, the enemy feels that we are going to stay there long
> enough for the South Vietnamese to be strong enough to handle their own
> defense, then I think they have a real incentive to negotiate, because if they
> have to negotiate with a strong, vigorous South Vietnamese government, the
> deal they can make with them isn't going to be as good as the deal they might
> make now.[7]

President Nixon sincerely believed at the time (and then saw subsequent
events confirm his view) that the Cambodian incursion rather than widening
the war actually hastened a negotiated settlement. He learned that despite
public opposition to the war he could use force as necessary. He saw public
reaction to the Cambodian incursion not in terms of its criticism for the

way he was handling the war but as a reaction—which he shared—to the needless loss of life at Kent State University, where four students had been killed by National Guardsmen at an antiwar demonstration. "The president realized," one aide who resigned in protest over the Cambodian incursion told me, "that he could still fight the war pretty well with fewer Americans." Another aide put it this way: "The president thought that there could never be meaningful negotiations unless U.S. power remained credible. And to do this, we had to take the war to the enemy every dry season just as they tried to take the war to us. The president was very mindful of Lyndon Johnson's experience: the gradual application of pressure simply didn't work on the North Vietnamese."

Only a few months after the Cambodian incursion, it was apparent that the Lon Nol government would barely survive the rainy season, only to be confronted by an even more substantial threat from both the North Vietnamese and indigenous Cambodian Communist forces. The news from Vietnam was equally ominous. The NVA had gone on the offensive despite the Cambodian incursion. Approximately two-thirds of Laotian territory was under the control of the Communist Pathet Lao. To the president, this signaled the need to think of peace on a regional basis and led to the October 1970 proposal for an Indochina-wide cease-fire-in-place. "The president was waking up every day to a nightmare," one aide recalled in an interview. "He inherited a mess from Lyndon Johnson, and it was getting worse. LBJ only had to think about negotiations for Vietnam. We had to think of what could be done to restore peace in three countries, and we had less troops, less diplomatic clout than LBJ had, and he failed."

THE SIGNIFICANCE OF A CEASE-FIRE-IN-PLACE

By the end of 1970, the U.S. embassy, the GVN, and even the opposition to Thieu agreed that a cease-fire would result only from the withdrawal of all North Vietnamese forces from the south. Any other cease-fire arrangement would leave North Vietnamese forces in control of territory they never would relinquish. Some Americans in the embassy and some in Washington agreed in theory with the South Vietnamese position but believed that the United States had no leverage left that could conceivably cause the North Vietnamese to withdraw. Significantly, these officials (whose views were well known to GVN officials) were detached to Kissinger's staff and participated in the secret negotiations with Hanoi. Initially they advocated an agreement that designated areas of Communist control to which all North Vietnamese forces would be regrouped. This would have the advantage of creating a more precise cease-fire line than would likely be the case if the soldiers of both sides simply stopped shooting and remained in place. This approach, its advocates maintained, would lessen the chances that forces on both sides would claim territory in dispute. The resulting regroupment zones would have to be those over which both sides had undisputed control.

Saigon officials feared, as one put it, that "this would be the beginning of a new war, this time without the Americans, rather than the end to the struggle. Regroupment would mean the beginning of the consolidation of Hanoi's control over South Vietnamese territory rather than a prelude to the gradual withdrawal of the NVA." Least acceptable to Saigon, of course, was a cease-fire-in-place that required not that North Vietnamese troops withdraw, only that they stop fighting. A high embassy official—who did not participate in negotiating the draft of the Paris Agreement, but who did have to present it later to Thieu—confirmed the South Vietnamese fears: "It was really no solution at all, just a face-saving way for us to withdraw before the Communists took over Saigon."

Henry Kissinger was in favor of the regroupment-zone approach. The difficulties inherent in the cease-fire-in-place concept, he pointed out in his *Foreign Affairs* article, were so numerous that

> negotiating a cease-fire may well be tantamount to establishing the preconditions of a political settlement. If there existed a front line with unchallenged control behind it, as in Korea, the solution would be traditional and relatively simple: the two sides could stop shooting at each other and the cease-fire line could follow the front line. But there are no front lines in Viet Nam; control is not territorial, it depends on who has forces in a given area and on the time of day. If a cease-fire permits the Government to move without challenge, day or night, it will amount to a Saigon victory. If Saigon is prevented from entering certain areas, it means in effect partition which, as in Laos, tends toward permanency. Unlike Laos, however, the pattern would be a crazy quilt, with enclaves of conflicting loyalties all over the country.

> This would involve the following additional problems: (1) It would lead to an intense scramble to establish predominant control before the cease-fire went into effect. (2) It would make next to impossible the verification of any withdrawal of North Vietnamese forces that might be negotiated; the local authorities in areas of preponderant communist control would doubtless certify that no external forces were present and impede any effort at international inspection. (3) It would raise the problem of the applicability of a cease-fire to guerrilla activity in the noncommunist part of the country; in other words, how to deal with the asymmetry between the actions of regular and of guerrilla forces. Regular forces operate on a scale which makes possible a relatively precise definition of what is permitted and what is proscribed; guerrilla forces, by contrast, can be effective through isolated acts of terror difficult to distinguish from normal criminal activity.

There would be many other problems: who collects taxes and how, who enforces the cease-fire and by what means. In other words, a tacit de facto cease-fire may prove more attainable than a negotiated one. By the same token, a formal cease-fire is likely to predetermine the ultimate settlement and tend toward partition. Cease-fire is thus not so much a step toward a final settlement as a form of it.[8]

Kissinger's diagnosis of the problems associated with a cease-fire-in-place proved cannily accurate. But by the end of 1970, he had come to think that, short of dumping Thieu, a cease-fire-in-place was the only concession the United States could reasonably offer to get Hanoi to sign an agreement. From his three rounds of secret talks with the North Vietnamese between 1967 and 1970, Kissinger had become convinced that the course he had recommended in his *Foreign Affairs* article would not work; Hanoi was simply unwilling to reach an agreement on ultimate goals without U.S. acquiescence to Pham Van Dong's four points. In Kissinger's view, a cease-fire-in-place offered Hanoi a reasonable prospect of victory (the key inducement required if Hanoi were to sign an agreement) since it would grant specific territory in South Vietnam to the Communist forces as well as granting the NVA the right to be there. This would also be consistent with the principle that the Communists should not gain through negotiations that which they could not achieve on the battlefield, just as Saigon could not hope to achieve through negotiations what ten years of warfare had failed to provide: a South Vietnam free from any Communist presence.

As with all major negotiating initiatives, the decision to offer the North Vietnamese a cease-fire-in-place depended on the president. Nixon saw things differently and operated on the premise that an agreement should be fundamentally in Saigon's interests; Kissinger believed any agreement had to be responsive primarily to Hanoi. "Before the Cambodian invasion, Nixon agreed with the . . . view [held by U.S. ambassador Ellsworth Bunker and General Creighton Abrams] that a cease-fire-in-place would pose too great a threat to the Thieu regime. But after that sixty-day spectacular, he developed considerable respect for ARVN's capabilities, and changed his mind."[9]

Kissinger thus made the U.S. offer of a cease-fire-in-place to the head of the North Vietnamese delegation in a secret meeting in Paris in September 1970. In making this offer to Hanoi, one U.S. participant told me in an interview, "We wanted to convey the impression that what we were offering gave Hanoi a fair crack at the south but that they could not expect us to abandon an ally of some twenty years and install a replacement government before our offer would be acceptable." Xuan Thuy, it was soon apparent, did not have instructions to go beyond accepting the U.S. proposal for transmission to

Hanoi. A second meeting was held, ostensibly to hear Hanoi's response to the new U.S. proposal. It "was yet another occasion on which Thuy would restate Hanoi's public position: agreement on the political solution—the four points—before the modalities of a cease-fire could be discussed," Kissinger's aide continued. "Kissinger knew that Thuy's response indicated that Hanoi had not authorized him to negotiate. Kissinger later explained only a member of the Politburo could negotiate. He told us 'In the future, I want to talk directly with Le Duc Tho.'"

Hanoi did not respond to the offer, and in October, consistent with Nixon's strategy of not keeping what was offered in the secret negotiations secret indefinitely, Ambassador David Bruce, the newly appointed head of the U.S. delegation to the Paris talks, made public what Kissinger had offered North Vietnam: a cease-fire-in-place, an immediate and unconditional prisoner release, a total withdrawal of U.S. forces thereafter, and an international conference to guarantee the settlement. What the proposal did not do was guarantee that the PRG would dominate South Vietnam after the American withdrawal. In Hanoi's view, such a guarantee would require that, while it still had leverage over Vietnamese politics, the United States arrange for a successor to President Thieu who would organize a coalition government. The resignation of Thieu and the creation of a coalition government before the cease-fire were still as essential to Hanoi as achieving a U.S. troop withdrawal.

Hanoi's refusal to consider the American offer in private or public was consistent with its own sense of timing and strategy. Internal Communist documents from this period suggest that from the leadership in Hanoi down to the local cadres, the growing strength of the GVN and its increasing administrative presence throughout the countryside alarmed the PRG. Saigon's counterintelligence program was beginning to take its toll of the indigenous PRG left after the Tet offensive, and in general, the Politburo was dissatisfied with the weaknesses in its own movement. The significance of this is that, however much an agreement specified that there would be a peaceful political evolution after the U.S. withdrawal, Hanoi knew that Saigon would never implement it. "It would also be," one Communist diplomat told me, "absurd to expect that in a life-and-death struggle both sides would renounce the use of force if they appeared to be losing. Then what guarantee have we that the Americans will not reintervene?" Only through expansion and then consolidation of control in the countryside could the PRG be assured of a secure base of operations; this would take time.

Saigon accepted the cease-fire-in-place offer fatalistically. "The war for the cease-fire line was on," one GVN official told me after the United States had made public the offer to Hanoi. "Now the North Vietnamese will try to take as much territory as possible and when their control appeared at its maximum point, they would accept the cease-fire. Then the Americans would leave. And then the war would start all over again."

SECRET TALKS RESUME

In the spring of 1971, following the expansion of the ground war into Laos in a Cambodia-type incursion, Henry Kissinger began a new round of secret meetings with the North Vietnamese. Elaborating on the basic U.S. proposal of September 1970, Kissinger added two inducements. The U.S. settlement plan now not only called for a cease-fire-in-place, but also assured Hanoi that all U.S. forces would be out of Vietnam within six months of signing an agreement. This aspect of the proposal was intended to show Hanoi that the United States had no plans to keep a residual military presence in Vietnam. The second new feature provided for the resignation of South Vietnamese president Thieu thirty days before a plebiscite was to be held to determine the political future of South Vietnam. This was as far as the United States could possibly go, Kissinger told Hanoi, toward meeting North Vietnamese insistence on an agreement that embodied both a military and a political solution to the conflict. But, Le Duc Tho told Kissinger, Hanoi still insisted that "any proposal that did not include political elements could not even be negotiated."[10]

A month later, the two negotiators met again for what was expected to be a routine discussion of the latest U.S. proposal. Instead, Le Duc Tho offered the following nine-point plan to end the war:

1. The withdrawal of the totality of U.S. forces and those of foreign countries in the U.S. camp from South Vietnam and other Indochinese countries should be completed within 1971.

2. The release of all military men and civilians captured in the war should be carried out in parallel and completed at the same time as the troop withdrawals mentioned in Point 1.

3. In South Vietnam the U.S. should stop supporting . . . [the GVN] so that there may be set up in Saigon a new administration standing for peace, independence, neutrality, and democracy. The Provisional Revolutionary Government of the Republic of South Vietnam will enter into talks with that administration to settle the internal affairs of South Vietnam and to achieve national concord.

4. The United States Government must bear full responsibility for the damages caused by the U.S. to the peace of the whole of Vietnam. The government of the Democratic Republic of Vietnam and the Provisional Revolutionary Government of the Republic of South Vietnam demand from the U.S. Government reparations for the damage caused by the U.S. in the two zones of Vietnam.

5. The U.S. should respect the 1954 Geneva Agreements on Indochina and those of 1962 in Laos. It should stop its aggression and intervention in the Indochinese countries and let their people settle by themselves their own affairs.

6. The problems existing among the Indochinese countries should be settled by the Indochinese parties on the basis of mutual respect for the independence, sovereignty, territorial integrity, and noninterference in each other's affairs. As far as it is concerned, the Democratic Republic of Vietnam is prepared to join in resolving such problems.

7. All the parties should achieve a cease-fire after the signing of the agreements on the above-mentioned problems.

8. There should be an international supervision.

9. There should be an international guarantee for the fundamental national rights of the Indochinese peoples, the neutrality of South Vietnam, Laos, and Cambodia, and lasting peace in this region.

The above points form an integrated whole and are closely related to one another.[11]

To Kissinger, this nine-point plan was the first time since 1965 that Hanoi had actually proposed the text of an agreement rather than simply reject the American formulation of one. "Henry thought we could live with Hanoi's formulation," an aide later recalled. By formulation, Kissinger meant the essential points enumerated and the sequence of events that their order implied. He saw each as subject to adjustment and believed that as far as point seven was concerned, Hanoi knew that the United States would only agree if all other provisions were implemented simultaneously with a cease-fire; he therefore reasoned that Hanoi was willing to reach the tacit or de facto cease-fire he had advocated in *Foreign Affairs.* And he believed that Thieu's offer to resign in favor of elections was an acceptable counter offer to what Hanoi wanted to achieve in the third point, which was, Kissinger believed, the beginning of a process that would set in motion a political accommodation between the GVN and the PRG. Again, this was what Kissinger had advocated in *Foreign Affairs,* and the North Vietnamese proposal seemed to confirm his idea of what a negotiated agreement should provide. Kissinger thus left the secret meeting for Washington in a hopeful mood. He began, one of his aides later told me, "to have his first taste of peace." It was to sour shortly.

On July 1, 1971, four days after the DRV had made their proposal in private, the PRG representative at the Paris talks offered a seven-point proposal for settlement that pertained only to South Vietnam. But the PRG proposal appeared to critics of the war in the United States to be a conciliatory step toward peace on the Communists' part, a step that made possible the

return of all U.S. POWs if U.S. forces left Vietnam by the end of 1971. The
PRG proposal contained the following elements:

1. The U.S. must "put an end to its war of aggression" in Viet-Nam; stop
Vietnamization; withdraw from South Viet-Nam all U.S./allied troops,
military personnel, weapons, and war materials; and dismantle all U.S. bases
in South Viet-Nam, "without posing any condition whatsoever." The United
States must set a terminal date in 1971 for the withdrawal of all U.S./allied
forces at which time the parties will agree on the modalities: (A) of the
withdrawal in safety of all such forces; and (B) of the release of all military
and civilian prisoners captured in the war (including American pilots
captured in North Viet-Nam). These two operations will begin and end on
the same dates.
A cease-fire will be observed between the South Viet-Nam People's
Liberation Armed Forces (Viet Cong) and the U.S./allied forces as soon as
the parties reach agreement on the withdrawal of all U.S./allied forces.
2. The United States must respect the South Viet-Nam people's right to
self-determination, end its interference in the internal affairs of South
Viet-Nam, and cease backing the Thieu government.
The political, social, and religious forces in South Viet-Nam aspiring to
peace and national concord will use various means to form in Saigon a new
administration favoring peace, independence, neutrality, and democracy.
The Provisional Revolutionary Government—PRG—(Viet Cong) will immediately enter into talks with that administration in order to form a broad
three-segment government of national concord that will assume its functions
during the period between the restoration of peace and the holding of
general elections, and to organize general elections in South Viet-Nam.
A cease-fire will be observed between the South Viet-Nam People's
Liberation Armed Forces and the Armed Forces of the Saigon administration as soon as a government of national concord is formed.
3. The Vietnamese parties will together settle the question of Vietnamese
armed forces in South Viet-Nam in a spirit of national concord, equality, and
mutual respect, without foreign interference.
4. On reunification of Viet-Nam and relations between the two zones:
a. Reunification will be achieved step by step, by peaceful means on
the basis of discussions and agreements between the two zones, without
constraint or annexation by either party, without foreign interference.
Pending reunification, the two zones will reestablish normal relations;
guarantee free movement, free correspondence, and free choice of residence; and maintain economic and cultural relations.
b. The two zones will refrain from joining any military alliance with
foreign countries; from allowing any foreign country to have military bases,
troops, and military personnel on their soil; and from recognizing the
protection of any country, of any military alliance or bloc.

5. South Viet-Nam will pursue a foreign policy of peace and neutrality, establish relations with all countries regardless of their political and social regime, maintain economic and cultural relations with all countries, accept the cooperation of foreign countries in the exploitation of the resources of South Viet-Nam, accept from any country economic and technical aid without any political conditions attached, and participate in regional plans of economic cooperation. After the war ends, South Viet-Nam and the United States will establish political, economic, and cultural relations.

6. The U.S. "must bear full responsibility for the losses and the destruction it has caused to the Vietnamese people in the two zones."

7. The parties will find agreement on the forms of respect and international guarantee of the accords that will be concluded.[12]

To many critics of the war, the proposal seemed to be the hoped-for breakthrough in the negotiations. Averell Harriman, for example, wrote the *New York Times* summarizing the views of many U.S. diplomats:

> The Administration has previously justified its refusal to negotiate a definite date for withdrawal of all American forces on three grounds—the safety of our forces, the release of our prisoners of war, and giving the South Vietnamese "a reasonable chance."

> Mrs. Binh's [the Chief PRG delegate at the Paris talks] seven-point proposal satisfies the first two reasons. The Administration should now explain what it means by giving South Vietnam "a reasonable chance," and what American vital interests are involved.[13]

What Harriman suspected was that the Nixon administration was still committed to the Thieu government. He feared that Thieu's intransigence might well sabotage another chance for an agreement, as it had in 1968. What Harriman did not know was that the North Vietnamese, in private, doggedly linked the cease-fire and the prisoner exchange to the overthrow of the Thieu government.

To those privy to the secret negotiations, however, the PRG proposal was not so much a negotiating document as it was a tactic to encourage doubts about the Nixon administration's sincerity in seeking an end to the war. When Kissinger called Le Duc Tho to clarify which of the two proposals now on the table should serve as the basis for future secret discussions, Tho replied that the secret proposal was the basis for future discussions. This confirmed the fears of Kissinger's aides that Hanoi would leapfrog its public and private positions and that a breakthrough in the negotiations had not occurred. As Kissinger himself later observed of Hanoi's negotiating strategy: "The great advantage of secret negotiations is that you can leapfrog public positions. . . . the resulting division [that Hanoi's leapfrogging caused in U.S.

politics] made the other side believe that the negotiations really were a form more of psychological warfare than of negotiations."[14]

In mid-August, Kissinger and Tho met again in what Kissinger hoped would at last be a turning point in the negotiations. He was prepared to pledge U.S. neutrality in the October 3 South Vietnamese presidential elections in which Thieu's likely opponent would be General Duong van Minh, a personality the Communists had long said would be an acceptable head of the Saigon government. Next, Kissinger promised that all U.S. forces would be withdrawn by August 1, 1972, if an agreement were reached by November 1, 1971. Kissinger finally stated that the United States was willing to agree to limit all future aid to the Saigon government if Hanoi's allies would do the same.

In response, Hanoi's representatives believed a "favorable opportunity" to end the war would be created if Washington discouraged Thieu from seeking reelection. Xuan Thuy, speaking on "Face the Nation" a year later, revealed that that is what Le Duc Tho told Kissinger. Thuy also said the DRV had even promised that the POWs would be released if only the United States would set a specific withdrawal date. This, of course, was precisely what Kissinger proposed to Le Duc Tho in secret, and precisely what Tho rejected. In early July, Thuy told Anthony Lewis of the *New York Times:* "To show our good will, we can settle the problem of Point 1 [of the PRG proposal calling for the total withdrawal of all U.S. forces and the prisoner exchange] separately." This pronouncement increasingly fueled opposition to the administration's policy, giving rise to charges that an important chance both to end the war and to get the prisoners back was lost. What Thuy did not tell Lewis was that, in private, Le Duc Tho refused to discuss any part of his nine-point proposal separately. Tho would only say that the nine-point proposal was an integrated whole and not an invitation to reach nine separate agreements.

On September 13, Hanoi informed Washington that it was ready to respond to Kissinger's latest offers. By then, all opposition to Thieu had withdrawn from the campaign; Hanoi merely noted that, in light of this, the U.S. pledge of neutrality in the election, which was then less than a month away, was meaningless. Hanoi was standing by its nine-point proposal, which was what Hanoi believed should be the outcome of the negotiations rather than their starting point. The North Vietnamese rebuffed an effort to hold another meeting in November.

KISSINGER'S ASSESSMENT: TALKING MAY NOT BE BETTER THAN FIGHTING

The North Vietnamese refusal to continue the Kissinger-Tho dialogue was an ominous development. It was a clear signal that U.S. strategy was not working. Intelligence forecasts, too, were discouraging because, by the end of

1971, it appeared that Hanoi still had not been dissuaded from prolonging the war or from pushing for a military victory. Some said that Hanoi was preparing for another dry-season military offensive. In October 1971, Soviet president Podgorny renegotiated a comprehensive arms assistance agreement in Hanoi. With the benefit of hindsight, this Soviet assurance must have been crucial to Hanoi's military planners in deciding on the scope and intensity for the dry season offensive they were about to launch. Soviet assurances were, of course, matched by those Hanoi received from the Chinese.

By the end of 1971, Kissinger also foresaw a rather rapid and dramatic decline of congressional willingness to fund the war effort. As he told journalists in background briefings, the defeat of the foreign aid bill on October 29, 1971, "was only the beginning," and the vote, coming as it did in the midst of the secret negotiations, "might have led the North Vietnamese to believe that U.S. economic support for Saigon could be ended without concession by Hanoi in the Paris Peace Talks." As Kissinger assessed the situation, Hanoi had gotten an end to the bombing and a U.S. pledge to withdraw without making a single concession: only the ouster of Thieu remained to be achieved. Hanoi had begun to receive tangible proof that its allies—despite détente—were not going to abandon the struggle in In-dochina; nor were they—because of détente—going to insist that Hanoi reach an agreement the terms or timing of which were not fully acceptable. Finally, Hanoi continued to be encouraged by the turmoil created in the United States by the administration's war policy.

For the next eight months there were to be no direct talks between Kissinger and Le Duc Tho. Thus, only after the apparent failure of secret negotiations did Kissinger finally move away from the negotiation scenario he had advocated in *Foreign Affairs*. By 1972, he realized that the continued warfare and the growing strength of the South Vietnamese army made it less possible to construct a settlement that proceeded from a basic agreement between Washington and Hanoi on ultimate goals. Kissinger later said he had realized by early 1972 that "rapid progress could be made only if the . . . North Vietnamese and we would negotiate about methods to end the war and if the political solution of the war were left to the Vietnamese parties to discuss among themselves."[15]

Kissinger aides report that in mid-December of 1971 there was a brief moment of hope that the long-sought-after second track of the negotia-tions—negotiations between the Saigon government and the Communists—might be established. The former foreign minister of South Vietnam, Dr. Tran Van Do, received word from a French friend saying that Xuan Thuy, whom he had seen recently, had specifically asked that his "best and warmest regards" be passed on to Dr. Do. Tran Van Do thought this was perhaps a signal that the Communists were interested in reaching a compromise on the status of the Saigon government despite the fact that Thieu had won an uncontested election to a second term. With the approval of President Thieu, Do arranged to meet Thuy. When they met, Thuy spoke about the need for peace, but suggested terms that required, in essence, the surrender of South Vietnam.

One explanation for this apparently pointless meeting is that it was sought before the North Vietnamese Politburo had decided on the Easter offensive. Perhaps at that time, Le Duc Tho and Xuan Thuy assessed the dynamics of the debate within the Politburo as slightly favoring a negotiation initiative over another military offensive. By the time the meeting was actually held, the Easter offensive was scheduled (intelligence analysts suggest that the decision to launch the Easter offensive was made in the first half of December), but some members of the Politburo may have thought going ahead with the Do-Thuy meeting might provide useful information on the mood of the Saigon intelligentsia concerning support for Thieu.

THE WAR RESUMES

Convinced that the secret talks were deadlocked, and deeply disturbed over Hanoi's repeated offers of a POW exchange for U.S. troop withdrawal—offers that Le Duc Tho denied in private—President Nixon once again revealed that there had been secret negotiations. Declaring in a January 1972 television address that "just as secret negotiations can sometimes break a public deadlock, public disclosure may help to break a secret deadlock," the president told of Henry Kissinger's effort to negotiate an agreement to end the war with Hanoi. The president believed that, if Hanoi could be discouraged from thinking that the American people, the Congress, and the forthcoming U.S. presidential election would obviate the need for any concessions, the negotiations would resume.

The day after the president's announcement, Kissinger proposed another secret meeting to the North Vietnamese and several weeks later they accepted by suggesting a meeting for mid-March. But, subsequently, Hanoi kept postponing the session. When they finally did accept a date, they did so only three days before the Easter offensive began.

Later Kissinger would observe: "Hanoi had 'decided to go military' back in October 1971, when Le Duc Tho had developed his diplomatic 'illness' [and left Paris]. From that moment on . . . their problem was to gear the negotiation in such a way that it would support their military objectives. Their delays were carefully calculated. 'It was very smart, tough bargaining on their part.' "[16]

Strangely enough, the Easter offensive provided the first clue that Hanoi might actually be ready for serious negotiations. As one participant in the secret negotiations told me later, "The dispersion of their attacks meant that the NVA was going largely for territory that, because it could not be held permanently (the supply lines just weren't there) could later be given up as concession if we got to bargaining over a cease-fire line."

By seizing the initiative, Hanoi was also demonstrating that it could always fight the war at a level the GVN was unable to contain. The Easter offensive taught the NVA that the GVN could not count on its soldiers to stand and fight if they feared being attacked by a superior force. Thus, Hanoi propagandists probably thought that, the more the ARVN knew about Communist military plans, the more frightened its soldiers would become. The fall of Quang Tri province to advance elements of the NVA who occupied the province capital for three days with only a token force symbolized the tenuous nature of ARVN morale. But even the Communists were surprised at the rapidity with which the GVN defenses collapsed and the ARVN soldiers abandoned their ground. There was considerable anxiety in Washington and Saigon that Quang Tri would only be the beginning. At the time, some U.S. officials feared that the disorderly route of the ARVN defenders and their pillage of Hue city might not be stopped. This was precisely what happened three years later.

From the North Vietnamese perspective, the Easter offensive was not a repeat of Tet 1968. Accounts of interviews with leaders in Hanoi suggest that the two offensives were different in scope and significance.

In the Tet offensive the communist leaders risked the near annihilation of their troops in the South in order to show the American people in the most dramatic way the futility of the U.S. military adventure. (The lesson of Tet was, to put it simply, that if the Americans did not withdraw from Vietnam in 1968 they would still be fighting the war in 1972.)

The current offensive has not followed the same pattern at all. Rather than the spectacular but militarily ineffective demonstration expected by U.S. commanders (who after four years have learned what the Tet offensive was about), it has begun as a conservative military campaign. The offensive will surely demonstrate to the American electorate the hollowness of Nixon's 1968 campaign promises to end the war. But it will do so only as a consequence of North Vietnamese military advances. The North Vietnamese may well have realized that it would be difficult for them to manipulate an American election when so few American lives are at stake and the U.S. aid and air support for the Saigon regime constitute such a small part of the U.S. budget. If so, they expected not that the offensive would result in a final victory by influencing the election but merely that it would push the electorate and the Administration further toward a recognition of the hopelessness of the cause of the Saigon regime. The North's offer of renewed secret negotiations was in all likelihood not a new initiative but merely an offer to discuss the softening or the actual surrender of the Nixon Administration's position.[17]

Politically, and of crucial importance for any future negotiations, the Easter offensive provided cover for the reorganization of the Communists' political infrastructure that began with the reinfiltration of experienced cadres during the attacks. ARVN units that had provided security to prevent precisely this from happening had to be rushed to the front, facilitating the PRG's, and with them, Hanoi's access to the Mekong Delta. By late summer 1972, and for the first time since the war began, internal Communist documents were beginning to sound as if the PRG had at last achieved the extent and depth of political control in the countryside that would permit acceptance of a cease-fire-in-place.

At the height of the offensive, President Nixon decided, with Kissinger's concurrence, that there was no alternative but to sharply increase pressure on the Soviet Union to stop its lavish support of the North Vietnamese offensive. Both men believed that the offensive could not have occurred without firm assurances from the Soviets that the materiel lost would be replaced. They wanted the Soviets to turn Hanoi toward negotiations by withholding future supplies. This was not as unreasonable a request as it may seem at first because Saigon, while it had launched a counteroffensive, was in no position to threaten seriously the North Vietnamese forces in the south—even with much of their heavy equipment (mainly tanks) destroyed. Kissinger's strategy was to blame the Soviet Union in public while offering further concessions to Hanoi if they would turn toward negotiations. This Kissinger would make clear when he met with Soviet leaders in Moscow at the end of April. Both Nixon and Kissinger also believed that Hanoi had to be shown that the United States would not shrink from using force to retaliate for aggressive military actions in the future. Hanoi was warned that American air power would, in the words of the chairman of the Joint Chiefs of Staff, "inch northward" until the offensive stopped. By the beginning of the second week of the offensive, American warplanes were bombing targets in North Vietnam that had been on the restricted list ever since November 1967. B-52 raids were resumed, and by the end of the month, more than 700 B-52 sorties had been flown over North Vietnam—this included a weekend of attacks on Hanoi and Haiphong. The objective of resuming the air war over North Vietnam was explained by a Kissinger aide: "We are trying to compress the amount of time the North Vietnamese have to decide whether the offensive is worth continuing and whether they have the means to continue it."[18]

SECRET TALKS RESUME—AND FALTER

Both the president and Kissinger believed the war had to be ended in the current dry season (by summer 1972). To wait until the next dry season would take the issue of the war into the president's second term. They both also believed that Hanoi was orchestrating its military actions with the U.S. election very much in mind. If the president showed the slightest sign of weakness as November approached, Hanoi would continue to hope that the war was either going to defeat Nixon or at least push him into making further concessions to ward off a George McGovern victory.[19] Consequently the president decided on a policy of applying maximum diplomatic and military pressure on Hanoi to reach an agreement. The president wanted to signal three things: (1) increased Communist aggression would be countered swiftly; (2) the United States was ready to sign an agreement to end the war before the next dry season, but after the U.S. election, the terms for a settlement were very likely to harden; and (3) Hanoi's allies saw the benefits of détente as so important that they were no longer willing to risk détente for the sake of the liberation struggle in Vietnam. "The president, after all, was not asking for Hanoi to surrender," one of the NSC staffers involved in the secret negotiations told me later. "He was asking them to permit an ending of the American involvement by lowering the level of warfare, and then to take their chances in a political struggle with Saigon." Another aide observed at the time, "It was the first time in the entire war that our use of force against Hanoi and our diplomacy with the Soviets and the Chinese were coordinated solely for its effect on the negotiations. The president no longer wanted to win the war, he wanted to end it."

In Moscow, Kissinger assessed the impact of the latest round of fighting in Vietnam—the Easter offensive and the resumption of the air war—on both Soviet willingness to pressure Hanoi into serious negotiation and the progress possible in Soviet-American relations if the war intensified. Kissinger told the Soviets that Washington no longer anticipated or required the eventual withdrawal of all North Vietnamese troops from South Vietnam—only those troops that had come into the south for the recent offensive should gradually be withdrawn. The U.S. position had changed from its maximum of a cease-fire-in-place with the expectation that most North Vietnamese forces would leave the south as the fighting wound down to the minimum of a cease-fire-in-place that left the North Vietnamese in position to continue the war if the progress made toward a political solution was satisfactory. Kissinger also suggested that the areas of the country in which the North Vietnamese troops were to remain need not be regarded as regroupment zones but as the territory of the PRG.

Kissinger made these points clear to Brezhnev, who probably realized what was conceded to the Communists' side and that Washington had probably reached its absolute minimum position on what was negotiable. At that time, one of Kissinger's aides told me, Brezhnev appeared to Kissinger to be both "the most understanding he had ever been of our sincerity in wanting to end the war, and not a little disappointed at Hanoi's intransigence."

Kissinger made clear to Brezhnev that further Vietnamese offensive action would have most serious consequences. Kissinger concluded that this threat had been clearly understood in Moscow: "I do not believe that there could have been any doubt in the minds of the Soviet leaders of the gravity with which we would view an unchecked continuation of a major North Vietnamese offensive and of attempts by the North Vietnamese to put everything on the military scales."[20]

In Moscow, Kissinger tried to argue that the progress of détente should be decoupled from the war if Hanoi persisted in its efforts to impose a military solution. Positive Soviet pressure on Hanoi to negotiate now, of course, would facilitate even further progress on the agenda that he and Brezhnev had discussed for the forthcoming Moscow summit. Kissinger thus left Moscow with a pledge of Soviet cooperation in transmitting the changes in the U.S. position to Hanoi and with a clear feeling for the likely Soviet reaction if further U.S. military action became necessary in the weeks ahead. In all probability, Kissinger must have known the Soviet Union was not prepared to cancel the scheduled summit if U.S. military pressure on North Vietnam intensified.

The détente diplomacy of April had little effect on Hanoi. On May 2, 1972, the day before the northernmost province of South Vietnam fell to the NVA, Henry Kissinger and Le Duc Tho met secretly for the thirteenth time. The loss of Quang Tri was a major test of Vietnamization and a major defeat for Saigon. It could not have come at a worse time in the negotiations; if anything, it suggested to Hanoi that Quang Tri might be to the United States in 1972 what Dien Bien Phu had been to the French in 1954.

Kissinger began the meeting by presenting the U.S. offer: if Hanoi would agree to a cease-fire and return the POWs, all U.S. forces in Indochina would be withdrawn no later than four months after an agreement was signed. But, as Kissinger was to tell the press only a week later: "We were confronted by the reading to us of the published Communist statement. It has [*sic*] taken us six months to set up the meeting . . . and when we got there, what we heard could have been clipped from a newspaper and sent to us in the mail."[21] Le Duc Tho read a formal statement outlining the DRV's already well-known demands—U.S. withdrawal and the creation of a coalition government. A sample of the dialogue that ensued is available from Kissinger's recollections in the Kalbs' book:

> KISSINGER: "How about de-escalation and a cease-fire?"
> LE DUC THO: "Wars aren't fought to have a cease-fire. Wars are fought to have victory."
> KISSINGER: "How about de-escalation alone?"
> LE DUC THO: "We don't fight to de-escalate."[22]

Two days after the secret talks broke down, the plenary sessions of the Paris talks were suspended because of, as the U.S. delegation head William Porter put it, the "complete lack of progress on every available channel."

AND THE FRUITS OF FORCE

A week later, President Nixon told a nationwide television audience that secret talks had broken down once again. He then announced the mining of Haiphong Harbor and other interdiction measures that were to remain in effect until the day the Paris Agreement was signed. The United States sought, the president announced, an internationally supervised cease-fire-in-place throughout Indochina plus a POW exchange. When these terms were accepted by Hanoi, U.S. forces would begin their final withdrawal from Vietnam and complete it within four months. Both Nixon and Kissinger were certain that Hanoi was likely to be dismayed by the reaction of its allies. Both knew that the mining and blockade would have a direct impact on the war effort in the south—Hanoi needed long supply lines to keep its offensive rolling. The mining would assure that Quang Tri would mark the end of the offensive, not the beginning of a GVN rout. Nixon and Kissinger believed, too, that this display of force would impact directly on the negotiations:

> What we are trying to prevent by this decision is an endless continuation of this process by which one attack after another takes place over a period of months without serious negotiations and without any prospect for a settlement. But we also want to be in a position that if our assessment of Hanoi's willingness to negotiate is incorrect and things should turn out not as well as we hope, that we have some bargaining position left on behalf of the Americans who will then be threatened and of the Americans who are now prisoners.[23]

More than twenty-two thousand telegrams and messages supporting the mining of Haiphong Harbor flooded the White House mail room the next day. Again, few Americans knew that the response had been organized by the Committee to Re-elect the President, just as a similar effort had been launched in 1969 when the president declared that the silent majority of the American people wanted to see the war ended with honor and were willing to wait until that goal was achieved. But to Nixon and Kissinger, the most important reaction to the mining took place in Moscow and Peking, not in the White House mail room. As one aide to Kissinger later recalled, "The whole tone of the internal debate over how to get Hanoi to negotiate changed. We were no longer worried about using force because the mining of Haiphong Harbor disproved the theories of those who had urged restraint for the sake of détente or because they feared Chinese or Soviet intervention. At last we had a free hand to use all our force to end the war."

FROM BREAKTHROUGH
TO BREAKDOWN

The origin of the Paris Agreement lies in the four sessions of the May 1972 Moscow Summit. Kissinger indicated to Soviet foreign minister Gromyko that Washington was at last prepared to be responsive to Hanoi's insistent demand that any agreement embody a political as well as a military solution: the United States was willing to sign an agreement calling for the creation of a tripartite commission to govern South Vietnam after the war.[1] This idea provided the foundation for a conceptual breakthrough in the deadlocked secret negotiations; it permitted Le Duc Tho to propose creating a three-party "National Council of Reconciliation and Concord" with little fear that it would be rejected by Washington. For Kissinger, the essence of the conceptual breakthrough was that he could see an agreement that, from Hanoi's point of view, embodied a political solution while, from Washington's point of view, it embodied a solution ambiguous enough to forestall the charge that the United States had overthrown Thieu.

During the summit, both the U.S. and Soviet governments explicitly agreed that the war should no longer impede the progress of détente between the great powers. While both agreed that an end to the war would be in their mutual interest, both acknowledged their limited ability to persuade Hanoi to negotiate. And both agreed that they had responsibilities to their allies that, in the absence of a negotiated settlement, would have to be fulfilled.

The United States was unable to reach a similar accommodation with China. One member of Kissinger's staff described the attempt this way: "Henry remarked to Chou En Lai that he wished he could get the president to stop doing what every president had done: to wake up and before breakfast read the combat and situation reports from Vietnam. This, Henry said, tended to put the war out of perspective, to inflate its importance, and to link to its settlement policies and decisions that should be independent of the war. Chou said that even if the president stopped reading daily reports, Vietnam would not go away. For her part, Chou continued, China had a principled foreign policy and this meant that it was always prepared to fulfill its duties to fraternal socialist allies. The mining of Haiphong had only increased North Vietnamese dependence on China and China would come to her assistance even though Hanoi at times rejected China's advice, such as when they launched the 1972 offensive."

Détente, however, promoted such intimate communications with the leaders of the Soviet Union and China that Nixon and Kissinger were convinced there was genuine feeling for what the United States was trying to do—negotiate an end to its involvement in a war it could not win with an adversary who, with each passing day, had less and less incentive to sign any agreement at all. Détente meant that Moscow and Peking would help as they could to arrange a negotiated settlement, and also that whatever the United States had to do militarily to achieve such a settlement would not be regarded as an expansion of the war. Nixon and Kissinger made it clear that the United States would not destroy North Vietnam. These ground rules were essential to Kissinger's conception of the relationship between détente and the war. "Kissinger always felt that the Vietnam war hurt his relations with China and the Soviet Union," one of his aides told me in an interview. "Kissinger impressed us from the beginning with how deeply he felt the war was wrong, that it was fought wrong, that it was dividing our society, and that it should be ended as quickly as possible. He was not interested in saving South Vietnam if it meant impairing relations with China and the Soviet Union. He believed that China, but particularly the Soviet Union, really needed better relations with the United States for economic reasons and that they would not intervene in Vietnam if Washington used greater force to get Hanoi to negotiate seriously." As a result, what the Nixon administration had established with détente was not necessarily a way to end the Vietnam war but a way of assuring that, if it continued, it would remain a local, limited war.

In mid-June, Soviet president Podgorny visited Hanoi to convey Washington's latest negotiating position, and U.S. officials believe that he urged Hanoi to consider a change in tactics. But while recommending negotiations, Podgorny did not tell Hanoi to compromise. Indeed, Moscow was confident that the U.S. withdrawal was irreversible and that this provided Hanoi with every chance to complete its liberation struggle successfully. Peking also did not favor compromise. In Mao's opinion, the liberation struggle in Vietnam had reached the stage at which negotiations would prove more profitable than continued fighting. Mao even told the PRG foreign minister, Madame Binh, that he had once written a book on the subject of the tactical uses of negotiations and that she should study it.[2]

But by this time, neither Moscow nor Peking was asking Hanoi to provide Washington with anything more than a face-saving way to withdraw its forces from the war.

THE SECRET TALKS SHOW SIGNS OF PROGRESS

By mid-July 1972, it appeared to those involved in the secret Kissinger-Tho talks that Hanoi was on the verge of serious negotiations. Hanoi's tone in the secret meetings changed from hostility to the same level of cordiality that had marked the early sessions when Kissinger had been hopeful of reaching a settlement. This time, however, U.S. officials knew from intelligence reports and captured Communist documents that Hanoi had begun to instruct its cadres in South Vietnam to prepare both for a cease-fire and for coping with the Thieu government. To Kissinger this meant that Hanoi was eventually going to stop insisting on Thieu's ouster before an agreement could be signed. Finally, NVA prisoner interrogation reports indicated that the PRG's military leadership had planned a series of land-grabbing operations in the early fall in anticipation of a cease-fire-in-place. Nevertheless, as Kissinger later told the press, ". . . between July nineteenth and October eighth . . . [Hanoi] constantly proposed various formulas for the institution of a coalition government which would replace the existing government in Saigon and which would assume governmental power. . . ."[3]

So certain was Kissinger that an agreement was at hand that he visited Saigon in late July to brief President Thieu on the search for a negotiated settlement. This was done partly to reassure Thieu that the speculation in the press about what was transpiring in the secret talks was groundless, and technically, of course, this was correct. But Kissinger did not indicate to Thieu that he personally expected an agreement to be reached. Instead, he led Thieu to believe that the Nixon administration might have to appear forthcoming in the negotiations for domestic political purposes, but that Hanoi's intransigence would be punished after the election. After these talks, the South Vietnamese leaders I saw said that Thieu became increasingly convinced that the GVN forces were going to go on the offensive in the next dry season which, in fact, they subsequently did.

Kissinger probably believed he had no choice other than to mislead Thieu. The United States had already offered Hanoi a cease-fire-in-place and a tripartite commission, and these Saigon had made clear it would reject. Trying to win Thieu's support before Hanoi was committed to a specific agreement would imperil the whole negotiating process that Kissinger expected to bear fruit shortly. Kissinger feared that Thieu would leak details of the expected agreement, rally public opinion against it, and denounce Hanoi. He thought Thieu would be easier to persuade if he were presented with a *fait accompli,* if he were given extensive military supplies before the agreement went into effect, and if the NVA were dealt a blow that assured there would be no offensive during the 1973 dry season. Kissinger doubted that Thieu would support the agreement without the above, even if the agreement were underpinned by understandings with Moscow and Peking that Hanoi would not be resupplied in order to launch another morale-shattering offensive.

Kissinger and Tho met twice in August. For the first time in ten years of secret talks, the North Vietnamese were talking about the reality of a South Vietnam where there were ". . . two armies, two administrations, and several political groupings." This was a further sign that Hanoi would not continue to insist on Thieu's ouster. Shortly after the second meeting ended, Tho returned to Hanoi for consultations. Kissinger believed that the Politburo would soon make a decision between war and peace. He again went to Saigon. It was then, Thieu's aides told me, that Thieu began to fear that Washington was very close to reaching an agreement with Hanoi. But, these aides suggested, Thieu believed Hanoi was still not inclined toward a negotiated settlement of the war. In a major speech to the National Defense College in Saigon in August 1972, Thieu set out what he thought was ahead: "There is only one way to force the Communists to negotiate seriously, and that consists of the total destruction of their economic and war potential. We must strike at them continuously, relentlessly, denying them any moment to catch their breath. . . . If our allies are determined, peace will be restored in Indochina. If they lack determination, the Communists will revert to their half-guerrilla–half-conventional warfare, and the war will go on in Indochina forever."

In Saigon, speculation that the secret negotiations had entered a critical stage was intense. The most commonly reported rumor was that Kissinger had come to tell Thieu to resign so that a new government of national union could be established to negotiate with the PRG; then the fighting would stop. A surprisingly large and diverse cross section of political leaders in South Vietnam believed that such a scenario would be a prelude to a coalition that the Communists would dominate. Many of these leaders privately expressed the wish that the United States would not force Thieu out. As one put it, "We are not yet ready for peace. We need a president who can lead us in war; we need to win more battles against the NVA. After that, we will find a president who can lead us into peace." While, I suspect, nearly all South Vietnamese wanted the war to end, many were uncomfortable with the idea of a negotiated settlement because they did not trust the North Vietnamese to honor it. "When the Americans leave," one close Vietnamese friend (whom I thought at the time was overly pessimistic) said, "The North Vietnamese will start planning again for war. Your troops did not prove to them that they would lose, you know, and our troops did not prove to them that we would win."

By 1972, the gap between Washington's and Saigon's expectations with respect to when, and on what terms, a negotiated settlement should be achieved was so wide that it could not be bridged. Kissinger sensed this during his discussions with Thieu, but he refused to consider the possibility that, when an agreement had been reached, Thieu would refuse to sign, or that President Nixon would permit Thieu to block a chance to have a negotiated settlement before the November election. Kissinger thought back to the Johnson-Thieu dispute over the bombing halt and the shape of the table in 1968. He could see why it had been important to act in concert with Thieu as the talks began. But surely, he reasoned, when an actual agreement was within reach, Thieu would have little basis on which to refuse to sign it and the president would have no qualms about signing even if Thieu balked.

Another indication that Hanoi was ready to reach a negotiated settlement came on September 11. On that day, the PRG released what it described as an "important statement on ending . . . the war . . . and restoration of peace. . . ." The essence of that statement was the following proposal:

> If a correct solution is to be found to the Viet Nam problem, and a lasting peace ensured in Viet Nam, the U.S. government must meet the two following requirements:
>
> 1. To respect the Vietnamese people's right to true independence and the South Vietnamese people's right to effective self-determination; stop the U.S. war of aggression in Viet Nam; stop the bombing, mining, and blockade of the democratic republic of Viet Nam; completely cease the Vietnamization policy; terminate all U.S. military activities in South Viet Nam; rapidly and completely withdraw from South Viet Nam all U.S. troops, advisors, military personnel, technical personnel, weapons, and war materiels and those of the other foreign countries in the U.S. camp; liquidate the U.S. military bases in South Viet Nam; stop supporting the Nguyen Van Thieu stooge administration.
>
> 2. A solution to the internal problem of South Viet Nam must stem from the actual situation: there exist in South Viet Nam, two administrations, two armies, and other political forces. It is necessary to achieve national concord: the parties in South Viet Nam must unite on the basis of equality, mutual respect, and mutual nonelimination; democratic freedoms must be guaranteed to the people. To this end, it is necessary to form in South Viet Nam a provisional government of national concord with three equal segments to take charge of the affairs of the period of transition and to organize truly free and democratic general elections.[4]

Kissinger detected in the PRG's proposal a willingness to settle for a cease-fire first, leaving internal political problems to an amorphous and evolutionary solution. He queried Brezhnev, himself fresh from talks with Le Duc Tho, and was assured that the PRG announcement signaled the end of deadlock in the negotiations. Kissinger's staff did not dispute the Soviet interpretation but they were divided over why Hanoi, acting through the

PRG, had turned toward the idea of an agreement now. Some believed that the president's interdiction measures against North Vietnam were having an effect on Hanoi. They argued that Hanoi would feint toward an agreement (perhaps even sign one) in order to have those restraints lifted. Then the war would resume. As support for their argument, they cited intelligence indications revealing that Hanoi was already instructing its cadres on how to violate the anticipated cease-fire-in-place.

Kissinger and Nixon believed otherwise. They attributed Hanoi's change in attitude to Soviet intervention. There was a crucial division, then, between Nixon and Kissinger and their Vietnam experts, and this accounted for their different expectations of the chances that a negotiated agreement would last. If, on Hanoi's part, an agreement to end the war was motivated by pressure from its allies, then the agreement would be respected and enforced by the emerging pattern of détente. A non-Communist government in South Vietnam would survive in spite of its inherent weaknesses. An agreement based largely on momentary and tactical considerations, Kissinger's Vietnam experts argued, would constitute nothing more than a face-saving way for the United States to withdraw before Hanoi went all-out to achieve a victory through force of arms. "We would have spent all of those years and all of those lives and within months of having signed the agreement found that it had brought neither South Vietnam peace nor the United States honor," one member of Kissinger's staff recalled.

When Kissinger and Tho met on September 15, Kissinger made a personal plea for progress in the negotiations. As it stood, Kissinger said, the PRG proposal was not acceptable to President Nixon because it still implied that the United States and not the South Vietnamese people would remove Thieu from office. If the North Vietnamese could be flexible on that point, Kissinger urged, they would find the president never more inclined to reach a negotiated settlement than at that moment. But, he warned, after the election the president's position might very well harden, the prospects of negotiations dim, and then the war would go on.

For reasons that will probably never be known with certainty, at the next secret meeting (September 26, 1972) Le Duc Tho broke the deadlock. In response to the U.S. proposal for a tripartite commission, Tho proposed creating a tripartite National Council of Reconciliation and Concord that, while composed of the three equal segments, was not to be considered a government (something the PRG wanted) and would operate on the principle of unanimity. Kissinger realized that this would be acceptable to President Nixon and that it should be far more acceptable to Thieu than Kissinger's own tripartite commission proposal. Prophetically, however, it was only three days later in a speech to Saigon University students that Thieu declared: "If the United States accepts to withdraw its troops unconditionally [i.e., without insisting that Hanoi do the same], the Communists will win militarily. If we accept a coalition, we will lose politically." Thieu never wavered in his conviction that, despite whatever the North Vietnamese called the organization to be created as part of a political settlement, it was a disguised coalition. Kissinger's staff never lost their suspicion that the United States was rushing too quickly into an agreement with Hanoi that Hanoi would later violate. But Kissinger, suddenly facing the first North Vietnamese concession in the negotiations, believed that for the first time in the long war peace could be at hand.

FROM BREAKTHROUGH TO BREAKDOWN
OF THE KISSINGER-THO TALKS

Kissinger and Tho met again on October 8. One of the U.S. negotiators described that meeting to me in the following terms:

> The session began without one hint that it would be any different than the others. Each side continued to ask the other for clarification of the latest proposals. I was let down, and expected that we would adjourn with nothing on the table than more questions. I was disappointed in Tho: he seemed more on the attack again as far the the Thieu issue was concerned, and he was insistent that there be a political solution before there could be a military solution. When the U.S. side had finished, and it appeared that we were about to conclude the proceedings, however, Le Duc Tho asked if he might be permitted to make an additional statement. He also asked for a brief recess. Kissinger agreed.
>
> Tho returned and began by saying that this had been a long war and had brought untold suffering to the Vietnamese and American people. He said there had been many opportunities to end the war, but the American government continually chose escalation. The DRV side had presented the U.S. with many sound and equitable proposals, Tho said, but always the U.S. refused. Then Tho said that his government was now going to make one last effort to end the war and restore peace through negotiations. This effort was in the form of a draft agreement Hanoi was prepared to sign. Tho then handed us an English-language version of his proposal.[5]

The proposal called for an immediate cease-fire and prisoner exchange, a withdrawal of U.S. forces from South Vietnam, and an end to all acts of war against the DRV, and prohibited the augmentation of the South Vietnamese armies (the NVA/PRG forces and the ARVN) that remained. Hanoi also agreed to separate the military from the political aspects of a settlement: while the proposed agreement addressed both types of problems, a cease-fire would come first and proceed according to a timetable that was not dependent on the progress made by the GVN and PRG toward a political settlement. A meeting was scheduled for the next day when the formal American response would be presented. This meeting had to be postponed twice because Kissinger had to negotiate not only with the North Vietnamese but also with his own delegation.

There was no argument within the U.S. negotiating team that a breakthrough had been achieved, but no member of Kissinger's staff dreamed that anything but several more months of hard bargaining lay ahead. The draft had been presented in English but described in Vietnamese. "The Vietnamese language was far more concrete and hard line than the way the text read in English," one of the American participants recalled, and as a result, when he sat down to draft what he thought would be the American reply he

> felt that unless we worked on every word, Hanoi was going to try to put over an agreement that sounded reasonable in English but would send Thieu and most South Vietnamese up a wall. Of greatest immediate concern was the fact that, in the point that called for the creation of an administrative structure to achieve national reconciliation and concord, the words for "administrative structure" in Vietnamese suggested that a parallel *governmental authority* would be set up. So we set to work on a very hard response to protect our position and the GVN's. Point by point we went over the implied ambiguities in English that had double or possible hidden meanings in Vietnamese. During this time, we did not see Kissinger. He had gone to telephone the White House in order to get the president's reaction to the proposal.
>
> When Kissinger returned and read our draft of a reply to the North Vietnamese proposal, he was furious. He dismissed most of our arguments as nitpicking and said that we failed to realize that after nearly four years of searching for a breakthrough, the last thing he was going to do was turn it down flat, as our draft response pretty much implied we would. "You don't understand," he shouted. "I want to meet their terms; I want to reach an agreement; I want to end this war before the elections. It can be done and it will be done."

Kissinger believed that Hanoi's formulation of an agreement permitted Washington and Hanoi to ". . . agree on some very general principles within which the South Vietnamese parties could then determine the political evolution of South Vietnam." Recounting to the press the significance of Hanoi's proposal, Kissinger observed that Hanoi

> dropped their demand for a coalition government which would absorb all existing authority. They dropped their demand for a veto over the personalities and the structure of the existing government. They agreed for the first time to a formula which permitted a simultaneous discussion of Laos and Cambodia. In short, we had for the first time a framework where, rather than exchange general propositions and measure our progress by whether dependent clauses

of particular sentences had been minutely altered, we could examine concretely and precisely where we stood and what each side was prepared to give.

Hanoi wanted the agreement signed by the end of the month, and Kissinger said he would do his utmost to comply.

> We believed that this was such an important step on the part of the North Vietnamese, that took into account so many of the proposals that we had made, and such a significant movement in the direction of the position consistently held by this administration, that we had an obligation, despite the risks that were involved, of working with them to complete at least an outline of an agreement, and we spent four days, sometimes working sixteen hours a day, in order to complete this draft agreement, or at least the outline of this draft agreement.[6]

Nearly every member of Kissinger's staff in Paris felt that the negotiations were moving far too rapidly. "There were still ambiguities and unresolved details," one recalled later, "that Henry wanted to include in the protocols or believed were just not important." Other advisors at the talks were alarmed at intelligence reports indicating that Hanoi was already instructing PRG cadres to prepare for a cease-fire any time after October 15 by seizing as much land as possible in the forty-eight-hour period before and after the cease-fire date was announced. The advisors believed that the draft agreement's provisions for inspection and supervision had to be considerably strengthened. However, another staffer recalled, "Virtually no one thought that Thieu would balk at the agreement. But he would have to be fully briefed while we were putting the finishing touches on the agreement. We were sure Thieu would realize that the agreement permitted him to remain in power and allowed for the continuation of military and economic assistance to the GVN." But neither the South Vietnamese ambassador in Paris, nor Thieu himself, had been briefed in any but the most general terms, and both said they had not been told that the United States and North Vietnam had actually gone so far as to have exchanged a draft of an agreement.

Kissinger and Tho concluded their negotiations over the draft on October 12, and Kissinger headed for Washington with a fifty-eight page document for the president, the secretary of state, and a handful of Vietnam experts in the CIA and the Department of State. Five days later, on the seventeenth, Kissinger was back in Paris with instructions to tighten up the draft's language and to proceed with getting it into final form. "Kissinger told us that he had assurances from Nixon," one of Kissinger's aides told me, "that the agreement was fine in principle, that we would sign it, but its ambiguities should be clarified."

What happened next and the developments that prevented Kissinger from initialing the agreement on October 22 in Hanoi as planned are extremely complex. See Appendix S for a chronology.

The Americans returning to Paris on October 17 considered that the negotiations had moved, as one put it, to the "mopping-up phase." North Vietnamese negotiators later said that on the seventeenth, Kissinger and Tho worked a twelve-hour day: "Both parties studied the text of the accords, chapter by chapter, article by article, sentence by sentence, word by word. This is why we think that there are no more questions of language or differences between the Vietnamese and the English [draft]."[7] "Article by article, phrase by phrase," one of the U.S. negotiators told me, "the agreement was reviewed and adjustments made. The president was fully informed of every step, every change, term by term."

But by the time Kissinger had to leave Paris for Saigon, two outstanding issues remained. These issues concerned (1) the degree of supervision to be applied over the replacement of war materiel once the agreement entered into force and (2) the relationship between the release of U.S. prisoners of war and of those Vietnamese civilians who had been detained in Saigon's jails as political prisoners. In his instructions, Xuan Thuy apparently did not have the negotiating flexibility that would allow him to resolve these problems without first consulting Hanoi; but Kissinger could not wait past 10:00 P.M. on the seventeenth if he was to reach Saigon in time to win Thieu's agreement and still initial the agreement by October 22. Kissinger was confident that the problem on these issues stemmed from Thuy's lack of instructions (Kissinger had run into this problem before with Xuan Thuy) and believed that the final details could be worked out by cable or possibly in Hanoi itself before the agreement was initialed.

On October 19, 1972, Kissinger presented Thieu with an English draft of the agreement and a three-and-one-half-hour explanation of its importance. He was, one of the South Vietnamese officials who attended these meetings later told me, "like a professor defending a thesis."

Kissinger wanted Thieu to understand three things: (1) that he had negotiated the agreement with Hanoi in good faith, keeping Saigon's and Washington's interests uppermost in mind; (2) that the agreement was realistic in terms of both its basic provisions and the understandings with China and Russia that made it possible; and (3) that it, along with U.S. support, provided Saigon with an excellent chance to survive the period ahead. "We told Thieu," one of the U.S. representatives at this first meeting told me later, "that we frankly felt it remarkable that Hanoi had itself proposed the National Council of Reconciliation and Concord idea that gave the Thieu government a full veto over any of the action that the council might take." The meeting ended, Americans who had been there told me, with no hint that the agreement was unacceptable to Thieu.

"But the next day," another participant recalled, "our meeting took a turn for the worse. Saigon did not agree with our interpretation of the agreement and did not see it in the least to their advantage to accept it. They read between the lines of each provision to find evidence of Hanoi's perfidy," just as, it will be recalled, Kissinger's staff had done when they first read the Vietnamese version of the draft Le Duc Tho had handed to Kissinger on October 8. The comments of both the U.S. interpreters and Thieu's closest advisors are remarkably similar when each group recalled its initial objections to the Vietnamese text. For example, Hanoi's draft called for the Vietnamese word for Paris to be the one that had come into vogue after the French defeat in 1954. In the provisions concerning troop withdrawal, the term for U.S. soldiers was actually slang that one Vietnamese official told me, "any kid on the street could tell Dr. Kissinger meant 'dirty yankee soldier.'" The formulation of many of the articles was such, in the South Vietnamese view, that the onus of the agreement seemed to rest entirely on the United States and the GVN. The provisions concerning inspection were weak. Of greatest concern was the absence of any reference to the status of the demilitarized zone and of any provision for what would happen if the two South Vietnamese parties were unable to reach a political settlement within the prescribed ninety days.

The technical, procedural, and linguistic objections of the GVN were compounded by the anti-Americanism of Thieu's two closest advisors. "We were being accused of both sabotaging an ally and of stupidity in letting the North Vietnamese sucker us into signing such a vile agreement," one of the U.S. participants told me. Within a day, Thieu's advisors had discovered some 129 textual changes that were "essential" before the document could be signed by the GVN.

Saigon also had fundamental objections to the principle of cease-fire-in-place on which the agreement rested. Despite the fact that Thieu had long suspected that this was what Washington was willing to settle for, he was no more inclined to accept it in 1972 than he had been when such suspicions had first arisen in 1969. "The agreement requires the North Vietnamese to give up nothing; it rewards their aggression," Thieu was reported to have said over and over again.[8] "They can stay in South Vietnam and do what they please behind their lines. They will not give the people democratic freedoms, yet they demand that we release the Communist agents from our prisons, that we must permit the VC to live freely in our cities. But our cadres would be killed by the VC if they went to live behind their lines." Thieu saw the agreement as promising continued warfare over precisely where the front lines were. One South Vietnamese participant at these meetings told me that "whenever Thieu raised this issue, Kissinger would ask what we were afraid of: we had a million-man army that was well-trained and well-equipped. But we would reply that we were a nation of only eighteen million people and that to maintain such a large defense force would mean we would have no resources for development and would always have to depend on U.S. aid. Kissinger only replied that he would try to do the best he could for us with the U.S. Congress." Thieu also was deeply suspicious of the administrative structure to be set up by the National Council of Reconciliation and Concord, and several times called it a disguised coalition.

As Thieu was considering turning down the draft agreement, Nixon was cabling Hanoi that "the United States side appreciated the goodwill and serious attitude of the DRVN. The text of the agreement can now be considered complete." The Nixon message also contained the caveat that the agreement would be signed only with Saigon's approval, which it was still expected Kissinger would get. Hanoi had repeatedly asked, when the negotiations got serious, if the United States was negotiating for Saigon as well as for Washington, and they were repeatedly told that Saigon would have to approve the agreement when it was finally drafted. One U.S. negotiator described what was happening: "You see, by this time we were all comfortable with talking past each other. They asked us to answer one question, and we would answer another slightly different question. Then the negotiations would continue. At base, I believe that Hanoi never really took Saigon seriously. To them, Saigon was merely a puppet—at times mischievous, but nonetheless a puppet—that could not in the final analysis stymie signing the agreement."

For the remainder of his visit, Kissinger tried a step-by-step approach in the negotiations. He treated each of the South Vietnamese objections to the agreement individually and made considerable progress in narrowing the scope of the controversy. Working from the more than one hundred changes Saigon desired down to a list of some twenty-six, Kissinger strove to build the confidence he knew he had never had in Saigon. By October 21, Kissinger had narrowed U.S.-GVN differences to six issues, but these were so fundamental and so crucial to the sovereignty of the GVN that, Kissinger's aides realized, Thieu would need time to digest them. "But, at that point, we still thought Thieu would sign," one of the U.S. negotiators later recalled.

Then Thieu produced a transcript of an interview that had been held between North Vietnam's premier Pham Van Dong and *Newsweek*'s senior editor Arnaud de Borchgrave in Hanoi on October 18. In this transcript, Thieu had all the ammunition he needed to torpedo the agreement.

Pham Van Dong began the interview with references to the failure of Vietnamization and the great victory the Easter offensive symbolized; he described the United States from that point on as being forced to liquidate its commitments to Saigon. When asked if South Vietnamese president Thieu could participate in the process of political settlement that would follow the war, Pham replied: "Thieu has been overtaken by events." De Borchgrave asked what would happen after a cease-fire. Pham replied: "The situation will then be two armies and two administrations in the south, and given that situation, they will have to work out their own arrangements for a three-sided coalition of transition. . . ."[9]

"The reference to a coalition was the final straw for Thieu," one of the U.S. negotiators recalled. "We had told him that the political settlement was not a disguised coalition, and now the premier of North Vietnam had said it was. Further argument would be fruitless."

To Thieu, in the face of such overwhelming evidence of North Vietnamese intent, the agreement as it stood was a sellout and he would not sign it. As one official who represented South Vietnam in every international negotiation since 1954 later reflected on what had happened: "We have watched the Communists win at the negotiating table what they could not on the battlefield. We have seen agreement after agreement guaranteed by the great powers fail to be honored. We have seen the Communists time and time again draft articles that read to the rest of the world as equitable, just statements but that in Vietnamese were propaganda victories. And most important of all, we have seen the great powers come to negotiations exhausted and ready to give in while the Communists came knowing that they had won or were about to win a great victory. We did not want this to happen again."

As Kissinger left Thieu's office, Saigon's objections to the agreement centered on these basic issues: (1) that the NCRC was a disguised form of coalition; (2) that the presence in South Vietnam of the NVA after the cease-fire was unacceptable; and (3) that the security and neutrality of the DMZ had to be established in order for any cease-fire to work. "The essence of our objections was this," one high GVN official explained: "As surprised as we were that the demand for an NVA withdrawal had been dropped, we were even more surprised that none of the counterbalancing measures we had discussed with Washington from time to time were included. These were, for example, provisions for respecting the DMZ and for autonomous inspection forces. We were not unwilling to see reality—we knew that the NVA would not leave of its own accord—but we wanted some provisions built into the agreement to provide us a way to deal with the problems that a cease-fire-in-place raised." Soon the number of basic objections would grow as all of the principals began to have second thoughts about the agreement.

On October 23, Kissinger called the president for fresh instructions and suggested that two steps be taken without delay. The first, suspension of all bombing north of the twentieth parallel, was designed as a gesture of good will toward Hanoi who would very soon learn that the original timetable for signing the agreement could not be kept. The second, cessation of all U.S. air support to the ARVN, was designed to put maximum pressure on Thieu. The president—for the first time in the entire negotiations process—made it clear to Kissinger that he was not about to make a separate peace with Hanoi. He told Kissinger to cable Hanoi both that the bombing was being suspended and that the U.S. side had encountered a delay in Saigon. But air support to the ARVN was to continue.

Kissinger (and later Nixon) and nearly all members of the U.S. delegation believed that Thieu was playing a dangerous game, holding out his approval of the agreement for as much as he could get in terms of concrete commitments of further U.S. support. Thieu and high South Vietnamese officials deny that this was their intention, and they took great pains in 1974 and 1975 to make clear that they had serious and valid objections to the way the agreement was formulated. As one GVN official put it, "It was not unreasonable to distrust the North Vietnamese, especially when the premier of North Vietnam gives an interpretation to the proposed agreement that was totally at variance with what Kissinger had characterized to be the North Vietnamese position."

The aura of urgency that Kissinger had brought to the negotiations with Hanoi and Saigon over the past several weeks was not, he learned back in Washington, shared by the White House. Kissinger was concerned that a delay extending beyond a few days might cause Hanoi to rethink the whole agreement. He believed Hanoi had insisted on the timetable it did, both because it felt an agreement concluded by the end of October would leave the NVA in a relatively strong military position and because the DRV leadership did not trust Nixon to hold to the offer of an agreement once he was reelected. Kissinger learned that the president was concerned not with the impact of delay on Hanoi but with avoiding a repeat of LBJ's handling of the 1968 bombing halt announcement. The president was satisfied with the agreement as it stood, but he insisted that Thieu agree as well. One of Nixon's aides later told me, "The president was looking at a timetable that stretched from the end of October until inauguration day."

Kissinger left the White House convinced that there was an effort afoot to sabotage the agreement he had negotiated. The culprits, he suspected, were H. R. Haldeman (the White House chief of staff) and John Erlichman (Nixon's chief domestic advisor). Both, Kissinger knew, took a harder line toward the North Vietnamese than he did, and both were increasingly distressed that he was getting nearly all the publicity from the negotiations. What Kissinger feared most was a delay that would encourage every agency still seeking military victory in Vietnam to critique the agreement and bring to bear on the president pressure (which he knew would be well orchestrated by Haldeman and Erlichman) to push for more than the North Vietnamese had already agreed to. If he had to face Le Duc Tho in November with a list of changes requested by Saigon *and* by Washington, Tho would lose face within the Politburo and the North Vietnamese might refuse to sign any agreement at all.

"In twenty-four hours," one NSC staffer later recalled, "the bottom fell out." On October 24, as Kissinger was briefing the president on his negotiations with Thieu, Thieu, in a series of speeches and meetings with political leaders, began to release portions of the draft agreement. Thieu did this, denouncing it as a North Vietnamese ruse designed to provide themselves time in which to recover from the failure of the Easter offensive, to resupply their troops, and to get ready to "strike the last blow" once the United States had withdrawn. That morning, a Saigon daily newspaper ran the following commentary outlining Thieu's reaction to the draft agreement:

President Thieu disclosed to the delegates from political parties what he said he has never disclosed to anyone. He cited the conditions put forth by the North Vietnamese Communists for a cease-fire: to force the Americans to withdraw completely, to stop their bombings, to stop their blockade, and to stop providing South Vietnam with all kinds of support. Meanwhile, the North Vietnamese Communists would seize the opportunity to restore their potential so as to strike the last blow.

In the political field President Thieu also disclosed the North Vietnamese Communists' conditions: that the entire southern administration resign, not just "Mr. Thieu" individually; the formation of a three-segment government from the central level to the infrastructure level, including the Saigon government and the "Viet Cong government," and that this government exist for approximately 6 months and after that a general election be held. The North Vietnamese Communists' intention definitely is to abrogate the constitution and to draft a new constitution, such as the constitution of the fourth French Republic, so as to create political disturbances aimed at seizing power. President Thieu also disclosed another detail: the Communists also demand the elimination of such organs as the national police and the Rural Construction Organization, demand freedom and democracy, and the return of all people to their native lands, meaning that there will be no war refugee problem.
President Thieu stated that the reason why the North Vietnamese Communists demand a cease-fire is that approximately 70 percent of their war potential has been lost, a cease-fire would benefit them, and would give them time to strengthen their forces and, after being a member of a three-segment government for 6 months, to resume the war with a deadly blow.[10]

That afternoon Thieu went on radio to further amplify his opposition to the draft agreement and to make clear his basic stand: North Vietnam had to withdraw its forces from South Vietnam. Only then could an internationally supervised plebiscite take place. Thieu proposed that Saigon and Hanoi negotiate directly to settle military problems and that Saigon and the PRG negotiate to arrange a political settlement. Thieu also declared, "We should make preparations so that if a cease-fire takes place, now or in a few months, we will not be in a disadvantageous position. Therefore we have planned measures to win over people and protect our land, wipe out enemy forces and ensure safety along communication lines . . . as well as security in the villages and hamlets. . . . I have also ordered that all Communist schemes to sow disturbances and foment uprisings must be nipped in the bud, that the Communist infrastructure must be wiped out quickly and mercilessly. . . ."

This declaration of war was not without impact on Hanoi. After negotiations marked by misunderstanding and mistrust, the little that had been achieved between Kissinger and Le Duc Tho was not sufficient to withstand the impact of Washington's request for yet another delay in initialing the agreement. In the early evening of the twenty-fourth, Radio Hanoi had alerted its listeners to be ready for an important announcement. Some seven hours later, while Washington slept, Hanoi released a summary of the basic points in the draft agreement, outlined the timetable for approval that had been set up, and then blasted the Nixon administration for sabotaging a chance to end the war.

The Kissinger–Tho Talks, 1972–1973

DRV-HOSTED MEETING SITE

Gif-Sur-Yvette, January 12, 1973. U.S. side, *top to bottom:* Mary Stifflemire (secretary), Peter W. Rodman, William H. Sullivan, Henry A. Kissinger, Winston Lord, David A. Engel (interpreter). DRV side, *top to bottom:* Tran Quang Co, Nguyen Dinh Phuong (interpreter), Nguyen Co Thach, Le Duc Tho, Xuan Thuy, Phan Hien, Pham The Dong. *(Courtesy of Peter W. Rodman)*

U.S.-HOSTED MEETING SITE

St. Nom la Breteche, January 13, 1973, the last day of the negotiations. *(Courtesy of Peter W. Rodman)*

ADJOURNMENT

Kissinger makes plans to see Le Duc Tho in Hanoi. *Left to right:* Nguyen Co Thach, Xuan Thuy, Nguyen Dinh Phuong (interpreter), Tho, Kissinger. *(White House photograph)*

AVENUE KLEBER

Initialing of the Paris Agreement, January 23, 1973. *(White House photograph)*

THE OPENING OF THE TALKS
Hanoi, February 10, 1973. *(Courtesy of Peter W. Rodman)*

WELCOME AT THE PRESIDENT'S HOUSE
Hanoi, February 10, 1973. *Left to right:* Bonnie Andrews, Peter W. Rodman, R. T. Kennedy, Winston Lord, William H. Sullivan, David A. Engel, Henry A. Kissinger, Pham Van Dong, Nguyen Dinh Phuong, Le Duc Tho, Nguyen Duy Trinh, Nguyen Co Thach, Herb Klein, John Ready. *(White House photograph)*

7

FROM THE BREAKDOWN
TO THE CHRISTMAS BOMBING

After years of making gratuitous statements about their readiness to reach a negotiated settlement, Washington, Saigon, and Hanoi now proved by their behavior that they were unready to accept one. And when an agreement finally was drafted, its provisions had been designed so that none of the principals would have to make compromises with respect to their ultimate goals or how those goals were to be achieved. Consequently, from October 26 onward, Kissinger found that he had to conduct negotiations at three levels: between himself and the Washington-based bureaucrats who opposed the terms of the agreement, between himself and Thieu in Saigon, and between himself and Hanoi.

KISSINGER'S NEGOTIATIONS WITH WASHINGTON

Governments have to mobilize for peace negotiations just as they do for war. In the fall of 1972, U.S. officials who dealt with the Vietnam war were uniformly appalled at and psychologically unprepared for the nature of the agreement Kissinger had negotiated with Le Duc Tho. There was cautious optimism that the war was again becoming winnable for the GVN, now that the United States had taken decisive action against North Vietnam by mining Haiphong Harbor. Peasant bicycles were no longer adequate to supply the T54 medium tanks and the heavy 130mm. guns that the NVA had moved south between 1969 and 1972. The pre-positioning of supplies, particularly POL (petroleum, oil, and lubricants) and ammunition, became crucial as the United States closed the port of Haiphong in what one member of the U.S Joint Chiefs of Staff described as the most effective operation of the war: "Not a single life was lost on either side and the flow of supplies into the south was dramatically reduced to a trickle." The NVA's Easter offensive had ground to a halt, and the Saigon command had mobilized a counterattack. The early rout of South Vietnamese forces in the northern provinces worked to Hanoi's immediate disadvantage; corrupt and incompetent ARVN generals were disgraced, fired, and replaced by those with a feel for the region and for their commands. The south's recovery of morale as a result of this offensive was dramatic compared with the aftermath of the 1968 Tet offensive, and never before had the NVA lost so much materiel that could not be easily replaced. These developments were all in the background as the draft agreement was being evaluated in Washington.

The more President Nixon focused on the agreement and considered it against the emerging battlefield situation and the prognoses of his military commanders, the more he toyed with the idea that he could actually do better. At one point, he even thought a token withdrawal of North Vietnamese forces might be possible. Only gradually did Nixon come to understand Kissinger's difficulties in negotiating with Hanoi. It was a certainty, Kissinger pointed out, that Hanoi would not agree to substantive changes in the agreement. Besides, he added, the agreement the North Vietnamese would sign did not seriously restrict the capability of the United States to continue to support South Vietnam or to respond if the North Vietnamese violated the agreement.

Nixon's growing dissatisfaction with the October draft centered on three key issues. First, intelligence reports confirmed that Hanoi had instructed its cadres in South Vietnam to launch a series of offensives against GVN positions in contested areas in order to expand PRG control as the cease-fire-in-place went into effect. Hanoi's strategy, these reports revealed, was to let the inspection mechanism (which in the October draft was only a token force of observers with limited mobility) decide who actually held control. Such inspection teams would take weeks to reach the scene of an incident, thus providing time for the PRG to consolidate its control. Nixon wanted the GVN to have time to prepare a defense against such operations and he wanted a more substantial supervisory and inspection mechanism created before the cease-fire agreement was signed.

Second, like Thieu, Nixon was disturbed that Pham van Dong had called the NCRC a coalition government. There could be no hint of a coalition. And other ambiguities had to be pinned down as well. As Nixon put it:

> Now, there are some who say: "Why worry about the details? Just get the war over!"

> Well, my answer is this: My study of history convinces me that the details can make the difference between an agreement that collapses and an agreement that lasts—and equally crucial is a clear understanding by all of the parties of what those details are.

We are not going to repeat the mistake of 1968, when the bombing-halt agreement was rushed into just before an election without pinning down the details.

We want peace: peace with honor, a peace fair to all, and a peace that will last. That is why I am insisting that the central points be clearly settled, so that there will be no misunderstandings which could lead to a breakdown of the settlement and a resumption of the war.[1]

Third and finally, Nixon did not want to be accused, as one of Kissinger's aides later recalled, of having "flushed Thieu down the election drain," by appearing to win reelection through breaking with an unpopular ally.

Kissinger regarded the Nixon reservations with increasing bitterness when he learned that Haldeman and Erlichman had begun to circulate a rumor that he had actually overstepped his negotiating instructions and reached a deal with Tho that Nixon would not support. The increasing confidence that Kissinger's aide, General Alexander Haig, had won with Nixon did not help matters since Haig reportedly felt that in the negotiations Kissinger had been too forthcoming with Hanoi, while giving President Thieu, an ally of many years, short shrift.

Most of the NSC staff and the members of the negotiating team sided with Kissinger. Whereas they had felt the agreement was negotiated too rapidly for their professional satisfaction, they believed that reopening issues of substance would imperil the whole process. In the then supercharged atmosphere of the Nixon White House, Kissinger's staff began to think that the president's objections to the agreement (particularly when negotiations with North Vietnam resumed in November) were based more on the Haldeman-Erlichman–Kissinger rivalry than on what was in the interest of either the United States or the South Vietnamese. While sources close to Nixon maintain that the president worked carefully over the draft agreement, sources close to Kissinger dispute this. As I was told by one NSC staffer who had been involved in the secret negotiations ever since they began: "Nixon hardly focused on the agreement, and we were frankly offended when he would continually say in public that he had been too busy working on peace terms so that he didn't have a moment for domestic politics. Bullshit. He was in there all the time with Haldeman and Erlichman talking politics. His only concern was that an agreement be reached. I don't think he even read the GVN's detailed reactions to the draft agreement. After the election Kissinger told me that Nixon had just said to him, 'Get this thing signed before the inauguration.' "

Outside the White House, the agreement was read from fault to fault. As one high State Department official told me, in terms that were echoed by officials of every agency involved: "It was a typical bureaucratic reaction.

Everybody tried to protect his position against the ambiguities of the agreement. The result was that everyone was calling for substantive changes in the terms of the agreement or a postponement of the signing." This reaction, in contrast to Nixon's, was not a surprise to Kissinger. Indeed, it was for this very reason that Kissinger had preferred to conduct all of the negotiations secretly and then present Washington with a *fait accompli.*

Some bureaucratic reactions were also anti-Kissinger. Having had Kissinger ask their high officials for advice at one point in the fall, and then having discovered that this advice was not taken, the offices and agencies asked to coordinate the draft agreement harked back to their original positions. The basic reference point was the NSSM-1 study. All agencies subscribed in varying degrees to what the Joint Chiefs of Staff described in NSSM-1 as "the essential conditions for a cessation of hostilities"; namely, "an effective cease-fire, verified withdrawal to North Vietnam of all North Vietnamese personnel (including those in Laos and Cambodia), verified cessation of infiltration, substantial reduction in terrorism, repatriation of U.S. prisoners, agreement to reestablish the demilitarized zone with adequate safeguards, no prohibition against U.S. assistance to ensure that the RVNAF is capable of coping with the residual security threat, and preservation of the sovereignty of the GVN." Such conditions were a prescription for victory on the battlefield; they implied not that Hanoi would make compromises but that they would give up the struggle to take over the south by force. Not all of these conditions, the JCS explained, might be achieved in the initial negotiations to end the war. The maintenance of the option for the United States to continue to assist the GVN militarily, despite any agreement that might be reached, was therefore essential.

So, critics of the October draft agreement made the strongest possible representations to the president that a stepped-up program of arms delivery ought to be instituted. This was necessary, the military argued, to assure that GVN forces were supplied and equipped at a high enough level so that the "one-for-one replacement" provision in the agreement would not unduly handicap ARVN operations.

Like so many U.S. assistance programs to Saigon, Operation Enhance and Operation Enhance-Plus (the crash programs that in six weeks' time provided the South Vietnamese with nearly $2 billion in supplies, materiel, and weapons) were designed not for what the South Vietnamese system could absorb and effectively maintain, but with reference to what North Vietnam would likely receive if the Soviets and the Chinese undertook a massive resupply effort to North Vietnam in 1973 and 1974. It was the Pentagon's way not of buying off Thieu, but of ensuring that, if congressional support for future military assistance began to wane, it would not be possible for our adversaries to think that the South Vietnamese had been abandoned and left defenseless. As one U.S. general put it, "We gave them the fourth largest air force in the world in a little over two months and such a superiority of firepower that if we had been giving this aid to the North Vietnamese they could have fought us for the rest of the century." I cite this statement, representative of many that I heard at the time, not because it should be taken as literal fact but because it illustrates that, at least to some elements in the Pentagon, Operation Enhance was genuinely regarded as the beginning of the end of U.S. assistance to Saigon.

Operation Enhance was greeted with mixed emotions by the negotiating team. Clearly, it did not reassure the North Vietnamese that the United States was sincere in its efforts to end its involvement in the war. It also created problems for the Soviets and the Chinese, who no doubt were asked to provide Hanoi with equivalent aid in 1973 in order to offset the effect of Operation Enhance. But it did help in the negotiations with Saigon by making it harder and harder for Thieu to hold out.

KISSINGER'S NEGOTIATIONS WITH SAIGON

"We were the prisoners of our own illusion," one NSC staffer told me. "After having said for years that the GVN was a sovereign, independent government, we now resented it acting that way by opposing what was from their point of view—and legitimately, I think—a poor agreement." The GVN did not want simply to end the war; it wanted to have the war won. Saigon did not want to negotiate with Hanoi about when the Communist soldiers would leave the south; it wanted the NVA to leave before negotiations began. Saigon did not want to separate the military and political issues involved in the conflict, for, GVN officials repeatedly told their U.S. counterparts, an effective cease-fire would depend on a meaningful political settlement. If a negotiated agreement did nothing to resolve the problems that had caused the war in the first place, then the war would go on. Most South Vietnamese governmental and political leaders were suspicious that the United States would ultimately seek a separate peace with Hanoi if domestic pressure became unbearable and most, including Thieu himself, believed that the United States would not hold out for a North Vietnamese troop withdrawal if that could not be forced by the course of the war. But in the fall of 1972, critics and supporters of Thieu alike rallied behind him, as they had in 1968 when he had initially refused to participate in the Paris talks.

Not surprisingly, the essence of Thieu's position was that the GVN was still too weak to survive a cease-fire-in-place. Thieu flatly refused to consider even preparing a map distinguishing between GVN and PRG zones of control based on a generous projection of the ARVN's defensive perimeters—an exercise that Kissinger said Hanoi had suggested. One American who participated in the negotiations with Thieu summarized the dynamics of the debate: "Thieu would say that the Communist infrastructure was still strong, the embassy would have to argue that it was weak. Thieu would say that Vietnamization was not yet fully effective and we would have to say (despite the fact that the ARVN was bogged down all over South Vietnam with full divisions trying to dislodge NVA companies) that it was a success. Thieu would say that the Communists would violate the cease-fire and there would be a bloodbath of terror, and we, ironically, would have to say that there would not be a bloodbath because the GVN's police force was strong and effective. We knew Thieu had the better case."

Thieu wanted three basic changes in the substance of the agreement. First, he objected to calling the National Council of Reconciliation and Concord an administrative structure since the Vietnamese words for this term implied that the Council would actually be a *governmental* structure; Pham Van Dong had called it a coalition of transition. Thieu also objected to having the NCRC composed of three equal segments (the GVN, the PRG, and a neutralist third force) since he believed that there were only two political tendencies in South Vietnam: the Communists and the non-Communists (the PRG and the GVN). Over and over again, Thieu would say, "There is no third force," and U.S. Vietnam experts tended to agree that the collection of anti-Thieu intellectuals, dissident religious leaders, and exiled politicians who called themselves the Third Force had little popular support. Thieu's fear was that officially recognizing a third force would permit the Communists to dominate two-thirds of the NCRC and claim that the GVN was a minority that opposed the will of the other political forces in Vietnam.

"Creating three political forces where there were only two," one of Thieu's advisors told me in an interview, "was an old Communist trick. They would quickly dominate the third force and then try to isolate us. Kissinger was saying not to worry because the NCRC could operate only on the basis of unanimity. But if our side continually vetoed what the NCRC wanted to do, then we and not the Communists would appear to be the real obstacles to peace." That this was in part Hanoi's intent was later confirmed by the conversations Murrey Marder, a *Washington Post* staff writer, had in Hanoi just after the Paris Agreement was signed. Marder observed:

> The North Vietnamese conceded that their underlying dual rationale for the "unanimity" rule was to prevent Thieu's forces from imposing their will on the Vietcong faction in the National Council, and to use the process to isolate Thieu's supporters by portraying them as the barriers to peace in South Vietnam.
>
> In a Vietnamese context, as alien as this may sound to Westerners, officials in Hanoi maintain that this form of political encirclement can prove quite effective.

The process, as explained by Hoang Tung, editor of the official newspaper *Nhan Dan*, and an alternate member of North Vietnam's Communist Central Committee, is that "first you try to get unanimity." If there are "differences between the various forces," he said, an attempt is then made to resolve them. Should that fail, the dissenters are then isolated and shown up to the public as intransigent obstructionists.

No one can risk "trying to block everything," Tung maintained.[2]

In the final text of the Paris Agreement (see Appendix C) the reference to the NCRC as an administrative structure was deleted and the extent to which this body would exist or be established outside the capital at local levels was left to further negotiations between the two South Vietnamese parties. But the NCRC did retain a tripartite composition.

Thieu's second major objection to the draft agreement was that it contained no specific reference to the status of the demilitarized zone. For Thieu, this was essential to the protection of both the cease-fire and the sovereignty of his country, the Republic of Vietnam, as a separate political entity pending the reunification of Vietnam. For both purposes, the DMZ had to be "airtight": no troops or supplies could pass through it, and if Hanoi agreed to this, then it would de facto have to recognize the sovereignty of the government in the south over that portion of the territory of Vietnam south of the DMZ line. These objections were finally met in the Paris Agreement by references to the demilitarized nature of the zone and a pledge by the signatories to respect it.

Third, Thieu objected to the method by which the agreement was to be signed. He refused to sign a document that specifically mentioned the PRG and that would require its signature along with that of the GVN. This, he felt, would have had the effect of conferring governmental status on the PRG, something the GVN assiduously sought to avoid. Consequently, when the Paris Agreement was finally signed, there were actually two ceremonies: one in which the United States and the DRV signed an agreement that mentioned the four belligerents by name and another that referred only to the "parties participating in the Paris conference" that all four participants signed.

Thieu remained fatalistic about the cease-fire-in-place. He consistently maintained that such a settlement simply perpetuated the war. Thieu was realistic about what could be achieved once it was clear that President Nixon wanted to sign the agreement. So Thieu's strategy was to push for changes with respect to the DMZ, the NCRC, and the language of the agreement while trying to secure a specific commitment from President Nixon on the nature and extent of future U.S. aid to the GVN.

Thieu tried to achieve this in several ways. Initially, he refused to deal with Henry Kissinger and insisted on negotiating directly with Nixon, believing at first that Nixon and Kissinger were divided over the agreement. Nixon sent General Alexander Haig to Saigon twice—in November and then in

December—to reassure Thieu by pointing out that signing the agreement
would make it easier for the United States to continue support to the GVN.
Participants at these meetings told me that the way Haig delivered his
message was as important as what was said: "Rabidly anti-Communist
himself, Haig won Thieu's confidence but misrepresented the extent of U.S.
support for the GVN." This occasioned one U.S. general later to say that this
had been a mistake. "Haig misled Thieu into thinking that the American
attitude toward Vietnam wouldn't change once this agreement was signed."
Haig was also continually in touch with the embassy in Saigon as ambassadors
Bunker and Whitehouse worked out the differences with Thieu. "Haig's
calls," one participant in the process recalled, "always stressed that the
president was for the agreement, wanted the agreement. I guess Haig wanted
to make sure that we gave no hope to Thieu that there was an exploitable
difference between Nixon and Kissinger on the cease-fire-in-place issue or
that, with the election over, the president would change his mind about
wanting the agreement."

Nixon followed up Haig's November visit with a personal letter to Thieu in
which he made clear for the record that the United States was set on
"remaining within [the] general framework" of the October draft. "As
General Haig explained to you," the letter continued, "it is our intention to
deal with this problem [the status of the NVA in the south] . . . by seeking
to insert a reference to respect for the demilitarized zone in the proposed
agreement and, second, by proposing a clause which provides for the
reduction and demobilization of forces on both sides in South Vietnam on a
one-to-one basis and to have demobilized personnel return to their homes."
Nixon urged Thieu to look at the "big picture":

> Above all we must bear in mind what will really maintain the agreement. It is
> not any particular clause in the agreement but our joint willingness to maintain
> its clauses. I repeat my personal assurances to you that the United States will
> react very strongly and rapidly to any violation of the agreement. But in order
> to do this effectively it is essential that I have public support and that your
> government does not emerge as the obstacle to a peace, which American public
> opinion now universally desires.[3]

Still not satisfied with the absence of a specific pledge of future aid, Thieu
sent his personal advisor, Nguyen Phu Duc, to see Nixon in Washington.
Again no specific commitment was forthcoming. Nixon consistently told
Thieu—by letter and through General Haig—only that the United States
would continue to give Saigon the aid it needed and would not stand idly by if
the North Vietnamese engaged in a wholesale violation of the agreement.
Thieu sensed through the delegations he dispatched to Washington that

Nixon's emissaries were underplaying or ignoring the difficulties they were likely to face in trying to get additional aid from Congress.

After the Paris Agreement was signed, Thieu continued to press his case for a fixed-aid commitment when he met with Vice-President Agnew in Saigon in February 1973 and with President Nixon in San Clemente that April. But even then, Nixon would go no further than to say, as he did in the joint communiqué issued at San Clemente on April 3, 1973, that it was "the United States' intention to provide adequate and substantial economic assistance . . . during the remainder of this year and to seek congressional authority for a level of funding for the next year sufficient to assure essential economic stability and rehabilitation as . . . [South Vietnam] now moved from war to peace." Based on his discussions with Agnew and Nixon, one of Thieu's aides told me, "President Thieu came back to Saigon convinced he had already been abandoned by the United States."

KISSINGER'S NEGOTIATIONS WITH HANOI

Kissinger initially expected to sign the agreement before election day; he later explained what had prevented him from doing so:

> The president and I were in complete agreement [before Kissinger returned to Paris on October 17] . . . that if it appeared at that particular moment that the cease-fire was too precarious, that we would not drive it through at all costs, especially because it was at the end of an electoral campaign and because we could not give the impression that we were doing it in order to gain votes.
>
> So, frankly, when I was in Saigon [October 19–23], and when we made the final decision that led to the delay, I knew what the president wanted, and it was not at all true that I pulled back.
>
> We had a public broadcast from Hanoi that was revealing in a slightly edited version some essential agreements which we had reached and demanding that we sign the agreement five days later on October 31. We had Saigon put itself into a position of opposition to the agreement, and what we had to make clear and make clear rapidly was, first, that we were not going to sign on October 31, but nevertheless we were not kicking over the agreement; that the agreement was essentially completed as far as we were concerned; and that it could be completed in a very brief period of time.
>
> When we said "peace is at hand," . . . we told Hanoi that we were fundamentally sticking to the agreement. We were telling Saigon that the agreement as it stood was essentially what we would maintain.
>
> . . . we thought it could be negotiated in four or five days.[4]

What had gone wrong?

In his theory, Kissinger was right: Hanoi would accept an agreement that embodied less than its maximum or even less than its publicly articulated demands. Later this was confirmed by the editor of Hanoi's *Vietnam Courier,* Nguyen Khac Vien, who observed: "It is certain that on our part, from the moment there was a workable agreement allowing us some advantages, we would end the war. Even if it were a compromise, so long as it allowed us to progress. Our most ambitious objective was to make the U.S. leave and to overthrow the Saigon regime. But on a practical level, at a given time, one must accept this or that according to the balance of forces."[5]

But, Le Duc Tho told Kissinger when they resumed talks in November, the Politburo had again put the issue of an agreement to a vote. All the years of mistrust and the enmity of warfare produced a decision that not only decommitted Hanoi from an agreement but also required Le Duc Tho to reopen issues that had been settled in the October negotiations. From the vantage point of Hanoi, the thirty-first of October represented more than a deadline; it represented the status quo on the battlefield in the south that could not be changed. Through delay, the North Vietnamese feared that Washington and Saigon would try to alter this situation; Operation Enhance was sufficient proof of U.S. perfidy. Basic to Hanoi's acceptance of any agreement was that it should in no way impair the capability of the NVA to operate in South Vietnam. Now, Hanoi would have to assess how drastically the military balance had changed before an agreement could again be considered.

In the weeks ahead, Washington and Hanoi were deadlocked over a number of key issues that still had to be negotiated either because of the ambiguities in the draft or because they had not been included in the original. When negotiations resumed in November, they did so in an atmosphere of hostility and mistrust. Le Duc Tho was now wary of Kissinger and his authority, thinking Kissinger had negotiated an agreement that exceeded his instructions. Tho's Politburo colleagues distrusted Nixon who was obviously, from their point of view, going to shift the balance of forces as much in Saigon's favor as possible through Operation Enhance. The U.S. side was increasingly alarmed about Communist plans to use the first few days and weeks of postagreement confusion as a screen for attacks against the GVN.

The Kissinger-Tho talks resumed on November 20 with Kissinger describing issues that had to be resolved. One set of issues, Kissinger told Tho, the United States was introducing for President Thieu; these issues represented Thieu's demands for linguistic and other changes in the agreement. Kissinger read sixty-nine such changes into the record, and then withdrew half before the North Vietnamese had a chance to respond. "So from the start," one U.S. official at these talks told me, "we encouraged Hanoi not to take Saigon seriously."

The other set of issues Kissinger was introducing represented the minimum demands of the United States: unless they were satisfied, Kissinger told Tho, an agreement could not be signed. These demands centered on the problems likely to occur in the first few weeks and months that the agreement was in force—problems raised by expected military operations aimed at extending PRG territorial control. It was essential that the cease-fire supervisory mechanism be in place and able to operate effectively when the agreement was signed. Equally essential was the clarification of the military status of the DMZ—an issue that Thieu wanted raised as a matter affecting the sovereignty of the GVN. Kissinger's approach was to downplay the sovereignty aspect of this issue and to discuss the DMZ in terms of its role in assuring that there would be a cease-fire. Consistent with its objective of retaining an unimpaired capability to resume the military struggle if the political evolution specified in the agreement did not occur, Hanoi had sought only the loosest of references to the DMZ.

As Kissinger later explained:

> We had to place stress [consequently] on the issue of the demilitarized zone because the provisions of the agreement with respect to infiltration, with respect to replacement, with respect to any of the military provisions would have made no sense whatsoever if there was not some demarcation line that defined where South Vietnam began. If we had accepted the proposition that would have in effect eroded the demilitarized zone, then the provisions of the agreement with respect to restrictions about the introduction of men and material into South Vietnam would have been unilateral restrictions applying only to the United States and only to our allies. Therefore, if there was to be any meaning to the separation of military and political issues, if there was to be any permanence to the military provisions that had been negotiated, then it was essential that there was a definition of where the obligations of this agreement began.[6]

Harking back to Nixon's proposal of early 1970, Kissinger expressed the president's concern that there be an Indochina-wide cease-fire-in-place. Hanoi, however, was reluctant to extend the scope of the agreement (as Washington was to learn in 1974, Hanoi lacked adequate influence over events in Cambodia). Ultimately, an understanding was reached "that the formal cease-fire in Laos will go into effect in a considerably shorter period of time than was envisaged in October, and since the cease-fire in Cambodia depends to some extent on developments in Laos, we expect the same to be true there."[7]

Finally, Washington and Hanoi differed over the size and capability of the cease-fire inspection and supervision force—the International Commission for Control and Supervision (ICCS)—and these differences persisted until after the Christmas bombing of Hanoi. Hanoi wanted the ICCS to be a relatively small force (no larger than 250 men) without independent communication or logistics, and, as Kissinger described it later in a press briefing, "dependent entirely on its authority to move on the party it was supposed to be investigating." Kissinger also pointed out that "over half of its personnel were supposed to be located in Saigon, which is not the place where most of the infiltration that we were concerned with was likely to take place." The cease-fire inspection force provided for in the Paris Agreement clearly reflected U.S. preferences, and to the U.S. negotiators the ICCS that was created increased their belief that the cease-fire would last. And at his January 24 press briefing, Henry Kissinger described what had been negotiated in considerable detail:

> . . . [The ICCS's] total number is 1,160 drawn from Canada, Hungary, Indonesia, and Poland. It has headquarters in Saigon. It has seven regional teams, twenty-six teams based in localities throughout Vietnam which were chosen either because forces were in contact there or because we estimated that these were the areas where the violations of the cease-fire were most probable.
>
> There are twelve teams at border-crossing points. There are seven teams that are set aside for points of entry, which have yet to be chosen, for the replacement of military equipment. That is for Article 7 of the agreement. There will be three on each side and there will be no legitimate point of entry into South Vietnam other than those three points. The other border and coastal teams are there simply to make certain that no other entry occurs and any other entry is by definition illegal. There has to be no other demonstration except the fact that it occurred.
>
> This leaves one team free for use; in particular, at the discretion of the commission and, of course, the seven teams that are being used for the return of the prisoners can be used at the discretion of the commission after the prisoners are returned.
>
> There is one reinforced team located at the demilitarized zone and its responsibility extends along the entire demilitarized zone. It is in fact a team and a half. It is 50 percent larger than a normal border team and it represents one of the many compromises that were made between our insistence on two teams, their insistence on one team, and by a brilliant stroke we settled on a team and a half. [Laughter]
>
> With respect to the operation of the international commission, it is supposed to operate on the principle of unanimity, which is to say that its reports, if they are commission reports, have to have the approval of all four members. However, each member is permitted to submit his own opinion so that as a practical matter, any member of the commission can make a finding of a violation and submit a report at the first instance to the party.

I have quoted Kissinger at such length here because U.S. negotiators genuinely believed that the provisions establishing the ICCS represented a practicable and effective mechanism for supervising the truce.

In addition to clarifying the provisions of the agreement that dealt with the implementation and inspection of the cease-fire, the United States sought concrete assurance from Hanoi that the cease-fire would be respected. The United States consequently, pushed for a token withdrawal of NVA forces from South Vietnam. This harked back to the previous May when Kissinger had asked Brezhnev to convey to Hanoi that, as part of a settlement, the United States expected there to be a gradual reduction of the NVA presence in the south as the cease-fire-in-place stabilized, a situation clearly expected by the Americans throughout the negotiations. "Hanoi had hinted to us all through October that it would withdraw the 40,000 troops that had come south for the Easter offensive," one U.S. negotiator later told me. "Now we were simply asking Hanoi to say so concretely." But Hanoi flatly refused and consistently took the position that the negotiations in Paris had been resumed not to write a new agreement but to clarify ambiguities in the October draft.

Kissinger's strategy for dealing with all of the linguistic problems posed by the agreement's translation into Vietnamese was to delete as many of the troublesome, ambiguous, or objectionable phrases as possible. Issues of principle that could not be included in the actual text of the agreement because Hanoi flatly refused to be committed to them publicly were left to a series of understandings that became part of the negotiating history. These were reached directly between Kissinger and Tho, read into the record, and contributed to Kissinger's initial confidence that the agreement, despite its ambiguities, would be honored by the North Vietnamese.

Through my interviews, I learned that Kissinger genuinely believed, as he stated on January 24, 1973, that "the problem of NVA forces will be taken care of by the evolution of events in South Vietnam." Kissinger believed that the agreement would make possible the normalization of U.S.-DRV relations. He believed that there would first be a "less-fire" but that this would evolve into a cease-fire within six to eight months. He believed Soviet and Chinese assistance supporting Hanoi's war-making capability would decline and that the three superpowers would henceforth act in a spirit of mutual restraint with respect to their allies in Indochina. For its part, the United States, declared Kissinger, was going to gear its future military aid to the GVN "to the actions of other countries and not to treat [such aid] as an end in itself." And, finally, Kissinger believed that Hanoi would keep the agreement, making the possible reinvolvement of U.S. forces in Indochina a "hypothetical situation that we don't expect to arise."[8] In essence, one NSC staffer put it, "Kissinger believed in the agreement, not in the ability of the GVN to defend itself."

During the first few weeks of the "less-fire," as the war continued at a high level, Kissinger reassured a national TV audience by saying that he "expected there would be continued fighting for a few weeks. It has gone on a little longer than I thought. . . . After all, how are the two sides going to establish their areas of control except by trusting each other?"[9] The expectation that there would be some weeks of fighting as both sides established regional lines led to an understanding between Kissinger and Tho that much of what would technically be called cease-fire violations would occur until the cease-fire-in-place had been stabilized.

Nearly every article of the Paris Agreement was the subject of understandings reached between Washington and Hanoi during the Kissinger-Tho meetings in Paris and between Washington and Saigon as part of the effort of General Alexander Haig (and later Vice-President Agnew) to persuade Thieu to accept the terms of the agreement. The essence of these understandings was that certain levels and types of military actions should be expected until the cease-fire became a reality. Thus, Washington told Hanoi that GVN reconnaissance flights over PRG territory would continue, and Hanoi assured Washington that if they did, PRG forces would fire on the aircraft. To avoid continued air war with South Vietnam, the DRV proposed that secure reconnaissance corridors be established for both sides, a suggestion the GVN flatly rejected since recognition of such corridors would tend to legitimize specific PRG territorial claims that the GVN disputed. Thus, both sides knew that the air war would continue.

The understandings reached between Kissinger and Tho recognized that the cease-fire itself would be an imperfect one. They agreed that while, as Article Three of the agreement provided, "All acts of force on the ground, in the air, and on the sea shall be prohibited. All hostile acts, terrorism, and reprisals by both sides will be banned," all other military actions not specifically prohibited could be expected. This understanding was particularly important to the GVN's military capability since it counted on freedom of action for the Police Field Forces, nearly 100,000 conventionally-armed soldiers seconded to the National Police.

Thus, as the GVN went on the offensive in 1973, and as the PRG did in 1974, Washington and Hanoi maintained that the actions of their respective allies were permissible in defense of the Paris Agreement.

As part of the negotiations over the protocols to the agreement, U.S. and DRV representatives could not agree on how to resolve the inevitable disagreement between the GVN and the PRG over areas of the countryside both claimed to control. The DRV proposed drawing a map of the cease-fire-in-place but this the GVN refused, again because it feared such a map would provide the PRG with more territory than it had won on the battlefield. U.S. negotiators proposed that the Two Party Joint Military

Commission (TPJMC) catalog the location of all military forces and use that as a guide to determining territorial control. This the DRV rejected. Thus, neither side expected either that the TPJMC would be able to act as a force for the pacific resolution of conflicting territorial claims or that the land-grabbing war would stop.

Articles Five and Six of the Paris Agreement provided that all military equipment belonging to the United States would be removed from South Vietnam and all U.S. bases would be dismantled. But what Hanoi was not told was that during the past eighteen months title to nearly all of the equipment and bases had been transferred to the GVN. U.S. negotiators deliberately chose not to so inform Hanoi for fear that it would make the issue of the transferred materiel central to the negotiations. "Getting Thieu to give all that stuff back," one of the U.S. negotiators recalled, "would have been a nightmare. So we decided to take our chances that when Hanoi noticed some sixty days later that a hell of a lot of U.S. equipment had fresh GVN paint on it, other provisions of the agreement—especially those relating to U.S. postwar assistance to the DRV—would be going into effect so that we would not find ourselves with Hanoi on the offensive again." Undoubtedly there were provisions of the agreement that Hanoi also construed to have double meanings, though in its public statements the DRV has consistently maintained that it strictly and literally interpreted the terms of the agreement while the United States, by behaving in precisely the ways Hanoi knew it would because of the understandings described above, consistently violated the agreement.

The point is that, from the very day the Paris Agreement was signed, none of the parties to it expected its implementation to be smooth or that it would end the war.

What Nixon and Kissinger were also not stressing publicly when discussing their expectations of the agreement was that each believed that its enforcement ultimately would depend on the United States maintaining the balance of military power in Indochina. "The threat of renewed and effective bombing," one of the U.S. negotiators told me, "was implied in all that we signed with Hanoi. The threat of bombing assured that there would be no major violations of the agreement such as the NVA invasion that took place during Easter 1972, and it reassured our South Vietnamese allies that they still had something of a shield behind which to continue with their efforts to strengthen their defenses and prepare for a political struggle. It was, frankly, less than Thieu wanted; he wanted the North Vietnamese militarily defeated before the agreement was signed. All we said we would do is make sure that the GVN could not be militarily defeated after the agreement came into force. We had not struggled all these years, after all, to write a document that in effect condemned our ally to death."

The basic changes and clarifications sought by Washington did not come easily. As Kissinger was methodically working through the U.S. agenda, the North Vietnamese were introducing new demands as the implied price for making the changes Washington sought. In the November meetings, for example, Hanoi reintroduced demands for the removal of Thieu as South Vietnam's president, the simultaneous release of political prisoners with the POWs, and a significant strengthening rather than diminution of the powers of the NCRC. Frequently, also, Hanoi would appear to drop its insistence on the wording of a particular article, only to have the objectionable wording appear in its November version of the understandings to be read into the negotiating history, and in December in the protocols to the agreement itself. "By the middle of our November meetings," one of the U.S. negotiators recalled, "there was clearly an attitude of dalliance on Hanoi's part, and it was then that Nixon told us to begin warning Hanoi in no uncertain terms that a failure to negotiate seriously would result in a renewal of the bombing. Serious negotiations from our perspective meant that Hanoi should cooperate in clarifying the linguistic ambiguities, working out the protocols, and staying within the framework of the October draft."

At the conclusion of their December session, however, Kissinger and Tho were farther away from reaching an agreement than they had been at almost any time since the negotiations over the October draft had begun. In both the November and December meetings, Kissinger warned Hanoi that, if the talks should break down, pressure on the president to use decisive force would be unbearable. Kissinger specifically warned Hanoi that the bombing—suspended in October only because, in the president's view, an agreement was near—could be resumed and that it would be quite unlike any the North Vietnamese had experienced. Increasingly, to Kissinger, it had become clear that the major obstacle to an agreement by December was not Saigon but Hanoi:

> The negotiations have had the character where a settlement was always just within our reach, and was always pulled just beyond our reach when we attempted to grasp it. . . . On December 4 . . . the meeting . . . began with Hanoi withdrawing every change that had been agreed to two weeks previously.
>
> We then spent the rest of the week getting back to where we had already been two weeks before. By Saturday, we thought we had narrowed the issues sufficiently where, if the other side had accepted again one section they already had agreed to two weeks previously, the agreement could have been completed.
>
> At that point the president ordered General Haig to return to Washington so that he would be available for the mission, that would then follow, of presenting the agreement to our allies. At that point we thought we were sufficiently

close so that experts could meet to conform the texts so that we would not again encounter the linguistic difficulties which we had experienced previously, and so that we could make sure that the changes that had been negotiated in English would also be reflected in Vietnamese.

When the experts met, they were presented with seventeen new changes in the guise of linguistic changes. When I met again with the special advisor [Le Duc Tho], the one problem which we thought remained on Saturday had grown to two, and a new demand was presented. When we rejected that, it was withdrawn the next day and sharpened up. So we spent our time going through the seventeen linguistic changes and reduced them again to two.

Then, on the last day of the meeting, we asked our experts to meet to compare whether the fifteen changes that had been settled, of the seventeen that had been proposed, now conformed in the two texts. At that point we were presented with sixteen new changes, including four substantive ones. . . ."[10]

Le Duc Tho later rejected this account entirely: "The DRVN side perseveringly maintained the principles [of the October draft] and at the same time made the utmost efforts [to resolve the problems Washington raised], so by December 13 only a few questions were left pending. The two sides agreed to make reports to their respective governments and to continue to exchange notes or to meet again if necessary to resolve these questions. . . . So, on December 13, the negotiations were still in progress and were likely to lead to an early conclusion."[11] Privately, Le Duc Tho told the U.S. negotiators that, within the Politburo, support for the agreement was uncertain; this meant to Tho that he could not show flexibility in the negotiations and had to return to Hanoi.

On December 14, Nixon and Kissinger sent a cable to Hanoi warning that grave consequences would follow if serious negotiations did not resume within seventy-two hours. On December 15, there was a meeting of the subdelegations drafting the protocols and dealing with other technical and linguistic issues. Hanoi again proposed fundamental changes in the agreement, including the demand that release of all U.S. POWs would be conditional on, rather than independent of, release of all political prisoners detained by Saigon. To Nixon and Kissinger, Hanoi was not negotiating seriously.

On December 16, Kissinger reviewed the status of the negotiations for the press. The agreement, he declared, "is 99 percent completed. The only thing that is lacking is one decision in Hanoi, to settle the remaining issues in terms that two weeks previously they had already agreed to." That decision was not to be made until several weeks later.

On December 17, Nixon's ultimatum expired. There was no assurance from Hanoi that serious negotiations would resume. "The impasse was created both by North Vietnamese rigidity and by their whole negotiating approach," Nixon later observed. "They kept a settlement continuously out of reach by injecting new issues whenever current ones neared solution. . . . In mid-December, therefore, we had little choice. Hanoi obviously was stalling for time, hoping that pressures would force us to make an unsatisfactory agreement. Our South Vietnamese friends, in turn, still had some strong reservations about the settlement. The more difficult Hanoi became, the more rigid Saigon grew. There was a danger that the settlement which was so close might be pulled apart by conflicting pressures. We decided to bring home to both Vietnamese parties that there was a price for continuing the conflict."[12]

THE CHRISTMAS BOMBING

On December 18, the president gave the order to execute Linebacker-2, the Christmas bombing of Hanoi. Consistent wih the incursion into Cambodia, the Laos invasion, and the mining of Haiphong (Linebacker-1), Kissinger defended the Christmas bombing of Hanoi in a way designed to cool emotions and to develop support for the move. "After a decision was made that he knew would be unpopular," one of Kissinger's aides later told me, "he would see his favorite journalists and let them believe that he was not initially for the decision. He did this in order to get their sympathy and attention. Then he would explain how difficult a decision it had been for the president and how it really had contributed directly to the search for peace."

By December 18, the negotiations had degenerated into what Kissinger and Nixon had most wanted to avoid: a deadlock beyond which loomed an indefinite delay and another dry-season Communist offensive. In Nixon's opinion, only a massive but controlled application of force could both forestall such an offensive and make an impression on those in the North Vietnamese Politburo who were again talking war and blocking an agreement that they had accepted in principle two months before. Kissinger later explained, "We had come to the conclusion that the negotiations as they were then being conducted were not serious; that for whatever reason, the North Vietnamese at that point had come to the conclusion that protracting the negotiations was more in their interest than concluding them. At the same time," Kissinger continued, "the more difficult Hanoi was, the more rigid Saigon grew; and we could see a prospect, therefore, where we would be caught between the two contending Vietnamese parties, with no element introduced that would change their opinion, with a gradual degeneration of the private talks between Le Duc Tho and me into the same sort of propaganda that the public talks in the Hotel Majestic had reached. . . . It was not generally recognized that when we started the bombing again of North Vietnam we also sent General Haig [General Alexander M. Haig, Jr., then deputy assistant to the president for National Security Affairs] to Saigon to make very clear that this did not mean that we would fail to settle on the terms that we had defined as reasonable. So we really moved in both directions simultaneously."[13]

Some participants in and observers of the negotiations at the White House, while not questioning the faith that both the president and Kissinger put in the bombing, have indicated that the decision was reached with much less coolness than the process described above suggests. Former presidential advisor Charles Colson alleges, for example, that Nixon believed Kissinger had become temporarily unstable with rage at Hanoi and advocated the bombing in a strongly worded telegram from Paris. Kissinger has denied this completely and his spokesmen have alleged that there is nothing in the record that would confirm the Colson charge. The records, unfortunately, are part of the Nixon Presidential Papers, impounded by an order of the U.S. District Court of the District of Columbia, and under the Freedom of Information Act they were not subject to release for review. In any case, at Paris, as one of the U.S. negotiators later recalled, "The level of acrimony had become so great that no one was really surprised by the bombing."

Militarily, the Christmas bombing was the most successful U.S. operation of the war. B-52 evasion tactics had decisively defeated the SAM (surface-to-air missile) defense system, and when the bombing ended, not a single SAM was left. The bombing also destroyed the vital military supplies that it had taken Hanoi months to get because of the naval blockade. So effective were these raids, in fact, that consensus was again growing within the highest circles in the Pentagon that a military victory, not peace, might be at hand in Vietnam.

THE BOMBING AND HANOI'S RETURN
TO THE OCTOBER DRAFT

But as the bombs fell on Hanoi, Washington pressed only for the return of Le Duc Tho and the completion of an agreement that still conformed to the basic principles in the October draft.

North Vietnamese accounts of the final days leading to the Paris Agreement stress that it was Washington, not Hanoi, that had to be persuaded to return to the October draft. From Hanoi's perspective, the key session appears to be that held on January 8: "Comrade Le Duc Tho reiterated his condemnation of the bombing and U.S. delaying tactics during a memorable private meeting on January 8, 1973, in a tone of severity and intensity that was unprecedented in the almost five years of negotiations. At times the U.S. representatives had to suggest that the comrade speak in a lower tone, lest newsmen waiting outside overhear. Embarking on this new meeting phase after the B-52 incident, on the conference table between us and the United States there remained a number of problems arising from the U.S. demand to change what had been agreed upon earlier." This much, of course, was true since the United States did want specific changes in the text agreed to in October. So did Hanoi. The DRV account of the January meetings then continues: "The U.S. advanced the proposal for civilian movement through the DMZ, which was actually a scheme to perpetuate the partition of our country and consolidate the puppet Saigon administration." In interviews, U.S. negotiators dismissed this charge as groundless, though there had been some talk that the freedom-of-movement provisions of the draft agreement could apply to travel between North and South Vietnam after the war.

Next, the DRV account alleged that the United States "did not want to return civilian prisoners [held by the GVN] and sought to prolong the timetable for a return." The U.S. position, of course, was that this issue should be separate from the return of POWs. "It wished to downplay the role of the National Council of Reconciliation and Concord," the DRV account continued (this was a reference to the changes in wording the United States sought for the provisions of the agreement concerning the relationship of the NCRC to the existing structure of the GVN). The DRV account also alleged that the U.S. side "proposed various methods of signing the agreement in an attempt to negate the role of the PRGRSV [Provisional Revolutionary Government of the Republic of South Vietnam]." American insistence on the separate signing ceremonies to placate the GVN did, of course, have this effect.

The DRV account then turned to the topic of troop withdrawal:

> One extremely heated topic of discussion dominated the conference table for five consecutive years and lingered on almost until the conclusion of the conference. This was the persistent U.S. demand for the withdrawal of northern forces from the south. Comrade Le Duc Tho pointed out that the U.S. could not place an aggressor on the same footing with those subjected to aggression, and that the Vietnamese people were authorized to fight their aggressor enemy anywhere in their country. The U.S. finally had to withdraw and give up this demand, and officially recognized that, from a political, spiritual, and legal standpoint it could no longer demand a withdrawal of northern forces.

The U.S. side did, nevertheless, expect that some NVA would be withdrawn as the level of violence subsided.

The DRV account concluded by alleging that the United States "tried to exclude its war compensation to us from the agreement. It used this issue as a bargaining card. We declared frankly that the dollar could not be used to buy or exchange, that the responsibility of the U.S. was to pay its debt owed to our people, and that we were determined to persistently collect this debt at all costs. The U.S. had to agree to acknowledge in the agreement a U.S.

contribution to healing the wounds of war in our country. This contribution really means reparation for the victims of aggression."[14] The sore point here was over Hanoi's last-minute insistence that the word *reparation* be used to characterize the U.S. pledge in Article Twenty-one to "contribute to healing the wounds of war and to postwar reconstruction" of the DRV.

Nor surprisingly, the U.S. negotiators have a totally different recollection of the last days of the secret Paris talks. As one of them told me later:

> When we returned on January 1 for a resumption of the technical talks, we were very strict with the North Vietnamese. We made it clear that Kissinger's return to the negotiations on schedule—on January 5—and the continued suspension of the bombing [Linebacker-2 stopped on December 31] would depend entirely on how serious and productive these talks were.
>
> We agreed to work a full eight hours per day and each night the president received a full report and assessment of the proceedings. Kissinger's return was ultimately delayed a bit because the president felt we were not making sufficient progress. When Kissinger did return, things moved very quickly, and at times we were able to negotiate a section or an article every hour.

Shortly after his return to Paris, Kissinger described the next phase of the negotiations in the following terms:

> It became apparent that both sides were determined to make a serious effort to break the deadlock . . . and we adopted a mode of procedure by which issues in the agreement and issues of principle with respect to the protocols were discussed at meetings between . . . Tho and myself, while concurrently an American team headed by Ambassador Sullivan and a Vietnamese team headed by Vice Minister Thach would work on implementation of the principles as they applied to the protocols.
>
> . . . Le Duc Tho and I then spent the week, first on working out the unresolved issues in the agreement and then the unresolved issues with respect to the protocols, and finally, the surrounding circumstances of schedules and procedures. Ambassador Sullivan remained behind to draft the implementing provisions of the agreements that had been achieved during the week.[15]

But throughout these negotiations, the United States never pressed Hanoi for more than was embodied in the October draft agreement. One member of the negotiating team later recalled asking Kissinger why, given the dramatic impact of the Christmas bombing, he wouldn't press Hanoi for more. Kissinger replied: "Look, you don't understand my instructions. My orders are to get this thing signed before the inauguration."

The agreement was signed on January 27, seven days after the deadline Nixon had set, and it embodied in principle no more than what Hanoi had wanted the United States to sign three months before. It was still an agreement for a cease-fire-in-place that, all parties to it realized, would require more than the stroke of a pen to achieve.

What had the delay and the Christmas bombing achieved? U.S. negotiators saw the bombing as serving a strictly limited purpose. As one put it, "Hanoi had refused to negotiate seriously by December, and the bombing was the only means we had left to get the negotiations going again." It was a fitting assessment of America's last battle in the Indochina war. The bombing symbolized what the United States had all along fought to achieve: the restoration of the status quo.

8

WHAT WENT WRONG?

Through the Vietnam negotiations the United States sought to legitimize the way it ended its decade of direct involvement in the war. To Henry Kissinger, what happened thereafter depended on whether the military stalemate that had made the Paris Agreement possible would last. As he observed in a press conference a year after the agreement had been signed:

> No settlement is self-enforcing. It is not possible to write an agreement whose terms, in themselves, guarantee its performance. Any agreement will last if the hostility of the parties is thereby lessened, if the parties have an incentive to observe it, and/or if the parties pay a penalty for breaking it.
>
> If those three conditions are not met, no matter what the terms of the agreement, there is a tendency toward erosion.
>
> In Viet Nam, in civil war conditions, the hostility of the parties does not significantly lessen.
>
> The incentives and penalties have been affected by many events of the past year [especially the U.S. Congress's cutoff of funds for the air war in Cambodia].
>
> So, at this moment, a great deal depends on the perception of the two sides of the existing military balance.

What had Kissinger initially expected? He initialed the Paris Agreement believing that he had achieved understandings with Le Duc Tho about the following: the future level of warfare in the south, that détente would involve a tapering off of Communist-country aid to Hanoi, that follow-up negotiations would occur if the ambiguities of the agreement created problems, and that U.S.-DRV relations would be normalized. But in mid-February 1973, when he visited Hanoi on what he called "an exploratory mission to determine how to move from hostility to normalization" of relations with the DRV, Kissinger had a disturbing meeting with North Vietnamese premier

Pham Van Dong. Pham suggested that most of the DRV's Politburo saw the Paris Agreement as little more than a face-saving instrument that permitted U.S. withdrawal. He called the NCRC a transitional coalition and said that the cease-fire was primarily with the Americans. As Pham put it, the cease-fire-in-place definitely would not be permitted to evolve into another way of partitioning Vietnam.

Nevertheless, Kissinger hoped that the Paris Agreement would eventually lead to a peaceful political settlement. After his Hanoi trip, for example, he told the press:

> The big problem is whether Indochina can be moved from a condition of guerrilla war or even open warfare to a condition in which the energies of the peoples of that region are concentrated on constructive purposes.
>
> If that objective can be achieved, if that process can start for a period of three or four years, then any decision to resume the conflict by any of the parties will have to be taken in an environment of peace and against the experience of the population in [war-like] tasks with which they have become almost totally unfamiliar.[1]

However, in a war in which time was a weapon and negotiation a tactic, the Paris Agreement proved neither a substitute for a military victory by Saigon nor a deterrent to the continued pursuit of military victory by Hanoi.

For Saigon, as one high GVN official remarked, the agreement permitted "continuing the war and improving our position on the battlefield with American help. The fact that there was an agreement took the edge off our American critics for a time." Saigon never believed that the causes of the war were negotiable, or that Hanoi would compromise unless it was defeated militarily in the south. Just as the war itself had seemed more important to the Americans fighting it than it did to the GVN in 1966 and 1967, so also the negotiations and the Paris Agreement were regarded by South Vietnamese officials as something far more desirable from Washington's standpoint than from Saigon's.

Throughout the negotiations, Thieu used them as a means of demonstrating his independence from the Americans and a chance to show his critics on the right, as well as the Communists, that he was no U.S. puppet. Thieu's intransigence delayed the start of substantive talks, accounted in part for the three-month delay that occurred after Henry Kissinger announced that peace was at hand, and necessitated the invention of a complicated signing ceremony in which, at Thieu's insistence, neither the GVN nor the PRG formally acknowledged the other's existence. The terms of the agreement were also not surprising to Saigon; by mid-1972 the GVN was prepared to continue the war regardless of what was agreed on in Paris. So, for Saigon, the negotiations provided time and the maximum amount of U.S. assistance possible to improve its position on the battlefield.

For Hanoi and the PRG, the negotiations provided a means to sustain the fighting, and the agreement provided a means eventually to win the war.[2] By 1969, the kind of war Hanoi wanted to fight required a secure and uninterrupted flow of supplies from its Communist allies into the north, and thence into the south via the Ho Chi Minh trail. The bombing suspension that accompanied the negotiations provided security for the NVA's rear bases. But, as a Hanoi radio commentary pointed out on August 13, 1972: ". . . in solving the South Vietnam problem one cannot deal only with the military problem. . . . To cease-fire or to release the captured soldiers are only concrete acts; the political objective is the only problem of decisive significance. Such a cease-fire cannot eliminate the cause of the war. Instead, such a cease-fire will permanently maintain the factors for waging war again at any time." And this is precisely what the Paris Agreement did.

Indeed, as one high-level U.S. official observed in a January 1975 interview in Saigon, "Hanoi basically saw the Paris Agreement as a generous and face-saving way for the United States to end its Vietnam involvement. They then expected Thieu to be ousted, PRG territorial control to be consolidated, and the National Council of Reconciliation and Concord to be established. They still expect this. They still expect the GVN to collapse. They feel the military balance is in their favor, that Saigon's soldiers know this, and that sooner or later Thieu and his generals will blunder into a defeat."

THE POSTWAR WAR, 1973–1974

As President Nixon wrote in his 1973 state of the world report, the Paris Agreement made it possible for the U.S. prisoners of war to be returned, and it provided Saigon with a "decent interval" of two years, in which "to demonstrate inherent strength." But the Paris Agreement did not end the war—and neither Washington, nor Saigon, nor Hanoi expected that it would. However, Kissinger did believe that the Paris Agreement would precipitate movement toward a political settlement. Speaking to newsmen shortly before the agreement was signed, he observed, ". . . it is not easy to achieve through negotiations what has not been achieved on the battlefield, and if you look at the settlements that have been made in the postwar period, the lines of demarcation have almost always followed the lines of actual control. . . . we have taken the position throughout that the agreement cannot be analyzed in terms of any one of its provisions, but it has to be seen in its totality and in terms of the evolution that it starts."[3]

But, since neither Saigon nor Hanoi gained in Paris all that they had gained on the battlefield, both believed that further fighting was essential to achieving their basic goals. For Saigon, continuing the war would prove to the north that it could not impose a military solution once U.S. forces left Vietnam. As President Thieu declared in a speech in June 1974:

> We will . . . not allow the Communists to use military means in lieu of the already agreed-to peaceful solution—the one provided for by the Paris Agreement, which calls for a cease-fire and an election. We will not let the Communists resort to war to solve the Vietnam problem. We must prove to them that they shall fail in their attempt to resort to military means, that their renewed aggression shall take them nowhere, and they had better sit down and negotiate seriously so that an election may soon be organized. All that we have done in reaction to Communist truce violations is only aimed at making the Communists realize the pointlessness of their use of force.

For Hanoi, continued fighting was essential to eliminating the "leopard spots" created by a cease-fire-in-place. As the lead editorial in the Hanoi journal *Vietnam Courier* declared in September 1973:

> The Paris Agreement recognizes the existence in South Viet Nam of two administrations, two armed forces, and two zones of control. Does this entail the threat of a new and permanent partition of Viet Nam, now split into three parts? Drawing lessons from their experiences of 1954, the Vietnamese negotiators dismissed all U.S.-Saigon proposals for regrouping belligerent forces into a number of well-defined areas: such an operation would facilitate the execution of Nguyen Van Thieu's plan to liquidate "Viet Cong pockets" at a given moment with the support of the U.S.A. or, if need be, to perpetuate the division of South Viet Nam. On insistence of the DRVN and PRG, the U.S.A. had finally to agree that the cease-fire be carried out on the spot, which makes the map of South Viet Nam look like a "leopard skin." But this very "leopard skin" must disappear within the shortest time. The existence of two zones, the recognition of which is imperative in the present phase in order to achieve a solution to South Viet Nam's internal problems, is not intended to last indefinitely.

> Certainly it is not a *complete* victory and this is also a question of the relation of forces reflecting itself in the Agreement concluded: the PRG . . . will have to coexist for a certain time with the puppet regime. . . . As shown by the events since January 1973, the situation "half-war, half-peace" will be the backcloth for a multisided struggle on the ground in South Viet Nam with its political, economic, and also its military aspects.

But as 1973 began, both sides were ill-prepared to expand their political support beyond areas they had controlled for decades. Much of the PRG's infrastructure was still weak: the prestige of, and latent sympathy for, the Communist movement had been much reduced by the brutality and the terrorist tactics used during and since the 1968 Tet offensive. For the non-Communists, political mobilization was still largely a product of the antagonisms among them, not a common cause designed to prepare the GVN for a political struggle with the PRG. When U.S. forces were removed from the equation, the countryside reverted to the patterns of control that each side had maintained rather consistently since the war began. It was in these areas that, the "postwar war," as my Vietnamese friends referred to it, was fought.

From the first speculations over the possibility of an agreement leading to a cease-fire-in-place through the end of the 1973 dry season (that is, from early October 1972 through spring 1973), both the PRG and the GVN concentrated on expandng the territory they controlled. Each accused the other of capturing key access points to South Vietnam, populated areas of the countryside adjacent or strategic to the defense of those areas, and certain provincial and district capitals. For the PRG, such land-grabbing made good sense; for the GVN, it was suicide.

In the first year after the Paris Agreement, Saigon alleged that it had been violated 35,673 times. The PRG charged Saigon with 301,000 violations: 34,266 land-grabbing operations, 35,532 artillery shellings, 14,749 aerial bombardments and reconnaissances, and 216,550 police and pacification operations. The initial intent of both sides was to take territory that would later have to be adjudicated by the Two Party Joint Military Commission (TPJMC) as provided for in Article 3(b) of the Paris Agreement (see Appendix C, pp. 188–97). When the TPJMC proved unable even to inspect contested areas, let alone to determine "the areas controlled by each party and modalities of [troop] stationing," both sides fought to regain the territory they had lost.

In the first eighteen months after the agreement, the PRG withdrew from more than 90 hamlets in which it had maintained a long-term presence and from some 300 others that had been seized during land-grabbing operations in January 1973. Through deploying its forces more thinly, the GVN claimed it had increased its control over nearly 1000 hamlets. The lack of Communist aggressiveness in the land-grabbing war had long-range tactical value: in attempting to assert control over areas long ruled by the PRG, the GVN was encouraged to overextend its forces. The more the government pursued this war, the more vulnerable it became. The more it appeared to be an aggressor, the less military aid it would receive from a rebellious U.S. Congress, and the less it appeared to the population of South Vietnam to be working toward peace. "If we attack our enemies," one captured Communist directive noted, "we will suffer politically. . . . If we permit them to move into our areas, then counterattack, our political image will remain intact." Reporting from such contested areas in 1973 and 1974, U.S. journalists pointed out that GVN control was increasingly restricted to the daytime hours—a pattern reminiscent of that prevailing during most of the 1960s.

On the GVN side, what was needed was both expansion of governmental services and effective security forces that would assure the government twenty-four-hour control and, thereby, a chance for its propaganda, pacification, and economic development programs to take root. Thieu sought to accomplish this through an official administrative revolution begun in mid-spring of 1973. This involved the centralization of all program management and decision-making in the hands of officials personally chosen by Thieu. As Ngo Dinh Diem had used the government structure as a substitute for popular political mobilization, so Thieu now tried to use it as an alternative both to accommodation with the PRG and to mobilization of the popular support that would be essential if the NCRC should be established. But territory seized by the South Vietnamese government in the last moments of the 1972 war did not prove to be fertile ground for "reforms." In this respect, Thieu imitated his predecessors: Saigon governments consistently tended to apply new programs and concepts to areas in which problems were the most acute, or to launch nationwide efforts that spread resources so thinly that the population was frequently alienated from the government rather than mobilized by it.

It was a familiar pattern. Hanoi had always used lulls in the war to consolidate and strengthen the bases of its support in the south. The Saigon government used these lulls to expand its territory rather than to bring competent administration and effective security to the areas already under its control.

Along with the land-grabbing war came the struggle over a series of besieged strategic military bases. These bases alternated as tempting targets for the NVA and as strategic outposts from which the GVN could harass and occasionally interdict infiltration from the Ho Chi Minh trail into the central and northern regions of South Vietnam. They had been the scene of heavy conventional fighting in the past. One such base, Tong le Chanh, was under attack for 411 days before it fell to the North Vietnamese. Most, of these bases, beginning with the fall of Le Minh base in western Pleiku on September 24, 1973, were lost to the North Vietnamese several times by the end of 1974. From the North Vietnamese viewpoint, attacks against these bases were designed as much to relieve pressure on supply routes as they were to test GVN morale and to produce in the average GVN soldier's mind the expectation of defeat.

The most intense fighting over these bases—more than 8000 soldiers on both sides were reported killed—occurred from early March through April 1974. By the first week in April, five GVN bases, many of them former U.S.

Green Beret outposts, had fallen to NVA assaults. Communist spokesmen hailed the attacks as "a necessary act in order to prevent and stop Saigon land-grabbing operations." The outposts taken secured infiltration routes from Cambodia and NVA use of a newly built road extending from the demilitarized zone to the Parrot's Beak (see map, p. 172).

As fighting over the strategic fire bases continued in northern and central South Vietnam, the PRG and the GVN were also fighting over the Mekong Delta's rice. There were no front lines in the rice war because the boundaries between zones of government and Communist control in the delta depended on the time of day and the season. Early in 1973, the GVN declared it would deny rice to PRG zones. That August, local GVN officials confiscated all rice in excess of a week's supply from each farming household in territory adjacent to PRG areas. Families were then given weekly withdrawal privileges from provincial storehouses. The excess rice of each household was sold to the government at prices averaging 10 to 50 percent below the market price.

The government's blockade proved ineffective: by paying two to three times the market price, the PRG retained unhindered access to all the rice it needed. Local officials meanwhile used their confiscation powers to increase their exactions from the farmers. Cash values of crops were downgraded arbitrarily, and payments were delayed for from one to several weeks. The net result of these developments was that Saigon, not the PRG, was denied access to rice. By early 1975, GVN officials estimated that fully 20 percent of the 1974 crop had been lost in this manner.

By the fall of 1974, the military balance began shifting to Hanoi's favor (see map, p. 172). There were then more North Vietnamese Army (NVA) regular combat forces in South Vietnam than at any time during the past decade. Estimates of total Communist troop strength ranged from 285,000 (preferred by most U.S. analysts) to 387,000 (suggested by GVN officials). Considerably more than half of these troops were deployed in regular infantry divisions in the area extending from the central highlands northward to the DMZ. U.S. officials feared that, if North Vietnam committed any of its estimated four to six reserve divisions to an offensive in the central highlands, or to a drive against the coastal cities of Hue or Danang, the GVN would have a less than equal chance of containing the attack. Communist artillery and armor equaled that of the GVN in number, while more than 10 percent of this inventory included weapons that could be fired completely out of the range of the ARVN's field guns. Enough ordnance had been stockpiled by the NVA to sustain an offensive at the 1972 level for a year.

Ranged against the North Vietnamese and PRG forces were 1.1 million GVN regular and paramilitary defense forces. While fully one-half to two-thirds of Saigon's forces were engaged in static defense missions, no more

VIETNAM: 1973-74

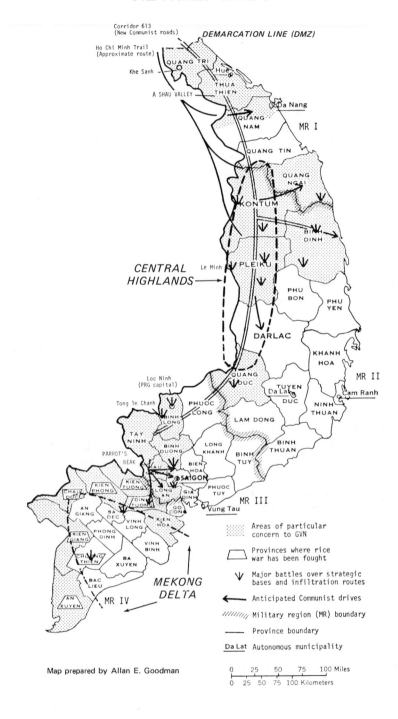

Corridor 613
(New Communist roads)

DEMARCATION LINE (DMZ)

Ho Chi Minh Trail
(Approximate route)

Khe Sanh

QUANG TRI

Hue

THUA
THIEN

A SHAU VALLEY

Da Nang

QUANG
NAM

MR I

QUANG TIN

QUANG
NGAI

KONTUM

BINH
DINH

CENTRAL
HIGHLANDS

Le Minh

PLEIKU

PHU
BON

PHU
YEN

DARLAC

KHANH
HOA

MR II

Loc Ninh
(PRG capital)

QUANG
DUC

TUYEN
DUC

Da Lat

Cam Ranh

Tong le Chanh

PHUOC
LONG

LAM DONG

NINH
THUAN

BINH
LONG

TAY
NINH

BINH
DUONG

LONG
KHANH

BINH
THUAN

PARROT'S
BEAK

BINH
TUY

BIEN
HOA

SAIGON

CHAU
DOC

KIEN
PHONG

KIEN
TUONG

LONG
AN

GIA
DINH

PHUOC
TUY

MR III

AN
GIANG

SA
DEC

DINH
TUONG

GO
CON

Vung Tau

KIEN
GIANG

PHONG
DINH

VINH
LONG

KIEN
HOA

Areas of particular
concern to GVN

CHUONG
THIEN

BA
XUYEN

VINH
BINH

Provinces where rice
war has been fought

BAC
LIEU

MEKONG
DELTA

Major battles over strategic
bases and infiltration routes

AN
XUYEN

MR IV

Anticipated Communist drives

Military region (MR) boundary

Province boundary

Da Lat Autonomous municipality

Map prepared by Allan E. Goodman

0   25   50   75   100 Miles

0   25 50 75 100 Kilometers

than 10 percent of the NVA forces were similarly deployed. Some ARVN commanders suggested that, as long as their troops had both to defend 90 percent of the population and to fight the North Vietnamese, even a delicate balance of forces no longer existed. They were right.

THE BREAKDOWN OF THE AGREEMENT

By 1974, both Hanoi and Saigon declared that military action was necessary to save the Paris Agreement. Their cease-fire had never been more than a less-fire. The International Commission for Control and Supervision (ICCS), and the Joint Military Commissions responsible for the maintenance of the cease-fire, were never permitted to determine which contested areas were controlled by the GVN and which by the PRG. The cease-fire and resupply inspection mechanisms were hamstrung from the start by the noncooperation of the PRG and Hanoi. The activities of the inspection forces ceased altogether after one unarmed U.S. member of the FPJMT, investigating, with the consent of the PRG, an air crash site where remains of MIAs were reported, stepped from his clearly marked helicopter and was shot dead.

Hanoi charged that it had been misled by the United States into thinking that all U.S. military installations in South Vietnam would be dismantled within sixty days of the agreement. The United States, instead, had transferred to the GVN title to all of its facilities before it signed the Paris Agreement. The North Vietnamese infiltrated additional military personnel into South Vietnam and introduced entirely new weapon systems into the south, while the United States provided Saigon with a few new F5-E fighter aircraft to replace and augment its force of F5-As. According to the terms of the agreement, both sides were permitted only to replace "armaments, munition, and war materiel which have been destroyed, damaged, worn-out or used up . . . on the basis of piece-for-piece, of the same characteristics and properties. . . ."[4]

The agreement provided for the return of all POWs, the release of political prisoners, and a full accounting for all soldiers listed as missing in action (MIA). Only the U.S. POWs were returned to the last man. There has never been a complete accounting by Hanoi of the U.S. MIAs. The GVN charged Hanoi with imprisoning 60,000 soldiers and civilians, while political prisoners in GVN jails were released only in April 1975 when the PRG captured Saigon.

The neutrality of Cambodia and Laos was not respected, nor was an Indochina-wide cease-fire realized. Hostilities in Laos stopped for a time, but this was largely because the United States no longer needed the up-country communications complex to guide bombers to targets in North Vietnam. The Laotian forces of the right, center, and left proclaimed a cease-fire on

February 21, 1973, and fourteen months later formed a coalition government. The coalition was soon dominated by the Communist Pathet Lao. Hostilities were resumed shortly thereafter, and the coalition collapsed in the wake of the fall of Phnom Penh and Saigon in the spring of 1975.

The Paris Agreement (Article 12[a]) had also provided that "the two South Vietnamese parties shall sign an agreement on the internal matters of South Vietnam as soon as possible and do their utmost to accomplish this within ninety days after the cease-fire comes into effect, in keeping with the South Vietnamese people's aspiration for peace, independence and democracy." Talks between the two parties began in late March 1973. Over a period of two years, the always acrimonious, sometimes stalled, and ultimately boycotted (after April 16, 1974) discussions revealed only that the GVN and the PRG favored establishing a National Council of Reconciliation and Concord. However, Saigon objected, as it had for the better part of a decade, to the provision in Article 12[a] that the council be composed "of three equal segments." Thieu saw this as giving the Communists undue advantage, even though the council was to function on the basis of unanimity. He argued that the third segment—called the third political tendency by its adherents in Saigon—would be dominated by the Communists, and he worked steadily to isolate, imprison, and generally weaken those associated with it.

Nor was a nationwide plebiscite held. Thieu did seek one shortly after the agreements were signed, propagandizing on banners over Saigon streets that the virtue of "quick elections" was "quick victory." If elections were held before the PRG's territorial control could be consolidated, he reasoned, the GVN would demonstrate both its legitimacy and its widespread support. The PRG declined to accept the challenge. It refused to participate in elections until Article 11 (which ensured "the democratic liberties of the people: personal freedom, freedom of speech, freedom of the press, freedom of meeting, freedom of organization, freedom of political activities, freedom of belief, freedom of movement, freedom of residence, freedom of work, right to property ownership, and right to free enterprise") was fully implemented. Thieu countered by demanding that all North Vietnamese troops be withdrawn from the south before Article 11 could be implemented.

In late March 1974, there was some speculation about a breakthrough in the GVN-PRG talks over a six-point PRG proposal and a four-point GVN counterproposal. At the forty-seventh session of the talks, the PRG proposed: (1) full implementation of the cease-fire, (2) return of all captured personnel within three months and an end to political imprisonment, (3) implementation of Article 11, (4) formation of the National Council for Reconciliation and Concord within ninety days, (5) general elections for a constitutional assembly within a year after the council was formed, for the purpose of drafting a new constitution, and (6) mutual troop reductions pending the establishment of a unified army by a new government.

Despite characterizing this proposal as "merely a rearrangement of a shopworn leaflet released on April 25, 1973, which the Communists have daily reiterated for more than a year," the GVN proposed forming joint working groups to set up procedures on implementation of Article 11, establishment of the National Council, organization of general elections, and demobilization. The groups were to complete their work within thirty days. Implementation of the cease-fire and prisoner exchanges, the GVN argued, should be left to the machinery established by the Paris Agreement. However, in mid-April 1974, the GVN began a boycott of all talks to protest the NVA/PRG military buildup. A month later, the PRG's participation in talks was suspended indefinitely as a counterprotest. By October 1974, the PRG side refused to negotiate further on any issue with Saigon until the Thieu government resigned.

In essence, what the agreement had left up to the two South Vietnamese parties to negotiate was not negotiable. The question of who was to have power in the south, both the GVN and the PRG concluded, could only be resolved on the battlefield, not at the conference table. Hoping that international pressure might prevent any resumption of large-scale warfare, the United States arranged a conference for February 26 to March 2, 1973, (see Appendix G) at which twelve countries were to guarantee the provisions of the Paris Agreement. When these signatories were later asked by the United States to urge Hanoi to halt its 1975 offensive in South Vietnam, not one agreed to do so. Kissinger's expectation that the level of military assistance reaching North Vietnam would decline also was not vindicated. By the end of 1974, Hanoi was receiving approximately twice as much aid as it had during the previous years of the war, twice what the United States was then authorized to provide Saigon.

Throughout the spring and early summer of 1973, U.S. and North Vietnamese representatives held talks on the creation of a Joint Economic Commission through which the U.S. would implement its pledge to contribute to the postwar reconstruction of the DRV. For the most part, negotiations were technical; they avoided charges and countercharges about violations of the agreement. The negotiators went relatively far in terms of talking about specific amounts and projects that would be appropriate for U.S. support. But in the fall of 1973, the U.S. Congress passed a law prohibiting any funds being given to Hanoi until Hanoi accounted for all of the U.S. MIAs. This Hanoi refused to do.

For nearly a week in June, Kissinger and Tho negotiated what they characterized as an amplification and consolidation of the original agreement.

Kissinger explained to the press why such follow-up negotiation had become necessary:

> . . . during the course of March and April the United States became quite concerned about the manner in which the cease-fire agreement was being implemented. We were specifically concerned about the following points:
>
> One, the inadequate implementation of the cease-fire.
>
> Secondly, the continued infiltration into South Viet-Nam and the continued utilization of Laos and Cambodia as corridors for that infiltration.
>
> Three, we were concerned about the inadequate accounting for the missing in action.
>
> Fourth, we were concerned about the violations of the demilitarized zone.
>
> Fifth, we were concerned about the inadequate cooperation with the international control commission and the slow staffing of the two-party military commission.
>
> Sixth, we were concerned about the violations of Article 20 requiring the withdrawal of foreign troops from Laos and Cambodia.[5]

But the resulting June communiqué (see Appendix H), read like the Paris Agreement's obituary. Kissinger and Tho had met nine times that week and the communiqué was the result of more than forty hours of their work. But the hopelessness of the situation was evident: throughout the June talks both Saigon and Hanoi continued to insist on many of the very issues that had stymied the negotiations in October, November, and December 1972. At the conclusion of the June negotiations, Kissinger said that he hoped "to be able to reduce my own participation in this process [of follow-up negotiations] in order to preserve my emotional stability."[6] In late June, the U.S. Congress voted to end all funds for U.S. air operations in Indochina on August 15, 1973. Throughout July, former White House counsel John Dean captured the nation's attention with his side of the Watergate story; by fall, the Nixon administration was under siege domestically, just as its foreign policy of détente was to face a challenge in the Middle East.

With the Cambodian bombing cut off, the president and Kissinger realized that the United States had lost its only means of enforcing the Paris Agreement. There had been debate within the administration in April 1973 over whether a resumption of the bombing of North Vietnam would be an appropriate response to, as Kissinger later put it, Hanoi's "flagrant violations of the agreements." But, Kissinger later said, "President Nixon . . . never made a final decision . . ."[7] Many U.S. officials believe that, when it did become clear that U.S. air power would no longer be used in Indochina, the last obstacle to an all-out Communist offensive was removed. Kissinger and Tho met once more in December, with little result. Their talks on December 20, 1973, were designed, from Hanoi's perspective, to see if further progress could be made toward implementing U.S. postwar assistance to the DRV. Kissinger reportedly took the position that one part of the agreement could not be implemented as long as other parts of it were being violated. He stressed the need for the level of military activity in South Vietnam to be reduced, for Hanoi to account for all of the American MIAs, and for the North Vietnamese troops to withdraw from Cambodia and Laos.

With the Paris Agreement moribund, Kissinger's most difficult negotiations were those he had with Congress over future aid to Vietnam. Both he and Nixon had assured Thieu that the United States would not stand idly by in the face of continuing pressure from the NVA and that U.S. aid to Saigon would continue at appropriate levels. In November and December 1972, and again during his state visit in 1973, Thieu pressed Nixon for a specific pledge, but Nixon continually responded by saying that only Congress could make such pledges. As late as the fall of 1974, however, senior U.S. officials were still telling their South Vietnamese counterparts that Saigon would get its aid.

But the U.S. Congress ultimately proved impervious to the pleadings of many that military assistance for the 1974–1975 fiscal year be appropriated, even at the authorized level. Administration spokesmen argued that Saigon spent at the level of the actual authorization ($1 billion) and geared its defense program to that ceiling rather than to the $700 million that was appropriated in September 1974 after a surprise cut was made during House debate. And of the $700 million then available for military aid, more than $400 million were charged off for shipping costs. At the end of the pipeline was less than $300 million in military assistance. Exclusive of their shipping costs, Moscow and Peking provided Hanoi nearly $400 million in war materiel. Interviews with a variety of GVN officials acknowledged that the U.S. cut, coupled with worldwide inflation, gravely affected Saigon's capability to respond to a North Vietnamese offensive. To these pleadings and assessments congressional leaders tended to respond as did Senator Hubert Humphrey, floor manager of the Foreign Assistance Act, in a speech he gave at the time:

After millions of words about the lessons of Vietnam, we ignore the most important lesson, that political battles cannot be resolved by force of arms.

We learned this lesson at great sacrifice to our nation. Yet our policy-makers now are engaged in a course of action which does not recognize this basic reality of Indochina. The United States has embarked upon a course of encouraging the funding of maximum military confrontation, hoping that somehow those we are supporting can prevail.

. . . How can the policy of military confrontation be sustained when it is clear that neither the Congress nor the American public is willing to fund the wars in Vietnam and Cambodia at high levels for the indefinite future?

Kissinger later told Barbara Walters, in an interview on the May 5, 1975, "Today Show," that he would never have negotiated the Paris Agreement if he had thought the U.S. Congress would have proved so difficult. Because of the restrictions placed on the use of American air power and the reluctance of Congress in 1974 to appropriate adequate aid for Saigon, Kissinger said he believed the resumption of the war by North Vietnam was inevitable. Ultimately, in the face of that prospect Saigon's army, and then its government, collapsed.

WITH THE END AT HAND

I originally thought it would be possible to end this study of the Vietnam negotiations with a prediction of how an eventual political settlement between the Communists and the non-Communists in South Vietnam could evolve. Such a settlement, I thought, was likely on the one hand, because of the strong anticommunism of substantial segments of Vietnamese religious and social forces, and on the other, because it was difficult for me to imagine the GVN collapsing overnight. But with a political settlement, I did expect the creation of a government not unlike the tripartite one hinted at in the Paris Agreement. Thereafter, I expected the gradual emergence of the PRG as the dominant political force in the south, just as, in 1945 and 1946, the Viet Minh—even though a minority in the north—came to dominate all other nationalist forces in the coalition government established there after World War II.

In retrospect I underestimated the PRG's prediction that the "internal contradictions" in the GVN would cause it to collapse, eliminating the need for Saigon's army to be defeated militarily. Such internal contradictions were abundant, even to the most casual observers: proclaiming an economic and social revolution, the GVN depended on the very elites who stood to lose the most from change. The peasant soldier was still led by ill-trained, urban-born scions of the elite, and army officer assignments were still largely determined by bribery. In 1975, nationalist political forces were as unprepared and unorganized for a political struggle with the PRG as they had been in 1965.

Yet, to my mind, each year that the GVN managed to survive made its collapse a little less likely. Moreover, the political opposition that Thieu faced in the fall of 1974 hardly compared with that against Diem in 1963, and the ARVN appeared to be equal to the military challenge it expected from the NVA in 1975. As one high U.S. embassy official put it that January: "We are talking about well-equipped experienced [ARVN] soldiers who know we won't do their fighting for them. The NVA is going to launch another offensive but all our indicators show that it will be nothing compared to what the ARVN withstood and pushed back at Tet 1968 or in the 1972 Easter offensive." With respect to the strength of the 1975 NVA offensive, the embassy official was right.

I traveled to Saigon in early January 1975 to conduct one last series of interviews for this book. Another dry season had begun in Vietnam and with it, the postwar war resumed against the backdrop of the breakdown of the Paris Agreement. I arrived on the eve of the fall of the provincial capital of Phuoc Long, although its loss was not confirmed by the GVN for several days. But the next day, a Vietnamese friend told me that when he saw the street banners go up proclaiming: "All compatriots support the heroic defenders of Phuoc Long," he knew the end was at hand. What I learned during the next three weeks convinced me that he was right.

After three weeks of interviewing Vietnamese officials and opposition political leaders, I concluded that the most well-organized segments of the South Vietnamese population actually expected a Communist victory. Their leaders began to use the word *accommodation* synonymously with *adaptation*. *Accommodation* had once referred to "live and let live" arrangements whereby GVN supporters coexisted with the NLF. But by January 1975, *adaptation* meant surviving while living under communism. Cabinet-level GVN officials believed that Phuoc Long was only the beginning. As one cabinet minister put it, "Much more of our territory will now be lost." I was repeatedly told that the boundary between North and South Vietnam was now, de facto, south of the seventeenth parallel and that there was to be a line drawn inside South Vietnam dividing it into eastern and western (Communist) regions.

The political opposition was equally pessimistic about both prospects for further partitioning of Vietnam and accommodation with the PRG. Consequently, the opposition was leaderless by January 1975 and no longer willing either to struggle for an alternative to Thieu or to participate in politics. The active opposition leaders who two years earlier were rarely in their offices due to their political activities in the countryside now were never in their offices due to having returned to private life. No one was coming forward to take their place.

When a strategic retreat was ordered from the central highlands in mid-March, the South Vietnamese soldiers panicked and in domino fashion abandoned outpost after outpost. They were reacting as much to the prospect of a fight with the NVA as to their future under the GVN. ARVN soldiers no longer believed (if they ever did) that they would eventually win against the NVA, and they no longer wanted war. As one U.S. embassy official put it in April 1975:

We should have asked ourselves long ago how an army can go on functioning when it is simply a business organization in which everything is for sale, from what you eat to a transfer or a promotion. We never encouraged the Vietnamese forces to fight aggressively, to take the offensive. We fought the war for them and made them over dependent on air support. We prepared them for conventional war when the Communists were fighting unconventionally, and then, when the Communists finally adopted conventional tactics, the South Vietnamese didn't know what to do. The fact they have no leadership is largely our fault; we made them followers, so successfully that even the soldiers who were willing to fight got killed or wounded as a result of incompetence, or lost by default. . . .[8]

From Ban Me Thuot in the central highlands, to Danang on the northern coast, and to the Mekong Delta in the south, retreating ARVN soldiers refused to believe that the future promised to them could be achieved by the government that the United States had supported in Saigon. America's lost peace in Vietnam came not only because of what was negotiated, but also because neither the process of negotiations nor the agreement itself produced a Saigon government that could end the war—through accommodation with the PRG or through victory over it.

I have not written this book with a view to apportioning responsibility for the whole chapter for history labeled "The Vietnam War." But such an accounting would certainly have to come to terms not only with what made a meaningful negotiated settlement unlikely, but also with the wisdom of the decision by successive American presidents to seek such a settlement, and the implications that this decision had for the strategy by which the war was fought. In retrospect, to be incremental in our military strategy and conciliatory in our negotiating strategy with an adversary who, from the outset, equated restraint with weakness, and to whom compromise was inconceivable, had the effect of obscuring what the costs of intervention in Vietnam were likely to be and, equally important, what the ultimate gains there might look like. But when U.S. policy-makers suddenly faced the end of the proverbial tunnel in Vietnam and witnessed the Saigon army fleeing the countryside—abandoning in a matter of days what it had taken a decade to secure and "pacify"—they realized there was no realistic option open that would have justified the investment. Probably there never was. Thus are the lives of men and women and the spirit of great nations wasted in adventures that ultimately bring neither the peace intended nor honor.

A Postwar War, 1973–1975

A busload of people who had fled what they feared would be another North Vietnamese offensive arrive in Saigon in January 1975. Some refugees had been constantly on the move since the Tet offensive of 1968. *(Photograph by the author)*

REFUGEES

THE BEGINNING OF THE END

The fall of Phuoc Long. Smaller headline is from Pacific *Stars and Stripes.* Both papers were published January 6, 1975. *(Photograph by the author)*

REMEMBRANCE

This monument to the U.S. war dead was purportedly one of
the first that the Communists demolished when they "liberated"
Saigon. *(Photograph by the author)*

THE VICTORS

A PRG village council meeting in Binh Dinh province. *(Courtesy of Charles
Benoît)*

LIBERATION?
Scene from a liberated village, Binh Dinh province. *(Courtesy of Charles Benoît)*

GRIM TASK
A meeting between U.S. and Communist negotiators in Hanoi, one of the last before collapse of the Paris Agreement. It was held to discuss arrangements for the return of the remains of the U.S. war dead. *(U.S. Army photograph)*

APPENDIXES

The purpose in collecting the documents that follow has been to provide a reference text of the Paris Agreement and the key statements concerning its implementation.

Human Costs of the War

Statistics compiled from January 1, 1961 (when official accounting begins) to March 29, 1973, when the last U.S. combat troops were withdrawn as per Article 5 of the Paris Agreement.

Cost to South Vietnam

ARVN killed in action	166,429
ARVN wounded in action	453,039
Civilians killed	415,000
Civilians wounded	935,000
Civilian refugees	8,819,700

Cost to North Vietnam and the PRG

NVA/PRG killed in action	937,562
NVA/PRG wounded in action	unknown
Civilians killed	unknown
Civilians wounded	unknown
Civilian refugees	unknown

Cost to United States (maximum troop level of 543,000 reached in April 1969)

Killed in action	45,943
Wounded in action	303,616
Missing in action	1,333
Died from noncombat causes	10,298

Hanoi's Proposal for a Kissinger-Tho Agreement

Translated by Radio Hanoi, October 25, 1972.

1. The United States respects the independence, sovereignty, unity and territorial integrity of Vietnam as recognized by the 1954 Geneva Agreements.

2. Twenty-four hours after the signing of the agreement, a cease-fire shall be observed throughout South Vietnam. The United States will stop all its military activities, and end the bombing and mining in North Vietnam. Within 60 days there will be a total withdrawal from South Vietnam of troops and military personnel of the United States and those of the foreign countries allied with the United States and with the Republic of Vietnam. The two South Vietnamese parties shall not accept the introduction of troops, military advisers and military personnel, armaments, munitions, and war material [*sic*] into South Vietnam. The two South Vietnamese parties shall be permitted to make periodical replacements of armaments, munitions, and war material [*sic*] that have been worn out or damaged after the cease-fire, on the basis of piece for piece of similar characteristics and properties. The United States will not continue its military involvement or intervene in the internal affairs of South Vietnam.

3. The return of all captured and detained personnel of the parties shall be carried out simultaneously with the U.S. troops withdrawal.

4. The principles for the exercise of the South Vietnamese people's right to self-determination are as follows: the South Vietnamese people shall decide themselves the political future of South Vietnam through genuinely free and democratic general elections under international supervision; the United States is not committed to any political tendency or to any personality in South Vietnam, and it does not seek to impose a pro-American regime in Saigon; national reconciliation and concord will be achieved, the democratic liberties of the people ensured; an administrative structure called the National Reconciliation and Concord of three equal segments will be set up to promote the implementation of the signed agreements by the Provisional Revolutionary Government of the Republic of South Vietnam and the Government of the Republic of Vietnam and to organize the general elections, the two South Vietnamese parties will consult about the formation of councils at lower levels; the question of Vietnamese armed forces in South Vietnam shall be settled by the two South Vietnamese parties in a spirit of national

reconciliation and concord, equality and mutual respect, without foreign interference, in accordance with the postwar situation; among the questions to be discussed by the two South Vietnamese parties are steps to reduce the military number on both sides and to demobilize the troops being reduced; the two South Vietnamese parties shall sign an agreement on the internal matters of South Vietnam as soon as possible and will do their utmost to accomplish this within three months after the cease-fire comes into effect.

5. The reunification of Vietnam shall be carried out step-by-step through peaceful means.

6. There will be formed a four-party joint military commission, and a joint military commission of the two South Vietnamese parties.

An international commission of control and supervision shall be established.

An international guarantee conference on Vietnam will be convened within 30 days of the signing of this agreement.

7. The government of the Democratic Republic of Vietnam, the Provisional Revolutionary Government of the Republic of South Vietnam, the government of the United States of America, and the government of the Republic of Vietnam shall strictly respect the Cambodian and Lao peoples' fundamental national rights as recognized by the 1954 Geneva Agreements on Indochina and the 1962 Geneva Agreements on Laos, i.e., the independence, sovereignty, unity and territorial integrity of these countries. They shall respect the neutrality of Cambodia and Laos. The government of the Democratic Republic of Vietnam, the Provisional Revolutionary Government of the Republic of South Vietnam, the government of the United States of America and the government of the Republic of Vietnam undertake to refrain from using the territory of Cambodia and the territory of Laos to encroach on the sovereignty and security of other countries. Foreign countries shall put an end to all military activities in Laos and Cambodia, totally withdraw from and refrain from reintroducing into these two countries troops, military advisers and military personnel, armaments, munitions, and war material [*sic*].

The internal affairs of Cambodia and Laos shall be settled by the people of each of these countries without foreign interference.

The problems existing between the three Indochinese countries shall be settled by the Indochinese parties on the basis of respect for each other's independence, sovereignty, and territorial integrity, and noninterference in each other's internal affairs.

8. The ending of the war, the restoration of peace in Vietnam will create conditions for establishing a new, equal, and mutually beneficial relationship between the Democratic Republic of Vietnam and the United States. The United States will contribute to healing the wounds of war and to postwar reconstruction in the Democratic Republic of Vietnam and throughout Indochina.

9. This agreement shall come into force as of its signing. It will be strictly implemented by all the parties concerned.

Agreement on Ending the War and Restoring Peace in Vietnam (The Paris Agreement)

Signed at the International Conference Center, Paris, Saturday morning, Paris time, January 27, 1973.

The parties participating in the Paris Conference on Vietnam,

With a view to ending the war and restoring peace in Vietnam on the basis of respect for the Vietnamese people's fundamental national rights and the South Vietnamese people's right to self-determination, and to contributing to the consolidation of peace in Asia and the world,

Have agreed on the following provisions and undertake to respect and to implement them:

CHAPTER 1
THE VIETNAMESE PEOPLE'S
FUNDAMENTAL NATIONAL RIGHTS
Article 1

The United States and all other countries respect the independence, sovereignty, unity, and territorial integrity of Vietnam as recognized by the 1954 Geneva Agreements on Vietnam.

CHAPTER 2
CESSATION OF HOSTILITIES—WITHDRAWAL OF TROOPS
Article 2

A cease-fire shall be observed throughout South Vietnam as of 2400 hours G.M.T., on January 27, 1973.

At the same hour, the United States will stop all its military activities against the territory of the Democratic Republic of Vietnam by ground, air and naval forces, wherever they may be based, and end the mining of the territorial waters, ports, harbors, and waterways of the Democratic Republic of Vietnam. The United States will remove, permanently deactivate or destroy all the mines in the territorial waters, ports, harbors, and waterways of North Vietnam as soon as this Agreement goes into effect.

The complete cessation of hostilities mentioned in this Article shall be durable and without limit of time.

Article 3

The parties undertake to maintain the cease-fire and to ensure a lasting and stable peace.

As soon as the cease-fire goes into effect:

a. The United States forces and those of the other foreign countries allied with the United States and the Republic of Vietnam shall remain in-place pending the implementation of the plan of troop withdrawal. The Four-Party Joint Military Commission described in Article 16 shall determine the modalities.

b. The armed forces of the two South Vietnamese parties shall remain in-place. The Two-Party Joint Military Commission described in Article 17 shall determine the areas controlled by each party and the modalities of stationing.

c. The regular forces of all services and arms and the irregular forces of the Parties in South Vietnam shall stop all offensive activities against each other and shall strictly abide by the following stipulations:

—All acts of force on the ground, in the air, and on the sea shall be prohibited;

—All hostile acts, terrorism and reprisals by both sides will be banned.

Article 4

The United States will not continue its military involvement or intervene in the internal affairs of South Vietnam.

Article 5

Within sixty days of the signing of this Agreement, there will be a total withdrawal from South Vietnam of troops, military advisers, and military personnel, including technical military personnel associated with the pacification program, armaments, munitions, and war material of the United States and those of the other foreign countries mentioned in Article 3(a). Advisers from the above-mentioned countries to all paramilitary organizations and the police force will also be withdrawn within the same period of time.

Article 6

The dismantlement of all military bases in South Vietnam of the United States and of the other foreign countries mentioned in Article 3(a) shall be completed within sixty days of the signing of this Agreement.

Article 7

From the enforcement of the cease-fire to the formation of the government provided for in Articles 9(b) and 14 of this Agreement, the two South Vietnamese parties shall not accept the introduction of troops, military advisers, and military personnel including technical military personnel, armaments, munitions, and war material into South Vietnam.

The two South Vietnamese parties shall be permitted to make periodic replacement of armaments, munitions and war material which have been destroyed, damaged, worn out or used up after the cease-fire, on the basis of piece-for-piece, of the same characteristics and properties, under the supervision of the Joint Military Commission of the two South Vietnamese parties and of the International Commission of Control and Supervision.

CHAPTER 3

THE RETURN OF CAPTURED MILITARY PERSONNEL AND FOREIGN CIVILIANS, AND CAPTURED AND DETAINED VIETNAMESE CIVILIAN PERSONNEL

Article 8

a. The return of captured military personnel and foreign civilians of the parties shall be carried out simultaneously with and completed not later than the same day as the troop withdrawal mentioned in Article 5. The parties shall exchange complete lists of the above-mentioned captured military personnel and foreign civilians on the day of the signing of this Agreement.

b. The parties shall help each other to get information about those military personnel and foreign civilians of the parties missing in action, to determine the location and take care of the graves of the dead so as to facilitate the exhumation and repatriation of the remains, and to take any such other measures as may be required to get information about those still considered missing in action.

c. The question of the return of Vietnamese civilian personnel captured and detained in South Vietnam will be resolved by the two South Vietnamese parties on the basis of the principles of Article 21(b) of the Agreement on the Cessation of Hostilities in Vietnam of July 20, 1954. The two South Vietnamese parties will do so in a spirit of national reconciliation and concord, with a view to ending hatred and enmity, in order to ease suffering and to reunite families. The two South Vietnamese parties will do their utmost to resolve this question within ninety days after the cease-fire comes into effect.

CHAPTER 4

THE EXERCISE OF THE SOUTH VIETNAMESE PEOPLE'S RIGHT TO SELF-DETERMINATION

Article 9

The Government of the United States of America and the Government of the Democratic Republic of Vietnam undertake to respect the following principles for the exercise of the South Vietnamese people's right to self-determination:

a. The South Vietnamese people's right to self-determination is sacred, inalienable, and shall be respected by all countries.

b. The South Vietnamese people shall decide themselves the political future of South Vietnam through genuinely free and democratic general elections under international supervision.

c. Foreign countries shall not impose any political tendency or personality on the South Vietnamese people.

Article 10

The two South Vietnamese parties undertake to respect the cease-fire and maintain peace in South Vietnam, settle all matters of contention through negotiations, and avoid all armed conflict.

Article 11

Immediately after the cease-fire, the two South Vietnamese parties will:

— achieve national reconciliation and concord, end hatred and enmity, prohibit all acts of reprisal and discrimination against individuals or organizations that have collaborated with one side or the other;

— ensure the democratic liberties of the people: personal freedom, freedom of speech, freedom of the press, freedom of meeting, freedom of organization, freedom of political activities, freedom of belief, freedom of movement, freedom of residence, freedom of work, right to property ownership, and right to free enterprise.

Article 12

a. Immediately after the cease-fire, the two South Vietnamese parties shall hold consultations in a spirit of national reconciliation and concord, mutual respect, and mutual non-elimination to set up a National Council of National Reconciliation and Concord of three equal segments. The Council shall operate on the principle of unanimity. After the National Council of National Reconciliation and Concord has assumed its functions, the two South Vietnamese parties will consult about the formation of councils at lower levels. The two South Vietnamese parties shall sign an agreement on the internal matters of South Vietnam as soon as possible and do their utmost to accomplish this within ninety days after the cease-fire comes into effect, in keeping with the South Vietnamese people's aspirations for peace, independence and democracy.

b. The National Council of National Reconciliation and Concord shall have the task of promoting the two South Vietnamese parties' implementation of this Agreement, achievement of national reconciliation and concord and ensurance of democratic liberties. The National Council of National Reconciliation and Concord will organize the free and democratic general elections provided for in Article 9(b) and decide the procedures and modalities of these general elections. The institutions for which the general elections are to be held will be agreed upon through consultations between the two South Vietnamese parties. The National Council of National Reconciliation and Concord will also decide the procedures and modalities of such local elections as the two South Vietnamese parties agree upon.

Article 13

The question of Vietnamese armed forces in South Vietnam shall be settled by the two South Vietnamese parties in a spirit of national reconciliation and concord, equality and mutual respect, without foreign interference, in accordance with the postwar situation. Among the questions to be discussed by the two South Vietnamese parties are steps to reduce their military effectives and to demobilize the troops being reduced. The two South Vietnamese parties will accomplish this as soon as possible.

Article 14

South Vietnam will pursue a foreign policy of peace and independence. It will be prepared to establish relations with all countries irrespective of their political and social systems on the basis of mutual respect for independence and sovereignty and accept economic and technical aid from any country with no political conditions attached. The acceptance of military aid by South Vietnam in the future shall come under the authority of the government set up after the general elections in South Vietnam provided for in Article 9(b).

CHAPTER 5
THE REUNIFICATION OF VIETNAM AND THE
RELATIONSHIP BETWEEN NORTH AND SOUTH VIETNAM
Article 15

The reunification of Vietnam shall be carried out step by step through peaceful means on the basis of discussions and agreements between North and South Vietnam, without coercion or annexation by either party, and without foreign interference. The time for reunification will be agreed upon by North and South Vietnam.

Pending reunification:

a. The military demarcation line between the two zones at the 17th parallel is only provisional and not a political or territorial boundary, as provided for in paragraph 6 of the Final Declaration of the 1954 Geneva Conference.

b. North and South Vietnam shall respect the Demilitarized Zone on either side of the Provisional Military Demarcation Line.

c. North and South Vietnam shall promptly start negotiations with a view to reestablishing normal relations in various fields. Among the questions to be negotiated are the modalities of civilian movement across the Provisional Military Demarcation Line.

d. North and South Vietnam shall not join any military alliance or military bloc and shall not allow foreign powers to maintain military bases, troops, military advisers, and military personnel on their respective territories, as stipulated in the 1954 Geneva Agreements on Vietnam.

CHAPTER 6

THE JOINT MILITARY COMMISSIONS,
THE INTERNATIONAL COMMISSION
OF CONTROL AND SUPERVISION,
THE INTERNATIONAL CONFERENCE
Article 16

a. The Parties participating in the Paris Conference on Vietnam shall immediately designate representatives to form a Four-Party Joint Military Commission with the task of ensuring joint action by the parties in implementing the following provisions of this Agreement:

—The first paragraph of Article 2, regarding the enforcement of the cease-fire throughout South Vietnam;

—Article 3(a), regarding the cease-fire by U.S. forces and those of the other foreign countries referred to in that Article;

—Article 3(c), regarding the cease-fire between all parties in South Vietnam;

—Article 5, regarding the withdrawal from South Vietnam of U.S. troops and those of the other foreign countries mentioned in Article 3(a);

—Article 6, regarding the dismantlement of military bases in South Vietnam of the United States and those of the other foreign countries mentioned in Article 3(a);

—Article 8(a), regarding the return of captured military personnel and foreign civilians of the parties;

—Article 8(b), regarding the mutual assistance of the parties in getting information about those military personnel and foreign civilians of the parties missing in action.

b. The Four-Party Joint Military Commission shall operate in accordance with the principle of consultations and unanimity. Disagreements shall be referred to the International Commission of Control and Supervision.

c. The Four-Party Joint Military Commission shall begin operating immediately after the signing of this Agreement and end its activities in sixty days, after the completion of the withdrawal of U.S. troops and those of the other foreign countries mentioned in Article 3(a) and the completion of the return of captured military personnel and foreign civilians of the parties.

d. The four parties shall agree immediately on the organization, the working procedure, means of activity, and expenditures of the Four-Party Joint Military Commission.

Article 17

a. The two South Vietnamese parties shall immediately designate representatives to form a Two-Party Joint Military Commission with the task of ensuring joint action by the two South Vietnamese parties in implementing the following provisions of this Agreement:

—The first paragraph of Article 2, regarding the enforcement of the cease-fire throughout South Vietnam, when the Four-Party Joint Military Commission has ended its activities;

—Article 3(b), regarding the cease-fire between the two South Vietnamese parties;

—Article 3(c), regarding the cease-fire between all parties in South Vietnam, when the Four-Party Joint Military Commission has ended its activities;

—Article 7, regarding the prohibition of the introduction of troops into South Vietnam and all other provisions of this article;

—Article 8(c), regarding the question of the return of Vietnamese civilian personnel captured and detained in South Vietnam;

—Article 13, regarding the reduction of the military effectives of the two South Vietnamese parties and the demobilization of the troops being reduced.

b. Disagreements shall be referred to the International Commission of Control and Supervision.

c. After the signing of this Agreement, the Two-Party Joint Military Commission shall agree immediately on the measures and organization aimed at enforcing the cease-fire and preserving peace in South Vietnam.

Article 18

a. After the signing of this Agreement, an International Commission of Control and Supervision shall be established immediately.

b. Until the International Conference provided for in Article 19 makes definitive arrangements, the International Commission of Control and Supervision will report to the four parties on matters concerning the control and supervision of the implementation of the following provisions of this Agreement:

—The first paragraph of Article 2, regarding the enforcement of the cease-fire throughout South Vietnam;

—Article 3(a), regarding the cease-fire by U.S. forces and those of the other foreign countries referred to in that Article;

—Article 3(c), regarding the cease-fire between all the parties in South Vietnam;

—Article 5, regarding the withdrawal from South Vietnam of U.S. troops and those of the other foreign countries mentioned in Article 3(a);

—Article 6, regarding the dismantlement of military bases in South Vietnam of the United States and those of the other foreign countries mentioned in Article 3(a);

—Article 8(a), regarding the return of captured military personnel and foreign civilians of the parties.

The International Commission of Control and Supervision shall form control teams for carrying out its tasks. The four parties shall agree immediately on the location and operation of these teams. The parties will facilitate their operation.

c. Until the International Conference makes definitive arrangements, the International Commission of Control and Supervision will report to the two South Vietnamese parties on matters concerning the control and supervision of the implementation of the following provisions of this Agreement:

—The first paragraph of Article 2, regarding the enforcement of the cease-fire throughout South Vietnam, when the Four-Party Joint Military Commission has ended its activities;

—Article 3(b), regarding the cease-fire between the two South Vietnamese parties;

—Article 3(c), regarding the cease-fire between all parties in South Vietnam, when the Four-Party Joint Military Commission has ended its activities;

—Article 7, regarding the prohibition of the introduction of troops into South Vietnam and all other provisions of this Article;

—Article 8(c), regarding the question of the return of Vietnamese civilian personnel captured and detained in South Vietnam;

—Article 9(b), regarding the free and democratic general elections in South Vietnam;

—Article 13, regarding the reduction of the military effectives of the two South Vietnamese parties and the demobilization of the troops being reduced.

The International Commission of Control and Supervision shall form control teams for carrying out its tasks. The two South Vietnamese parties shall agree immediately on the location and operation of these teams. The two South Vietnamese parties will facilitate their operation.

d. The International Commission of Control and Supervision shall be composed of representatives of four countries: Canada, Hungary, Indonesia and Poland. The chairmanship of the Commission will rotate among the members for specific periods to be determined by the Commission.

e. The International Commission of Control and Supervision shall carry out its tasks in accordance with the principle of respect for the sovereignty of South Vietnam.

f. The International Commission of Control and Supervision shall operate in accordance with the principle of consultations and unanimity.

g. The International Commission of Control and Supervision shall begin operating when a cease-fire comes into force in Vietnam. As regards the provisions in Article 18(b) concerning the four parties, the International Commission of Control and Supervision shall end its activities when the Commission's tasks of control and supervision regarding these provisions have been fulfilled. As regards the provisions in Article 18(c) concerning the two South Vietnamese parties, the International Commission of Control and Supervision shall end its activities on the request of the government formed after the general elections in South Vietnam provided for in Article 9(b).

h. The four parties shall agree immediately on the organization, means of activity, and expenditures of the International Commission of Control and Supervision. The relationship between the International Commission and the International Conference will be agreed upon by the International Commission and the International Conference.

Article 19

The parties agree on the convening of an International Conference within thirty days of the signing of this Agreement to acknowledge the signed agreements; to guarantee the ending of the war, the maintenance of peace in Vietnam, the respect of the Vietnamese people's fundamental national rights, and the South Vietnamese people's right to self-determination; and to contribute to and guarantee peace in Indochina.

The United States and the Democratic Republic of Vietnam, on behalf of the parties participating in the Paris Conference on Vietnam, will propose to the

following parties that they participate in this International Conference: the People's
Republic of China, the Republic of France, the Union of Soviet Socialist Republics,
the United Kingdom, the four countries of the International Commission of Control
and Supervision, and the Secretary General of the United Nations, together with the
parties participating in the Paris Conference on Vietnam.

CHAPTER 7
REGARDING CAMBODIA AND LAOS
Article 20

a. The parties participating in the Paris Conference on Vietnam shall strictly
respect the 1954 Geneva Agreements on Cambodia and the 1962 Geneva Agreements on Laos, which recognized the Cambodian and the Lao peoples' fundamental
national rights, i.e., the independence, sovereignty, unity, and territorial integrity of
these countries. The parties shall respect the neutrality of Cambodia and Laos.

The parties participating in the Paris Conference on Vietnam undertake to refrain
from using the territory of Cambodia and the territory of Laos to encroach on the
sovereignty and security of one another and of other countries.

b. Foreign countries shall put an end to all military activities in Cambodia and
Laos, totally withdraw from and refrain from reintroducing into these two countries
troops, military advisers and military personnel, armaments, munitions and war
material.

c. The internal affairs of Cambodia and Laos shall be settled by the people of each
of these countries without foreign interference.

d. The problems existing between the Indochinese countries shall be settled by the
Indochinese parties on the basis of respect for each other's independence, sovereignty, and territorial integrity, and non-interference in each other's internal affairs.

CHAPTER 8
THE RELATIONSHIP BETWEEN
THE UNITED STATES AND
THE DEMOCRATIC REPUBLIC OF VIETNAM
Article 21

The United States anticipates that this Agreement will usher in an era of
reconciliation with the Democratic Republic of Vietnam as with all the peoples of
Indochina. In pursuance of its traditional policy, the United States will contribute to
healing the wounds of war and to postwar reconstruction of the Democratic Republic
of Vietnam and throughout Indochina.

Article 22

The ending of the war, the restoration of peace in Vietnam, and the strict
implementation of this Agreement will create conditions for establishing a new,
equal and mutually beneficial relationship between the United States and the

Democratic Republic of Vietnam on the basis of respect for each other's independence and sovereignty, and non-interference in each other's internal affairs. At the same time this will ensure stable peace in Vietnam and contribute to the preservation of lasting peace in Indochina and Southeast Asia.

CHAPTER 9
OTHER PROVISIONS
Article 23

This Agreement shall enter into force upon signature by plenipotentiary representatives of the parties participating in the Paris Conference on Vietnam. All the parties concerned shall strictly implement this Agreement and its Protocols.

Done in Paris this twenty-seventh day of January, One Thousand Nine Hundred and Seventy-Three, in Vietnamese and English. The Vietnamese and English texts are official and equally authentic.

[Separate Numbered Page]*

For the Government of the
United States of America

For the Government of the
Republic of Vietnam

William P. Rogers
Secretary of State

Tran Van Lam
Minister for Foreign Affairs

[Separate Numbered Page]

For the Government of the
Democratic Republic of Vietnam

For the Provisional Revolutionary
Government of the Republic of
South Vietnam

Nguyen Duy Trinh
Minister for Foreign Affairs

Nguyen Thi Binh
Minister for Foreign Affairs

---

*The signatures appear on separate pages in the original document. —Author

Agreement on Ending the War and Restoring Peace in Vietnam (The Afternoon Version)

Signed at the International Conference Center, Paris, Saturday afternoon, Paris time, January 27, 1973.

The Government of the United States of America, with the concurrence of the Government of the Republic of Vietnam,

The Government of the Democratic Republic of Vietnam, with the concurrence of the Provisional Revolutionary Government of the Republic of South Vietnam,

With a view to ending the war and restoring peace in Vietnam on the basis of respect for the Vietnamese people's fundamental national rights and the South Vietnamese people's right to self-determination, and to contributing to the consolidation of peace in Asia and the world,

Have agreed on the following provisions and undertake to respect and to implement them:

[Text of Agreement, Chapter I–VIII, pp. 188–97]

CHAPTER 9
OTHER PROVISIONS
Article 23

The Paris Agreement on Ending the War and Restoring Peace in Vietnam shall enter into force upon signature of this document by the Secretary of State of the Government of the United States of America and the Minister for Foreign Affairs of the Government of the Democratic Republic of Vietnam, and upon signature of a document in the same terms by the Secretary of State of the Government of the United States of America, the Minister for Foreign Affairs of the Government of the Republic of Vietnam, the Minister for Foreign Affairs of the Government of the Democratic Republic of Vietnam, and the Minister for Foreign Affairs of the Provisional Revolutionary Government of the Republic of South Vietnam. The Agreement and the protocols to it shall be strictly implemented by all the parties concerned.

Done in Paris this twenty-seventh day of January, One Thousand Nine Hundred and Seventy-Three, in Vietnamese and English. The Vietnamese and English texts are official and equally authentic.

For the Government of the   For the Government of the
United States of America   Democratic Republic of Vietnam

_____   _____

William P. Rogers   Nguyen Duy Trinh
Secretary of State   Minister for Foreign Affairs

Text of Communist Clandestine Radio Broadcast "On the Signing of the Paris Agreement" January 28, 1973

Translated by Foreign Broadcast Information Service.

Dear compatriots and combatants, the NFLSV [*National Front for the Liberation of South Vietnam*] Central Committee and the PRGRSV solemnly declare before all compatriots:

On January 27, 1973, the foreign ministers, plenipotentiaries of the DRV Government, the PRGRSV, the U.S. Government and the RVN Government, signed the Agreement on Ending the War and Restoring Peace in Viet-Nam. The main contents of the Agreement are:

The United States and all other countries undertake to respect the independence, sovereignty, unity and territorial integrity of Viet-Nam.

The United States will end the war of aggression completely, end its military involvement and intervention and the internal affairs of South Viet-Nam, respect the right to self-determination and guarantee the rights to freedom and democracy of the South Vietnamese people.

The South Vietnamese people will decide for themselves their own political future through a truly free and democratic general election.

The reunification of Viet-Nam shall be carried out step by step through peaceful means.

Dear compatriots and combatants, the U.S. imperialists' war has ended and peace has been restored in our country. This great victory is the result of 18 years of violent fighting and enduring tens of thousands of sacrifices, difficulties and hardships by all our heroic people and by our Southern armed forces and people, who have fought on persistently, who were the first to fight and the last to win and who have always been worthy of being the brass fortress of the Fatherland.

All our nation is the victor. Anyone with Vietnamese blood in his veins, who truly loves the country and the people, has the right to be proud and share the glory.

Glory first of all belongs to the people's elite children—the war heroes who have sacrificed for the Fatherland. Glory belongs to the heroic Liberation Armed Forces that have scored many brilliant armed exploits and to all stalwart and brave children of the country who have braved terrorism and imprisonment, resolutely struggled and fought the Americans for national salvation to liberate the South.

This victory of the Vietnamese people is also the victory of the three fraternal countries' peoples of the Indochina Peninsula, who united in fighting the common enemy. This is also the victory of all independence- and freedom-loving nations and all progressive mankind, including the peace- and justice-loving Americans.

The great victory of our Vietnamese people proves that in today's era a nation with a small land and population but having a correct revolutionary line and knowing how to unite the entire people and effect international solidarity and with the determination to fight and win can surely defeat any aggressive enemy.

Dear compatriots and combatants, the dawn of peace and the glory of victory are illuminating all mountains and rivers in our country. Before the eyes of our people opens a new stage, a new situation very favorable for our completion of the national and democratic revolution.

However, our people's struggle is still full of difficulties and complications. The reactionary, militarist, fascist and satellite forces still nurture many dark schemes of sabotaging peace and opposing independence, democracy and national concord. Therefore our people's present duty is to strive in the spirit of national concord to unite the entire people, resolutely maintain true peace, independence and sovereignty, implement the rights to freedom and democracy, improve the people's living conditions, build a peaceful, independent, democratic and prosperous South Viet-Nam and advance toward peace and national reunification.

The NFLSV and the PRGRSV solemnly declare that they will seriously and actively carry out all provisions of the signed Agreement and perseveringly struggle for their full implementation.

All compatriots and combatants; brother and sister workers and laborers; brother and sister peasants; brother and sister youths; students; our friendly intellectuals, teachers and civil servants; scholars; industrial and commercial men, compatriots of various religions; compatriots of various nationalities; brother and sister of Vietnamese residents abroad, a peaceful, independent, democratic and prosperous life is a deep aspiration and an urgent demand of the compatriots of all strata. A new weapon in our hands is the signed Agreement. Our people's uncheckable strength is the great solidarity among the entire people in the spirit of national concord. Great solidarity and national concord are our nation's noble tradition and the unchanged, clear-cut and resolute policy of the NFLSV and the PRGRSV.

Any Vietnamese who had no opportunity to participate in the resistance to protect the Fatherland can now contribute to our people's common struggle. The NFLSV and the PRGRSV warmly welcome and are ready to cooperate with all who want peace, independence, democracy and national concord, regardless of their past activities.

Bloodsealed affection and compatriotism must be respected. Let us shake hands, as we are the members of the same family. Let us eradicate all hatred and suspicion and cooperate in building a life full of love and happiness.

Let the PLAF cadres and combatants continue to struggle under the banner of protecting peace, independence, democracy and the signed Agreement. Let them correctly implement the cease-fire order, and in all contacts with the brother RVN troops treat them like brothers and advance the great cause of national concord.

Friends, officers and troops of the army of the Saigon administration, restoration of peace is our common victory. To maintain peace firmly is to love one's country and people and is your vital happiness. We hope you will cooperate with brother liberation combatants, seriously implement the cease-fire and avoid any regrettable incidents.

The policy of the Front, Government and our people is clear and correct. Their attitude shows good will and sincerity. In this dignified hour in our history, the PRGRSV hopes the Saigon administration will place the Fatherland's interests above all, meet the requirements of our compatriots of various strata, through sincere consultations quickly set up the National Council of National Reconciliation and Concord of three equal segments at all echelons, and quickly proceed toward organizing truly free and democratic general elections so that the Southern people can freely decide on their political regime.

Let both sides conduct serious negotiations on all conditions and clauses of the Agreement, fully implement all the people's free and democratic rights, heal the war wounds, care for our compatriots' livelihood so they can live a happy, decent life soon, quickly establish normal relations in all aspects with the North and promote negotiations with the DRV government so as to proceed toward peace and reunification of the Fatherland.

Dear kith and kin Northern compatriots, faced with our people's glorious victory, the Southern compatriots and combatants have engraved in their minds the blood-sealed love and great service of the heroic Northern compatriots and combatants in the anti-U.S. national salvation resistance. The Southern people have complete confidence that the 22 million compatriots who are building and strengthening the North in all aspects will serve as a support for all our people's struggle to firmly maintain peace, achieve independence and democracy and proceed toward peacefully reunifying our country.

The National Liberation Front and PRGRSV express their sincere gratitude to the fraternal Cambodian people under the leadership of the NUFK and RGNUC and to the fraternal Lao people under the leadership of the Lao Patriotic Front for their wholehearted support and valuable assistance to the Vietnamese people's national salvation resistance. Let the noble solidarity among the people of our three countries of the Indochina Peninsula become increasingly steadier.

The National Liberation Front and PRGRSV express their deep gratitude to the governments of friendly countries, international organizations and all peace- and justice-loving people all over the world for their zealous support and generous assistance to the Vietnamese people's resistance.

The National Liberation Front and PRGRSV convey their warm greetings to the American progressives for the common victory they have achieved for peace and for the interests of the people of both countries.

The PRGRSV, the sole genuine representative of the South Vietnamese people, declares that it will firmly maintain and develop friendly relations with those countries that have diplomatic relations with the PRGRSV, and is ready to establish diplomatic relations with all other countries on the basis of respect, sovereignty, equality and mutual interest.

Dear compatriots and combatants, in celebrating our success today, all of us earnestly recall the great service of venerable and beloved President Ho. His sacred testament has always lighted the path to certain victory for our people. To be worthy of his great love for us, let our Southern armed forces and people pledge to always uphold the flag of peace, independence, democracy and national concord and resolutely struggle to achieve new successes.

Together with the compatriots throughout our country, let the 18 million Southern compatriots uphold the national flag of victory and, with their increasingly greater posture and force, closely unite more than ever, resolutely struggle for consolidating peace, developing their successes and achieving a peaceful, independent, democratic and prosperous South Viet-Nam and proceed toward peacefully reunifying the Fatherland.

Let the heroic Southern compatriots and combatants elatedly advance!

Text of Joint Communiqué Issued after Kissinger's Visit to Hanoi February 10–13, 1973

Released by the White House on February 14, 1973.

Dr. Henry A. Kissinger, Assistant to the President of the United States, arrived in Hanoi on February 10, 1973, and left Hanoi on February 13, 1973. He was accompanied by Mr. Herbert G. Klein, Director of Communications for the Executive Branch, Ambassador William H. Sullivan, Deputy Assistant Secretary of State, and other American officials.

During his stay in Hanoi, Dr. Henry A. Kissinger was received by Premier Pham Van Dong, Special Advisor Le Duc Tho, and Vice Premier Nguyen Duy Trinh. The DRVN [*DRV*] side and the U.S. side had frank, serious, and constructive exchanges of views on the implementation of the agreement on ending the war and restoring peace in Vietnam which was signed in Paris on January 27, 1973, as well as post-war relations between the Democratic Republic of Vietnam and the United States, and other subjects of mutual concern. Special Advisor Le Duc Tho and Dr. Kissinger also held discussions in a continuation of their meetings which took place in Paris during the past four years. In addition to these working sessions, Dr. Kissinger and his party visited a number of points of interest in Hanoi.

The two sides carefully reviewed the implementation of the Paris Agreement on Vietnam in the recent period. They discussed various imperative measures which should be taken to improve and expedite the implementation of the agreement, and also agreed that they would continue to have periodic exchanges of views in order to ensure that the agreement and its protocols are strictly and scrupulously implemented, as the signatories have undertaken.

The two sides welcomed the discussions between the two South Vietnamese parties for the purpose of carrying out the provisions concerning self-determination in South Vietnam, in accordance with the stipulations of the Paris Agreement on Vietnam.

The Democratic Republic of Vietnam and the United States declared that the full and scrupulous implementation of the Paris Agreement on Vietnam would positively contribute to the cause of peace in Indochina and Southeast Asia on the basis of strict respect for the independence and neutrality of the countries in this region.

The two sides reaffirmed that the problems existing between the Indochinese countries should be settled by the Indochinese parties on the basis of respect for each other's independence, sovereignty, and territorial integrity, and non-interference in each other's internal affairs. They welcomed the negotiations between the parties in Laos, which are intended to produce a peaceful settlement in that country.

The two sides exchanged views on the manner in which the United States will contribute to healing the wounds of war and the post-war economic reconstruction in North Vietnam. They agreed to establish a DRVN-U.S. Joint Economic Commission. This Commission, which will be composed of an equal number of representatives from each side, will be charged with the task of developing the economic relations between the Democratic Republic of Vietnam and the United States.

The two sides also exchanged views on the convening of [*the*] International Conference on Vietnam, as provided for in Article 19 of the Paris Agreement on Vietnam. They will continue their consultations with the other participants in the conference so as to prepare the ground for a successful meeting.

The two sides considered the post-war relationship between the Democratic Republic of Vietnam and the United States, and examined concrete steps which can be taken to normalize the relations between the two countries. They agreed on certain general principles which should govern their mutual relations.

—All provisions of the Paris Agreement on Vietnam and its protocols should be fully and scrupulously implemented.

—The Democratic Republic of Vietnam and the United States should strive for a new relationship based on respect for each other's independence and sovereignty, non-interference in each other's internal affairs, equality and mutual benefit.

—The normalization of the relations between the Democratic Republic of Vietnam and the United States will help to ensure stable peace in Vietnam and contribute to the cause of peace in Indochina and Southeast Asia.

Dr. Kissinger and his party expressed warm appreciation for the hospitality extended by the Democratic Republic of Vietnam. Both sides hope that this visit will mark the beginning of new bilateral relations.

Text of the Act
of the International Conference
on Viet-Nam

Signed in Paris, March 2, 1973.

The Government of the United States of America; The Government of the French Republic; the Provisional Revolutionary Government of the Republic of South Viet-Nam; the Government of the Hungarian People's Republic; the Government of the Republic of Indonesia; the Government of the Polish People's Republic; the Government of the Democratic Republic of Viet-Nam; the Government of the United Kingdom of Great Britain and Northern Ireland; the Government of the Republic of Viet-Nam; the Government of the Union of Soviet Socialist Republics; the Government of Canada; and the Government of the People's Republic of China;

In the presence of the Secretary-General of the United Nations; with a view to acknowledging the signed Agreements; guaranteeing the ending of the war, the maintenance of peace in Viet-Nam, the respect of the Vietnamese people's fundamental national rights, and the South Vietnamese people's right to self-determination; and contributing to and guaranteeing peace in Indochina;

Have agreed on the following provisions, and undertake to report and implement them;

Article 1

The Parties to this Act solemnly acknowledge, express their approval of, and support the Paris Agreement on Ending the War and Restoring Peace in Viet-Nam signed in Paris on January 27, 1973, and the four Protocols to the Agreement signed on the same date (hereinafter referred to respectively as the Agreement and the Protocols).

Article 2

The Agreement responds to the aspirations and fundamental national rights of the Vietnamese people, i.e., the independence, sovereignty, unity, and territorial integrity of Viet-Nam, to the right of the South Vietnamese people to self-determination, and to the earnest desire for peace shared by all countries in the world. The Agreement constitutes a major contribution to peace, self-determination, national independence, and the improvement of relations among countries. The Agreement and the Protocols should be strictly respected and scrupulously implemented.

Article 3

The Parties to this Act solemnly acknowledge the commitments by the parties to the Agreement and the Protocols to strictly respect and scrupulously implement the Agreement and the Protocols.

Article 4

The Parties to this Act solemnly recognize and strictly respect the fundamental national rights of the Vietnamese people, i.e., the independence, sovereignty, unity, and territorial integrity of Viet-Nam, as well as the right of the South Vietnamese people to self-determination. The Parties to this Act shall strictly respect the Agreement and the Protocols by refraining from any action at variance with their provisions.

Article 5

For the sake of a durable peace in Viet-Nam, the Parties to this Act call on all countries to strictly respect the fundamental national rights of the Vietnamese people, i.e., the independence, sovereignty, unity, and territorial integrity of Viet-Nam and the right of the South Vietnamese people to self-determination and to strictly respect the Agreement and the Protocols by refraining from any action at variance with their provisions.

Article 6

a. The four parties to the Agreement or the two South Vietnamese parties may, either individually or through joint action, inform the other Parties to this Act about the implementation of the Agreement and the Protocols. Since the reports and views submitted by the International Commission of Control and Supervision concerning the control and supervision of the implementation of those provisions of the Agreement and the Protocols which are within the tasks of the Commission will be sent to either the four parties signatory to the Agreement or to the two South Vietnamese parties, those parties shall be responsible, either individually or through joint action, for forwarding them promptly to the other Parties to this Act.

b. The four parties to the Agreement or the two South Vietnamese parties shall also, either individually or through joint action, forward this information and these reports and views to the other participant in the International Conference on Viet-Nam for his information.

Article 7

a. In the event of a violation of the Agreement or the Protocols which threatens the peace, the independence, sovereignty, unity, or territorial integrity of Viet-Nam, or the right of the South Vietnamese people to self-determination, the parties signatory to the Agreement and the Protocols shall either individually or jointly, consult with the other Parties to this Act with a view to determining necessary remedial measures.

b. The International Conference on Viet-Nam shall be reconvened upon a joint request by the Government of the United States of America and the Government of the Democratic Republic of Viet-Nam on behalf of the parties signatory to the Agreement or upon a request by six or more of the Parties to this Act.

Article 8

With a view to contributing to and guaranteeing peace in Indochina, the Parties to this Act acknowledge the commitment of the parties to the Agreement to respect the independence, sovereignty, unity, territorial integrity, and neutrality of Cambodia and Laos as stipulated in the Agreement, agree also to respect them and to refrain from any action at variance with them, and call on other countries to do the same.

Article 9

This Act shall enter into force upon signature by plenipotentiary representatives of all twelve Parties and shall be strictly implemented by all the Parties. Signature of this Act does not constitute recognition of any Party in any case in which it has not previously been accorded.

Done in twelve copies in Paris this second day of March, One Thousand Nine Hundred and Seventy-Three, in English, French, Russian, Vietnamese, and Chinese. All texts are equally authentic.

For the Government of the United States of America, The Secretary of State, William P. Rogers.

For the Government of the French Republic, The Minister for Foreign Affairs, Maurice Schumann.

For the Provisional Revolutionary Government of the Republic of South Viet-Nam, The Minister for Foreign Affairs, Nguyen Thi Binh.

For the Government of the Hungarian People's Republic, The Minister for Foreign Affairs, Janos Peter.

For the Government of the Republic of Indonesia, The Minister for Foreign Affairs, Adam Malik.

For the Government of the Polish People's Republic, The Minister for Foreign Affairs, Stefan Olszowski.

For the Government of the Democratic Republic of Viet-Nam, The Minister for Foreign Affairs, Nguyen Duy Trinh.

For the Government of the United Kingdom of Great Britain and Northern Ireland, The Secretary of State for Foreign and Commonwealth Affairs, Alec Douglas-Home.

For the Government of the Republic of Viet-Nam, The Minister for Foreign Affairs, Tran Van Lam.

For the Government of the Union of Soviet Socialist Republics, The Minister for Foreign Affairs, Andrei A. Gromyko.

For the Government of Canada, The Secretary of State for External Affairs, Mitchell Sharp.

For the Government of the People's Republic of China, The Minister for Foreign Affairs, Chi Peng-Fei.

Text of U.S.-DRV Communiqué Following Negotiations to Strengthen the Paris Agreement June 13, 1973

Signed in Paris.

The Parties signatory to the Paris Agreement on Ending the War and Restoring Peace in Viet-Nam, signed on January 27, 1973,

Considering that strict respect and scrupulous implementation of all provisions of the Agreement and its Protocols by all the parties signatory to them are necessary to ensure the peace in Viet-Nam and contribute to the cause of peace in Indochina and Southeast Asia,

Have agreed on the following points (in the sequence of the relevant articles in the Agreement):

1. In conformity with Article 2 of the Agreement, the United States shall cease immediately, completely, and indefinitely aerial reconnaissance over the territory of the Democratic Republic of Viet-Nam.
2. In conformity with Article 2 of the Agreement and with the Protocol on mine clearance:
    a. The United States shall resume mine clearance operations within five days from the date of signature of this Joint Communiqué and shall successfully complete those operations within thirty days thereafter.
    b. The United States shall supply to the Democratic Republic of Viet-Nam means which are agreed to be adequate and sufficient for sweeping mines in rivers.
    c. The United States shall announce when the mine clearance in each main channel is completed and issue a final announcement when all the operations are completed.
3. In implementation of Article 2 of the Agreement, at 1200 hours, G.M.T., June 14, 1973, the High Commands of the two South Vietnamese parties shall issue identical orders to all regular and irregular armed forces and the armed police under their command, to strictly observe the cease-fire throughout South Viet-Nam beginning at 0400 hours, G.M.T., June 15, 1973, and scrupulously implement the Agreement and its Protocols.

4. The two South Vietnamese parties shall strictly implement Articles 2 and 3 of the Protocol on the cease-fire in South Viet-Nam which read as follows:

Article 2

a. As soon as the cease-fire comes into force and until regulations are issued by the Joint Military Commissions, all ground, river, sea and air combat forces of the parties in South Viet-Nam shall remain in place; that is, in order to ensure a stable cease-fire, there shall be no major redeployments or movements that would extend each party's area of control or would result in contact between opposing armed forces and clashes which might take place.
b. All regular and irregular armed forces and the armed police of the parties in South Viet-Nam shall observe the prohibition of the following acts:
   1. Armed patrols into areas controlled by opposing armed forces and flights by bomber and fighter aircraft of all types, except for unarmed flights for proficiency training and maintenance;
   2. Armed attacks against any person, either military or civilian, by any means whatsoever, including the use of small arms, mortars, artillery, bombing and strafing by airplanes and any other type of weapon or explosive device;
   3. All combat operations on the ground, on rivers, on the sea and in the air;
   4. All hostile acts, terrorism or reprisals; and
   5. All acts endangering lives or public or private property.

Article 3

a. The above-mentioned prohibitions shall not hamper or restrict:
   1. Civilian supply, freedom of movement, freedom to work, and freedom of the people to engage in trade, and civilian communication and transportation between and among all areas in South Viet-Nam;
   2. The use by each party in areas under its control of military support elements, such as engineer and transportation units, in repair and construction of public facilities and the transportation and supplying of the population;
   3. Normal military proficiency training conducted by the parties in the areas under their respective control with due regard for public safety.
b. The Joint Military Commissions shall immediately agree on corridors, routes, and other regulations governing the movement of military transport aircraft, military transport vehicles, and military transport vessels of all types of one party going through areas under the control of other parties.
5. The Two-Party Joint Military Commission shall immediately carry out its task pursuant to Article 3(b) of the Agreement to determine the areas controlled by each of the two South Vietnamese parties and the modalities of stationing. This task shall be completed as soon as possible. The Commission shall also

immediately discuss the movements necessary to accomplish a return of the armed forces of the two South Vietnamese parties to the positions they occupied at the time the cease-fire entered into force on January 28, 1973.

6. Twenty-four hours after the cease-fire referred to in paragraph 3 enters into force, the commanders of the opposing armed forces at those places of direct contact shall meet to carry out the provisions of Article 4 of the Protocol on the cease-fire in South Viet-Nam with a view to reaching an agreement on temporary measures to avert conflict and to ensure supply and medical care for these armed forces.

7. In conformity with Article 7 of the Agreement:
   a. The two South Vietnamese parties shall not accept the introduction of troops, military advisers, and military personnel, including technical military personnel, into South Viet-Nam.
   b. The two South Vietnamese parties shall not accept the introduction of armaments, munitions, and war material into South Viet-Nam. However, the two South Vietnamese parties are permitted to make periodic replacement of armaments, munitions, and war material, as authorized by Article 7 of the Agreement, through designated points of entry and subject to supervision by the Two-Party Joint Military Commission and the International Commission of Control and Supervision.

      In conformity with Article 15(b) of the Agreement regarding the respect of the Demilitarized Zone, military equipment may transit the Demilitarized Zone only if introduced into South Viet-Nam as replacements pursuant to Article 7 of the Agreement and through a designated point of entry.
   c. Twenty-four hours after the entry into force of the cease-fire referred to in paragraph 3, the Two-Party Joint Military Commission shall discuss the modalities for the supervision of the replacements of armaments, munitions, and war material permitted by Article 7 of the Agreement at the three points of entry already agreed upon for each party. Within fifteen days of the entry into force of the cease-fire referred to in paragraph 3, the two South Vietnamese parties shall also designate by agreement three additional points of entry for each party in the area controlled by that party.

8. In conformity with Article 8 of the Agreement:
   a. Any captured personnel covered by Article 8(a) of the Agreement who have not yet been returned shall be returned without delay, and in any event within no more than thirty days from the date of signature of this Joint Communiqué.
   b. All the provisions of the Agreement and the Protocol on the Return of Captured Personnel shall be scrupulously implemented. All Vietnamese civilian personnel covered by Article 8(c) of the Agreement and Article 7 of the Protocol on the Return of Captured Personnel shall be returned as soon as possible. The two South Vietnamese parties shall do their utmost to accomplish this within forty-five days from the date of signature of this Joint Communiqué.
   c. In conformity with Article 8 of the Protocol on the Return of Captured Personnel, all captured and detained personnel covered by that Protocol shall

be treated humanely at all times. The two South Vietnamese parties shall immediately implement Article 9 of that Protocol and, within fifteen days from the date of signature of this Joint Communiqué allow National Red Cross Societies they have agreed upon to visit all places where these personnel are held.

    d. The two South Vietnamese parties shall cooperate in obtaining information about missing persons and in determining the location of and in taking care of the graves of the dead.

    e. In conformity with Article 8(b) of the Agreement, the parties shall help each other to get information about those military personnel and foreign civilians of the parties missing in action, to determine the location and take care of the graves of the dead so as to facilitate the exhumation and repatriation of the remains, and to take any such other measures as may be required to get information about those still considered missing in action. For this purpose, frequent and regular liaison flights shall be made between Saigon and Hanoi.

9. The two South Vietnamese parties shall implement Article 11 of the Agreement, which reads as follows:

    "Immediately after the cease-fire, the two South Vietnamese parties will:

    —achieve national reconciliation and concord, end hatred and enmity, prohibit all acts of reprisal and discrimination against individuals or organizations that have collaborated with one side or the other;

    —ensure the democratic liberties of the people: personal freedom, freedom of speech, freedom of the press, freedom of meeting, freedom of organization, freedom of political activities, freedom of belief, freedom of movement, freedom of residence, freedom of work, right to property ownership and right to free enterprise."

10. Consistent with the principles for the exercise of the South Vietnamese people's right to self-determination stated in Chapter IV of the Agreement:

    a. The South Vietnamese people shall decide themselves the political future of South Viet-Nam through genuinely free and democratic general elections under international supervision.

    b. The National Council of National Reconciliation and Concord consisting of three equal segments shall be formed as soon as possible, in conformity with Article 12 of the Agreement.

    The two South Vietnamese parties shall sign an Agreement on the internal matters of South Viet-Nam as soon as possible, and shall do their utmost to accomplish this within forty-five days from the date of signature of this Joint Communiqué.

    c. The two South Vietnamese parties shall agree through consultations on the institutions for which the free and democratic general elections provided for in Article 9(b) of the Agreement will be held.

    d. The two South Vietnamese parties shall implement Article 13 of the Agreement, which reads as follows:

    "The question of Vietnamese armed forces in South Viet-Nam shall be settled by the two South Vietnamese parties in a spirit of national reconciliation and concord, equality and mutual respect, without foreign interference, in accordance with the postwar situation. Among the questions to be discussed by the two South Vietnamese parties are steps to reduce their military effectives [*sic*] and to demobilize the troops being reduced. The two South Vietnamese parties will accomplish this as soon as possible."

11. In implementation of Article 17 of the Agreement:

   a. All the provisions of Articles 16 and 17 of the Protocol on the cease-fire in South Viet-Nam shall immediately be implemented with respect to the Two-Party Joint Military Commission. That Commission shall also immediately be accorded the eleven points of privileges and immunities agreed upon by the Four-Party Joint Military Commission. Frequent and regular liaison flights shall be made between Saigon and the headquarters of the Regional Two-Party Joint Military Commissions and other places in South Viet-Nam as required for the operations of the Two-Party Joint Military Commission. Frequent and regular liaison flights shall also be made between Saigon and Loc Ninh.

   b. The headquarters of the Central Two-Party Joint Military Commission shall be located in Saigon proper or at a place agreed upon by the two South Vietnamese parties where an area controlled by one of them adjoins an area controlled by the other. The locations of the headquarters of the Regional Two-Party Joint Military Commissions and of the teams of the Two-Party Joint Military Commission shall be determined by that Commission within fifteen days after the entry into force of the cease-fire referred to in paragraph 3. These locations may be changed at any time as determined by the Commission. The locations, except for teams at the points of entry, shall be selected from among those towns specified in Article 11(b) and (c) of the Protocol on the Cease-Fire in South Viet-Nam and those places where an area controlled by one South Vietnamese party adjoins an area controlled by the other, or at any other place agreed upon by the Commission.

   c. Once the privileges and immunities mentioned in paragraph 11(a) are accorded by both South Vietnamese parties, the Two-Party Joint Military Commission shall be fully staffed and its regional commissions and teams fully deployed within fifteen days after their locations have been determined.

   d. The Two-Party Joint Military Commission and the International Commission of Control and Supervision shall closely cooperate with and assist each other in carrying out their respective functions.

12. In conformity with Article 18 of the Agreement and Article 10 of the Protocol on the International Commission of Control and Supervision, the International Commission, including its teams, is allowed such movement for observation as is reasonably required for the proper exercise of its functions as stipulated in the Agreement. In carrying out these functions, the International Commission, including its teams, shall enjoy all necessary assistance and cooperation from the parties concerned. The two South Vietnamese parties shall issue the necessary instructions to their personnel and take all other necessary measures to ensure the safety of such movement.

13. Article 20 of the Agreement, regarding Cambodia and Laos, shall be scrupulously implemented.
14. In conformity with Article 21 of the Agreement, the United States–Democratic Republic of Viet-Nam Joint Economic Commission shall resume its meetings four days from the date of signature of this Joint Communiqué and shall complete the first phase of its work within fifteen days thereafter.

Affirming that the parties concerned shall strictly respect and scrupulously implement all the provisions of the Paris Agreement, its Protocols, and this Joint Communiqué, the undersigned representatives of the parties signatory to the Paris Agreement have decided to issue this Joint Communiqué to record and publish the points on which they have agreed.

Excerpts from Hanoi's Analysis of One Year of Implementation of the Paris Agreement on Viet Nam

Published in English by the Ministry of Foreign Affairs, DRV, Hanoi, January 1974.

1. PROVISIONS ALREADY IMPLEMENTED

Under Articles 2, 3, and 5 of the Agreement, the United States has ceased all its acts of war in South Viet Nam, stopped the bombing, ended the mining of the territorial waters, ports, harbors, and waterways of the Democratic Republic of Viet Nam, deactivated or destroyed the mines it had laid along ten channels in the latter's territorial waters, and withdrawn from South Viet Nam its troops and those of the other foreign countries allied with it.

The return of the captured and detained military personnel and foreign civilians of the parties under Article 8(a) of the Agreement was carried out simultaneously with U.S. troop withdrawals. Pursuant to Article 8(a), the Government of the Democratic Republic of Viet Nam and the Provisional Revolutionary Government of the Republic of South Viet Nam returned to the United States all the U.S. military personnel and all foreign civilians captured in North and South Viet Nam, totaling 588 persons. During the same period, the Provisional Revolutionary Government of the Republic of South Viet Nam returned 5,016 captured and detained military personnel of the Saigon Administration. The U.S. and Saigon Administration side returned to the Provisional Revolutionary Government of the Republic of South Viet Nam 26,508 military personnel captured and detained by it, and is still detaining a number of prisoners.

The ending of the U.S. war of aggression against the Vietnamese people in both zones and the withdrawal of the U.S. expeditionary corps from South Viet Nam which put an end to a 115-year-long occupation of Vietnamese territory by foreign troops, constitutes a historic event of great political significance. This victory is inspiring the Vietnamese people in their persistent struggle to ensure respect for, and a scrupulous implementation of, all the provisions of the Paris Agreement, and to secure the Vietnamese people's fundamental national rights and the South Vietnamese people's right to self-determination.

2. THE UNITED STATES AND THE SAIGON ADMINISTRATION
HAVE BEEN SYSTEMATICALLY VIOLATING
MANY ESSENTIAL PROVISIONS OF THE AGREEMENT
The Cease-Fire Is Not Yet Effective in South Viet Nam

Article 2 of the Paris Agreement on Viet Nam clearly stipulates: A cease-fire shall be observed throughout South Viet Nam as of 2400 hours GMT on January 27, 1973, and the complete cessation of hostilities shall be durable and without limit of time.

Article 3 of the Agreement stipulates: The Parties undertake to maintain the cease-fire and to ensure a lasting and stable peace. As soon as the cease-fire goes into effect, the armed forces of the two South Vietnamese parties shall remain in-place, stop all offensive activities against each other, and strictly abide by the following stipulations:

—All acts of force on the ground, in the air, and on the sea shall be prohibited.
—All hostile acts, terrorism, and reprisals by both sides will be banned.

The Protocol concerning the cease-fire has given further precision on the above provisions, and laid down concrete steps to maintain the cease-fire and ensure lasting peace in South Viet Nam; for instance, it prohibits armed patrols into areas controlled by opposing armed forces and flights by bomber and fighter aircraft of all types, armed attacks against any person either military or civilian, by any means whatsoever, all combat operations on the ground, on rivers, on the sea, and in the air, all hostile acts, terrorism, or reprisals, and all acts endangering lives or public or private property. The Protocol also makes clear that the above-mentioned prohibitions shall not hamper or restrict the civilian supply, freedom of movement, freedom to work, freedom of the people to engage in trade, and civilian communication and transportation between and among all areas in South Viet Nam.

On January 27, 1973, the Command of the South Viet Nam People's Liberation Armed Forces ordered all regular, regional and guerrilla units to cease fire throughout South Viet Nam, to remain in-place and stop all offensive activities.

The military delegation of the Democratic Republic of Viet Nam and the military delegation of the Provisional Revolutionary Government in the Four-Party Joint Military Commission and subsequently, the military delegation of the Provisional Revolutionary Government in the Two-Party Joint Military Commission have made many proposals and put forward many steps for a strict implementation of the cease-fire, for instance, the three steps proposed on March 17, 1973, to end the hostilities, and the five points of May 11, 1973, for ending hostilities. On April 25, 1973, the delegation of the Provisional Revolutionary Government of the Republic of South Viet Nam to the Consultative Conference in La Celle–Saint Cloud (Paris) made a proposal for immediate cessation of all hostilities, and strict observance of all the provisions concerning a cease-fire that is durable and without limit of time.

In contrast, the Saigon Administration has frenziedly sabotaged the cease-fire with U.S. encouragement and assistance. On January 28, 1973, one hour before the cease-fire went into effect, Nguyen Van Thieu, the chieftain of the Saigon Administration, bluntly declared that "the cease-fire does not mean the end of the war," that "the cease-fire does not mean real peace." At the same moment, great infantry forces of the Saigon Army with air, tank and artillery support, launched operations against areas under the control of the Provisional Revolutionary Government of the Republic of South Viet Nam.

As pointed out by *U.S. News and World Report* of January 29, 1973, the purpose of such operations was "to move into contested areas—even communist controlled regions—and reduce the number of people and territory dominated by Reds."

The Saigon Administration's sabotage of the cease-fire is part of an overall plan called "territory-invading plan" which includes four stages: preparations, pre-cease-fire actions, actions concomitant with the cease-fire, and post-cease-fire actions. Under this plan, the Saigon Administration's armed forces have been ordered:

—to expand military operations aimed at "securing control over 100 per cent of the population and territory" in the preparatory stage;

—to expand to a maximum the sphere of control and "launch simultaneous attacks against enemy units, inflict maximum losses on them or pin them down in remote places" before the cease-fire;

—to achieve increased "coordination among units while invading territory" as the ceasefire is ordered;

—"to secretly invade the territory or cut off the enemy-controlled area" after the cease-fire.

Since that time, the Saigon Administration has launched operation upon operation to grab lands in the area controlled by the Provisional Revolutionary Government of the Republic of South Viet Nam; at the same time, it has stepped up police and "pacification" operations in the area under its control. What is particularly serious, of late, the Saigon Administration has conducted large-scale operations in the provinces of Binh Dinh, Quang Ngai, Quang Duc, Kontum, Gia Lai, Tay Ninh, Chuong Thien, etc. It has also launched savage air strikes against many areas lying deep in the liberated zone, razing many villages, and committing countless crimes against the South Vietnamese people.

From January 28 to December 15, 1973, the Saigon Administration committed 301,097 violations, comprising:

34,266 land-grabbing operations (including 37 division-size operations and 5,250 regiment-size ones);

35,532 artillery shellings;

14,749 aerial bombardments and reconnaissances;

216,550 police and "pacification" operations.

The Saigon Administration has killed or injured over 6,000 civilians.

In response to the profound aspirations of all social strata in South Viet Nam, on October 15, 1973, the Command of the South Viet Nam People's Liberation Armed Forces called on the Saigon Administration to strictly observe the cease-fire and to scrupulously implement the Paris Agreement; at the same time, it asserted the legitimate right of the Provisional Revolutionary Government of the Republic of South Viet Nam to take appropriate measures against the sabotage of the Agreement:

—to give resolute ripostes to the Saigon Administration war acts, to defend the liberated zone, protect the people's lives and property, to safeguard the Agreement.

—to resolutely fight back at any place, with appropriate forms and forces so long as the Saigon Administration continues its war acts, to compel the other side to scrupulously and strictly implement the Paris Agreement on Viet Nam, and stop all its acts of violation and sabotage of the Agreement.

The implementation of the Paris Agreement must be coupled with the struggle against any U.S. and Saigon action in violation of the same, and with due punishment inflicted on the Saigon Administration's sabotage of the cease-fire.

Hundreds of Thousands of Political Prisoners
Are Still Languishing in Prisons and Detention
Camps of the Saigon Administration

Article 8(c) of the Paris Agreement on Viet Nam stipulates: The two South Vietnamese parties will do their utmost to resolve the question of the return of the Vietnamese civilian personnel captured and detained in South Viet Nam within ninety days after the cease-fire comes into effect.

The Protocol concerning the Return of Captured Military Personnel and Foreign Civilians and Captured and Detained Vietnamese Civilian Personnel stresses that each party shall return all captured persons without denying or delaying their return for any reason, and shall facilitate their return and reception. Pending their return, all Vietnamese civilian personnel captured and detained in South Viet Nam shall be treated humanely at all times, and in accordance with international practice . . .

Pursuant to Article 8(c) of the Agreement, the military delegation of the Provisional Revolutionary Government of the Republic of South Viet Nam has repeatedly stated its willingness to return to the Saigon Administration all the Vietnamese civilian personnel captured and detained by the Provisional Revolutionary Government of the Republic of South Viet Nam, and to complete this operation within ninety days as provided for by the Paris Agreement on Viet Nam.

But, at U.S. instigation, the Saigon Administration has refused to return all political prisoners captured and detained by it. Although it is detaining over 200,000 Vietnamese civilian personnel belonging to the National Front for Liberation, the Provisional Revolutionary Government of the Republic of South Viet Nam, and various political and religious tendencies, which do not side with either party in South Viet Nam, Nguyen Van Thieu has bluntly stated: "There are no political prisoners in South Viet Nam. There are only two kinds of prisoners: 21,000 common-law convicts and 5,081 communist prisoners" (Nguyen Van Thieu's letter to Pope Paul VI dated April 9, 1973).

Shortly before the cease-fire, the Saigon Administration already resorted to many perfidious tricks in an attempt to avoid the return of prisoners. For instance, it sent detainees from one prison to another, dispersed prisoners to various jails, registered political detainers as "common-law" convicts, compelled detainees to sign "release certificates," brought many prisoners to unknown destinations, or secretly killed them.

Speaking at the U.S. Senate, Senator E. Kennedy said: "The Thieu Government may choose any label it desires for civilians detained for political reasons, but by every international standard what are commonly called 'political prisoners' exist in South Viet Nam today" (*Congressional Record,* Wash. June 4, 1973).

Public opinion in South Viet Nam, many national and international organizations, well-known personalities, and Western press have exposed the cynical lies of Nguyen Van Thieu and his agents.

On February 21, 1973, 30 political organizations in Saigon urged the Nguyen Van Thieu Administration to release the 200,000 political prisoners still kept in custody. Father Chän Tin, a representative of the Committee to Reform the Prison System in South Viet Nam and deputy Ho Ngoc Nhuän denounced that Adminstration for its continued detention of 202,000 political prisoners.

The U.S. magazine *Newsweek* of Dec. 18, 1972, wrote: "Nearly 45,000 South Vietnamese have been tried, convicted and jailed for political offences, and up to 100,000 others have been arrested and thrown into prisons established everywhere, including Poulo Condor, without trial. They are men and women who are writhing and languishing in the prisons . . . for their political activities did not please Thieu."

After a trip to South Viet Nam, U.S. Bishop Thomas J. Gumbleton asserted: "I can state unequivocally that there are political prisoners in Saigon's jails and in jails throughout the provinces. They are in jail not for any crime, but simply because they are in political opposition to the present government. The proof is overwhelming, and it is clear that these prisoners are subjected to inhuman treatment, including deliberate and prolonged torture" (*National Catholic Reporter,* May 11, 1973).

Speaking before the U.S. Congress on September 18, 1973, Fred Branfman, Co-director of the Indochina Resources Center in Washington, said: "The Government of the Republic of Viet Nam is clearly attempting to avoid the release of the vast majority of its political prisoners, in clear violation of the Paris Accord. . . . I was given a prison by prison breakdown totalling 202,000 political prisoners prepared by the Committee to Reform the Prison System . . .

"The main device used by the Government of the Republic of Viet Nam to justify holding political prisoners has been reclassification. This has been an attempt to change their status to that of common-law criminals. . . . The U.S. Embassy in Saigon confirmed this practice to Senator E. Kennedy in a letter dated April 3, 1973."

Even for the 5,081 Vietnamese civilian personnel whose detention has been admitted by it, the Saigon Administration has returned so far to the Provisional Revolutionary Government only over 1,500.

In the meantime, it has jailed tens of thousands of persons who desire peace and stand for national reconciliation and concord.

The civilian personnel kept by the Saigon Administration in "tiger cages" or other jails are living in inconceivable conditions. As the U.S. magazine *Time* of March 19, 1973, put it, "It is not really proper to call them men any more. 'Shapes' is a better word—grotesque sculptures of scarred flesh and gnarled limbs."

Former U.S. Senator George Murphy has said that the long story of the Saigon Administration's inhuman treatment of prisoners in South Viet Nam is well-known to broad segments of public opinion around the world (*Reuter,* June 7, 1973).

The 3rd International Conference of Catholics in Solidarity with the Peoples of Viet Nam, Laos, and Cambodia held in Turin (Italy) from November 1 to 4, 1973, unanimously passed an appeal in which it condemned the policy of sabotage of the

Paris Agreement pursued by the United States and the Nguyen Van Thieu Administration, exposed the regime of repression and terror imposed by Saigon which has turned the areas under its control into a huge prison, and denounced the continued detention of 200,000 political prisoners in South Viet Nam (*AFP*, Turin, November 4, 1973).

Thus, a year after the signing of the Paris Agreement on Viet Nam, and at variance with its explicit provisions, hundreds of thousands of political prisoners are still languishing in prisons and detention camps of the Saigon Administration.

It is to be stressed that the United States is the builder of the police organization and the system of prisons and detention camps in South Viet Nam.

On April 30, 1971, U.S. Senator W. Anderson, speaking before the U.S. Congress, denounced that the United States had spent at least $266,000 to build more "tiger cages" in Poulo Condor. On September 9, 1973, Senator E. Kennedy denounced the U.S. Government for violation of the Paris Agreement on Viet Nam by continued financial support for the police apparatus and prison system in South Viet Nam.

Heavy responsibility rests with the U.S. Government for the fate of the political prisoners now being detained by the Nguyen Van Thieu Administration.

The South Vietnamese People's Democratic Liberties Continue to Be Trampled Upon

Article 11 of the Agreement stipulates: "Immediately after the cease-fire, the two South Vietnamese parties will:

— Achieve national reconciliation and concord, end hatred and enmity, prohibit all acts of reprisal and discrimination against individuals or organizations that have collaborated with one side or the other;

— Ensure the democratic liberties of the people: personal freedom, freedom of speech, freedom of the press; freedom of meeting, freedom of organization, freedom of political activities, freedom of belief, freedom of movement, freedom of residence, freedom of work, right to property ownership, and right to free enterprise."

In the Appeal of January 28, 1973, the Central Committee of the South Viet Nam National Front for Liberation and the Provisional Revolutionary Government of the Republic of South Viet Nam stated that they would fully guarantee the democratic liberties to the people, achieve national reconciliation and concord so that all South Vietnamese people could end hatred and enmity, and jointly shape a new life, and rebuild the country, and demanded that the Saigon Administration do the same. On June 28, 1973, the Delegation of the Provisional Revolutionary Government of the Republic of South Viet Nam to the La Celle–Saint Cloud Conference proposed specific measures aimed at guaranteeing the democratic liberties, and among other things, that the two parties "issue a decision to the effect that all persons belonging to all political tendencies or religious beliefs will be allowed freedom of activities in both zones of the two South Vietnamese parties, and that newspapers belonging to all tendencies will be freely circulated between the two zones." It was also proposed that the two parties immediately enact laws to guarantee full democratic liberties to the people, as a first step to speed up the settlement of the internal political questions of South Viet Nam in a spirit of national reconciliation and concord.

At the same Conference, on July 8, 1973, the Delegation of the Provisional Revolutionary Government of the Republic of South Viet Nam put forward a proposal about "fundamental stipulations to guarantee democratic liberties to the South Vietnamese people" for the two South Vietnamese parties to agree upon and undertake to enact at once in the zone under their respective control.

With its extremely fascist and warlike nature, the Nguyen Van Thieu Administration has ignored these constructive proposals and continued to trample underfoot the people's democratic liberties as if it had not made any commitment in Paris.

One day only after the signing of the Agreement, Nguyen Van Thieu bluntly stated that "as for all our affairs, laws, administration, we'll do exactly as in the past, nothing is changed. . . . If Communists enter the village, they will be shot dead on the spot."

One day only after the four parties signed the June 13, 1973, Joint Communiqué, the Saigon Administration's spokesman stated: "The Government of the Republic of Viet Nam reserved its right to maintain restrictions to democratic liberties."

On March 1, 1973, the *Washington Post* remarked that the Saigon Administration "had restricted democratic liberties more than it had done before the Agreement came into effect." That is a well-grounded remark in view of the fact that shortly before and after the signing of the Agreement, the Saigon Administration has enacted dozens of new "decrees" such as:

—The "decree on local security" banning all market strikes and demonstrations and allowing the police to open fire on the spot;

—The "new press decree" stifling freedom of the press, and resulting in dozens of newspapers being closed down;

—The "decree" abolishing village elections. All chiefs of province are to be appointed by Nguyen Van Thieu, the administrative apparatus at grass-roots level is in the hands of officers loyal to Thieu;

—The "decree on the status of parties" aimed at eliminating 26 political parties in South Viet Nam, leaving in existence only the so-called "Democratic Party" and other organizations belonging to Thieu;

—The "decree" on the setting up of nine new criminal courts in Saigon and a number of provinces;

—The "decree N° 090" repressing anyone regarded as "dangerous" by the Saigon Administration.

Everything, from the tribunals to the press, is in the hands of Nguyen Van Thieu's army and police. Over 7,000 army and police officers of the Saigon Administration have been sent to various provinces to strengthen the apparatus of coercion and repression.

Hundreds of police operations are conducted each day with a view to purging, arresting, or killing people, herding them into concentration camps, or preventing them from returning to their native villages. The "accelerated pacification" and "Phoenix" programs which are carried on and expanded by the Saigon Administration in the areas under its control with a force of 125,000 policemen is merely a protracted campaign of white terror directed by the SAAFO [*Special Assistant to the American Ambassador for Field Operations*], which was formerly CORDS [*Civil Operations and Rural Development Support*].

Anyone suspected of communist or neutralist convictions or even of sympathy with neutralism, is considered "dangerous" and may be jailed or shot dead.

The so-called "crop-protecting plan" now being carried out by the Saigon Administration is merely a plan for plunder of rice, even in places recently devastated by typhoons and floods, and for economic blockade of the zone under the control of the Provisional Revolutionary Government of the Republic of South Viet Nam.

According to still incomplete figures, in nearly one year from the signing of the Paris Agreement on Viet Nam to December 15, 1973, the Saigon Administration conducted hundreds of thousands of police and "pacification" operations in the course of which it "purged" over 3 million people, arrested and tortured over 36,000 persons, plundered hundreds of thousands of tons of rice, tens of thousands of head of cattle, forcibly took away 145 billion South Vietnamese piasters, and herded over 920,000 people into concentration camps.

It is clear that the purpose of the Saigon Administration is not to ensure democratic liberties and achieve national reconciliation and concord, but to make its regime more fascist in crude violation of Article 11 of the Paris Agreement on Viet Nam, thus turning the zone under its control into a huge concentration camp, a hell on earth.

That is precisely the reason why the various social strata in Saigon and other Saigon controlled areas have been intensifying further and further their struggle for peace, democracy, a better life, and national reconciliation and concord.

No Progress Has Been Recorded
in the Settlement of the Internal Matters
of South Viet Nam

Article 9 of the Agreement asserts that the South Vietnamese people's right to self-determination is sacred, inalienable, and it stipulates that the South Vietnamese people shall decide themselves the political future of South Viet Nam through genuinely free and democratic general elections under international supervision.

Article 12 of the Agreement clearly points out that the two South Vietnamese parties shall hold consultations in order to set up a National Council of National Reconciliation and Concord of three equal segments. According to the fundamental spirit of these provisions, the two South Vietnamese parties shall jointly settle the internal matters of South Viet Nam in a spirit of national reconciliation and concord, mutual respect, without annexation of either side by the other, and without foreign interference.

National reconciliation and concord are a deep aspiration of the South Vietnamese people, the realistic way to maintain lasting peace and to achieve the South Vietnamese people's right to self-determination.

Proceeding from the policy of great national unity clearly expounded in its program of action and in the Political Program of the South Viet Nam National Front for Liberation, the Provisional Revolutionary Government of the Republic of South Viet Nam has repeatedly stated its willingness to cooperate with all people—whatever their past—who stand now for peace, independence, democracy and national concord, to end hatred and suspicion with a view to jointly building a life of love and happiness. It has called upon the Saigon Administration to place the interests of the

Fatherland above all, to respond to the demands of people from all walks of life, to rapidly set up through sincere consultations the National Council of National Reconciliation and Concord of three equal segments, and to organize at an early date genuinely free and democratic general elections to allow the South Vietnamese people to freely decide their political regime.

On April 25 and June 28, 1973, at the La Celle–Saint Cloud Conference, the Provisional Revolutionary Government of the Republic of South Viet Nam put forward reasonable and sensible proposals aimed at ensuring a total cease-fire and the return of all captured civilian personnel, guaranteeing the people's democratic liberties, setting up the National Council of National Reconciliation and Concord, holding genuinely free and democratic general elections in order to realize the South Vietnamese people's genuine right to self-determination, and resolving the question of the Vietnamese armed forces in South Viet Nam.

The Government of the Democratic Republic of Viet Nam has declared its full support to the policy and constructive proposals of the Provisional Revolutionary Government of the Republic of South Viet Nam.

The attitude of the U.S. Government and the Saigon Administration in this question is completely at variance with the spirit and letter of the Paris Agreement.

The Agreement clearly stipulates: "Foreign countries shall not impose any political tendency of personality on the South Vietnamese people" (Article 9c). However, U.S. President R. Nixon has openly declared to recognize the Nguyen Van Thieu Administration as the only legal administration in South Viet Nam. And as a matter of fact, the U.S. Government continues to maintain and strengthen this administration as an instrument of U.S. neo-colonialism in South Viet Nam.

As for the Saigon Administration, right from the beginning, it has not concealed its opposition to the Paris Agreement. It has evaded the most fundamental and urgent questions, namely to achieve a total cease-fire, to return all captured civilian personnel, and to ensure democratic liberties in order to create favourable conditions for resolving the internal matters of South Viet Nam as provided for in the Agreement; at the same time, it has sought every means to sabotage the achievement of national reconciliation and concord.

It has rehashed the unreasonable U.S. demand for the so-called "withdrawal of North Vietnamese troops" which has been rejected by the Paris Agreement and considered it a prerequisite for the settlement of the political questions in South Viet Nam.

With regard to the functions of the National Council of National Reconciliation and Concord, the Paris Agreement has explicitly stipulated: promoting the two South Vietnamese parties' implementation of the Agreement, achievement of national reconciliation and concord, ensurance of democratic liberties, and organization of the general elections. Yet the Saigon Administration wants to turn the National Council of National Reconciliation and Concord into a mere electoral commission in the framework of the so-called "Constitution" of the Thieu regime.

The Paris Agreement has explicitly stipulated that the National Council of National Reconciliation and Concord is composed of three equal segments. However, the Saigon Administration has tried hard to deny the existence of political and religious tendencies which stand on neither side in South Viet Nam, in an attempt to prevent these political forces from participating in the political life in South Viet Nam.

With a view to deceiving public opinion, the Saigon Administration has made a proposal concerning a specific date for the general elections, thus pretending to have at heart the implementation of the South Vietnamese people's right to self-determination. As is known, the shooting has not stopped in South Viet Nam, the people in the Saigon-controlled zone have continued to be denied all democratic liberties, hundreds of thousands of political prisoners belonging to various political and religious tendencies have remained in detention, opposition forces have continued to be subjected to repression and terror. General elections held in such conditions would be a mere farce as had been done in South Viet Nam, and which would result in giving a legal cover to Nguyen Van Thieu's dictatorial regime and eliminating the Provisional Revolutionary Government of the Republic of South Viet Nam. To hold such general elections is in fact to deny the South Vietnamese people's right to self-determination, and to act at variance with the Paris Agreement on Viet Nam.

In view of the aforesaid obstinate attitude of the Saigon Administration, no progress has been recorded as yet in the settlement of the internal matters of South Viet Nam.

The United States Is Not Willing to Put a Complete End to Its Military Involvement and Interference in the Internal Affairs of South Viet Nam

The Paris Agreement clearly stipulates: The United States will stop all its military activities against the territory of the Democratic Republic of Viet Nam by ground, air and naval forces wherever they may be based . . . (Article 2); will not continue its military involvement or intervene in the internal affairs of South Viet Nam (Article 4); within sixty days of the signing of the Agreement, there will be a total withdrawal from South Viet Nam of troops, military advisers, and military personnel including technical military personnel and military personnel associated with the pacification program, advisers to all paramilitary organizations and the police force, armaments, munitions, and war material of the United States and those of the other foreign countries allied with it (Article 5).

The Agreement also explicitly stipulates that the dismantlement of all military bases in South Viet Nam of the United States and of the other foreign countries allied with it shall be completed within sixty days of the signing of the Agreement (Article 6), and the two South Vietnamese parties shall not accept the introduction of troops, military advisers, and military personnel including technical military personnel, armaments, munitions and war material into South Viet Nam (Article 7). The two South Vietnamese parties shall be permitted to make periodic replacements of armaments on the basis of piece-for-piece, of the same characteristics and properties, under the supervision of the Joint Military Commission of the two South Vietnamese parties and of the International Commission of Control and Supervision.

The United States has seriously violated all the above-mentioned provisions.

Before the signing of the Paris Agreement on Viet Nam, the United States had already evaded the Agreement by establishing the biggest airlift in the history of the wars in Indochina to urgently introduce into South Viet Nam hundreds of aircrafts, tanks, artillery pieces, and tens of thousands of tons of other armaments and munitions at the average rate of 700 tons a day.

The troops of the United States and of its allies withdrawing from South Viet Nam, did not bring away with them their armaments, munitions and war material. This amounts in fact to illegally introducing hundreds of thousands of tons of armaments and war material into South Viet Nam in violation of the provisions of Article 7. The United States has also failed to dismantle its military bases in South Viet Nam, as stipulated by Article 6 of the Agreement.

Over the past year, the United States has illegally brought on repeated occasions armaments, munitions, aircraft, tanks, and artillery pieces into South Viet Nam to lend a helping hand to the Saigon Administration in its sabotage of the cease-fire and of the Agreement. In the face of the condemnation by public opinion, it has claimed by way of excuse that its actions "are consistent with Article 7 of the Agreement." In fact, Article 7 prohibits the introduction of armaments, munitions and war material into South Viet Nam and allows the two South Vietnamese parties to make replacements of armaments only under the supervision of the Two-Party Joint Military Commission and of the International Commission. As long as the two South Vietnamese parties have, not reached any agreement on the date of replacement of armaments, the kinds of armaments to be replaced, and the modalities of replacement and supervision, the United States is not permitted to bring into South Viet Nam any kinds of armaments, munitions and war material whatsoever.

What is particularly serious, the United States has left behind tens of thousands of military personnel disguised as civilians, and has not ceased to secretly bring thousands more into South Viet Nam. At present, there are already over 24,000 U.S. military personnel disguised as civilians working in the various services of the Defense Ministry, the various branches and services of the army, the police organizations, intelligence agencies and pacification services of the Saigon Administrations.

To direct and manage this system of "advisers," the United States has disguised its former military organizations as "civilian" agencies. D.A.O. [*Defense Attaché Office*] is a variant of the former MACV [*Military Assistance Command in Viet Nam*], S.A.A.F.O. [*Special Assistant to the Ambassador for Field Operations*] is as a matter of fact the former CORDS [*Civil Operations and Rural Development Support*] in a disguised form to assume continued direction of the "pacification" and "Phoenix" programs; U.S.A.I.D. [*United States Agency for International Development*] is nominally an economic agency, but has been for a long time now responsible for training, equipping, and giving advice to the police force of the Saigon Administration. As for the four U.S. "consulates general" in Da Nang, Nha Trang, Bien Hoa, and Can Tho, and the U.S. provincial "consulates" established since the signing of the Paris Agreement on Viet Nam, they are in fact U.S. commands in the various military regions and provinces of South Viet Nam.

With such an organization system, the United States is actually directing the war and repressive machine of the Nguyen Van Thieu Administration in the conduct of land-grabbing and "pacification" operations in South Viet Nam.

What is particularly significant, the U.S. military aid to the Saigon Administration after the signing of the Paris Agreement is even bigger than in war-time. Elliot

Richardson, former U.S. Defense Secretary, reported to the Defense Appropriations Committee of the U.S. House of Representatives that in the 1973–1974 fiscal year, the U.S. military aid to South-East Asia is not a mere 2.9 billion dollars, but actually 4.069 billion, surpassing by far the 2.735 billion dollars of military aid to South-East Asia in the 1972–1973 fiscal year. According to figures given in the Record of the U.S. Senate Armed Services Committee, out of this 4.069 billion dollars, the appropriations for "the use, maintenance, and purchase of arms" in South Viet Nam alone accounted for over 3 billion dollars. This does not include the military expenditures concealed under other headings, and the aid to the police organization and prisons in South Viet Nam.

It is clear that the United States, although compelled to withdraw its troops from South Viet Nam, is not willing to put a complete end to its military involvement and intervention in the internal affairs of South Viet Nam, and has not given up its design of strengthening and consolidating the Saigon Administration and army, and clinging to South Viet Nam through military aid and the system of disguised "military advisers."

With regard to the Democratic Republic of Viet Nam, in the carrying out of its obligations concerning the removal, permanent deactivation or destruction of mines in the territorial waters, ports, harbors and waterways of North Viet Nam, the United States deliberately created delays and obstacles in an attempt to prolong in practice the blockade of the territorial waters of the Democratic Republic of Viet Nam. It failed to carry out its obligation of removing the deactivated mines and to provide all appropriate facilities for the removal of mines in the waterways of the Democratic Republic of Viet Nam.

On the other hand, the United States has not stopped its encroachments on the sovereignty, territory and security of the Democratic Republic of Viet Nam. From the signing of the Paris Agreement to December 15, 1973, it sent on 39 occasions aircraft to intrude into the airspace of the Democratic Republic of Viet Nam for espionage activities over many places in North Viet Nam such as Vinh Linh, Quang Binh, Ha Tinh, Nghe An, Thanh Hoa, Hoa Binh, Yen Bai, Vinh Phu, Ha Bac, Tuyen Quang, Lang Son, Son La, Quang Ninh, and even Ha Noi and Hai Phong. It has also repeatedly sent warships to waters adjacent to the Democratic Republic of Viet Nam.

In the meantime, in application of the so-called "strategy of deterrence," the United States maintains big air and naval forces in Thailand and South-East Asia in an attempt to intimidate the Vietnamese people and the other peoples of Indochina.

The United States Has Delayed the Carrying Out of Its Obligation with Regard to the Healing of the Wounds of War in the Democratic Republic of Viet Nam

Article 21 of the Paris Agreement on Viet Nam stipulates: The United States will contribute to healing the wounds of war and to postwar reconstruction of the Democratic Republic of Viet Nam and throughout Indochina.

The DRVN-U.S. Joint Economic Commission was formed on March 1, 1973, and held its first meeting on March 15, 1973. After over one month of discussions, on its own, the U.S. side suspended sine die on April 19, 1973, the work of the Commission and of the group of experts. Thus, it acted at variance with the agreement reached between the two sides to the effect that the Commission's work would be completed on April 30, 1973, that is 60 days after the formation of the Commission.

The firm struggle of the Democratic Republic of Viet Nam brought the United States back to the meetings of the Joint Economic Commission on June 18, 1973. This time, the United States agreed with the Democratic Republic of Viet Nam on the amount of the credit and its use for the five-year plan and the plan of the first year of the U.S. contribution to healing the wounds of war and to postwar reconstruction in the Democratic Republic of Viet Nam; however, it posed political conditions for the signing of the document on the agreed points in an attempt to delay it.

This is clearly an attempt to shirk its responsibility and obligation under Article 21 of the Paris Agreement.

As is well-known, in the criminal air and naval war of destruction it conducted against the Democratic Republic of Viet Nam, the United States destroyed virtually all towns and cities, devastated many villages, hospitals, schools, factories, state farms, and other economic installations. It is a matter of course that the United States is duty-bound to contribute to healing the wounds of war in the Democratic Republic of Viet Nam, and the United States itself has accepted this under Article 21 of the Agreement. The Vietnamese people, international law, the conscience of the world's peoples, and of the progressive people of the United States will not allow Washington to shirk this responsibility and obligation incumbent on it.

Communiqué of the Ministry of Foreign Affairs of the Republic of Viet-Nam Marking One Year of Negotiation at the La Celle-Saint Cloud Conference between the Two South Vietnamese Sides, Saigon March 19, 1974

The two South Vietnamese sides have been negotiating for exactly one year at the La Celle–Saint Cloud Conference without making any progress. Over that period, in South Viet-Nam, the sound of gunfire has continued to be heard, soldiers of the Republic of Viet-Nam have continued to fall on the battlefields, and the South Vietnamese people have been forced to endure additional suffering, mourning, and hardships.

This tragic situation is due entirely to the bad faith of the Communists. On the occasion of the first anniversary of the negotiation at La Celle–Saint Cloud, the Government of the Republic of Viet-Nam deems it necessary to explain to the people of the world the efforts the Republic of Viet-Nam has made during the past year to solve the problems of South Viet-Nam and to contrast those initiatives with the negative attitude of the Communist side.

At the La Celle–Saint Cloud Conference, the Delegation of the Republic of Viet-Nam has made concrete and constructive proposals which show clearly its desire to reach a peaceful solution for South Viet-Nam, in accordance with the spirit and letter of the Paris Agreement.

Concerning the form in which the negotiations should be held, the Republic of Viet-Nam's Delegation has proposed that:

—Both sides stop criticizing each other so as to create a tranquil and conciliatory atmosphere.

—Both sides discuss together every matter that needs to be settled with a view to reaching a global solution for South Viet-Nam.

This approach would allow both sides to examine each other's matters of concern and demands, thus facilitating bargaining and compromise in a spirit of mutual concession.

Such bargaining and compromise can only take place in discreet talks free of propaganda. For this reason, the Republic of Viet-Nam's Delegation has proposed that in addition to open talks at the La Celle–Saint Cloud palace, the two sides should hold restricted and closed meetings during which they could talk openly and frankly.

As for the substance of the negotiations, the Republic of Viet-Nam holds that the solution reached by the two sides must absolutely respect the right to self-determination of the people of South Viet-Nam and that this right must be exercised as soon as possible. Therefore at the La Celle–Saint Cloud Conference, the Delegation of the Republic of Viet-Nam has three times proposed to hold general elections in South Viet-Nam at an early date.

On April 25, 1973, the Delegation of the Republic of Viet-Nam proposed that general elections be held on August 26, 1973.

Then, on June 28, 1973, the Delegation of the Republic of Viet-Nam proposed that general elections be carried out on December 25, 1973.

Finally, on January 18, 1974, the Delegation of the Republic of Viet-Nam proposed that general elections be held on July 20, 1974.

On each occasion, along with the proposal for general elections, the Delegation of the Republic of Viet-Nam suggested that the two sides meet in order to settle—prior to the general elections—all pending problems including the establishment of the National Council of National Reconciliation and Concord, the guarantee of democratic liberties, and the disposition of Vietnamese armed forces in South Viet-Nam.

Outside the scope of the La Celle–Saint Cloud Conference, the Government of the Republic of Viet-Nam has initiated other efforts to implement the Paris Agreement and to achieve reconciliation between the two sides. On January 26, 1974, the Minister of Foreign Affairs of the Republic of Viet-Nam solemnly declared that he was ready to meet the North Vietnamese Foreign Minister, or another high ranking representative of the Hanoi administration, to negotiate the normalization of relations between South and North Viet-Nam, and to discuss any other measures which might serve to ease tensions in South Viet-Nam, as well as measures to preserve the long-range interests of the Vietnamese people in both zones.

To this maximum goodwill and these practical, open-minded and constructive proposals of the Republic of Viet-Nam, the Communist side has responded with an extremely negative and uncompromising attitude.

It did not respond to the Republic of Viet-Nam's proposal to put an end to propagandistic criticisms. Neither did it agree to hold restricted or closed sessions to faciliate open and frank exchanges between the parties. It refused to discuss together problems which need to be solved simultaneously. It arranged matters for discussion in a rigid order and contended that problems must be settled successively according to that order. It systematically turned down the Republic of Viet-Nam's proposals for holding general elections and thereby delayed the day that the South Vietnamese people can decide their own political future.

The Communists' attitude at the La Celle–Saint Cloud Conference shows that:

—They want to use the Conference solely as a propaganda platform and not for frank and open-minded talks.

—They never think of bargaining or compromise in a spirit of mutual concession, but want the Republic of Viet-Nam to accept unconditionally all their demands. This is why they have arranged all problems in a rigid order and insisted that they be solved separately. In that manner, the Communists would agree to discuss a question only after the Republic of Viet-Nam had accepted all their demands on the previous one.

The preconditions set by the Communists, along with their attempts to reduce the La Celle–Saint Cloud Conference to a mere propaganda platform, show clearly that they do not sincerely desire a political solution for South Viet-Nam in a spirit of reconciliation. They want only to prolong the current talks at La Celle–Saint Cloud while trying to seize more land and control more population in their attempt to win militarily in South Viet-Nam.

The Communists' actions during the past year in South Viet-Nam are clear proof that they have neither abandoned aggressive designs nor changed their bellicose attitude. Over this period they have:

—Repaired and enlarged at least twelve military airfields and openly built more infiltration corridors south of the 17th Parallel.

—Introduced from the North more than 100,000 troops into South Viet-Nam, one SAM-2 missile regiment, 600 tanks, 600 pieces of artillery, and a massive quantity of other war material.

—Continued their military interference and maintained their troops on the territories of the Kingdom of Laos and of the Khmer Republic in flagrant violation of Article 20 of the Paris Agreement.

—Formed new combat divisions made up of former prisoners of war returned to them by the Republic of Viet-Nam; in the meantime they still have not accounted for 70,255 civilian and 26,645 military personnel of the Republic of Viet-Nam.

—Never stopped their systematic violations of the cease-fire provisions of the Paris Agreement. These violations now exceed the 39,000 mark. Not only did the Communists attack or shell the Republic of Viet-Nam's buses such as Tong-Le-Chan, Le-Minh, Khiem-Hanh, Bu-Prang, Bu-Dong, Kien-Duc, and Daksong, they also engaged in terrorist activities, killing thousands of innocent civilians. A most tragic and barbarous case was their shelling of the Cai-Lay primary school on March 9, 1974, that took the lives of 32 school children and wounded 34 others, plus one lady teacher and two relatives of students.

The Communists cannot deny their responsibility for the above actions, because their own leaders in orders No. 02/CT73/TUC/MN and 03/CT73/TUC/MN issued on January 19, 1973, and on March 30, 1973, respectively, and in resolution No. 4R, had instructed Communist units to increase their fighting potential in order to seize more land and control more people in South Viet-Nam.

The Communists' perfidy was also revealed by their attempts to make the International Commission of Control and Supervision inoperative by firing at the Commission's aircraft, shelling its Headquarters, demanding unceasingly a reduction in its personnel and making cuts in its budget. If the Communists did not have the deliberate intention of violating the Paris Agreement, they would not have tried so brazenly to paralyze the body whose duty is to supervise the implementation of that Agreement.

The Communists' bad faith is therefore fully evident. However, because of the earnest aspirations for peace among the people of South Viet-Nam, the Government of the Republic of Viet-Nam affirms that it will respect and implement seriously all the provisions of the Paris Agreement, and continue its attempts to achieve national reconciliation on the basis of the sacred right to self-determination of the people of South Viet-Nam.

The Government of the Republic of Viet-Nam, however, deems it necessary to denounce strongly before the people of Viet-Nam and the world's people, the Communists' schemes of aggression and their attempts to sabotage the peace. The Government of the Republic of Viet-Nam appeals to all freedom-loving peoples to support actively the efforts of the Republic of Viet-Nam aimed at securing a lasting and stable peace for South Viet-Nam, by compelling the Communists to accept the right of the people of South Viet-Nam to decide their own political future through free general elections under international supervision, as prescribed by the Paris Agreement of January 27, 1973.

Saigon's View One Year after the Joint Communiqué of June 13, 1973: Statement of the Foreign Ministry of the Republic of Viet-Nam, Saigon June 13, 1974

Exactly one year ago, the Parties to the Paris Agreement of January 27, 1973, signed a Joint Communiqué reaffirming their pledge to observe strictly and implement seriously the Paris Agreement and its related Protocols.

Although it had solemnly signed the two above documents, the Communist side has not hesitated during the past year to violate repeatedly and grossly every important provision of the Agreement and its Protocols.

Concerning the *cease-fire:* In opposition to Articles 2, 3, and 10 of the Agreement and the entire Protocol on the cease-fire in South Viet-Nam, the Communists have daily violated the cease-fire by launching attacks to grab more land and control more population; encircling, shelling and overrunning bases held by the Republic of Viet-Nam Armed Forces, perpetrating acts of terrorism against the civilian population. Typical cases of the recent cease-fire violations by the Communist side include its seizure of Tong-Le-Chan (April 12, 1974) and Dak-Pek bases (May 16, 1974); its major offensive along the Cambodian-Vietnamese border, in the Highlands and coastal area of Central Viet-Nam, and in Binh-Duong province; its artillery bombardments of the primary schools of Cai-Lay (March 9, 1974) and Song-Phu (May 4, 1974), which caused the death of a great many school-children and civilians, and its shelling of the urban center of Bien-Hoa (June 3, 1974). Thus, the Communist side has clearly trampled under foot the Cease-Fire Agreement and resumed its armed aggression against the Republic of Viet-Nam.

Concerning the problem of *infiltration:* In disregard of Article 7 of the Paris Agreement, the Communists have introduced into South Viet-Nam, from the signing of the Agreement until now, some 150,000 troops and cadres, one SAM-2 regiment, about 600 tanks and 600 pieces of heavy artillery. The level of Communist infiltration for this period is even higher than during the war. In order to carry out these illegal acts, the Communists have openly enlarged corridors of infiltration and built a strategic supply route going from the Demilitarized Zone to Loc-Ninh. Consequently, the military potential of the Communist side in South Viet-Nam is now even greater than in 1972.

To hide their active preparations for a renewed war, the Communist side has obstinately refused to implement Article 7 (concerning the designation of points of entry for the replacements of war material and munitions) and Article 11 (concerning the deployment of regional teams of the Joint Military Commissions) of the Protocol on the cease-fire. It has also refused to let the ICCS [*International Commission for Control and Supervision*] teams operate in the Communist side's temporary troops-stationing areas, in disregard of the entire Protocol on the ICCS.

Concerning the *return of captured personnel* and the *search for those missing in action:* The Communists are still detaining 26,645 military personnel and 70,255 civilian personnel of the Republic of Viet-Nam captured before January 28, 1973, although the Republic of Viet-Nam has provided a complete list of these persons and the deadline for the return has long passed. By so doing, the Communist side has obviously violated Articles 8 (A) and 8(C) of the Paris Agreement as well as the entire Protocol concerning the return of captured personnel. The Communist side is also uncooperative in the gathering of information regarding the personnel of the various parties missing in action. They even shot at teams engaging in the search for these missing persons, therefore trampling on the spirit and letter of Article 8(B) of the Agreement and Article 10 of the related Protocol.

Concerning the *exercise of the South Vietnamese people's right to self-determination* provided for in Articles 9 to 13 of the Paris Agreement, the Communist side has rejected all concrete proposals of the Republic of Viet-Nam to hold free general elections in South Viet-Nam. Worse still, the Communist side has recently decided to suspend indefinitely the meetings between the two South Vietnamese Parties at the La Celle–Saint Cloud Conference, thereby blocking all possible progress in the implementation of the South Vietnamese people.

As for the *relations between South and North Viet-Nam,* in accordance with Article 15(C) of the Paris Agreement, the Minister for Foreign Affairs of the Republic of Viet-Nam has twice proposed to meet the North Vietnamese authorities with a view to normalizing the relations between the two zones and to reducing the tensions in South Viet-Nam.

On both occasions, the Communist authorities in Hanoi have rejected this proposal without any justifiable ground.

Moreover, the North Vietnamese Communist administration had disregarded Articles 15(A) and 15(B) of the Agreement by daily violating the military demarcation line as well as the Demilitarized Zone (DMZ) separating the two parts of Viet-Nam.

Vis-à-vis *the ICCS and the Joint Military Commissions* established on the basis of Articles 16 to 18 of the Paris Agreement, the Communist side has always showed an uncooperative and hostile attitude. It has constantly obstructed and sabotaged the plans of deployment and the investigative work of these bodies. The Communists have shot at ICCS aircrafts, shelled its headquarters, arrested and detained its members. They have refused to contribute their share to the ICCS budget. Lately they have unfoundedly criticized and dared the Indonesian and Iranian delegations to withdraw from the Commission. Besides, they had unilaterally suspended their participation in the meetings of the Two-Party Joint Military Commission and of the Four-Party Joint Military Team for some time, thus paralyzing the work of these bodies.

Regarding *Cambodia and Laos:* Ignoring the clear provisions of Article 20 of the Paris Agreement, the Communists have continued their military operations on the national territories of these neutral countries, and kept using them to infiltrate troops and weapons into South Viet-Nam. On several occasions, the Government of the Khmer Republic has denounced the illegal interference in Cambodia by North Viet-Nam. As for Laos, Defense Minister Sisouk Na Champassak of the Provisional Government of National Union of Laos has just criticized North Viet-Nam for not withdrawing its troops from the Laotian territory in conformity with the Paris and Vientiane Agreements.

In short, although it signed the Paris Agreement of January 27, 1973, and the Joint Communiqué of June 13, 1973, the Communist side has daily committed serious violations of all the provisions of that Agreement.

For its part, the Government of the Republic of Viet-Nam has always strictly observed and seriously implemented the Paris Agreement of January 27, 1973, and the related Protocols. The Government of the Republic of Viet-Nam demands that the Communist side respond by a serious attitude.

More concretely, the Communist side must:

— immediately put an end to all its cease-fire violations and illegal infiltrations.

— return to its troops-stationing positions before January 28, 1973.

— withdraw to North Viet-Nam its troops and cadres, weapons and war material that have been illegally introduced into South Viet-Nam.

— return immediately all the military and civilian personnel of the Republic of Viet-Nam captured before January 28, 1973, and start talks for the return of all personnel captured thenceforth.

— show its goodwill for peace by concrete acts, and negotiate seriously with the Republic of Viet-Nam side with a view to reaching an overall solution for the problems of South Viet-Nam.

Only in this way could the war be ended rapidly and peace restored in Viet-Nam. Otherwise, the tension here will persist and the Communist side shall have to bear full responsibility for all the consequences resulting from this situation.

The Communists' View: "Advancing the Revolution by Means of Peace or War, Violence or Negotiation" (Resolution of Binh Dinh Province Party of the PRG), September 1974

Captured by South Vietnamese forces and made available in Saigon in unofficial English translation.

[PART 1.]
[INTRODUCTION]
Section 1.
The Development of the Situation since the Signing of the Paris Agreement

The American imperialists, defeated in aggressive war, were forced to sign the Paris Agreement and withdraw their troops from Vietnam. They changed from using American troops to using puppet troops, the Puppet Government and U.S. advisors to continue the war. The principal strategem is "Pacification" (Binh Dinh) by encroaching (Lam Chiem) to seize land and people, eradicating (Koa Han) the disputed areas (Vung Tranh Chap) and those under our control (Vung Ta Lam Chu), pushing us from the lowlands and forcing a clear line between our areas and theirs. (In Binh Dinh Province) the main object has been "encroaching" on our "liberated and governed areas" (Vung Kep, i.e., GVN controlled) in the southern districts.

The Americans and Puppets combined military, political, economic and psywar [psychological warfare] tricks to attack our infrastructures and neutralize (Vo Hieu Hoa) our organizations and cadre in the hamlets and villages. The enemy established strong points (Dong Chot), expanding step by step from one area to another. The enemy has introduced confusing ideas to sow suspicion, illusions and hope among our people, cadre and troops, has exploited (the spirit of) national conciliation (Chinh Sach Hoa Hop Dan Toc) to plant spies in our areas, has attacked our entry-exit points to sabotage our economy. (Also) the enemy is building up his regional forces so that his regular forces can be more mobile, consolidating his village government and police system, developing the Democracy Party, assigning military personnel to village government, building his economy while harassing ours. He is suppressing the people's struggle movements and preventing the third force from coming into being. He is trying to remove the "leopard skin position" (Da Bao).

During the first seven or eight months of the cease-fire our people resisted and to some extent limited the enemy's Pacification and Encroachment Program; however, the three-pronged attack (Ba Mui Giap Cong—political, military and military proselyting) was weak and the enemy achieved a number of results. Following Resolution of A.15 (Region 5 Committee), which set forth the party mission as "Counterpacification and Encroachment" (Chong Binh, Lam Chiem), we have moved to a new state of leadership. First, we overcame rightest (Nuu Khuynh) attitudes and during September and October 1973 stopped in part the enemy's pacification and expansion, restoring a number of areas taken by the enemy in the north of the province and consolidating our illegal forces in the South and reactivating them. This stopped enemy encroachment in certain areas but he continued pacifying and encroachment in other places. In early 1974 the enemy regrouped and continued his program, encroaching in the North and pacifying in the controlled and contested areas in the South. Although we resisted, we did not overcome the rightist attitude entirely, overemphasizing defense and failing to make the best use of (our forces). The momentum of our attack was not strong, and the enemy continued his program. Neither side achieved a clear cut advantage.

In April 1974, following the March Conference of the Province Committee's Current Affairs Committee to study the guidance of the Regional Committee, the leadership from the Province Committee down to the village committees underwent considerable change: the enemy and friendly situations were evaluated more correctly; we realized the enemy continued the war and that we had to wage war to defeat him, rightist attitudes and illusions of peace were more effectively overcome; our perceptiveness was increased; our dedication to attacking the enemy and complying with the plans of higher echelons was improved; and we combined, throughout the Province, attacks with uprisings in the rural areas creating opportunities to develop movements in the towns and cities. We destroyed his defenses, defeated his expansion and one step of his pacification, retook lost areas and liberated a number of new areas, pushed the enemy into a more defensive and confused position, strove to consolidate our areas and improve our strength. All of which has created favorable opportunities for local force attacks and people's uprisings. Our attacks and uprisings were slightly better in the northern area with Koai Nhon District being the best. Political struggle and military proselyting obtained new developments, some population was returned to the liberated areas. There has been new progress in the development of liberated areas. The revolutionary pride of the Party Headquarters, the Army and the people has been heightened.

The summer–autumn (May–June and July–August) victory is only the initial step, but it (heightens) the possibility of defeating the enemy's encroachment and pacification program. Our main force is superior to the enemy's in destructive power. Our local forces and people can intimidate the enemy, annihilate key positions, destroy the enemy's oppressive system piece by piece and liberate large areas during a combined campaign. This summer–autumn victory has proved that the policy of the Central Committee is sound and that the evaluation of the friendly and enemy situation by the region and province committees is sound and accurate, promoting the unit, confidence, enthusiasm and determination of the Party Headquarters, Army and People.

Section 2.
Present Enemy and Friendly Situation

A. ENEMY SITUATION

Prior to the summer–autumn campaign, although our attacks were weak, we preserved our territory and created the opportunity for the victories we won during the campaign. During the campaign the enemy continued his pacification effort but had to spread his forces thinly. This was ineffective and enemy morale was low. Many of his key positions were destroyed or abandoned. We stopped encroaching. His pacification efforts were limited and weak. He strove to defend his territory, but it was taken back by our attacks or by mass risings. In many areas puppet officials ran for their lives, showing the people how loose enemy control over them was.

It is true that the enemy is still large, has strong firepower, has a strong defense system, controls many populated areas and is still supported by the Americans. Yet these strengths have been drastically reduced. The basic weaknesses of the enemy are: the withdrawal of American and Korean troops had political military, ideological and economic impact on the puppet troops resulting in about 7,500 troops less and considerable loss of firepower; the enemy's main force has been spread out, limiting his ability to mass and maneuver; he has reduced reserves; his outposts are weaker than before; his territorial forces are at full strength but still cannot control the people and defend the area; his air and artillery are weak; and his rear services are experiencing difficulties.

Politically Thieu and the Americans are flagrantly sabotaging the Agreement, carrying out a fascist policy, terrorizing the masses and oppressing the opposition forces. The economic crisis is making life more miserable and promoting dissension. The Americans and Thieu are more isolated politically (from the people) and the internal conflicts develop more acutely. Opposition forces to Thieu are stronger and more active. These problems and the resignation of Nixon have created difficulties and demoralized the puppet troops and government. Economically the crisis worsens day by day because of the costs of supporting a huge bureaucratic war machine. Reduced aid speeds inflation, affecting social welfare, triggering unemployment and lawlessness. In brief, the enemy's basic flaws are weakening him and frustrating his development.

B. FRIENDLY SITUATION

At the beginning of the new phase (post-cease-fire) we could not understand the nature of the enemy's strategy or his basic weakness. Also, we could not clearly see what the capabilities of the revolution were after the withdrawal of American troops. Rightist attitudes and illusions of peace were still a problem and defense was overemphasized. At times we were weak in attacking and counterattacking, and our movement met difficulties. But step by step, mainly since March 1974, the concepts and leadership of the Party have been improved significantly. Military activities have been emphasized. The summer–autumn campaign was carried out, winning a victorious step forward. Our forces have incapacitated 6,600 enemy soldiers, destroyed or forced withdrawal from 67 key positions and 28 temporary (Trai) positions, captured 393 weapons of all types and destroyed (assorted equipment, vehicles and aircraft). Almost 40 of these key positions were dislodged by guerrillas and uprising masses who also destroyed 17 resettlement areas, taking hundreds of people into our areas. We have gained control of almost 25,000 people, increasing the liberated and autonomous population to more than 130,000 people and widening the contested areas and those where enemy control is lossening [sic]. We also have enlarged the areas of operation for our next series of activities. However, our counterpacification activities are weak, and the victories of the summer–autumn campaign limited. The general movement in the province was not simultaneous–it was especially weak in An Nhon and Tuy Phuoc districts and in Qui Nhon City.

The movement in the enemy controlled areas recently took a new direction. With the people's resentment over the economic situation and the enemy's fascist policy, (exacerbated by) the effect of our victories and the results of the work of our cadre in certain areas, the struggle movement demanding social welfare and democracy, the return of sons and husbands, and freedom to travel and work has developed. When our forces were attacking, the people of certain areas rose and destroyed several enemy resettlement areas, repatriating to their villages in our areas. Armed propaganda and tyrant annihilation activities have been good, and various action units have been strengthened. The contested area and that where the enemy is losing control have been enlarged. We have persuaded 1,500 enemy soldiers, including one entire territorial company, to desert. One regular platoon deserted at our call. We have persuaded three territorial companies and nine platoons to take anti-war positions and resist operational orders. In the urban areas workers struggle movements demanding lower prices and more social services have taken place continuously. The Buddhist movement for peace held prayer sessions, there have been protests over the province and city council elections.

The political situation in the enemy area is developing in favor of the Revolution; the situation is chaotic; the people are annoyed by the standard of living and the fascist policy of Thieu. The intermediary stratum and third forces are massing against Thieu. This could lead to uprisings in the cities and in the countryside. Nevertheless, our activities, particularly in the urban areas, are weak in many aspects.

We have carried out in part the task of creating the armed forces, giving them "good maturity" in ideology, combat techniques and tactics and arms. Our forces are deployed in important areas of operation with motorized transport and a road system which facilitates reinforcement and supply. All types of our forces have progressed, as evidenced by their performance during the summer–autumn campaign. Our local forces are still weak, but together with the uprising of the masses they gained control of many villages during the campaign. Yet certain weaknesses still exist. District local forces and guerrillas are weak, poor in quantity and quality. Reinforcements are short, and rear services do not effectively support continuous and long term attacks.

Our liberated area has been enlarged and improved. It has been generally stabilized in all respects, has increased its production supporting the people's livelihood and the armed forces. We have overcome the damage inflicted by the typhoons of the fall of 1974 and the drought of 1974. Since the Agreement we have farmed and cultivated 78,438 mau (circa 5,000 square meters) of rice paddy and arable land and cleared and revived 9,000 hectares more. The (spring) rice harvest was good. Animal husbandry has been restored. The standard of living has not only stabilized but improved in certain areas. The North–South truck route has been developed. Refugees of 1973 are now supporting themselves. Life in the mountains has been improved. Access to indispensable supplies such as salt, fabric, and farming tools has improved. This development of our areas has made people in the enemy area more confident in our policies and the ultimate victory of the Revolution. Weaknesses, however, still exist: development of the mountain base is slow, forestry work is only slightly advanced, maintenance of the roads and vehicles is poor and wasteful, food supply in combat areas is not adequate, the ideology of both party members and people in the base areas is developing too slowly with too many signs of pessimism and too much recurrence of backward, depraved customs which affect unity, production, public order and security. Although we have made progress in building up the Party, including recruiting 1,300 new members, the work has progressed at "a snail's pace" and the quality of the cadre and the capability of the leadership have not been up to expectations. There are fewer party chapters in the enemy areas and the development of Party members, particularly in the cities and the enemy areas, is slow. (The work) has not gone well. Although the Party has achieved some results in understanding policy, overcoming rightist attitudes and false hopes for peace and evaluating the enemy situation, much more must be done.

Section 3.
Good and Weak Points Regarding the Leadership of Party Headquarters

Since the enemy did not adhere to the cease-fire, the Province Current Affairs Committee has ordered all (echelons) to focus on defeating the encroachment and pacification programs of the enemy and defending and enlarging our territory. We have held fast and developed agents in the enemy area, including the cities. Our movement has improved one step there, and in some places even more. The liberated area is enlarged and improved. Morale has been improved. We have made an important change in the ideology of the party, army and people (i.e., to accepting the need for further war) and developed and consolidated our Party chapters. (All this has) proved the correctness of Province and Regional Committee Guidance. The causes of this victory are: correct policy of the Province Committee and firm leadership of the Region Committee toward us; the brave Party Headquarters, troops and people in the Province; the determination of staying close and attacking the enemy; all levels of the Party united and agreed to carry out the mission assigned from above; reinforcements from above and from main force units in the area; and the support of others in the common battlefield. The weak points are: opposition to pacification and encroachment is still weak and, having lost land and people at the beginning, the restoration is slow; the movement in the enemy area is still poor and needs further organization, not being publicly, legally, and widely developed, particularly the third force; we still have fewer people than the enemy; development of the people's livelihood is too slow; cadre and soldiers have not been reformed completely; economic development is too slow and filled with difficulties; party organization is slow; some areas, Van Canh for instance, are deteriorating; the establishment of local forces and guerrillas has not kept up, main district and village units are still weak; the guerrilla organization is not strong and regulars and replacements are a problem; rightist attitudes have been clearly seen, false hopes for peace, fear of war atrocities, deviation from policy; many village organizations are still weak; and cadre are being produced too slowly. The degree of organization realized at all levels is weak.

These weaknesses exist because: in the beginning the enemy strategy was not understood; rightist attitudes, persistent pacifism and poor understanding of the attack strategy existed; understanding of the focus of activities was inadequate; lethargy in overcoming weaknesses; recruitment in combination with attack was weak; and the establishment of the organization was weak.

PART 2.

EXPERIENCES FOR GUIDANCE OF THE INITIAL STEP OF THE NEW PHASE

From practical experience in guiding the implementation of the first step of the new phase, we have drawn a number of lessons as follows:

Section 1.
Assessment of the Enemy and Ourselves

It is extremely important to assess accurately the nature and schemes of the enemy and at the same time to assess accurately the balance of forces between the enemy and ourselves during the new revolutionary phase. At the beginning we did not make a complete assessment of the enemy's stubborn nature and his strategic scheme to continue "Vietnamizing" the war by signing the Paris Agreement and at the same time continuing the war. We did not fully realize that the changes in the balance of forces were on our side after the withdrawal of the American troops. This made us hesitate and the lack [sic] determination in attack, particularly not recognizing clearly the role and the objective of the military attack.

In the past we have at times made incomplete assessments of the enemy and we have not fully seen our own shortcomings. After the signing of the Paris Agreement sometimes our review of the situation has been subjective. As a result many comrades in the local areas and units also have been subjective and made exaggerated assessments of the enemy's strength. As a result during the recent past we have made a very high estimate of the enemy and we have not fully seen all the basic weak points of the enemy. As for our side we have seen difficulties and weak points in all aspects, and we have not clearly realized that our position and power have been in the process of development. This has influenced our determination in attacking the enemy.

The present situation, compared to that before the withdrawal of the American forces, has changed a lot and the balance of forces between the enemy and ourselves is also evolving. The weak points of the enemy have become more obvious from day to day and our basic strong points are in the process of development. Of course, we cannot overlook the temporary strong points which the enemy may exploit to attack us. The withdrawal of the American forces after the signing of the Paris Agreement has been a big change, making the Puppet Government encounter many difficulties and manifest many shortcomings and weak points in the military, political and economic fields. All these areas are on the decline. Particularly the present economic crisis has made the Puppet Government feeble. These economic difficulties have led to a political and military weakness and are leading to a political crisis for the Saigon regime. In the military field, although the enemy is still numerous, his weapons still abundant and his defense systems dense, we have seen clearly from the summer–autumn campaign that the morale of the local units has been weaker than before, his air strikes and artillery have been feeble, as a result his previously solid defense positions have become weaker than before. At times the enemy maneuvered his entire force to implement its pacification program and to expand and encroach on our territory, yet we did not use our entire forces to counter them. Still we won an initial victory and that is significant.

The evaluation of the people is not simple. We must first bear in mind that the revolutionary work is about the people. We ought to thoroughly realize the revolutionary potential of the people in order to exploit and develop it. At the same time we must realize that after years of "Vietnamization" of the war, the situation of the people in the enemy held areas has many complexities. Their relationship with the enemy and with us is complicated, their thoughts and sentiments have been influenced a great deal. In many respects they are passive. We ought to be very patient in educating, motivating deeply, activating, propagandizing, and correctly implementing our policy in order to make them active. In practice when we began to enlarge our areas and our cadre began to contact the people, we discovered that the people were uncooperative and afraid of the Revolution; they did not listen to the cadre; the cadre despaired after talking to the people a couple of times; there were even cadre who gave orders to or were harsh with the people. These attitudes only make the people misunderstand us more and be more afraid of us. This creates a separation between revolutionary cadre and the people which the enemy can try to exploit.

We must realize that the families of enemy soldiers are related to the enemy, but nevertheless they are farmers and workers who bear a grudge against and have suffered from the enemy, their sons and brothers were sent to die for Thieu and the U.S., and they had in the past bound their interest up with the Party. As for the old agents, some people still believed and relied on them because of their past achievements and did not realize that they are now passive and are being influenced, undermined, and neutralized by the enemy. A number of comrades have tried to motivate the people by classifying them into two categories (Revolutionary Families and Soldiers' Families—Gia Dinh Cach Mang Voi Gia Dinh Binh Si), but this discrimination has raised suspicion and tension among the people.

With regard to the targets of motivation, we must realize the old people have much knowledge and deep feelings toward the Revolution, yet they are cowardly, pacifistic, and afraid of the enemy so they dare not act quickly; while the young people are always a bit afraid of us at the beginning because they have been brainwashed by the enemy but once they are close to us and understand us they boldly join us and operate actively.

In fact, most of the families in the countryside nowadays are families of enemy soldiers, and they are our targets of motivation. Only when we have succeeded in controlling the enemy soldiers' families will we be able to hold fast the people after the expansion of our controlled area.

In general, when we evaluate the enemy and ourselves we must not look merely into the quantity, into a few aspects, into the quiet appearance of the situation, but we must examine the situation totally. The accurate evaluation and comparison of balance of forces between the enemy and ourselves, and recognition of the trend of development of the present situation has a very great significance because it provides us with a basis to affirm our determination to attack the enemy in the future.

Section 2.
Advancing the Revolution by Means of Peace or War, Violence or Negotiation

In the past this matter has not been thoroughly understood. After the Paris Agreements, the trend of thought inclined to the illusion of peace and it was imagined that political struggles and diplomatic struggles would advance the Revolution. Experience in the past has taught us a lesson which is: American imperialism is still forcing neo-colonialism on South Vietnam, the persistent schemes of the Americans are on the one hand to sign the Paris Agreements and on the other hand to hold on to the Thieu Puppet Government by continuing to aid it with weapons, money and advisers to continue the "Vietnamization" of the war, so as to use the war to eliminate our revolutionary achievements and liquidate the Revolution. The "Pacification" program is used to encroach on our lands, to terrify the people, and repress all the forces against them and thus have made the war even more fierce. Experience has proven that the nature of the present revolutionary struggle is both to liberate the people and at the same time to conduct a strong and meaningful class struggle. The capitalist, "comprador" (Mai Ban), bureaucratic, militarist, fascist clique that is led by Nguyen Van Thieu is the natural child of the U.S. Its economic, political and military organizations are based on a foundation of the most reactionary social class. It will try to protect its class rights to the end. What it did in the past has proven it is the most reactionary, extremist and blood-thirsty clique. We must not delude ourselves that we can negotiate peace or national reconciliation with the Thieu clique. We ought to struggle decisively to defeat the new colonialism of the American imperialist and decisively conduct a class struggle to overthrow the Thieu clique. Only thus can national reconciliation and concord be achieved. Thus we have no other choice but to use violence, start the war to totally win the "Vietnamization" war of the enemy and to advance the Revolution. For that reason, to think of attaining peace by negotiation is to entertain an illusion. We must be prepared for violence. We can only achieve peace by defeating the enemy through war.

The signing of the Paris Agreements denoted a gigantic victory achieved by our people who had defeated the aggression of the American imperialist army which was compelled to pull out of Vietnam. Yet peace has not been restored in South Vietnam because of the enemy. Hence we must on one hand propagandize the people, especially the people in the enemy-controlled areas and enemy soldiers, that our slogan is peace, independence, democracy, food and clothing, and national reconciliation and concord, point out that the enemy continues the war, and on the other hand start a war to win the war caused by the enemy. Only when we have thwarted

"Pacification" and encroachment by the enemy and have caused the Saigon Regime to be faced with a danger of collapse and are ourselves in a better position and stronger will there be the possibility of a cease-fire. But a cease-fire is only a postponement; it is not the permanent peace longed for by our people.

Our people have undergone 20 years of war against the Americans for national salvation in which we have sacrificed, suffered so much that everyone longs for peace. That is an earnest and legitimate aspiration. However, the kind of peace we want must exist in independence and freedom. We must now master the concept of violence, above all the violence of war to defeat the enemy. Only when the capitalist, comprador, bureaucratic, militarist, and fascist American Puppet government clique is overthrown and replaced by another force which is willing to implement the Paris Agreement is there a possibility that peace can be restored. In order to have real and persistent peace, the entire enemy army and government must be totally expunged and the government put into the hands of the people. We should master this concept so that we will not be confused or deluded again, even if there will be conferences or the signing of another Agreement in the future.

The Geneva and Paris Agreements are gigantic victories gained by our people. Twice the enemy seriously violated these Agreements. We have no other choice but to start the war to defeat the "Vietnamization" war of the enemy in order to have the Agreements implemented.

Section 3.
Through Understanding of the Concepts of Revolutionary Progress (Tien Cong)

Revolution is progress. Progress is revolutionary activity, the development of revolutionary movements. Ceasing to make revolutionary progress means the decline of the movement. Only revolutionary progress weakens the enemy, makes the basic weaknesses of the enemy still weaker and exposes them clearly. Only revolutionary progress makes us stronger and develops our basic strong points. Revolutionary progress is the process of our evaluating the enemy and ourselves more accurately, and our finding better ways to attack the enemy more effectively. The power of revolutionary progress is in the complete coordination of the political and military struggle, the three armed forces, the three prong attack throughout the three strategic areas. Only when we take care in organizing these forces, give them proper leadership, know how to closely coordinate all our forces and all our fronts of attack, will we be able to develop enough strength to launch major attacks. On the contrary, if our forces lack coordination, or one of the forces, or one of the aspects, or one of the three strategic areas is weak or stands still, our attack on the enemy will be incoherent, weakening our entire force.

Recently, we have not clearly defined the role of the military attack, and have not coordinated attacks against the enemy with the organization and consolidation of our forces; we have put more emphasis on defense than on offense. We have not developed the three types of forces and the three prong attack very well, our attacks against the enemy's rear area have been weak; in some areas our troops and cadre have retreated to the rear and action units have narrowed their operational areas, enabling the enemy to take advantage of us and attack and encroach upon our land.

The fact that the enemy has succeeded in implementing a part of the "pacification" encroachment, and setting up blocking positions, has not been due to the enemy's strength, but because our attacks against the enemy have not been strong enough. Where our forces, even if only district and guerrilla forces, stay close to the enemy, the situation is different. But where our forces withdraw to the rear, the enemy attacks and encroaches upon us, causing us difficulties; but when our forces counterattack, even lightly, the enemy must pull back and the situation changes again.

The recent lesson teaches the concept of the revolutionary progress. Full understanding of the concept of revolutionary progress must be shown in the coordination of attack against the enemy with the building of our forces aimed at attacking the enemy harder each time. We already have the experience of combining attacks against the enemy with the building of our forces, and only in this way will we be able to attack the enemy, hold land and people, maintain our position on the battlefield, and create good conditions to continue to progress.

Section 4.
Decisively Defeating the Primary Strategy of the Enemy, Which is "Pacification," Expansion Encroachment, and Helping the People Gain Control, Expanding Our Areas, and Steadily Advancing the Revolution Step-by-Step

The enemy continues to implement the "Vietnamization" of the war and use "pacification" as its primary strategic measure to hold on to and expand its area of control, increase its strength and weaken ours. We must defeat the strategy of the enemy in order to win over people, put the people in control, expand our areas, increase our strength in all respects, and fundamentally change the balance of forces between the enemy and ourselves, in order to overthrow the enemy. The defeat of the enemy's primary strategic measure will lead to the overthrow of the enemy. That is the key objective, and it is the axis of the entire apparatus of the life-and-death struggle between the enemy and ourselves in the new phase. We must combine three methods: initiate a high tide of attack and uprising in the rural areas, coordinate this with the attacks of our main forces to annihilate the enemy and liberate each and every area, and intensify the political movement in the towns and cities leading to severe political crisis there.

The summer–autumn campaign has shown that although the enemy realized we would attack, it continued to implement its "pacification" and encroachments to firmly hold the countryside, while at the same time maneuvering its mobile forces to relieve pressure on battlefields held by our regular forces. But the enemy could not realize its intentions. When attacked by us, the enemy was compelled to mobilize its regular forces to liberate and block the battlefields of our main forces. Even so, the strength of the enemy was limited and it was afraid of being exterminated by us. The enemy was hurt badly, many of its key positions eliminated and its defensive lines penetrated; it only brought in regiment-size units for rescue, and these reinforcements were made drop by drop. The enemy was passive and confused and its primary concern was to hold off our attacks; it was unable to counterattack to retake lost areas. The regular army units had to deploy thinly to hold people and rural areas. Then, when attacked by us, the regular army units had to be brought over for rescue operations on battlefields held by our main forces. This leaves many gaps in many rural areas, and the enemy's local forces are not capable of standing up to our local forces and guerrillas. The enemy's firepower, mobility, and rear service activities have decreased greatly in comparison with the past. For this reason, its morale and combat effectiveness is obviously on the decline. Our main force troops have the capability of destroying outposts, district towns, and subsectors provided with strong fortifications; of destroying battalions and regiments coming as relief forces; and of destroying the enemy on a medium or large scale. We can liberate the various areas successively, starting with the mountain and border areas, to create favorable conditions for the local forces to attack and the people to rise up. Recently, we have destroyed and forced withdrawal from hundreds of outposts of oppressive control. The people have risen up, breaking loose the enemy's control, annihilating and disintegrating the enemy's local forces and auxiliary forces, and winning control, portion by portion, of land area. Had we been better prepared we would have been able to coordinate our attacks by our main force units to push forward strongly the three-pronged attack, to conduct attacks and uprisings to win control of large portions of land, and to create the opportunity for a spontaneous uprising to recapture large rural areas.

The movements in the urban areas are presently weak. Yet they have many new capabilities, especially as a result of our two attacking blows: the main force attacking and destroying the enemy and the rural attack and uprising. If the leadership of the movement in the cities knows how to coordinate with the above combined campaign of the two attacking blows, how to motivate the people's struggle movement, how to coordinate with the Buddhist Movement, how to manipulate and develop the third force under the slogan of demanding peace, democracy, better living conditions and the implementation of the Paris Agreement, this may bring about a political high tide.

Section 4. [sic]
Staying Close to the Population and to Areas of Operation

The enemy is carrying out his "pacification" and expansion fiercely and persistently. In doing so he has mobilized all his forces, used any means, and employed the most cruel and cunning tricks with the primary objective of destroying our infrastructure and neutralizing our basic village organizations and agents. He has made use of our every tiny deficiency to attack us and fight for the control of each single civilian and each inch of land. When we retreat, the enemy advances. If we don't attack, the enemy attacks us. During the most critical period of resistance against the U.S., our cadres, soldiers, and the people of our area had the tradition and experience of realizing the four "stay-close" principles with the slogan, "abandon not one milimeter of land." Thanks to this we were able to hold the land, the people, and defeat the U.S. invaders. Since signing the Paris Agreement, in many places, often due to pacificism and relaxation, our capability of staying close has been weak. Many units, action teams, and cadre operating in enemy areas have left their area of operations and withdrawn to rear areas. In other areas they stayed close to the people but failed to make necessary preparations as in the past, so they were forced to leave the people when they were fiercely attacked by the enemy. Therefore the movement in some areas at some times has met with difficulty. But in the places where the troops, cadre and action teams have stayed close to the area of operation and gone on the offensive, propagandized and indoctrinated the people to attack the enemy and exterminate tyrants, then the enemy has withdrawn and the people's enthusiasm for struggle has increased and the movement developed well. To carry out the "staying close" tactic, we must resolve the following matters: to constantly keep the cadre and the action teams well indoctrinated, to make necessary preparations so that they can hold their areas when the enemy launches attacks and sweep operations, to attack the enemy and liquidate tyrants continually, to cause the enemy to retreat, to activate the thoughts of the people and organize and guide them to struggle against the enemy, to achieve the organization of local and interior leadership and to coordinate the interior force with the exterior force in attacking the enemy exterminating tyrants, and leading the people in struggle. We must increase our activities to attack the enemy, eliminate tyrants, punish enemy spies, and force the enemy to withdraw if we are to stay properly close to the people. Recent experience shows that where we do stay properly close, we are able to exploit opportunities to launch attacks and uprisings, counterattack when the enemy attacks, maintain the people's control, and continue our attacks to expand the areas we control.

Although the enemy continues the "Vietnamization" of the war, we keep on pushing forward the people's warfare to defeat him. However, the development of the situation after the signing of the Paris Agreement has some new characteristics: the enemy has become weak militarily, politically, and economically. Although the war is still fierce, the capability of the puppet army is limited, so the intensity of the fighting is now different than before the signing of the Paris Agreement when the U.S. troops were present in South Vietnam. Our strength has been consolidated and developed; the balance between our forces and the enemy's has changed significantly; our bases and liberated areas have been gradually stabilized and enlarged; our road system has been developed rapidly and now connects with North Vietnam. The aid from North Vietnam for our region has been larger and larger; we have good conditions to step up the reconstruction of liberated areas in all respects, to restore and develop the economy. The operational requirements in enemy controlled areas, especially in the cities, have become greater and more complicated. The situation is developing whereby the requirements for revolutionary operations must become more and more systematic, broadly based, and complex. Therefore, the leadership at all levels and in all branches is required to solve many big and complex problems in order to concentrate forces to defeat enemy "pacification" and encroachment, intensify operations of the armed forces, initiate coordinated campaigns, develop the movements in enemy controlled areas, especially in the cities, and at the same time quickly develop our areas to restore and develop the economy and resolve the rear service problems there. We have many fairly complicated problems concerning ideology, organization, implementation, policies, and regulations. For this reason, the heightening of the capability for total leadership, organization and implementation at all levels is a major problem affecting the development of the movement.

The leadership at all levels must understand our emphasis and supervise closely the military, political, economic, cultural and social aspects, including the attack in the front lines and the development of the rear areas. They must concentrate on all three strategic areas. Besides the leadership's carrying out our primary mission, conducting operations in enemy controlled areas, motivating the people, and developing the Party, the direction and development of the economy and the development of the armed forces has become progressively more important and larger scale, encountering more complicated technical and scientific problems. This then demands a heightening of leadership capability, more timely decision making, better organization of our apparatus, judicious deployment of cadre, and the formulation of truly appropriate policies.

We must develop democracy, we must develop collective intellectual astuteness, but we must also emphasize concentration in order to increase the effectiveness of our organization. We must avoid dispersion, relaxation, and tardiness in our activities. The organization of our apparatus at all levels and in all branches and the training and development of cadre must be methodical and simple. Quality must be high in order to respond to the requirements of leadership in the new situation and to guarantee the completion of our mission in all three areas, the mountains, the countryside and the cities. We must organize our apparatus appropriately, particularly the economic branches, in order to increase the efficiency of our apparatus, particularly in organizing activities requiring close contact with people, with our work, and with our most productive assets. We must improve our leadership in the technical fields and must improve our technical and scientific cadre. We must put forth and make timely adjustments in our policies in order to respond to the new situation.

PART 3.
POLICY AND MISSION
Section 1.
The Forthcoming Enemy Scheme

American imperialism failed in its war of aggression and as a consequence Americans were forced to sign the Paris Agreement to end the war and withdraw American and satellite troops from Vietnam. It is the strategic plan of American imperialism in South Vietnam to continue to use the Saigon Puppet Government as a tool for realizing the Nixon-Doctrine-Without-Nixon and neocolonialism. The U.S. is continuing to assist Nguyen Van Thieu's Puppet Government by providing military, financial and economic assistance and advisers in order to strengthen enemy forces in every respect, and to continue the "Vietnamization" of the war, advocating "pacification" and land encroachment as the priority strategic measure in an aim to exterminate our forces, to take control of people and land, and to wipe out our areas.

Recently in our province the enemy was hurt badly, part of its forces were reduced, its morale was heavily agitated, certain areas under its oppression were breached, its controlled areas were reduced, and at present the entire 22nd Division has had to be brought in. The enemy will continue to "pacify" areas controlled by us and disputed areas in order to eliminate the leopard skin state, to expand and encroach upon liberated areas, and to drive us out of the lowlands. At the same time the enemy will also endeavor to carry out pacification and communist-denunciation activities in areas they presently are encroaching upon or control. The immediate effort of the enemy will be to try to retake the areas which they lost during the summer–autumn campaign. They will use rangers and regular forces coordinated with tanks, air, artillery and regional forces to try to recapture important positions in southern and northern Phu Cat, southeastern Phu My, western Hoai Nhon, and eastern Hoai An to dislodge our troops and then assign regional forces there and have tyrants and military officers take people back to these areas to pacify and control them. In areas they have no capability to recapture, they may use air and artillery to launch fierce attacks to cause the people to move to their areas, then round up the people and evacuate them to other places. They will also increase espionage and commando activities and will conduct air and artillery attacks into our rear corridors and storage areas. They will step up their psywar activities in order to threaten and create suspicion among the people. Especially in the Van Canh mountainous area, they will continue to attract and move people to their areas.

In the South, they blockaded the swamp areas and attacked the border areas to establish a blocking line to keep us out. Inside, the enemy are increasing their oppressive forces to control hamlets and villages, using fascist measures coordinated with their psywar tactics to prevent and repress the people's struggle movement; they are increasing police operations, assigning pacification teams, military officers and police to hamlets and villages to conduct communist-denunciation and purging activities, defoliating, and then calling on our people to surrender and rally in order to neutralize the revolutionary infrastructure and drive our illegal forces to distant positions. They are also endeavoring to track down deserters, conduct conscriptions, and upgrade units in order to develop the PSDF [Popular Self Defense Force] and to improve the regional forces to give it the strength to effect pacification and oppression (civilian defense companies and regional force groups may be formed).

They will also actively increase taxes, steal rice, encircle our corridors and entry-exit points, blockade coastal areas and eradicate our economy in order to carry out their economic plans.

In the cities, they will try to prevent and repress the third force, to defoliate and clear surrounding areas, and to set up defensive systems to prevent us from penetrating them.

Although the enemy is very obstinate, possesses malicious plans, numerous troops, many weapons, and thick defensive systems; and even though he still controls many important areas, with a large population and considerable property; and is still being assisted by the U.S. with money and weapons—his strength is limited and he is becoming weaker and weaker. During the summer–autumn campaign, even though the enemy only suffered the first step of defeat, his weakness has been revealed and it is obvious that it will be difficult for the enemy to develop his current strong points as he would like. On the contrary, his basic weak points are growing more and more obvious. Especially his morale, his combat capability, his means of mobility, and the guarantee of materials to the Puppet Army have seriously decreased. The enemy's machinery of oppression in the hamlets and villages would be difficult to maintain in the face of strong attacks and uprisings by us. He is suffering considerable economic difficulties, his problems of inflation and unemployment are becoming aggravated; he is isolated politically and torn by internal conflicts. The crisis in the U.S., the reduction of U.S. assistance, and Nixon's resignation have greatly affected the Puppet Government and its troops.

Recently, we conducted the summer–autumn campaign, exterminated part of the enemy strength and a number of enemy companies, destroyed a number of bases we attacked and rose up and thereby exterminated and overran a number of enemy strong-points. We liberated, gained control of, or made contested a number of the enemy's areas, cut off sections of a number of important roads and attacked rear bases and airfields. Although the enemy concentrated a fairly intense level of mobile units in our Province, they are still on the defensive, in a difficult position and can only react cautiously. They aimed mostly at stopping us, but at the same time they exposed their shortcomings in many places and were attacked by us; the morale of their soldiers declined, especially the regional force units. In the forthcoming period, if we conduct larger scale operations, if the uprising movement within enemy areas is stronger, and if we attack their rear bases and communications continuously, they will become weaker, more disorganized, and more bogged down in a difficult and defensive position; if their main force troops withdraw, their regional forces will lose their support, and we will thus acquire a new advantageous opportunity.

OUR ADVANTAGES AND DIFFICULTIES

Advantages:

—The enemy is weakened. When we attack, the mobile forces of the enemy will have to be dispersed and the regional forces will thus lose their support, will become weaker and weaker, and will have no capability to hold the people and the land.

—Through past combat our armed forces have matured a step further, our combat capability grows better and better, our troop strength is gradually being increased, and we are developing a firm foothold in our operating areas.

—In the enemy area, action teams are being reinforced. They have succeeded in staying close to their operating areas. Old agents are being consolidated and new agents are being developed, and the people have an enthusiastic belief in the Revolution.

—The liberated and base areas are being enlarged. With each day they are being more and more consolidated and progress has been made in every respect. The living standards of the people are gradually being normalized, thus creating a material base to serve the front lines.

—Our recent victory has increased the revolutionary fervor of the people, elevated their spirit and augmented the unity and unanimity within the entire ranks of the Party, military and people. A step has been taken towards resolving the expression of rightist thinking.

—Leadership by the region's current affairs committee is strong.

—All echelons have acquired some experience for organization of leadership for the realization of the main mission.

Difficulties:

—Rightist thought, passivity, fear of the fierceness of war, loss of morale before the prospects of a long struggle, and reliance on others still continue to be obstacles that affect several aspects of our operations. Expressions of individualism, corruption, authoritarian attitudes, giving orders, licentiousness, and violation of policy have not been overcome, but are in fact still increasing.

— Political knowledge, ideology, and combat techniques in the armed forces still do not meet requirements. There is still difficulty in replacing troop strength. The guerrilla warfare movement is still very weak.

— Organization in the hamlets and villages is still weak. The Revolutionary strength within enemy areas, especially within cities and towns, is still too weak.

— Enemy main forces are still numerous, they continue to conduct counterattacks and attacks. After this prolonged dry season, there may be floods and then the livelihood of the people will not be stable. This will influence all aspects of our activities.

— Leaders of various echelons still do not have a thorough understanding of our main mission and the organization for its implementation still has many shortcomings.

Section 2.

Forthcoming Duties

From the above analysis of the enemy's and our situation, we can foresee a new trend advantageous to our development which we must comprehend thoroughly in order to continue to attack and push the enemy into a still weaker position and to elevate the movement in the Province a step further. Therefore, the forthcoming duties of the (Province) Party Chapter will be: to expand upon the recent victories by the three types of forces, to push strongly the three pronged attack, to attack the enemy in all three areas, to defeat the encroachments on our land, to take an important step toward defeat of the enemy's attempt at pacification, to push the enemy into a weaker position, to recapture the areas the enemy has encroached upon, to firmly maintain the results obtained already, to enlarge the liberated and controlled areas (including the mountains), to strengthen our movement in enemy territory, especially in the cities and towns, to improve our forces in every respect, to develop our areas — especially to develop and improve our economy, and to create conditions and opportunities for achieving greater victories.

Section 3.

In Order to Implement the Above Duties We Must Strive to Achieve the Following Five Objectives

a. To be resolute in recapturing the areas the enemy has encroached upon (including the old and newly encroached areas); to concentrate on the heavily populated areas, the rich areas, the areas bordering the cities and market towns, the areas along various strategic communication routes; to elevate the movements within enemy controlled areas one step further.

b. To kill or cause to desert 15,000 of the enemy (not to include the destruction of the main force); to cause enemy outposts in rural areas to be ineffective; to attack and create damage to war facilities; to cut many different portions of important communication routes for periods of several days; to force the enemy on the defensive straining to cope in several places at one time.

c. At the same time with our combat activities, to develop and elevate the quality and quantity of the various types of forces; to strengthen the local units and the guerrillas; to concentrate on developing a strong guerrilla warfare movement; to ensure the coordination with the people in attacking and uprising to defeat the RF [*Rural Forces*] and to firmly maintain our areas.

d. To continue strengthening the movement in the cities and towns; to gather large numbers of people; to try to take over and develop the role of the third force; to develop the revolutionary strength (in the cities); to take initiative in elevating the movement; to be flexible in creating our conditions and take advantage of any opportunity for bringing about a revolutionary high tide in the cities and towns; to give a strong boost to the three pronged attack; to enlarge the controlled areas and to increase the revolutionary strength in the enemy's area; to reinforce the various action units so that they can stay very close to their operational areas; and to create conditions for a large attack and uprising.

e. To formulate firm step-by-step plans for developing the liberated and base areas in every respect, economically, politically, militarily, and culturally; to develop strong village and hamlet organizations; to continue to stabilize and improve the living standards of the people step-by-step; to increase production work with emphasis on agricultural and forest products; to advance to the point of having a rear service capability that by the end of 1976 will guarantee sufficient grain and most other foodstuffs and have reserve stores as well, and by 1977 will have the funds for almost full local financial self-sufficiency, thus establishing a long-range material base; to develop expeditiously the newly liberated areas, to stabilize quickly the living standard of the people, their security and public order; to develop the guerrilla and security forces, the people's organizations and the government; to develop party chapters and to train cadre; to be resolute in defeating the enemy's attempts to encroach upon our land.

Section 4.

Leadership Guidelines

a. To have a firm understanding of the concept of violence and to thoroughly understand the various aspects of attacking and developing. To have a firm knowledge of the principles of our people's warfare, which are as follows: coordination of the two forces, military and political; the three types of forces; the three pronged attack; the attack and the uprising; the destruction of the enemy and winning over of the people; the return of power to the people; the coordination of all three areas; the three punch attack.

b. To have a firm knowledge of offensive strategic concepts, to develop the initiative, the resolution to attack and counterattack the enemy, to consider attacking as the main objective. The main direction of attack will be the areas controlled by the enemy and disputed areas, both rural and urban, with the rural areas to be considered the main objective, yet at the same time the urban areas not ignored.

c. To have a firm knowledge of the various relationships, to coordinate closely attacking the enemy with developing ourselves, to intensify our attacks while stepping up our development, to step up our development to be able to attack more strongly. To endeavor to firmly develop our areas that they might serve our attack on the enemy, and to develop the movement within the enemy's area. To coordinate tightly among the three areas and between the lines and the rear base.

d. The leadership must be based on a firm knowledge of our central points, but must also pay appropriate attention to various other important matters. Best use must be made of reinforcement from higher levels. Self-sufficiency and autonomous production must be emphasized, and guarantee of rear service support should be considered as the primary economic objective.

PART 4.

SPECIFIC MISSIONS
Section 1.
Military

The coming mission of the armed forces is to join with the political struggle, military proselyting and popular uprising efforts to defeat pacification and encroachment, to enlarge our areas of control, to develop a firm position for attack, and to recruit more district forces and hamlet/village guerrillas. To fulfill this mission efforts must be made to achieve the following: annihilate and deactivate 15,000 enemy troops, reducing two-thirds of their auxiliary forces and a quarter of the RF. Province forces are to destroy key positions (outposts) and battalion size units (RF), district forces to liquidate companies (RF) and village guerrillas to annihilate platoons (PF) [Popular Forces]. Develop guerrilla warfare to continuously attack the enemy. Strengthen our armed forces for higher combat requirements and insure in 1975 that district forces and guerrillas are sufficient to carry out attacks and defend their areas.

In particular, take the initiative in attacking the enemy and countering his offensives. Attack rear storage areas and communications facilities. Interdict (National) Highways 1 and 19. Promote and develop popular uprising and armed action teams. Rear base sappers are to eliminate cruel people such as detached officers and policemen. Make everyone perform military duty. Assign young persons and guerrillas to district and province units to maintain troop strength. Master the concept of eliminating the enemy and gaining control of the population. Improve the quality of the armed forces through combat training and political education.

Section 2.
People's Uprising for Gaining Power

Establish corridors and springboards near district towns and cities and develop legal agents and cadre to propagandize, motivate and lead people to rise up. Coordinate the separate uprisings to create conditions for large uprisings to gain control over the population. Take people back to our area and prepare to support them. Liberate 15,000 people.

Section 3.
Operations in the Enemy Area, Political Struggle and Military Proselyting

—Push forward the people's struggle movement and create instability.

—Demand the return of the people to native villages, the implementation of the Paris Agreement, and the improvement of the welfare of the people.

—Oppose confiscation of property, terrorism, troop upgrading and conscription. Push forward military proselyting to sow dissension.

—And motivate soldiers to oppose the war and refuse to take part in military operations.

Section 4.
Operations in District Towns and Cities

Try to control public organizations of workers, youth, students and women to make them into the assault force of the movement. Struggle to control the Buddhist and Catholic forces. Control the third force and other forces against Thieu. Coordinate with the rural area, military and political operations to confuse and disturb the enemy and create the opportunity for a revolutionary high tide.

Section 5.
Development and Economic Restoration of our Area

Immediately, develop our areas as rear bases to serve the attack against the enemy to which we can bring people from the enemy area. Create a guerrilla force to protect our area. Improve agricultural and forestry production to serve immediate needs and to form the basis for future development. Realize self-sufficiency in provisions and food. Improve people's living conditions. Organize transportation facilities to serve the fighting. Advance commercial activities to serve the people and encourage production. Develop culture, educational, entertainment, public health and gradually solve illiteracy.

Section 6.
Civilian Proselyting Operations

Make the people aware of our recent victories and our strong development of the Revolution in all aspects, while pointing out the enemy's weaknesses and failures. Raise national, local and personal pride and defeat the enemy's psywar. In enemy areas of control, enlarge the struggle front and prepare for the big attack and uprising in the rural area leading to the revolutionary high tide in the city. Improve cadre performance of front groups in village organizations.

Develop the role of the National Liberation Front. Strive to bring together all the forces opposed to Thieu into a struggle front. Create divisiveness among and strive to control the religious leaders, especially the Catholics and Buddhists. We must make an effort to develop key elements among the members of the religious groups, particularly the Buddhists.

Text of a Telegram from the U.S. Embassy, Saigon, to the Secretary of State on the Negotiations with Hanoi and the PRG on Implementing Article 8(b) of the Paris Agreement Concerning Information to Be Supplied on Soldiers and Civilians Missing in Action

Sent on December 2, 1974. Throughout the telegram, the term "PRG" appears in quotation marks by order of U.S. Ambassador Graham Martin, who maintained that the PRG was wholly a creature of, and subservient to, Hanoi.

1. The purpose of this message is to provide summary background information on the current boycott by the DRV and "PRG"—now in its 23rd week—of Two Party Joint Military Commission (FPJMC) [*sic*] and Four Party Joint Military Team (FPJMT) meetings to be drawn on in discussing this subject.

2. The alleged impediment to negotiations in the TPJMC (RVN and "PRG") and the FPJMT (US, RVN, DRV and "PRG") is the question of privileges and immunities (P&I). This question is discussed in detail below. However, this is not the real barrier to progress in implementing the obligations undertaken in the Paris Agreement with respect to the TPJMC and FPJMT. The P&I question is a subterfuge designed to frustrate the talks. What Hanoi and its "PRG" puppet really seek is passive agreement to a set of demands (which they call adequate P&I) which would amount to recognition of the "PRG" as a legitimate government. It is an artificial and fabricated tactic, involving the presentation of these so obviously unacceptable demands in order to stall the talks, and—at the same time—to try to place the onus for this on the US/RVN.

3. This point was graphically illustrated by a captured "PRG" document informing their cadre that the talks would be suspended on May 30, 1974. In the most revealing portion of that document Viet Cong cadre were informed that "we have

decided to cancel all FPJMT meetings effective May 30, 1974. Furthermore, we have released a series of communiques condemning the US for continuing military aid to Thieu's belligerent clique, thus enabling them to perpetuate hostilities; maintaining military bases in Thailand, thus creating war threats; failing to withdraw US military personnel and Thai troops from Laos; and continuing to interfere in Cambodia." VC cadre were instructed to "indoctrinate subordinate personnel and the people on this circular and increase their (military) activities to support effectively our diplomatic offensive." Subsequently, the DRV/"PRG" did, in fact, walk out of the FPJMT talks on May 30 and the TPJMC talks on May 10. Both bodies met briefly in June; the FPJMT met June 11, 13, 18 and 20, and the TPJMC June 14, 18 and 21. The continuing boycott of both bodies began then. Having found that the US is not willing to "barter for bones," and will neither cease its support for the RVN nor collude with the DRV/"PRG" in the overthrow of the RVN Government the DRV/"PRG" decided to stalemate the talks and pursue their objectives through other means.

4. Thus, it is clear that P&I is not the issue. The P&I question is just one of the current ploys of Hanoi and its puppet to try and bring about the demise of the Republic of Viet Nam as a sovereign nation. The following is a synopsis of the P&I question:

   a. The Agreement on Ending the War and Restoring Peace in Viet Nam (the Paris Agreement) stipulates that the two joint military commissions (The TPJMC, and the Four Party Joint Military Commission (FPJMC) which was superceded after 60 days by the FPJMT as specified in the Paris Agreement) "shall agree immediately" on the organization, procedure and measures to carry out their tasks. The Protocol to the Paris Agreement concerning the cease-fire in South Vietnam and the joint military commissions provided that this should include, *inter alia,* "privileges and immunities equivalent to those accorded diplomatic missions and diplomatic agents" while the commissions were carrying out their tasks—essentially military in nature—of implementing the provisions of the Agreement.

   b. A subcommission of the FPJMC developed a set of "eleven points pertaining to privileges and immunities" which were then agreed upon by the delegation chiefs as sufficient to carry on the work of that body.

   c. These eleven points of P&I were adopted by the FPJMT in a minute of agreement on May 3, 1973. It was agreed in the Paris communique of June 13, 1973, that the TPJMC should "immediately be accorded the eleven points of P&I agreed upon by the FPJMC."

   d. The FPJMT and TPJMC operated satisfactorily under these P&I until April 1974. In addition to the agreed-upon P&I, the RVN also granted—unilaterally—additional privileges, including a weekly press conference for the "PRG" and open use of the civilian telephone system in Saigon.

   e. An RVN aircrew member was killed by "PRG" ground fire during a TPJMC prisoner exchange flight March 7, 1974. In reaction to this, and after refusal of the "PRG" to provide a guarantee of safety, the RVN on April 16, 1974, withdrew the main additional P&I they had unilaterally granted, namely DRV/"PRG" use of open common user telephone lines throughout the Saigon metropolitan area and suspension of the "PRG" weekly press conference. The Saigon/Loc Ninh liaison flight was also suspended because no guarantee of safety was forthcoming from the "PRG." From April 18 to May 30, the DRV/"PRG" paralyzed the plenary sessions with the P&I issue. In accordance with their prearranged plan, on May 30 the DRV/"PRG" walked out of the meetings. After the DRV/"PRG" boycotted sessions of 4 and 6 June, the RVN notified the DRV/"PRG" on June 7 in a gesture of good will that it had decided to restore all P&I (the eleven plus the additional points) as they had existed prior to April 16.

f. As the captured document referred to above illustrates, the DRV/"PRG" had by this time decided to boycott all further talks. To this end, on June 18, 1974, the "PRG" introduced draft minutes of agreement which if agreed to would amount to *de facto* recognition of the "PRG" as a separate government. They insisted that their demands be discussed at plenary sessions notwithstanding the fact that the original eleven points of P&I had been worked out at subcommittee level of the FPJMC. The US/RVN proposed that the P&I question (which is procedural) be discussed at the deputy or secretary level (in accordance with the precedent set by the FPJMC subcommittee that originally agreed on P&I) so that the plenary sessions could continue to negotiate issues of substance. The DRV/"PRG" refused and began their boycott. The last meeting of the FPJMT was June 20, 1974, and the TPJMC June 21, 1974.

g. At the present time, the US continues to provide a weekly Saigon/Hanoi liaison flight, even though the substantial purposes of this flight (exchange of information on missing and dead) have not been met. The RVN continues to provide a twice weekly Saigon/Loc Ninh liaison flight for the "PRG." The US continues to provide vehicular support for the DRV/"PRG." The RVN continues to supply billets, electricity, water and other supplies to the DRV/"PRG." RVN continues to allow communication by the DRV/"PRG" with other delegations, with the ICCS, and through the Saigon public telephone circuits. Perhaps the most striking P&I that RVN provides is one not specified in the minute of agreement, that is the weekly press conference of the "PRG."

h. In blatant abuse of the "privileges and immunities equivalent to those accorded diplomatic missions and diplomatic agents," the "PRG" have on a number of occasions since October 12, 1974, used this press conference to call for, *inter alia,* the overthrow of the constitutionally-elected president and Government of the Republic of Vietnam. This action is a major violation of diplomatic protocol which would not be tolerated by any other host government, and in a normal diplomatic context would constitute ample basis for breaking relations.

5. The US and RVN remain on the record as agreeing to discuss the P&I issue as it has been discussed before, while the DRV/"PRG" remain firm in boycotting the sessions entirely until their demands are met.

6. Foregoing background is provided addressees in unclassified form in order to be of maximum benefit in discussing the TPJMC and FPJMT negotiations, stalled since June because of the preconditions to resumption insisted upon by the DRV/"PRG." As noted above, these preconditions now include a call for the overthrow of the GVN. This is in sharp contrast to the recent GVN call to resume negotiations in Saigon and Paris without preconditions.

[U.S. AMBASSADOR GRAHAM A.] MARTIN

A South Vietnamese View
of the Future of Vietnam
circa January 1975

Excerpts from the text of a memorandum of conversation between a U.S. Embassy official and a South Vietnamese Senator, transmitted to Washington on January 16, 1975.

2. I asked him what eventual scenario he envisioned for an end to the struggle between North and South. Predictably, he responded, that it depended upon continuation of substantial American support. That, he said, is the most crucial factor. The resignation of President Nixon was a blow to Vietnamese confidence and morale, he said, because President Nixon had demonstrated his courage in support of the South Vietnamese and his power with the U.S. Congress. The new President in Washington does not have that strength and is faced with an opposition Congress, he observed.

"One of our greatest mistakes," the Senator said, "was not to establish and maintain continuous liaison between Vietnamese and American Parliamentarians, independent of the official exchanges between our two governments at the highest levels. At this point there followed a long digression about the Asian Parliamentarian Association of which the Senator is Vice-President. During their meetings, there are always opportunities to encourage outside support to the GVN by presenting the true situation of the country, he said. Reverting to the idea of liaison between VN and US senators, he said, "There are issues, there are policies about which we might come closer to agreement with the American politicians than with the public policies of either or both governments. It would have strengthened understanding and mutual confidence if we had maintained an unofficial dialogue between Parliamentarians in Saigon and in Washington."

3. Comparing the relative strength of South Vietnam versus North Vietnam the Senator began by saying that, "there is now more nearly an equilibrium between North and South than there was at the time of Independence in 1954." "The North," he said, "began with an aura of military invincibility as a result of the victory over the Japanese occupation forces and the French colons. The North already had, in the structure of the Viet Minh command, a strong government that, if it was repressive, was none-the-less in absolute control and could implement national policies. However, the North lacked natural resources to keep its small industrial facilities in

operation. It has never, even with the most brutal policies of the government, been able to produce enough food to feed its population. But the most crucial factor is its proximity to China," he said. "There the North Vietnamese, with a population of scarcely 20 million, sit in fear behind an indefensible frontier from China with 700 millions of people and vast resources."

4. Furthermore, the Senator said, the leaders in the North were old, they are passing one by one. With vast support from the communist world, they have failed throughout thirty years of ceaseless military and political struggle to have their way in the South. Their economy is totally dependent upon support from outside—much more than ours, he said. They could not survive six months without it, he said.

5. The South began in 1954 without a government, without armed forces of any kind, without a single Vietnamese university (only one French university with only foreign professors). However, we were far from China, the land is naturally rich so there has never been a shortage of essential foodstuffs, we have great forests, and now we believe we have great petroleum reserves. Our government is young and now strong, our army has proved its capability even without the promised support from the USG and we still have our liberty. The balance between North and South, he continued, is very precarious. It can be upset by other countries who support, or who fail to support, one side or the other. The presence of the PRG in South Vietnam, is a great embarrassment, and continues to be a cover for NVA [North Vietnamese Army] invaders but, with a continuation of reasonable support from America, we will gain on the North because our strength is growing while theirs is waning.

6. "Before 1954—you were here, you must remember—most of our people were barefoot, uneducated. Now we have twelve universities and still there is not place for all the qualified students. A generation or two have been educated, some abroad— mainly in America—and they have come back to work in government. Before, we had no diplomatic traditions. Now we have some very bright and highly trained young men in the ministry of foreign affairs, in the ministries of economics and agriculture. Our agriculture has been put on a more scientific basis and is producing more than before, though there are still potentials we have not reached. All this has been accomplished during the war years. It is not only with ideas and guns that we fight the North. We have improved the quality of our youth and the standard of living of our people and the new generations we are forming now are very much more capable than mine was at the moment of independence," the Senator declared.

7. "In five to ten years, provided essential support continues, the equilibrium between North and South will shift heavily in favor of South Vietnam. As, this happens, opportunities for negotiation on a realistic basis will occur," he said.

"There is much criticism of the GVN in the United States because it is not a true democracy and it is not understood in America that the whole concept of democracy is new to us and, one must frankly state, it is contrary to much of our social traditions," he explained. "The Vietnamese tradition is that with great responsibility go certain rights, certain prerogatives. The VN people expect the government to be strong, to take initiatives, to establish social discipline, to impose order. They would consider a government weak that did not do these things that are so often criticized in the US," he said. "These traditional attitudes go far back in our history and are absorbed by children within the strong bonds of the family. They are rooted in the history of our ceaseless struggle against the Chinese, against the colonials, against the Japanese, against the communists. They represent the basic strength of our society," he said with conviction. "However, the Vietnamese people are very flexible, quick to absorb foreign ideas when they seem better than our own. We have taken the best from the Chinese, the best from the French and we have surely absorbed a great deal of administrative, technical, political and economic ideas from the Americans. As education becomes more general and security improves, we will see a new social system emerging and then, perhaps, true democracy can become possible," he said. End text.

Directive NR. 08/CT74 from Hanoi's Central Office for South Vietnam on Military Operations in 1975

Captured by South Vietnamese forces and made available in Saigon with unofficial English translation.

Section 1.
Highlights of the Situation during the First Half of CY 1974

After 6 months of implementation of the Central (Trl.: Short for "Central Executive Committee of the Lao Dong Party") Resolution 21 and the COSVN [Central Office for South Viet Nam] Resolution 12, we scored major gains while the enemy suffered another serious decline.

There have arisen, in the friendly vs. enemy situation as well as that of the population, new factors requiring timely assessment so that requirements can be formulated and appropriate action taken if far greater gains are to be achieved in the near future.

The following facts stand out in the struggle between us and the enemy:

a. Our entire Party Headquarters is in full agreement with the Central Committee's Resolution 21 and COSVN Resolution 12. Great achievements have been obtained in the conduct of military operations to frustrate enemy land-grab operations, expand our liberated areas and establish more military bases. *Cadre and Party members have turned their will to fight, their revolutionary attitude, their concept of using violence and their confidence in the people, into realistic actions by developing the people's revolutionary movement throughout all the three areas (mountainous, lowland and urban).*

1. In many areas, the tasks of disrupting pacification and inroads, gaining control of the population, and dominating the forward rural area achieved results that exceeded the requirements for restoring our posture prior to 28 January 1973 and for the entire CY 1974.

    We put out of action 102,000 enemy troops, dislocated 24,000 of them, dismantled 1,389 military posts, liberated eleven villages, 332 hamlets, and 244,600 inhabitants exclusive of 80,000 people who had gone over to the liberated area, turned 668 hamlets in the weak area (Trl.: i.e., area where the

GVN is in ascendancy) into hamlets with limited dominance by us. Compared with the accomplishments in the second half of CY 1973, the results achieved in the battles exceeded all norms. Dismantled military posts (in the second half of CY 1974) exceeded those in the whole CY 1973. One noteworthy fact is that the *previously weak localities—outskirts of the Saigon capital such as Binh Chanh Thu Duc, Hoc Mon, Go Vap etc., have now taken a turn for the better. The drive to strike the enemy with the three-prong tactics at the grassroots has been developing fairly evenly in all fields of battle. The populace* have taken fresh and effective initiative in the political struggle. Guerrillas have been present everywhere. *District (units) have been able to wipe out strings (of outposts). Guerrillas also destroyed outposts, captured enemy troops, and seized weapons.* (In the Mekong Delta, guerrillas dismantled 10 percent of the total number of destroyed military posts.)

In some regions where the main force units took turns to undergo training, the district local force and village and hamlet guerrillas intensified their activities, designed to destroy the enemy, dismantle military people, seize land, and liberate the population. The activities in one month were more numerous than those in the previous month.

The main force units at regions played their strike role of disrupting pacification, massed and dispersed their troops in a flexible manner, effected good coordination with local areas, waged continuing attacks against the enemy, created conditions for the on-the-spot expansion of the three-prong movement, and at the same time held the enemy up for the "R" main force to execute deep penetrations and hit the enemy right at the border area, *opening up our main force's new possibility* not only to fight junble [sic] and mountain battlefields *but also to destroy the enemy and hold defensive positions in the plains and even at the doorsteps of Saigon like Rach Bap and Ghiniel [sic].*

Aside from the ever-widening mass movement struggling continually in different ways for their legitimate rights, such as demanding rice, salt, and relief aid; resisting oppressive grip, [missing word] of terror, forced conscription, and confiscatory taxation; and asking to return to their old homes and lands, etc. (at many places, the local government officials and civilian self-defense members complied with such demands of the masses), *there have been emerging vigorous mass movements* in areas where our structures are weak, *which resorted to violence* to oppose the forcing into the army of religious personalities and monks in the Hoa Hao and Khmer (minority dominated) areas.

2. In cities and towns, people of all walks of life—even refugees, disabled veterans, troops dependents—expressed *their dissatisfaction with Thieu.* In their discussions they condemned Thieu for undermining the agreement, causing deaths and hard living conditions and *wanted peace to work for a living and improved living standards.* The mass struggle for their legitimate rights *is likely to spread more vigorously and regularly than it did in 1973.* The level of our agent penetration into the population mass, interference with leadership matters, and domination of mostly spontaneous agitations, has been steadily increasing. A number of agitations instigated or dominated by us served as a

core for the common movement, such as the movement for the relief of unemployed people, flood victims in Central Vietnam, and the May 1, 1974, movement.

Our in-place structure has achieved a slow but firm development.

The struggle front has been further widened. There have been movements at wards, firms, schools, markets, and branches; and among high school and university students, notables, intellectuals, and the Third Force; which, despite enemy hindrance, have kept emerging, and are depending on the masses to build up their forces, secure legitimacy, demand the release of political prisoners, urge implementation of the agreement, and drive Thieu to further isolation.

3. *Our liberated and base areas are more secure and widened than they were previously.* Numerous enclaves and liberated patches have been formed. The population has increased markedly. The achievements accomplished in 1973 (?), plus the aid in cadre personnel, workers, technicians, equipment and materials have improved. *The look of the liberated areas in Regions 1 and 6 has changed visibly:* The revolutionary government has been formed and consolidated; living conditions have stabilized; security and order have improved; production has been developed one step further; our market is less dependent on the enemy's than it was in the past; public health, cultural and social activities are intensified; and revolutionary potentialities are better than they were before.

b. *Having suffered setback in 1973, the enemy realigned his encroaching plans for 1974.* An augmentation of the III Corps mobile force was affected in conjunction with the construction of ditches, alteration of terrain features, etc., in the middle-line area for the defense of the northern and northwestern sectors of Saigon. At the same time, he conducted relocation of population, inroads, widening of the blocking line in the east (Ba Ria, Long Khanh and Region 6 areas); and massed his forces to occupy the Plain of Reeds area and block the frontier, creating conditions for widening the scope of encroachment and achieving his basic schemes.

1. *The enemy did score some results.* He has succeeded in relocating the inhabitants, grabbing certain areas in Regions 1 and 6, especially in Binh Tuy, occupying the heartland of Kien Tuong, and blocking a section of our transportation corridor at the border. He still maintains his coercive apparatus, draws recruits, and collects taxes. (His activities during the first 5 months of CY 1974 were five times as much as those during the first 5 months of CY 1973). *Even if he has caused us certain difficulties, he has from the outset been beset with failures, driven to the defensive, and plagued by fresh shortcomings.*

The enemy succeeded in marshalling his mobile force, making inroads into the heartland of the Plain of Reeds area, and relieving our pressure from "quoc 3" [*sic*]. But being stranded here, he was unable to defend other localities. Strings of his outposts were forced to withdraw to avoid annihilation. His support for the plan of encroaching upon and pacifying the (capital) city outskirts and the middle-line area was cut down. His project of re-occupying Highway 2 at Ba Ria was temporarily dropped. His plan of relocating the population and striking our bases could not be carried out as expected.

2. *The Saigon regime's financial-economic structure was seriously shaken.* Industrial and agricultural production dropped sharply. Imports amounting to 614 million dollars were fifteen times as much as exports. Excesses in expenditures for CY 1973–1974 amounting to 195 billion SVN [South Vietnam] piasters were greater than the whole 1970 budget (187 billion piasters). There was a galloping inflation (the money in circulation in 1974 reached an unprecedentedly high level—30 billion South Vietnamese piasters, or six times the quantity of money in circulation in 1966). The piaster was subjected to repeated devaluations during the first half of CY 1974. U.S. military aid to Saigon dropped from 2.2 billion dollars in FY 1972–1973 to 1.6 billion dollars in FY 1973–1974, and to 700 million dollars in FY 1974–1975. Economic aid from 748 million dollars in FY 1972–1973 was down to 6.9 [*sic*] million in FY 1973–1974, and to 420 million in FY 1974–1975.

   The deteriorating financial-economic situation fraught with grave political significance affected all aspects of enemy military, political, economic, cultural and social activities and the livelihood of all strata of the population living in the area under temporary enemy control.

3. *The puppet troops' morale has been falling off sharply.* The incidence of mass desertion and defiance of order was high. Even army officers disapproved of Thieu's violation of the agreement. The self-defense troops were in sympathy with and lent support to the masses' struggle.

4. *As a counter-measure and in implementation of his fundamental plans, the enemy resorted to a number of new tricks and tactical measures* consistent with his capabilities such as pacification and encroachment through relocation of population, administrative revolution, assignment of officers to hamlet and village administrations, redeployment of the outposts under pressure to avoid annihilation, appeal for a Vietnamese way of waging the war, accelerated forced conscription directed even at religious circles, scrounging to the extreme limit through taxation and acts of banditry at the expense of the population, etc. But such acts, *which are simply the product of a posture of defeat and defensive,* can achieve certain temporary results *without solving the actual situation, while generating deep conflict between the enemy and the population and within the ranks of the puppet army and administration.*

The following conclusion can be drawn from the real situation of the movement in the last six months.

1. During the first six months of the year we *scored major full-scale and firm gains,* blunted the enemy—initiated dry-season rice-looting plan, and set back and defeated by one major step his pacification and encroaching project. Those facts were evidence of the "Central" and COSVN resolutions that deeply reflect the realities of the movement and can produce major strength-generating effects.

   A number of shortcomings and weaknesses adversely affecting our gains were the slow building-up of our forces that failed to meet the requirements, spotty three-pronged offensive at the grassroots, imbalance among the three types of forces (Trl.; i.e., main, local, and guerrilla forces), slow growth of the movement at urban centers and weak areas.

The enemy still has strong points such as a numerically large army and control over populous and rich areas. This thus permits him to continue sweeping off resources and pressing people into his army. The U.S. is still striving to provide aid to Thieu. (Those strengths definitely hamper the development of the revolution.) *However, developments resulting from the evolution of the situation are greatly in our favor.* Our weaknesses can be entirely overcome and they are being effectively reduced step-by-step. The enemy's strong points are temporary ones with internal conflicts. (These strengths) can not develop and become weaker than before.

2. *Our posture and force is being developed steadily, stronger than at the time we embarked on the '73–'74 dry season, stronger even than at the time we made preparations for the offensive in 1968 and 1972.* Meantime, U.S. aggressor troops are no longer present on the battlefield; enemy air and artillery support has presently decreased a great deal as compared with that received in the days of the Americans' presence. With our steadily increasing material facilities for battlefields (our liberated areas and bases being connected with the "greater rear base" (Trl.: NVN) and receiving large assistance from it), *we have achieved a very high level of unity of spirit within the whole Party, the whole army, and the whole people revolving around the resolutions of* the Party's Central Committee and COSVN. The Party's policies correctly reflect the aspirations and pressing needs of the masses such as those in "weak" *areas inhabited by the refugees and ethnic minorities,* where up to now, revolutionary activities have been weak because of the small and inadequate number of our infrastructures. New developments have taken place there; the masses hate the enemy, have a better understanding of the revolution, and are ready to help and support our infrastructures. This is a condition greatly advantageous to the stronger and larger development of our posture and force.

3. *The Nguyen Van Thieu's puppet army and government although not yet being reduced to collapse, continue to face increasing difficulties in all respects and keep on declining both quantitatively and qualitatively in terms of posture and force.* However, the U.S. and the puppet government are very stubborn; they continue to brazenly display their reactionary intent of aggression and (working) class hatred.

Although they have *tried to regain freedom of action from their defensive posture and changed tactics and schemes to cope with the new situation, their schemes and tactics have been conceived from a defensive posture* and consequently present numerous shortcomings and weaknesses.

The material facilities for the survival of the Nguyen Van Thieu's puppet government are being seriously shaken as they have to nurture an excessively heavy war and administrative machinery with over one and a half million non-productive personnel, with expenses for military require-ments that keep increasing in the face of our concerted offensives on all battlefields, and with measures to meet the living needs of the population in areas under enemy control and of the people gathered in large numbers by the enemy. Meantime, production in agriculture and industry has declined seriously, and the life of the Thieu's regime depends entirely on U.S. aid which in the near future will be further reduced. To remedy this situation, the Saigon puppet government has only one alternative—to resort to inflation and robbery practices to the utmost at the expense of people from all social strata (practices that are carried on concurrently with brazenly conducted forced induction). To this end, there is the *need to further apply fascism to its oppressive machinery,* to put down whatever opposition (opposition that may come from the people or from the Third Force), and as a consequence, this generates bitter and irreconcilable antagonisms between every social class and the Saigon government and will certainly lead sooner or later to a new, widespread and strong movement of the people of all social strata. The possibility that the enemy's internal differences might become so critical that internecine strife could happen within his den is not ruled out.

4. The current contest of strength between us and the enemy is occurring within the context of the world's situation, of the situation in Indochina, and even in the U.S., and is *highly favorable to our side and greatly disadvantageous to the enemy.*

The three revolutionary trends are still directing their attacks against the imperialist camp and new-style colonialism. Pro–U.S. anti-revolutionary forces in urban masses in Portugal, Ethiopia, Greece, and Thailand are forced to pull back one step; in Indochina, the revolutionary force in Cambodia continues its offensive and succeeds in securing great gains; the Neo Lao Kak Sak Front [*sic*] becomes more consolidated within the recently established coalition government in Laos.

In the U.S. in particular, Nixon's resignation adversely affects the Saigon situation in all respects and drives henchman Nguyen Van Thieu and his clique into a state of confusion.

All the above points confirm clearly that from the present situation are emerging highly favorable new factors that will permit us to achieve in an overriding manner the remainder of the 1974 plan and will offer new advantageous possibilities allowing the raising of previously set performance criteria intended for 1975 and some ensuing years. This will constitute a turning point of a decisive character, as it will tip off the balance of power to our advantage and create very basic conditions that will lead toward the achievement of total victory.

Section 2.
Enemy Scheme

1. The basic scheme of U.S. imperialists in Vietnam continues to be the implementation of the Nixon doctrine, imposition of neo-colonialism in the South, destruction of armed liberation forces, and eradication of liberated areas and the revolutionary government. The U.S. keeps on providing advisory assistance and

military, economic, and financial aid to the Saigon puppet government to strengthen its forces in all respects and at the same time goes on using tricky diplomatic maneuvers to enlist aid from reactionary countries to cope with us.

2. To carry on the aforementioned basic scheme, the enemy gradually implements immediate steps that are the following:

   a. Use of the Saigon puppet government to continue to undermine the Agreement, to keep on waging the war at levels or in areas advantageous to his side, and to avoid a big war that would force U.S. direct intervention and would bog down the U.S.

   b. The scheme for pacification and land encroachment still remains the enemy's No. 1 central scheme. He has a plan for stepping up all-aspect implementation through coordination of efforts: military, political, economic, psywar, and espionage; for seizure of villages and hamlets one-by-one with the intent to occupy the whole liberated and contested areas, to eliminate the state of enclaves, to wholly control the rural and urban populations, to create every condition favoring the move forward for gradual occupation of liberated base areas.

   c. He endeavors to build strong regional forces, tries to consolidate and develop the Civilian Self-Defense Force, reinforce the police, and develop the Regional Force Units up to battalion and regiment-size levels so that they can pacify localities by themselves, thus permitting more mobility for the regular units. The enemy also built a stronger air force.

   d. To continue the collection of taxes and rice, to build the economy in areas under his control and at the same time to lay an economic blockade against us, the enemy is capable of launching major military operations against our base areas to destroy our storage facilities and cut our communications corridors in places where we lack vigilance, etc.

   We must fully understand the realistic situation up to the present time despite the above enemy scheme. However, in keeping abreast of the situation we come to realize that recently when we stepped up the people's warfare in the lowlands and the border area, raiding their bases or destroying their sub-sectors, district seats, infantry battalions and battle groups the puppet army met with lots of difficulties and the U.S. did not dare intervene openly.

   If in coming years we alter the balance of forces in our favor and the puppet side is weakened and encounters additional troubles they may either partially carry out the Agreement to bide time, seek accommodation, overcome their difficulties only to later resume the sabotage of the Accord by all possible means, (or) keep on attacking us to resume war in South Vietnam. In short, so long as the mandarinistic, militarist, fascist, U.S. lackey administration has not been toppled yet they surely cannot implement the Agreement's basic provisions and will try to renew the hostilities. In case the enemy risks being reduced to a crumbling state U.S. Air Force and Navy can be called for to come to his rescue. Though the possibility of an intervention in the South and an offensive against the North by U.S. ground forces is slim, we must, nevertheless, be on the look-out and make sound estimates. We must apply preventive measures and an appropriate strategy so as not to leave room for a U.S. intervention or a U.S. timely intervention. However, we must not entertain defeatism in the eventuality of an American involvement in the hostilities. We must resolutely defeat them to have the Revolution in the South continually take a step ahead.

Section 3.
Policy and Missions in the Coming Period

a. *The basic mission of the Revolution in the South in the forthcoming stage is to carry on with the strategy of people's democratic and national revolution, unite all people in a struggle against U.S. imperialists and against mandarinistic, militarist, fascist, U.S. lackey, mercantile bourgeois, eradicate neo-colonialism, set up a national, genuinely democratic administration, carry out national concord, entirely get rid of U.S. dependence and achieve a peaceful, independent, democratic, neutral and prosperous South Vietnam to advance toward peace and national reunification.*

b. Our immediate mission is to unite all people in the political, military and diplomatic fronts in the most active and flexible way, and, depending on the conditions at each place or each period, appropriately coordinate these fronts to force the enemy to correctly implement the Paris Agreement on Vietnam. We must maintain and develop the revolutionary force in all respects, win victories step-by-step and keep the initiative under all circumstances so as to help the Revolution in the South proceed forward.

c. There exist two capabilities in the development of the Revolution in the South. They are:

—If in the coming period the balance of force between the enemy and us tilts to our side and the enemy meets with increased difficulties they are compelled to cling to the Agreement and implement small parts of it to impede our advancement, save their deteriorating situation and sabotage the Accord.

—In case they do not want to carry out the Accord and the present war gradually widens into a large scale one we again have to wage a decisive revolutionary war to defeat the enemy to win total victory.

—These two capabilities exist side by side and are in the process of development. We must take advantage of Capability 1 and ready ourselves for Capability 2 and grasp revolutionary violence to secure victory regardless of what development will happen. The road to success for the Revolution in the South is the road of violence based on political and military forces.

d. The nature of the present war in South Vietnam differs from that of recent anti-French and anti-U.S. struggles for national emancipation. In the past, French colonialists invaded our country with their old colonialism; they directly ruled our people and used French expeditionary troops and hirelings to repress the Revolution. Unlike the French, the Americans invaded our country with their neo-colonialism. To come to the rescue of the puppet forces who ran the risk of being totally defeated, since 1965 the U.S. has substantially

poured satellite troops into South Vietnam, the first time with a strength of 500,000, allegedly at the request of the Saigon government for assistance. In this way the Americans could not hide the face of an aggressor. Now that the U.S. has pulled out its troops, nevertheless its scheme of aggression against South Vietnam is still carried out. They have been sending in advisers, providing military, economic and financial aid to help the Saigon puppet administration build up its forces from all aspects with a view to wiping out revolutionary forces and eliminating the people's government. Nominally there is no longer a U.S. expeditionary army here, but it is apparent that the Americans have masterminded the scheme and that the puppet Army and Administration are but U.S. lackeys and tools of U.S. neo-colonialism in the prosecution of the war under U.S. orders. Fòr this reason, the present war is still a decisive one between the Vietnamese people and U.S. imperialism. In order to stage an aggression against Vietnam the Americans have relied on mandarinistic, militarist, fascist, mercantile bourgeois and feudal landowners to represent their interests and these social classes are directly ruling the people in their controlling areas and are directly waging war.

The latter's interests are closely linked with the Americans'; as a consequence the present war is a life-and-death struggle between various Vietnamese social strata and the mercantile bourgeois, feudal, mandarinistic, militarist, fascist, U.S. lackey ruling clique, to achieve the national democratic revolution in the South.

Thus, the present war bears the characteristics of a national war and a marked social class struggle and in this dual capacity it is both a struggle for national emancipation and a civil war between our Party-led revolutionary clique [*sic*].

e. The rules for success in this war still are:
—Coordination of military, political and diplomatic efforts;
—Military offensive and uprising, uprising and military offensive;
—Enemy destruction for population control and right to be the master;
—Combination of three areas, three prongs and three punches.

Development of national strength including the Northern socialist force and the Southern national, democratic, revolutionary force to overthrow the mandarinist, militarist, fascist, U.S. lackey ruling clique and eliminate neo-colonialism.

f. Our missions in the period ahead:
The armed forces must in the coming period closely coordinate with the political, diplomatic and legal struggles with a view to fulfilling the following missions:
1. Vigorously pressing forward the gaining of the population and the population's control of their land in the lowlands and city-bordering areas; thwarting an important step in the enemy pacification, land-grabbing and boundary-delineating plan; recovering the areas occupied, pacified and expanded by the enemy; expanding and connecting penetration areas and disputed ones; turning the enemy-controlled areas into disputed and

liberated ones; building up our reserve forces, manpower and material resources.

2. Our main forces must, on the one hand, engage in combat to wipe out the enemy, hold, expand and improve liberated areas and base areas, attract and hold the enemy, in support of the gaining of the population in the lowlands, and, on the other, build up, strengthen and improve themselves in every respect in order to get prepared for a large-scale offensive when the need arises.

3. Vigorously pushing forward the urban movement, consolidating and developing mass organizations, rallying great numbers of the populace from all walks of life in various forms, pressing forward, step by step, the overt political struggle. Our operations in the lowlands as well as those of the main forces are geared to the backing of the urban movements so that it can move forward.

4. Strengthening and building up liberated areas and base areas actively, urgently and step-by-step; stabilizing the populace's living conditions, setting up on-the-spot rear service facilities, enlarging corridors, meeting immediate requirements and maintaining reserves; foiling the enemy plan of imposing a blockage against our economy; frustrating the economic development plan of the enemy, causing his economy to increasingly deteriorate.

5. Consolidating unity with Laos and Cambodia. A fullfillment of the five above-mentioned missions, taking the first mission of gaining the population and the population's control, thwarting the enemy plan of pacification, land-grabbing and boundary delineating in the lowlands as the No.1 Central one, will result in a shift in posture and strength to our advantage, thereby rendering us stronger, weakening the enemy, compelling him to implement, step-by-step, the Paris Agreement, reducing his capability to wage a large-scale war, and at the same time insuring our victory when the enemy risks resuming major hostilities.

GUIDELINES AND MODUS OPERANDI
Guidelines:

It is necessary to master the concept of offensive and to make creative use of attack and counter-attack guidelines. Generally speaking, we must primarily be on the offensive on the battlefield, for the lowlands are populous, and only by attacking could we gradually turn disputed areas into liberated ones, and enemy-controlled areas we must resolutely attack and foil the enemy land-grabbing operations. On the other hand, we must take the initiative in launching attacks so as to enlarge and consolidate liberated areas and simultaneously coordinate with the thwarting of the pacification in the lowlands.

Mastering the guideline of annihilating the enemy is to create conditions for the mass movement to develop, to insure the population's uprising, and at the same time to carry out an all-out offensive with the combined strength of the three areas.

Modus Operandi:

Attention must be paid to the following modus operandi:

—Vigorously pressing forward operations on a regular and continuous basis in combination with wave of "high points"; regular and continuous operations must be regarded as the basis.

—Initiating combined campaigns at all levels in conjunction with the campaign of coordination of combat arms and services in jungle and mountainous areas, with the annihilating of local tyrants, the breaking of the oppressive control, the setting up of structures, the establishment of the mass political organizations in weak areas, thereby creating conditions for the liberation of these areas, at the same time attacking and sabotaging storage facilities, bases, airfields and ports.

—Constantly enlarging the scope of the three-front attack at villages and hamlets.

Text of U.S. Diplomatic Note
on the Viet-Nam Situation

Released on January 13, 1975, by the Department of State.

The Department of State of the United States of America presents its compliments to (the Ministry of Foreign Affairs/Ministry of External Affairs of the Union of Soviet Socialist Republics, People's Republic of China, Great Britain, France, Hungary, Poland, Indonesia, Iran, and Secretary General of the UN Kurt Waldheim) and has the honor to refer to the Agreement on Ending the War and Restoring Peace in Viet-Nam signed at Paris January 27, 1973, and to the Act of the International Conference on Viet-Nam signed at Paris March 2, 1973.

When the Agreement was concluded nearly two years ago, our hope was that it would provide a framework under which the Vietnamese people could make their own political choices and resolve their own problems in an atmosphere of peace. Unfortunately this hope, which was clearly shared by the Republic of Viet-Nam and the South Vietnamese people, has been frustrated by the persistent refusal of the Democratic Republic of Viet-Nam to abide by the Agreement's most fundamental provisions. Specifically, in flagrant violation of the Agreement, the North Vietnamese and "Provisional Revolutionary Government" authorities have:

—built up the North Vietnamese main-force army in the South through illegal infiltration of over 160,000 troops;

—tripled the strength of their armor in the South by sending in over 400 new vehicles, as well as greatly increased their artillery and anti-aircraft weaponry;

—improved their military logistics system running through Laos, Cambodia and the Demilitarized Zone as well as within South Viet-Nam, and expanded their armament stockpiles;

—refused to deploy the teams which under the Agreement were to oversee the cease-fire;

—refused to pay their prescribed share of the expenses of the International Commission of Control and Supervision;

—failed to honor their commitment to cooperate in resolving the status of American and other personnel missing in action, even breaking off all discussions on this matter by refusing for the past seven months to meet with U.S. and Republic of Viet-Nam representatives in the Four-Party Joint Military Team;

—broken off all negotiations with the Republic of Viet-Nam including the political negotiations in Paris and the Two Party Joint Military Commission talks in Saigon, answering the Republic of Viet-Nam's repeated calls for unconditional resumption of the negotiations with demands for the overthrow of the government as a pre-condition for any renewed talks; and

—gradually increased their military pressure, over-running several areas, including 11 district towns, which were clearly and unequivocally held by the Republic of Viet-Nam at the time of the cease-fire. Their latest and most serious escalation of the fighting began in early December with offensives in the southern half of South Viet-Nam which have brought the level of casualties and destruction back up to what it was before the Agreement. These attacks—which included for the first time since the massive North Vietnamese 1972 offensive the over-running of a province capital (Song Be in Phuoc Long Province)—appear to reflect a decision by Hanoi to seek once again to impose a military solution in Viet-Nam. Coming just before the second anniversary of the Agreement, this dramatically belies Hanoi's claims that it is the United States and the Republic of Viet-Nam who are violating the Agreement and standing in the way of peace.

The United States deplores the Democratic Republic of Viet-Nam's turning from the path of negotiation to that of war, not only because it is a grave violation of a solemn international agreement, but also because of the cruel price it is imposing on the people of South Viet-Nam. The Democratic Republic of Viet-Nam must accept the full consequences of its actions. We are deeply concerned about the threat posed to international peace and security, to the political stability of Southeast Asia, to the progress which has been made in removing Viet-Nam as a major issue of great-power contention, and to the hopes of mankind for the building of structures of peace and the strengthening of mechanisms to avert war. We therefore reiterate our strong support for the Republic of Viet-Nam's call to the Hanoi—"Provisional Revolutionary Government" side to reopen the talks in Paris and Saigon which are mandated by the Agreement. We also urge that the (Addressees) call upon the Democratic Republic of Viet-Nam to halt its military offensive and join the Republic of Viet-Nam in re-establishing stability and seeking a political solution.

Kissinger's View of the Paris Agreement on the Fall of Saigon

Response of Secretary of State Henry A. Kissinger at a press conference on April 29, 1975, to the questions: "Do you consider the United States now owes any allegiance at all to the Paris Pact? Are we now bound in any way by the Paris Agreements?"

Well, as far as the United States is concerned, there are not many provisions of the Paris Agreement that are still relevant. As far as the North Vietnamese are concerned, they have stated that they wish to carry out the Paris Accords, though by what definition is not fully clear to me . . .

Do you favor American aid in rebuilding North Viet-Nam?
No, I do not favor American aid for rebuilding North Viet-Nam.

South Viet-Nam?
With respect to South Viet-Nam, we will have to see what kind of government emerges and indeed whether there is going to be a South Viet-Nam. We would certainly look at particular specific humanitarian requests that can be carried out by humanitarian agencies, but we do believe that the primary responsibility should fall on those who supply the weapons for this political change.

A Chronology of Major Developments in the Air War against North Vietnam, 1965–1968

Adapted from chronologies printed in Pentagon Papers.

1965	
February 6	Soviet Premier Kosygin arrives in Hanoi for a state visit that will deepen Soviet commitment to the DRV, and expand Soviet economic and military assistance.
February 7	Well-coordinated NLF attacks hit the U.S. advisors' barracks at Pleiku and the helicopter base at Camp Holloway. The NSC is convened in the evening (February 6, Washington time), and with the recommendation of McGeorge Bundy, Ambassador Taylor and General Westmoreland from Saigon, decides on a reprisal strike against the north in spite of Kosygin's presence in Hanoi.
February 13	Approval is given for the dispatch of 30 B-52s to Guam and 30 KC-135s to Okinawa for contingency use in Vietnam. The president decides to inaugurate ROLLING THUNDER (sustained bombing of the north) under strict limitations with programs approved on a week-by-week basis.
February 24	In a meeting in Warsaw, the Chinese are informed that while the U.S. will continue to take those actions required to defend itself and South Vietnam, it has no aggressive intentions toward the DRV.

February 28	The U.S. and the GVN make simultaneous announcement of decision to open a continuous limited air campaign against the north in order to bring about a negotiated settlement on favorable terms.
March 2	104 USAF planes attack Xom Bang ammo depot and 19 VNAF aircraft hit the Quang Khe Naval Base in the first attacks of ROLLING THUNDER.
March 20	The administration approves the separation of the anti-infiltration bombing in the Laotian panhandle from the BARREL ROLL strikes in support of Laotian forces. The former are now called STEEL TIGER.
March 29	In a daring bombing of the U.S. Embassy, the NLF kill many Americans and Vietnamese and cause extensive damage.
March 31	CINCPAC recommends a spectacular attack against the north to retaliate for the bombing of the embassy. The president rejects the idea.
April 5	The JCS [Joint Chiefs of Staff] report confirmation of the construction of a SAM missile site near Hanoi and request authority to strike it before it becomes operational. Their request is not acted on at the time.
May 6	Commenting, at the president's request, on CIA Director McCone's parting memo on Vietnam, DCI Rayborn agrees with the assessment that the bombing had thus far not hurt the north and that much more would be needed to force Hanoi to the negotiating table. He suggests a pause to test DRV intentions and gain support of world opinion before beginning the intensive air campaign he believes will be required. The chairman of the JCS recommends to the secretary that the SAM sites already identified be attacked.
May 10	The president informs U.S. ambassador to Saigon Maxwell Taylor of his intention to call a temporary halt to the bombing and asks Taylor to get P. M.

	Quat's concurrence. The purpose of the pause is to gain flexibility either to negotiate if the DRV shows interest, or to intensify the air strikes if they do not. He does not intend to announce the pause but rather to communicate it privately to Moscow and Hanoi and await a reply.
May 11	U.S. ambassador Foy Kohler in Moscow is instructed to contact the DRV ambassador urgently and convey a message announcing the pause. Simultaneously, Rusk was transmitting the message to the Soviet ambassador in Washington.
May 12	In Moscow, the DRV ambassador refuses to see Kohler or receive the message. A subsequent attempt to transmit the message through the Soviet Foreign Office also fails when the Soviets refuse their assistance.
May 14	Westmoreland, with Taylor's concurrence, recommends the use of B-52s for patterned saturation bombing of NLF headquarters and other area targets in South Vietnam.
May 18	After five days of pause the bombing resumes in the north.
	On the evening of the resumption, the DRV Foreign Ministry issues a statement describing the pause as a deceitful maneuver to pave the way for further U.S. acts of war.
	Somewhat belatedly, the DRV representative in Paris, Mai Van Bo, discusses the four points with the Quai, somewhat softening their interpretation and indicating that they are not necessarily preliminary conditions to negotiations.
June 3	In a meeting in Hanoi with DRV foreign minister Pham Van Dong, ICC Commissioner Seaborn (Canada) confirms Hanoi's rejection of current U.S. peace initiatives.
June 15	McNamara disapproves the JCS recommendation for air strikes against the SAM sites and IL-28s at DRV air bases since these might directly challenge the Soviet Union.

August 4–6	At the Senate Armed Services Committee, McNamara defends bombing with restraint, pointing to the risks of escalation if POL lines, air fields, or the Hanoi-Haiphong area brought wider massive attack.
November 3	McNamara urges the approval of the bombing pause he first suggested in a July 20 memo to test NVN's intentions.
November 9	A State memo to the president, written by U. Alexis Johnson with Rusk's endorsement, opposes a pause at a time when Hanoi has given no sign of willingness to talk. It would waste an important card and give them a chance to blackmail us about resumption.
December 24	37-day bombing pause begins.
1966	
January 18	JCS argues that "offensive air operations against NVN should be resumed now with a sharp blow and thereafter maintained with uninterrupted, increasing pressure." Specifically, the chiefs called for immediate mining of the ports.
January 31	Bombing pause ends.
March 1	Focusing their recommendations on POL, the JCS call it "highest priority action not yet approved." It would have a direct effect in cutting infiltration.
April 27	General Taylor in a major memo to the president discusses the problem of negotiations describing the bombing and other U.S. military actions as blue chips to be bargained away at the negotiation table, not given away as a precondition beforehand.
May 4	W. Bundy, commenting on Taylor's blue chip memo, takes a harder position on what we should get for a bombing halt—i.e. both an end of infiltration and a cessation of NLF/NVA military activity in the south.
May 6	W. W. Rostow urges the attack on POL based on the results such attacks produced against Germany in World War II.
June 3	The president, having decided sometime at the end of May to approve the POL attacks, informs U.K.

	Prime Minister Wilson. Wilson urges the president to reconsider.
June 7	Rusk, traveling in Europe, urges the president to defer the POL decision because of the forthcoming visit of Canadian ambassador Ronning to Hanoi.
June 14–18	Canadian ambassador Ronning goes to Hanoi and confers with top DRV leaders.
June 29	North Vietnamese POL facilities are struck.
July 8	McNamara informs Admiral Sharp (CINCPAC) that the president wants first priority given to strangulation of the NVN POL system.
August 1	70% of North Vietnam's bulk POL storage has been destroyed.
September 4	ROLLING THUNDER mission is directed away from POL to attrition of men, supplies, equipment.
November 22	JCS once again oppose holiday standdowns for Christmas, New Year's, and Tet, citing the massive advantage of them taken by the DRV during the 37-day pause.
December 13–14	A series of air attacks on targets in Hanoi in early December culminated in heavy strikes on December 13–14. In the immediate aftermath, the DRV and other Communist countries claimed extensive damage in civilian areas. The attacks came at a time when contact with the DRV through the Polish government had appeared promising.
December 23	In response to the worldwide criticism of the attacks on civilian areas, a 10 n.m. [nautical mile] prohibited area around Hanoi was established with a similar zone for Haiphong. Henceforth attacks within it could only be by specific presidential authorization.
December 24	A Christmas truce and bombing pause (48 hours) is observed.
December 31	New Year's truce (48 hours). Heavy Communist resupply efforts are observed during the standdown.

1967

January 18	JCS renew their opposition to the Tet truce.
	Admiral Sharp recommends six priority targets for RT in 1967: (1) electric power, (2) industrial plants, (3) the transportation system in depth, (4) military complexes, (5) POL, and (6) Haiphong and the other ports.
February 8	The president invites Ho to indicate what reciprocity might be expected from a bombing halt. The letter is transmitted in Moscow on February 8.
February 8–14	While the Tet truce was in effect, efforts were undertaken by U.K. Prime Minister Wilson and Premier Kosygin in London to get peace talks started. In the end, these failed because the enormous DRV resupply effort forced the president to resume the bombing.
February 15	Replying to the president's letter, Ho rejects the U.S. conditions and reiterates that unconditional cessation of the bombing must precede any talks.
February 22	The president approved the aerial mining of the waterways and the attack on the Thai Nguyen iron and steel works.
February 27	The first aerial mining of the waterways begins.
March 10	The Thai Nguyen iron and steel complex is hit for the first time.
May 19	The power plant, one mile from the center of Hanoi, is hit for the first time.
June 11	The Kep airfield attacked for first time; 10 MIGs are destroyed.
June 12	Three bombing programs are offered in Pentagon's Draft Presidential Memo: (1) intensified attack on Hanoi-Haiphong logistical base; (2) emphasis south of 20°; (3) extension of the current program. (McNamara, Vance, and SecNav favor the second; JCS favor the first; SecAF favors the third.)
August 11–12	New targets, including the Paul Doumer bridge, are struck in Hanoi.
August 24–September 4	All attacks within Hanoi's 10-mile zone suspended.

September 7	Suspension of such attacks extended indefinitely.
September 29	The president makes public the San Antonio Formula: U.S. will stop bombing if assured that productive discussions will follow and that Hanoi will not take military advantage of the cessation.
October 20	San Antonio Formula rejected by DRV.
October 25	Phuc Yen Mig airfield attacked for first time.
November 17	Bac Mai airfield (near center of Hanoi) attacked for first time.
November 28	McNamara's resignation reported in press.
December 24	Christmas truce (24 hours).
December 31	New Year's truce (24 hours).

1968

January 3	Bombing prohibited within 5 nautical miles of central Hanoi and Haiphong.
January 29	Tet truce begins.
January 31	Tet offensive begins.
February 10	Haiphong bombed.
March 18–19	The president convenes informal "Council of Wisemen," who recommend against further escalation.
March 31	The president announces end of all bombing north of 20th parallel.
November 1	The president announces end to all bombing of the DRV.

From Breakthrough to Breakdown: A Chronology

1972	
October 17	Kissinger, Deputy Assistant Secretary of State William Sullivan, and State Department Legal Advisor George Aldrich return to Paris to meet with Xuan Thuy. Le Duc Tho is in Hanoi.
October 20	Nixon informs Hanoi that the draft agreement is acceptable to the U.S.
October 19–23	Kissinger and Sullivan visit Saigon; five meetings are held with Thieu.
October 24	Thieu briefs political party and government officials on the objectionable provisions of the draft agreement.
October 25	Hanoi radio broadcasts details of the draft agreement.
	GVN Senate votes to reject a tripartite government of national concord as part of an overall settlement. Similar action is taken in the lower house on October 27, 1972.
October 26	Kissinger declares peace is at hand, explaining that one more negotiating session with Hanoi is required.
October 27	DRV releases additional details about the negotiating process, contradicting Kissinger's account and accusing the U.S. of reneging on its pledge to sign the agreement.
November 7	Nixon reelected.

November 9–10	General Alexander Haig visits Saigon to reassure Thieu of full U.S. support and to secure GVN support of the agreement.
November 15	Saigon proposes that additional negotiation tracks be created so it could deal directly with the PRG.
November 20–25	Kissinger-Tho talks resume.
November 25	Le Duc Tho returns to Hanoi.
November 29– December 1	Nixon meets with Thieu's personal emissary, Nguyen Phu Duc.
November 30	The JCS approve the terms of the draft agreement.
December 4–13	Kissinger-Tho talks resume; experts held technical talks on the protocols December 10–12.
December 15	Technical talks resume.
December 15–16	Le Duc Tho visits Moscow.
December 16	Kissinger reviews the status of the negotiations: the "agreement is 99 percent completed."
December 17–18	Le Duc Tho visits Peking.
December 18–30	Linebacker 2: the Christmas bombing of Hanoi.
December 19–20	General Haig visits Indochina and Thailand to win support for the draft agreement and to begin discussions on what U.S. aviation will remain in Southeast Asia.
December 23	Technical talks adjourned by DRV representatives protesting the Christmas bombing.
December 24	Xuan Thuy (on ABC's "Issues and Answers") declares DRV will not resume talks until air strikes north of twentieth parallel are halted.
December 27	Technical talks scheduled for this date called off by DRV in protest.
December 30	Linebacker 2 ended with announcement that technical talks would resume on January 2, 1973.
1973	
January 2–5	Technical talks between Sullivan and DRV Deputy Foreign Minister Nguyen Co Thach.
January 6	Le Duc Tho returns to Paris.

January 8–10	Technical talks resume.
January 8–13	Kissinger-Tho talks resume.
January 13	Negotiations are concluded.
January 15	Bombing of North Vietnam completely halted.
January 13–20	General Haig briefs allies in Indochina and Asia on the agreement.
January 23	Kissinger and Tho initial agreement.

NOTES

CHAPTER 1.

1. For a detailed, historical treatment of this topic, including numerous citations from North Vietnamese sources, see my article "Fighting While Negotiating" in Joseph J. Zasloff and MacAlister Brown, eds., *Communism in Indochina: New Perspectives* (Lexington, Mass.: D. C. Heath, 1975), pp. 81–108.

2. Joint U.S. Public Affairs Office (Saigon), "The Position of North Vietnam on Negotiations," *Viet-Nam Documents and Research Notes,* no. 8 (October 1967), p. 4.

3. Truong Chinh, *Primer for Revolt* (New York: Praeger, 1963), pp. 112–13.

4. I have found the following particularly helpful both in sorting out the attitudes of Hanoi's allies toward the war and for assessment of Hanoi's attitude toward the Sino-Soviet dispute: Donald S. Zagoria, *Vietnam Triangle* (New York: Pegasus, 1967); D. P. Mozingo and T. W. Robinson, *Lin Piao on "People's War": China Takes a Second Look at Vietnam,* Rand Corporation Research Memorandum RM-4814-PR (November 1965); Alexander Woodside, "Peking and Hanoi: Anatomy of a Revolutionary Partnership," *International Journal* 24 (Winter, 1968–1969), pp. 65–85; and, Charles B. McLane, "The Russians and Vietnam: Strategies of Indirection," ibid., pp. 47–64.

5. Throughout this book I shall be using NLF (National Liberation Front) or PRG (Provisional Revolutionary Government) to refer to the Communist movement in South Vietnam. Most Americans called the NLF "Viet Cong" or "VC," neither of which was generally used by the Vietnamese. In June 1969 the NLF and assorted Communist-dominated organizations united to form the PRG. When discussing the major developments in the negotiations I have, unless specifically noted, treated the PRG's position as if identical with Hanoi's.

6. GVN—Government of Vietnam—is the abbreviation used by U.S. officials throughout the war to refer to the government in Saigon.

7. U.S. Congress, U.S. Senate, *Two Reports on Vietnam and Southeast Asia to the President of the United States by Senator Mike Mansfield,* 93d Congress, 1st session, April 1973, p. 14.

8. Henry Brandon, *Anatomy of Error* (Boston: Gambit, 1969), p. 60.

9. *The Pentagon Papers,* the Senator Gravel edition, 4 vols. (Boston: Beacon Press, 1972), 2: 277.

10. Ibid., 2:319.

11. George W. Ball, "Top Secret: The Prophecy the President Rejected." *The Atlantic* (July 1972), p. 43.

12. Ibid.

13. Chester Cooper, "Fateful Day in Vietnam—10 Years Ago," *Washington Post* (February 11, 1975), p. 14.

14. Oleg Hoeffding, *Bombing North Vietnam: An Appraisal of Economic and Political Effects*, Rand Corporation Research Memorandum RM-5213-1-ISA (December 1966), p. v.

15. *Pentagon Papers*, vol. 3, p. 101.

CHAPTER 2.

1. *Pentagon Papers*, the Senator Gravel edition, 4 vols. (Boston: Beacon Press, 1972), 3: 212.

2. Lyndon Baines Johnson, *The Vantage Point* (New York: Holt, Rinehart and Winston, 1971), p. 250.

3. Saigon wanted far more than such discussions, and put forward its own four-point stand in a June 1965 statement by Foreign Minister Tran Van Do. These points remained central to the GVN position for nearly a decade thereafter:

    a. the north must terminate its aggression and subversion, dissolve the National Liberation Front and withdraw infiltrated troops and agents;

    b. the future of South Vietnam must be decided by the people of the south in conformity with democratic principles and without any foreign interference from whatever source;

    c. as soon as aggression from the north has ceased, South Vietnam and the nations that have come to its aid will be able to suspend military measures beyond the boundaries of the south. The South Vietnamese Government would be prepared to ask friendly nations then to remove their military forces from South Vietnam, but reserves its right to call again for foreign assistance if necessary;

    d. the independence and freedom of the people of South Vietnam must be effectively guaranteed.

4. *Pentagon Papers*, vol. 3, p. 366.

5. Chester L. Cooper, *The Lost Crusade* (New York: Dodd, Mead and Company, 1970), p. 295.

6. See Walt W. Rostow, "Victory and Defeat in Guerrilla Wars: The Case of South Vietnam," *Pentagon Papers*, vol. 3, pp. 381–82.

7. *United States* v. *Ellsberg and Russo*, vol. 91 (March 15, 1975), p. 16,021.

8. Ronning testimony, *United States* v. *Ellsberg*, vol. 91, pp. 16,016–19.

9. Johnson, *Vantage Point*, p. 252.

10. Wilfred Burchett, *Washington Post* (December 1968). For details of a similar episode involving the Hungarian Government as an intermediary, see Janos Radványi, "Astonishing revelations about how the Hungarian foreign minister perpetrated a peace hoax," *Life*, (March 22, 1968), pp. 60–74.

11. David Kraslow and Stuart H. Loory, *The Secret Search for Peace in Vietnam* (New York: Vintage, 1968), p. 81.

12. Ibid., p. 54.

13. *Pentagon Papers*, vol. 4, p. 137.

14. President Johnson, press conference, February 2, 1967.

15. Reported in Joint U.S. Public Affairs Office (Saigon), "The Position of North Viet-Nam on Negotiations," *Viet-Nam Documents and Research Notes*, no. 8 (October 1967), p. 4.

16. Harold Wilson, *The Labour Government, 1964–1970* (London: Weidenfeld and Nicolson, 1971), pp. 346–47.

17. Cooper, *Lost Crusade,* pp. 355–56.

18. Johnson, *Vantage Point,* p. 253.

19. Cooper, *Lost Crusade,* p. 354.

20. Wilson, *Labour,* p. 351.

21. Ibid., pp. 357–58.

22. Ibid., p. 359.

23. Ibid., p. 360.

24. Ibid., p. 364.

25. Cooper, *Lost Crusade,* pp. 367–68.

26. All quotations from Johnson, *Vantage Point,* p. 255.

27. *Pentagon Papers,* vol. 4, p. 175.

28. Ibid., p. 176.

29. Johnson, *Vantage Point,* p. 266.

30. Ibid., p. 267.

31. Ibid., p. 268.

CHAPTER 3.

1. Henry A. Kissinger, "The Vietnam Negotiations," *Foreign Affairs* 47 (January 1969): 215–16.

2. Lyndon Baines Johnson, *The Vantage Point* (New York: Holt, Rinehart and Winston, 1971), p. 591.

3. For a detailed account of the Tet attacks and their aftermath, see Don Oberdorfer, *Tet!* (Garden City, N.Y.: Doubleday, 1971).

4. Harry McPherson, *A Political Education* (Boston: Little, Brown, 1972), p. 422. For an excellent account of Tet's impact on the U.S. domestic scene, see Thomas Powers, *The War at Home* (New York: Grossman, 1973).

5. Text of the study is in *Pentagon Papers,* the Senator Gravel edition, (Boston: Beacon Press, 1972), 4:218–20.

6. *Pentagon Papers,* vol. 4, p. 583.

7. "A Conversation with Clark Clifford—Vietnam and Its Aftermath," program transcript for "Bill Moyers' Journal: International Report," WNET (New York), April 10, 1975, p. 11.

8. Reported in Marvin Kalb and Elie Abel, *Roots of Involvement* (New York: Norton, 1971), p. 260.

9. Ibid., p. 260.

10. Reported in Stuart H. Loory, "Secret Bomb Halt Sessions Revealed," *Los Angeles Times* (March 9, 1969).

11. See "Behind the Bombing Halt: An Account of Bargaining," *New York Times* (November 11, 1968), pp. 1, 20.

12. U.S. Congress, Senate, Committee on Foreign Relations, *Legislative Proposals Relating to the War in Southeast Asia,* 92d Congress, 1st session, April and May 1971, p. 502.

13. Ibid., pp. 502–3.

CHAPTER 4.

1. See "President Nixon's Record on Vietnam, 1954–1968," in *Legislative Proposals Relating to the War in Southeast Asia,* 92d Congress, 1st Session, April and May 1971, pp. 295–99.

2. Richard M. Nixon, "Asia after Vietnam," *Foreign Affairs* 46 (October 1967), pp. 111–12.

3. Printed in Richard Whalen, *Catch the Falling Flag* (Boston: Houghton Mifflin, 1972), p. 287.

4. "Nixon Replies," *The New Republic* (October 26, 1968), pp. 11–15.

5. Ibid., p. 15. As president, of course, Nixon quickly dropped his insistence on linking the progress of détente to the Vietnam negotiations when he realized that Moscow had very little leverage over Hanoi.

6. Whalen, *Falling Flag,* p. 289.

7. Henry A. Kissinger, "The Vietnam Negotiations," *Foreign Affairs* 47 (January 1969), p. 234.

8. Ibid., p. 214.

9. Ibid., p. 212.

10. Ibid., p. 220.

11. Ibid., p. 221.

12. Ibid.

13. Ibid., p. 225.

14. Ibid., pp. 233–34.

15. Kissinger to CBS diplomatic correspondent Marvin Kalb in a TV interview on February 1, 1973.

16. Kissinger, press conference, October 26, 1972.

17. Kissinger, "The Vietnam Negotiations," p. 230.

18. Richard M. Nixon, *U.S. Foreign Policy for the 1970s: The Emerging Structure of Peace* (Washington: The White House, February 9, 1972), p. 113.

19. Kissinger, "The Vietnam Negotiations," p. 230.

20. Joint U.S. Public Affairs Office [JUSPAO] (Saigon), "NLF Thoughts on Peace Negotiations, World Policies: A Cadre's Notes on a High Level 1967 Reorientation Course," *Viet-Nam Documents and Research Notes,* no. 14 (January 1968), p. 9.

21. Joint U.S. Public Affairs Office, " 'Decisive Victory': Step by Step, Bit by Bit," *Viet-Nam Documents and Research Notes,* nos. 61–62 (June 1969), pp. 5–6.

22. Quoted in Goodman, "Fighting While Negotiating," in Joseph J. Zasloff and MacAlister Brown, eds., *Communism in Indochina: New Perspectives* (Lexington, Mass.: D. C. Heath, 1975), p. 91.

23. Henry A. Kissinger, *Nuclear Weapons and Foreign Policy* (New York: Norton, 1957) pp. 50–51.

CHAPTER 5.

1. Henry A. Kissinger, "The Vietnam Negotiations," *Foreign Affairs* 47 (January 1969), p. 211.

2. Henry Kissinger, press conference, May 9, 1972.

3. Printed in Kalb and Kalb, *Kissinger* (Boston: Little, Brown, 1974), p. 134.

4. Throughout the war, official and academic experts in Vietnam and in the United States continually tried to identify which members of the Politburo favored which strategy in the war and the negotiations. Such knowledge was essential, many experts argued, to evaluating the sincerity of Hanoi's public and private offers in the negotiations and to gauging U.S. responses to North Vietnamese military actions. There were, however, so many conflicting interpretations of Politburo dynamics based on such slim evidence—since, as one intelligence specialist put it, "Nearly all we had to go on was the public statements of North Vietnamese leaders"—that an advocate for a negotiations initiative or one for an escalation of the war could find equally ample support for his case. An example of the imprecision of official U.S. assessments of the North Vietnamese Politburo can be seen in the differences between U.S. intelligence agencies summarized in NSSM-1. Probably the most influential of the assessments available to both high U.S. officials and the general public can be found in Douglas Pike's excellent short book *War, Peace and the Viet Cong* (Cambridge, Mass.: MIT Press, 1969). See especially pp. 164–67.

The only thing that can be reasonably concluded from the various attempts to fathom who in Hanoi favored what is that (a) each member of the Politburo probably had several different and not necessarily consistent opinions about the war between 1960 and 1975; (b) individual opinions always had to be accommodated within the Politburo as a whole; (c) the Politburo itself is striking as an institution for its tradition of political unity and the nearly total lack of any purges of its membership; and (d) each major decision about the war reached in Hanoi always was taken in part with the hope that it would produce U.S. concessions in the negotiations. For a detailed study of the publicly known positions of Politburo members on several key turning points in the war—one that is typical of those also available to U.S. officials—see Robert F. Rogers, "Risk Taking in Hanoi's War Policy: An Analysis of Militancy Versus Manipulation in a Communist Party-State's Behavior in a Conflict Environment" (Ph.D. dissertation, Georgetown University, April 1974).

5. Le Duc Tho, a specialist in party organization, became a member of the Politburo in 1951 when he replaced Le Duan as head of the Viet Minh resistance movement in the South where he remained until 1954. In a February 1973 TV interview with CBS diplomatic correspondent Marvin Kalb, Henry Kissinger characterized Tho in the following terms:

> Le Duc Tho is an impressive man who joined the Communist Party as a very young man, a man therefore driven in the context of this time by a certain missionary zeal; spent seven years at extreme hard labor in a French prison; organized guerrilla movements; and finally after long struggle, wound up in the Politburo of a country that then found itself at war almost immediately.

> He is a man who has never known tranquility; and where we fight in order to end a war, he fights in order to achieve certain objectives he has held all his life. He holds values quite contrary to ours, and I never had any illusions about that. I didn't convert him to our point of view.

6. Reported in Hedrick Smith, "Cambodia Decision: Why President Acted," *New York Times* (June 30, 1970), p. 14.

7. "A Conversation with the President on Foreign Policy," July 1, 1970, and printed in *Congressional Record* (July 27, 1970), p. S12134.

8. Kissinger, "The Vietnam Negotiations," pp. 226–27.

9. Kalb and Kalb, *Kissinger,* pp. 172–73.

10. Ibid., p. 180.

11. From the official DRV text.

12. From the official PRG text.

13. Reprinted in the *Congressional Record* (July 15, 1971), p. H6836.

14. Kissinger, press conference, January 26, 1972.

15. Ibid., October 26, 1972.

16. Kalb and Kalb, *Kissinger,* p. 285.

17. Frances Fitzgerald, "The Offensive," *The New York Review of Books* 18 (May 18, 1972), p. 11.

18. Kalb and Kalb, *Kissinger,* p. 291.

19. Le Duc Tho later told Kissinger that his Politburo colleagues never thought McGovern had a chance of being elected president.

20. Kissinger, press conference, May 9, 1972.

21. Ibid.

22. Kalb and Kalb, *Kissinger,* p. 299.

23. Kissinger, press conference, May 9, 1972.

CHAPTER 6.

1. This account closely parallels the one in Tad Szulc's "How Kissinger Did It: Behind the Vietnam Cease-Fire Agreement" (*Foreign Policy,* no. 15 [Summer 1974], pp. 21–69), reflecting the fact that we both interviewed many of the same sources. I have constructed my story from these interviews rather than from the Szulc article because we differ in emphasis and interpretation.

2. Mao Tse-Tung, *On the Chung King Negotiations* (Peking: Foreign Languages Press, 1961).

3. Kissinger, press conference, October 26, 1972.

4. From the official PRG text.

5. See Appendix B for text.

6. All quotations are from Kissinger's press conference, October 26, 1972.

7. DRV press spokesman Nguyen Thanh Le, press conference, November 1, 1972.

8. For a point-by-point representation of the GVN's view of the weaknesses of the draft agreement, written by a South Vietnamese who was shortly to enter Thieu's cabinet, see Nguyen Tien Hung, "Settling the War on Hanoi's Terms," *Washington Post,* Outlook Section (November 19, 1972), p. 1.

9. "Exclusive from Hanoi," *Newsweek* (October 30, 1972), p. 26.

10. *Chinh Luan,* (October 20, 1972), p. 1.

CHAPTER 7.

1. "Look to the Future," Radio Address to the Nation, November 2, 1972.

2. Murrey Marder, "Hanoi Regards Unanimity Rule as Useful Tool," *Washington Post* (February 5, 1973), p. 16.

3. All quotations are from a text of the Nixon letter made public by a former GVN cabinet minister and printed in the *New York Times,* May 1, 1975.

4. Kissinger to "Today Show" hostess Barbara Walters on NBC-TV, February 25, 1973.

5. *Jeune Afrique,* February 10, 1973.

6. Kissinger, press conference, January 24, 1973.

7. Ibid.

8. Ibid., January 24, 1975.

9. Kissinger, on the "Today Show," NBC-TV, February 22, 1973.

10. Kissinger, press conference, December 16, 1972.

11. Le Duc Tho, press conference, reprinted in *New York Times* (January 7, 1973).

12. Richard M. Nixon, *U.S. Foreign Policy for the 1970s: Shaping a Durable Peace* (Washington: The White House, 1973), p. 56.

13. Henry Kissinger, in a TV interview with Marvin Kalb, February 1, 1973.

14. Hong Ha, "Paris: A Year Ago Today, and the Final Days Leading to the Paris Agreement on Vietnam," Hanoi Radio Broadcast, January 27, 1974.

15. Kissinger, press conference, January 24, 1973.

CHAPTER 8.

1. Kissinger, press conference, February 22, 1973.

2. This assertion is, of course, swathed in controversy. Supporters of the PRG maintain that it sincerely accepted and implemented the agreement but that the violations of the GVN caused it to break down. This view is painstakingly reported and documented in D. Gareth Porter, "The Paris Agreement and Revolutionary Strategy in South Vietnam," in Zasloff and Brown, eds., *Communism in Indochina: New Perspectives* (Lexington, Mass.: D. C. Heath, 1975), pp. 57–80. For an equally detailed and differing interpretation, see James M. Haley and Jerry M. Silverman, "The Provisional Revolutionary Government and the National Liberation Front since the 1973 Paris Agreements" (manuscript, Saigon, January 1974).

3. Kissinger, press conference, January 24, 1973.

4. For statements on each side's assessment of the other's violations of the Paris Agreement, see the documents reproduced in the Appendix.

5. Kissinger, press conference, June 13, 1973.

6. Ibid.

7. Ibid., April 29, 1975.

8. Quoted in Robert Shaplen, "Letter from Saigon," *The New Yorker* (April 21, 1975), p. 127.

INDEX

Washington Post, 21, 148, 221
Washington Special Action Group, 95
Watergate, 4, 176
Westmoreland, William (General), 58,
    275, 277
Weyand, Fred C. (General), 10
Whitehouse, Ambassador, 150
Wilson, Harold, 25, 47, 48, 49, 50, 51,
    52, 53, 279, 280

Xom Bang, 276
Xuan Thuy, 67, 91, 92, 102, 109, 110,
    115, 116, 117, 132, 140, 141, 282, 283

Yen Bai, 226